ESSENTIALS OF
COMPUTING

H. L. CAPRON

The Benjamin/Cummings Publishing Company, Inc.
Redwood City, California • Menlo Park, California
Reading, Massachusetts • New York • Don Mills, Ontario
Wokingham, U.K. • Amsterdam • Bonn
Singapore • Tokyo • Madrid • San Juan

Sponsoring Editor	Michelle Miceli-Baxter
Developmental Editors	Pat Waldo and Jamie Northway
Production Editor	Jean Lake
Art & Design Manager	Michele Carter
Cover and Text Designer	Vargas /Williams /Design
Illustrations	Illustrious, Inc.
Photo Editor	Cecilia Mills
Photo Researcher	Susan Friedman
Copy Editor	Toni Murray
Composition and Film	York Graphic Services
Printing and Binding	R. R. Donnelley & Sons Company

Library of Congress Cataloging-in-Publication Data

Capron, H. L.
   Essentials of computing/H. L. Capron.
      p. cm.
      Includes index.
      ISBN: 0-8053-1060-6
       1. Electronic data processing.   I. Title.
QA76.C359   1992
004—dc20   91-34531
                                  CIP
ISBN 0-8053-1060-6

   3 4 5 6 7 8 9 10   DO   96 95 94 93

The Benjamin/Cummings Publishing Company, Inc.
390 Bridge Parkway
Redwood City, CA 94065

- **Lecture Support Software** by J. Huhtala. This seven-disk package for IBM PCs, PS/2s, or compatibles provides 280 color screens containing animation and text that summarize the key concepts for each section of the book. The accompanying student workbook (300 pages) supports the software with additional text, learning objectives, key terms, review questions, and completion questions. The software and workbook can be used in lecture or lab. The Instructor's Guide contains a reference guide to help you incorporate these materials.

- **Test Bank** by S. Langman (224 pages). The test bank contains 1800 items. There are five types of questions: multiple choice, true/false, matching, completion, and situational essay questions. Each question is referenced to the text by page number, and the answers are provided. The test bank is available both as hard copy and in a computerized format for the IBM PC (and compatibles), IBM PS/2, and Macintosh computers.

- **Color Transparency Acetates.** The 100 full-color transparency acetates include artwork and diagrams taken directly from the text plus additional outside sources.

- **Videotapes.** Benjamin/Cummings makes available to qualified adopters free videotapes from our library of commercially produced videos. Use this valuable resource to enhance your lectures on concepts presented in the text. Your Benjamin/Cummings sales representative has details about this offer.

- **Lab Manuals.**

  Computing Fundamentals Series. This series consists of brief tutorials that introduce beginners to specific software packages, operating systems, and programming languages. The books cover the fundamental functions necessary to start using a particular application successfully. The titles include Davis, *Concepts, Third Edition*; Davis, *WordPerfect 5.0/5.1*; Davis/Schreiner, *dBASE III PLUS*; Byrkett, *Lotus 1-2-3 Release 2.01/2.2*; Wood, *PC-DOS and MS-DOS*; Davies, *PageMaker for the Macintosh*; Davies, *PageMaker for the IBM PC*; Gorman/Haggard, *Microsoft Word 5.0*; Davis/Schreiner, *dBASE IV*.

  Hands-On by Larry Metzelaar and Marianne Fox. An ideal introduction to four major software applications for the IBM PC, these books cover the most recent releases: *Hands-On PLUS: MS-DOS, dBASE IV, WordPerfect 5.1, Lotus 1-2-3*; *Hands-On WordPerfect 5.1*; and *Hands-On: MS-DOS, dBASE III PLUS, WordPerfect 5.0, Lotus 1-2-3, Second Edition*; and *Hands-On: dBASE IV* or *Hands-On: Word Perfect 5.1*.

Software for the Instructor

- **LotusWorks from Lotus Development Corporation.** This two-disk integrated package offers a spreadsheet, database, word processor, and communications service. The package includes a tutorial booklet and a reference book with quick-reference guide. The software is available in PC or PS/2 formats.

- **University Gradebook.** This class record-keeping software is available for the IBM PC and compatible computers.

Of Related Interest

- *The Student Edition of Lotus 1-2-3, Second Edition* (509 pages); *The Student Edition of dBASE IV* (704 pages); *The Student Edition of Framework II* (372 pages); *The Student Edition of PageMaker* (370 pages).

Brief Table of Contents

• • • • • • • • • • • •

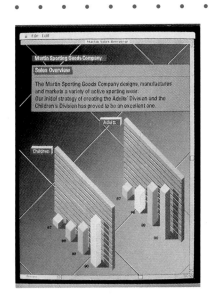

Detailed Table of Contents

• • • • • • • • • • • • •

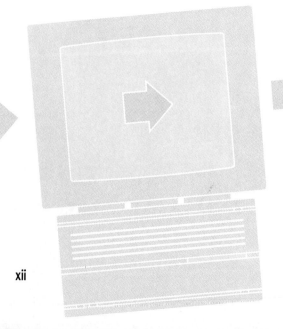

GALLERY
Computer Graphics
Follows page 96

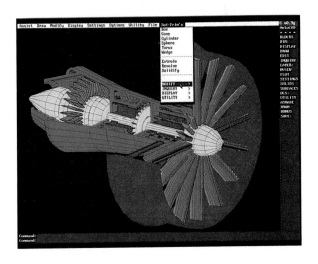

GALLERY
How to Buy Your Own Personal Computer
Follows page 192

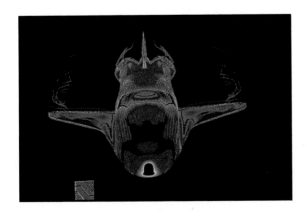

CHAPTER 12
WORD PROCESSING AND DESKTOP PUBLISHING: PREPARING PRINTED COMMUNICATIONS   234

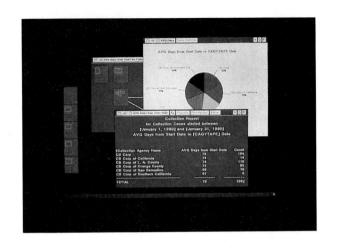

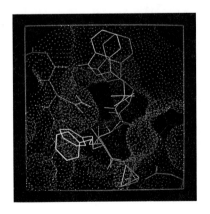

GALLERY

Computer Graphics

Color and Content

Follows page 96

In this photo essay we explore the colorful world of computer graphics, from realistic and abstract art to the new realm of virtual reality.

BUYER'S GUIDE

How to Buy Your Own Personal Computer

Follows page 192

This special eight-page section presents issues and questions to consider before buying a personal computer and software. If you are thinking about buying a personal computer now or in the future, read this section carefully.

▽ PREFACE

• • • • • • • • • • • •

Exploring the world of computers can be both informative and exciting. For those students taking an introductory course who are just beginning to discover computers, *Essentials of Computing* will make the process of discovery enjoyable and educational. For those who are not entirely comfortable with computers, this textbook provides blocks of information presented within the framework of the user's environment. This introduction to computers is written in a friendly and engaging style that sparks the reader's interest.

We believe that, in *Essentials of Computing*, you will find all you need to ensure that students understand and retain what they have read. We offer up-to-date coverage of computer concepts and an explanation of popular software packages. Though comprehensive in scope, each topic presents practical, day-to-day applications of computers. In addition, the integrated instructional support package and accompanying software provide you with all the elements you need to teach an introductory computer course.

KEY THEMES

- **Extensive personal computer coverage.** Although we discuss all types of computers, we place a strong emphasis on personal computers, reflecting their continuing prominence in business and education. Two chapters focus specifically on issues related to the personal computer: Chapter 3, "Personal Computers: An Introduction," and Chapter 9, "Personal Computers on the Job: For Information Systems Managers and Everyone Else." In addition, we incorporate a wide variety of personal computer examples throughout the text.

- **Focus on computers in business settings.** We provide several features that focus on the uses of computers in the business environment. Each of the four parts of the text begins with a personal interview, in which individuals from a variety of industries discuss their use of computers on the job. Part 3, Computers and Business, is devoted to issues of current interest in business computing. Topics include the use of personal computers; the role of the information systems manager; security, privacy, and ethics; and artificial intelligence, expert systems, and robotics.

- **Appealing style.** When students enjoy what they read, they remember it. The text's friendly style encourages the reader and increases students' comprehension and confidence. For example, each chapter begins with an engaging story that leads the student into the material. The real-world applications included throughout the text pique student interest as well as illustrate key points from the chapter.

SPECIAL FEATURES

- **The Microsoft Windows graphical user interface** is introduced in three featured essays that focus on special elements of this popular operating environment, including multitasking, automatic updating, and desktop publishing applications. Additional coverage of the Windows environment is included in Chapter 8, "Operating Systems: The Underlying Software."

- **The Macintosh computer** is highlighted in several chapters through brief discussions of the Macintosh operating environment. The text covers topics such as graphics, HyperCard, and PageMaker desktop publishing software.

- **Built-in study guide.** To allow students to review essential concepts easily and to confirm their comprehension of the material, each chapter concludes with a student study guide. This Chapter Review provides an end-of-chapter summary of core concepts and key terms, followed by a self-test that includes true/false, matching, and completion questions. Answers to odd-numbered questions are provided for the student at the end of the self-test; a complete set of answers is included in the Instructor's Edition with Annotations.

- **Buyer's Guide.** Students and their families are making important economic decisions about the purchase of a computer for their educational needs. This concise eight-page guide with checklist offers students the information they need to answer questions about hardware and software purchases.

- **Personal Computers in Action.** Each chapter includes a feature article on personal computers that demonstrates the range of tasks personal computers perform. The articles include topics such as the use of personal computers in retail stores, on cruise ships, and in hospital emergency rooms.

- **Computing Highlights.** To give students a glimpse at the great variety of roles computers can play, each chapter provides a brief essay that focuses on issues and trends in the world of computing. Examples include subjects such as self-serve businesses, software glitches, and computer security and privacy.

- **Photo gallery.** A full-color photo essay on computer graphics vividly illustrates the increasing sophistication of computer graphics and the wide variety of uses for graphics applications.

- **Margin notes.** To further engage student attention, margin notes are carefully placed throughout the text. The margin notes extend the text material by providing additional information and highlighting interesting applications of computers.

In-Text Learning Aids

Each chapter includes the following pedagogical support:

- A chapter **preview** that outlines key concepts
- **Key terms** boldfaced throughout the text
- A **built-in study guide** (chapter review) that includes extensive **summaries** of core concepts and boldfaced key terms and a **self-test** that students can use to check their comprehension of essential concepts
- An extensive **glossary** and comprehensive **index**

Organization of the Text

The text is divided into four parts:

- **Part 1** offers an overview of computer systems and their uses in our society, and an introduction to the personal computer.
- **Part 2** explores computer hardware and software, including coverage of the central processing unit, input/output, storage, communications, programming and languages, and operating systems.
- **Part 3** looks at personal computers in the workplace; management of information systems; security, privacy, and ethics; and artificial intelligence, expert systems, and robotics.

- **Part 4** includes three chapters on applications packages: word processing (WordPerfect 5.1) and desktop publishing, spreadsheets and business graphics (Lotus 1-2-3 version 2.2), and database management systems (dBASE IV).

- **Appendices** include coverage of dBASE III PLUS database management software for those who prefer to use this application package instead of dBASE IV, a discussion of the history of computing, and information on number systems.

A COMPLETE SUPPLEMENTS PACKAGE

- **Instructor's Edition with Annotations** by S. Langman with H. L. Capron. This special edition contains annotations for lecture preparation and includes supplementary material not found in the Instructor's Guide. The annotations include chapter outlines with key terms for lecture, lecture objectives, lecture activities, discussion questions, lecture hints, test-bank references, transparency references, answers to end-of-chapter study guide questions, and student projects.

- **Instructor's Guide and transparency masters** by H. L. Capron (250 pages). Each chapter contains learning objectives, a chapter overview, a detailed lecture outline, and a list of key words. The Instructor's Guide also includes ten transparency masters, a reference guide to the Lecture Support Software screens, a guide to incorporating the videotape offerings into lectures, and an answer sheet for all end-of-chapter problems from the study guide within *Essentials of Computing*.

- **Lecture support software** by J. Huhtala. This seven-disk package for IBM PCs, PS/2s, or compatibles provides 280 color screens containing animation and text that summarize the key concepts for each section of the book. The accompanying student workbook (300 pages) supports the software with additional text, learning objectives, key terms, review questions, and completion questions. The software and workbook can be used in lecture or lab. The Instructor's Guide contains a reference guide to help you incorporate these materials.

- **Test bank** by S. Langman (224 pages). The test bank contains 1800 items. There are five types of questions: multiple choice, true/false, matching, completion, and situational essay questions. Each question is referenced to the text by page number, and the answers are provided. The test bank is available both as hard copy and in a computerized format for the IBM PC (and compatibles), IBM PS/2, and Macintosh computers.

- **Color transparency acetates.** The 100 full-color transparency acetates include artwork and diagrams taken directly from the text and outside sources.

- **Videotapes.** Benjamin/Cummings makes available to qualified adopters free videotapes from our library of commercially produced tapes. Use these valuable resources to enhance your lectures on concepts presented in the text. Your Benjamin/Cummings sales representative has details about this offer.

LAB SUPPORT

Lab Manuals.

Computing Fundamentals Series. This series consists of brief tutorials that introduce beginners to specific software packages, operating systems, and programming languages. The books cover the fundamental functions required to begin using a particular application successfully: Davis, *Concepts, Third Edition;* - Davis, *WordPerfect 5.0/5.1; Davis/Schreiner, dBASE III PLUS; Byrkett, Lotus 1-2-3 Release 2.01/2.2;* Wood, *PC-DOS and MS-DOS;* Davies, *PageMaker for the Macintosh;* Davies, *PageMaker for the IBM PC;* Gorman/Haggard, *Microsoft Word 5.0;* Davis/Schreiner, *dBASE IV.*

Hands-On Series by Larry Metzelaar and Marianne Fox. An ideal introduction to four major software applications for the IBM PC, these books cover the most recent releases: *Hands-On PLUS: MS-DOS, dBASE IV, WordPerfect 5.1, Lotus 1-2-3; Hands-On WordPerfect 5.1;* and *Hands-On: MS-DOS, dBASE III PLUS, WordPerfect 5.0, Lotus 1-2-3, Second Edition;* and *Hands-On: dBASE IV* or *Hands-On: WordPerfect 5.1.*

SOFTWARE FOR THE INSTRUCTOR

LotusWorks from Lotus Development Corporation. This two-disk integrated package offers a spreadsheet, database, word processor, and communications service. The package includes a tutorial booklet and a reference book with a quick-reference guide. The software is available in PC or PS/2 formats.

University Gradebook. This class record-keeping software is available for the IBM PC and compatible computers.

OF RELATED INTEREST

The Student Edition of Lotus 1-2-3, Second Edition (509 pages); *The Student Edition of dBASE IV* (704 pages); *The Student Edition of Framework II* (372 pages); *The Student Edition of PageMaker* (370 pages).

SPECIAL NOTE TO THE STUDENT

We welcome your reactions to this book. It is written to open up the world of computing for you. Expanding your knowledge will increase your confidence and prepare you for a life that will be influenced by computers. Your comments and questions are important to us. Write to the author in care of Computer Information Systems Editor, Benjamin/Cummings Publishing Company, 390 Bridge Parkway, Redwood City, California 94065. All letters with a return address will be answered by the author.

ACKNOWLEDGMENTS

We would like to thank some of the key people who contributed to the success of this project: Developmental editors Jamie Northway and Pat Waldo ensured superior consistency and quality with their attention to detail in the preparation of this book. Jean Lake directed the efforts of many people to keep the book on its extraordinary schedule, permitting greater currency than would otherwise be possible. Toni Murray has, yet again, done a superb copyediting job. Cecilia Mills played a significant role in photo research, and Lisa Weber and Kathy Galinac contributed quality research and supplementary materials in a timely manner. We appreciate the many contributions of Mark Sheehan at Indiana University. Michelle Miceli-Baxter provided the coordination and inspiration that guided this book on its path to success.

Reviewers and consultants from industry and academia have provided valuable contributions that improved the quality of the book. Their names are listed in the following section, and we wish to express our sincere gratitude to them.

REVIEWERS

· · · · · · · · · · · · · ·

Doris Edwards
National Education Center
Sacramento, California

Kate Goelz
Rutgers University
New Brunswick, New Jersey

Roger Hammond
Morehead State University
Morehead, Kentucky

Sally Ann Hanson
Mercer City Community College
Doylestown, Pennsylvania

Jon Huhtala
Ferris State University
Big Rapids, Michigan

Shelley Langman
Bellevue Community College
Bellevue, Washington

Margery Meadows
Heald College
San Francisco, California

Jo Ruta
Chattanooga State Technical Community College
Chattanooga, Tennessee

Mark Sheehan
Indiana University
Bloomington, Indiana

Rod Southworth
Laramie County Community College
Cheyenne, Wyoming

Jane Varner
Montgomery College
Rockville, Maryland

Larry Waldrop
Raymond Walters College
Cincinnati, Ohio

SURVEY PARTICIPANTS

· ·

David Barros
Tarrant County Junior College
Fort Worth, Texas

Aaron Finerman
University of Michigan
Ann Arbor, Michigan

Tom Lyons
Mississippi County Community College
Blytheville, Arkansas

Micky Miller
Skyline College
San Bruno, California

Louis Pryor
Garland Community College
Hot Springs, Arkansas

K. W. Wen
University of Connecticut
Storrs, Connecticut

THE PRISM PUBLISHING PROGRAM

• • • • • • • • • • • •

The Benjamin/Cummings Publishing Company is pleased to announce its new PRISM Publishing Program, an innovation in publishing. PRISM is our response to your request for textbooks tailored to your course. We believe it is an unprecedented opportunity for educators to evaluate flexible text components and build them into a customized teaching support system suitable for individual course configurations.

A TEXT WITH CONCEPTS AND CUSTOMIZED APPLICATION COVERAGE

With the PRISM Publishing Program you can combine the concepts coverage in *Essentials of Computing* (Chapters 1 through 11 and appendices) with your choice of hands-on instructional modules. The modules you select along with Chapters 1 through 11 are bound into one convenient, durable text. We offer the following selection of modules:

Item	Item Number	Pages	Authors
1. Projects for DOS and Windows 3.0	31088	128	Fox/Metzelaar/ Scharpf
2. Projects for Lotus 1-2-3	31089	128	Fox/Metzelaar
3. Projects for WordPerfect 5.1	31096	128	Fox/Metzelaar
4. Projects for dBASE III PLUS	31093	128	Fox/Metzelaar
5. Projects for dBASE IV	31094	128	Fox/Metzelaar
6. Projects for Paradox	31059	128	Fox/Metzelaar
7. Projects for Excel (IBM Version)	31091	128	Scharpf
8. Structured BASIC for Programmers	31090	96	Appelt/ Whittenhall

Each of the modules, written by an experienced author and instructor, follows a consistent, pedagogically sound format. The modules begin with an introduction to basic concepts for each software application—concepts such as using the program, getting help, and an explanation of the conventions the modules use. The student then learns problem-solving techniques by completing seven or more increasingly challenging projects. The approach both enhances and reinforces comprehension of the specific software application package.

These projects are the core of the student's learning process. They are designed to motivate by offering both general-interest examples and business-related documents. Each project title identifies the functional context within which specific commands are mastered. The student gains an appreciation of both the conceptual and keystroke levels of a software application. Also included are student objectives, appropriate keyboard instructions, screen captures, and check documents. After the student has successfully completed the project, it is briefly summarized along with a list of key terms. Student study questions (true/false, completion, and discussion) and review exercises follow the list. Each module concludes with additional projects, a command reference chart, an extensive glossary, and an index. The modules are intended for the first-time computer user, but they contain selected advanced topics for the more experienced student.

The Advantages of PRISM Publishing

The PRISM Publishing Program brings you and your students many advantages:

- **Flexibility.** Now you can adapt your textbook to your curriculum instead of the other way around. You can choose *any* combination of the modules you prefer. And if your course should change next term, you can choose a new selection of modules to meet your new course needs. Each semester, Benjamin/Cummings will introduce additional modules that will contain new releases and new software or programming applications. If we don't currently publish modules for the specific software packages you need, contact your Benjamin/Cummings sales representative or call 800/854-2595. We will be happy to work with you to address your textbook requirements.

- **Convenience.** The PRISM Publishing Program gives you computer concepts plus the exact lab coverage you want all in one text and from one publisher. And with our low minimum-order policy, we can offer the PRISM Publishing concept to almost every educator. Also, your students will like the ease of carrying only one text for both lecture and lab.

- **Affordability.** Each module is individually priced. Because you select just those modules you plan to teach, your students pay for only what they need. And because we offer the text and modules bound into one volume, they aren't paying for additional costly binders and packaging.

- **Improved Instructional Package.** With computers so much a part of our daily lives, your students deserve the best preparation possible. PRISM Publishing and *Essentials of Computing* give you up-to-date coverage of computer concepts by the best-known author in computer information systems; pedagogically consistent, customized lab instruction; and the most complete instructional support available.

    In addition to the complete instructional support package for the *Essentials of Computing* textbook, we will make available to qualified adopters an Instructor's Guide for the modules with transparency masters, and a test bank for each of the modules. The student study questions and review exercises can serve as a student study guide if you elect to distribute to your class the answer key provided in the Instructor's Guide.

Complimentary Review Copies

We have prepared the following materials for review and adoption consideration:

The Instructor's Edition with Annotations of *Essentials of Computing*
This edition contains the complete contents of the student text plus nine types of margin annotations to support instruction. The student version of the PRISM edition of *Essentials of Computing* contains only Chapters 1 through 11 plus appendices from the Instructor's Edition and without the blue margin annotations.

    To avoid duplication of applications concepts contained within the modules, Chapters 12, 13, 14, and the appendix on dBASE III PLUS do not appear in the PRISM edition of *Essentials of Computing*.

    Important note: The Instructor's Edition with Annotations is marked with a blue stair-step symbol *(see margin)* in the bottom right corner of each right-hand page in Chapters 12, 13, 14, and the appendix on dBASE III PLUS. This symbol indicates that all of this chapter is *not* included in your PRISM edition of *Essentials of Computing*.

DOS/Windows, Lotus 1-2-3, dBASE III PLUS, and WordPerfect 5.1

These four modules are bound separately as a sample for your review. Once adopted, the PRISM edition (Chapters 1 through 11, plus appendices) is bound with the modules you have selected. The four modules on dBASE IV, Paradox, Excel, and BASIC are available for your review from your sales representative.

Ordering and Pricing Information

Your Benjamin/Cummings representative will be happy to work with you and your bookstore manager to outline the ordering process and provide pricing and delivery information. To take advantage of the PRISM Publishing Program, you can call Benjamin/Cummings Publishing Company at 800/854-2595. This special HOTLINE number is attended by service representatives ready to answer your inquiries and provide you with additional complimentary or desk copies.

PHOTO CREDITS

• • • • • • • • • • • •

Frontispiece: ©Melvin Prueitt.

Title page: ©Richard Tauber 1991.

Text Photo Credits

Chapter 1

Chapter 2

Chapter 3

Chapter 4

Chapter 5

ESSENTIALS OF
· · · · · · · · · ·
COMPUTING

PART ONE

INTERVIEW: Steve Schaefer—Golden State Warriors

One doesn't usually associate computers with sports. How does an NBA basketball team use computers?

The biggest area is running the business. That includes writing letters; writing for our publications, such as *Warriors Playbook* magazine and our media guide; doing proposals for advertisers; writing press releases; dealing with game operations. Our account executives use the computer to follow up on leads to sell tickets.

We also use the computer for desktop publishing: postcards, sales presentations, sponsor recaps, newsletters, mailings, forms. We use Lotus 1-2-3 for financial planning and our souvenir merchandise inventory, because we sell all our own souvenirs. There's the BASS system, which has to do with our ticket sales. When I send out the *Playbook,* there's a complete list of ticket holders in the system. We print out all 5,000 accounts in zip-code order for bulk mail.

There's the scoreboard, which is run by a minicomputer. Ours is a matrix board rather than a huge TV screen—it's little dots. Some of the displays are animations: One shows a player hitting the ball off the rim, and it says, "Brick!" The operator just hits a couple of keys and it plays out.

There's the StatMan program, which is used during the game to keep track of all the game action. Instead of somebody writing everything down on a pad and saying, "How many rebounds you got, Frank?" it's all right on the screen. They print it out, and the reporters can immediately run off and write their stories.

Then there's the NBA computer. It links all the teams to each other and to the central office in New York. Any trade or injury information can be relayed to everybody. Instead of sending out 27 telexes or faxes, someone in the office just types in the information, hits Enter, and sends it off. It's computers as they should be, making things quicker and easier.

Tell us a little about your background. How did you come to be in your current position with the Warriors?

I fell into this job completely by accident. There are people waiting in line to work for a sports franchise. I never had anything to do with sports in my life—I flunked out of Little League. I had an English degree from San Francisco State. I worked in the rare-book business for seven years, and that is where I first learned about word processing and databases. Later I became a temp word processor to make some money, and I was sent here for my first job. Eventually I was hired permanently. Since then I've gone through a few different jobs here. A year and a half ago I took on the publications manager position, running the magazine. I've been involved with the computer network since it was installed three years ago.

Have you taken any computer courses?

I took a class called "Introduction to Computers" in 1983. I briefly considered getting more involved in mainframe stuff, because some of my friends were doing it, but I hated it. I didn't want to do that, just working with data, data, data all

▲
Steve Schaefer is publications manager and network administrator for the Golden State Warriors NBA basketball franchise. In this interview, Steve describes how computers are becoming important players in the fast-paced world of professional sports.

A First Look At Computers

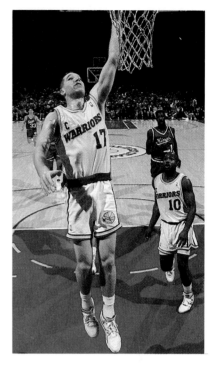

the time and running jobs. I took a one-day class three years ago in network administration, which confused me more than helped. Where I've learned how to do anything is from the system engineers who come out, and I look over their shoulders.

What are your primary responsibilities as network administrator?

Basically, I make sure that the computer network is up and running. If there is a problem that I can't solve, I'll call our vendor, and the vendor will send someone out to help me. I also have hot lines that I can call for information. I update software versions. I supervise the desktop publishing. I order and install supplies. I also work with cabling companies, who run the lines. If there is someone who needs to go to training, I send them. People have to develop good file-cleaning habits. So I send out memos periodically: "Kill off your old files." I don't go in and do it. I'm not the czar of the network; I'm just the manager.

Where do staff members get their computer knowledge? Do you provide training for them?

I'd say that the people that we've brought in have known something already. We've had a few people who really don't know anything, and you just say, "Here's the keyboard," and start them going. It's training by immersion. Getting in and out of the network is a few keystrokes. Usually they teach themselves the basics, and then we help them out. The only weak spot in that method is

that people work only to the level of what they absolutely require and they don't know the other options.

You do desktop publishing. What are the advantages and disadvantages compared to traditional printing methods?

It allows you to have a little type shop in your office. Now there's never a reason something has to look like it came out of a typewriter if you don't want it to. It's given us the ability to re-

> *The thing about a sports organization that people often don't think about is that it's a business.*

spond and communicate better with our season ticket holders. For example, recently we had to get information out really fast. We wanted people to wear white to the first home game of the play-offs. So I used the computer to make a postcard in the afternoon and then took it to the printer in the morning, and they got them done by about four o'clock. Then we stuck 5,000 labels on them, and I got them to the post office at 6:15. We actually turned a postcard around in 26 hours, and it cost me nothing to design it. Peo-

ple got it in time—and the whole place was white when we got there for the first game. So, that was really a success.

How have computers changed the way sports organizations operate?

I think it's made everything quicker. When I first came here five years ago, sending out the season tickets meant counting things out by hand and putting them in envelopes. Now they just have a big machine that prints all the sheets. It's also a lot easier to give season ticket holders better seats, because we now know exactly who is here and who is not here at the end of each season. Computers have given us the ability to upgrade the look of everything. Having the NBA network has been helpful, to spread information around the league. I guess that's what it's all about—communication, speed, and efficiency.

The thing about a sports organization that people often don't think about is that it's a business. I don't know how representative my situation is, but every team is using computers in some way. It's just the thing to do. But it's because we're a business, not because we're a sports franchise. It takes a lot of people doing these things behind-the-scenes to get those twelve guys out there playing ball every game. □

CHAPTER 1

OVERVIEW

The Ongoing Revolution
What the Future of Computers Holds for You

Frank Munoz was excited when the student employment office placed him in a temporary job at the local public television station. The station needed help recording on computer the pledges called in during their annual fund-raising drive. Frank's interest in journalism and his high school exposure to computers made him a good candidate for the job.

Although Frank knew his way around a computer keyboard, this was the first time he had used a computer for work. However, he quickly learned to enter names, addresses, pledge amounts, and viewer comments into the system. After the project was completed, the station manager asked Frank to stay on and help with the activities that followed the fund drive.

Frank learned to use the computer to sort the information he had previously entered. The station's staff then used the sorted information to print mailing labels. Later, he helped to create a form letter acknowledging viewers' pledges. He learned how to use the computer to merge viewers' names and addresses into the letters, creating personalized messages from the station manager thanking each viewer for contributing. (He had always wondered how advertisers were able to do that!)

Frank was encouraged by his success with computers, but he knew he still had a lot to learn about the machines and programs he was using. So, when he enrolled for classes in the spring, he decided to include a course in computer literacy in his schedule.

That was four years ago. What began as a temporary job soon became a career. Frank now puts computers to work producing news documentaries for a major cable network. ❏

THE REVOLUTION THAT WON'T WAIT

The Industrial Revolution changed human society on a massive scale. To live in the rapidly changing period between 1890 and 1920, for instance, was to live with the dizzying introduction of electricity, telephones, radio, automobiles, and airplanes. Like the Industrial Revolution, the Computer Revolution is bringing dramatic shifts in the way we live, perhaps even in the way we think. This revolution, however, is happening a great deal more quickly than the Industrial Revolution.

The Computer Revolution is unfinished; it will probably roll on into the next century. Nevertheless, perhaps we can glimpse the future now. Let us see how far we have come, first in society and then on a more personal level.

The Information Age: Forming a New Society

Computers have gone beyond acceptance—they are shaping society in fundamental ways. Traditionally, economics courses taught that the cornerstones of an economy were land, labor, and capital. That tenet is now being challenged, and we speak of *four* key economic elements: land, labor, capital, and information. We have converted from an industrial society to an information society. We are moving from physical labor to mental labor, trading muscle power for brain power. Just as people moved from the farms to the factories when the Industrial Revolution began, so must we adjust to the information age. You have already taken that first step, just by taking a computer class and reading this book. But how will computers become a part of your life beyond the classroom? Let us look at some of the ways in which we're already adjusting to this information age.

How You Will Use a Computer

Personal computers have moved into many facets of our lives. In the home, they are being used not only as playthings but also for keeping track of bank accounts, writing term papers and letters, learning foreign languages, designing artwork, turning on lawn sprinklers or morning coffee, monitoring temperature and humidity, presenting math and reading skills to children, and organizing mailing lists or directories. Many people are also using computers on the job, whether they sit at a desk from 9 to 5 or run a farm. Personal computers are now used for writing letters and reports; forecasting and updating budgets; creating and maintaining files; and producing charts, graphs, and newsletters. Almost any job you hope to obtain in the future will involve a computer in some way. Clearly, the computer user no longer has to be a Ph.D. in a laboratory somewhere. We are all computer users (Figure 1-1).

▲
Figure 1-1   Personal computer users.
All these people—whether at home, at work, or at school—are making use of the personal computer.

COMPUTER LITERACY FOR ALL

. . . .

Why are you reading this book? Why are you studying about computers? In addition to curiosity, you probably recognize that it will not be easy to get through the rest of your life if you do not know anything about computers.

We offer a three-part definition of **computer literacy**:

- **Awareness.** As you study computers, you will become aware of their importance, their versatility, their pervasiveness, and their potential for good and ill in our society.

- **Knowledge.** You will learn what computers are and how they work. This requires learning some technical jargon that will help you deal with the computer and with people who work with computers.

- **Interaction.** Computer literacy also means learning to use a computer for some basic tasks, or applications. By the end of this course, you should feel comfortable sitting down at a computer and using it for some suitable purpose.

Note that no part of this definition suggests that you must be able to write the instructions that tell a computer what to do. That would

CLIMB ABOARD

Is it really that important to be computer literate? Yes. But people have not always thought so. In the early days of the Computer Revolution, the average person worried about the disadvantages of computers but failed to recognize the advantages. The situation was similar to that in the early 1900s, when cars were first introduced. Historians tell us that the reaction to that newfangled contraption was much the same as people's reactions to computers. Today's traffic crush, however, is a good indication that attitudes changed somewhere along the way.

The analogy between cars and computers is illuminating. In the very near future, people who refuse to have anything to do with computers may be as inconvenienced as people who refuse to learn to drive.

be akin to saying that everyone who plans to drive a car should become an auto mechanic. Someone else can write the instructions for the computer; the interaction part of the definition merely implies that you should be able to make use of those instructions. For example, a bank teller should be able to use a computer to see if an account really contains as much money as a customer wishes to withdraw. Computers can also be used by an accountant to prepare a report, a farmer to check on market prices, a store manager to analyze sales trends, or a teenager to play a video game. We cannot guarantee that these people are computer literate, but they have at least grasped the "hands-on" component of the definition—they can interact with computers.

Since part of the definition of computer literacy is awareness, let us now look at what makes computers so useful. We will then turn to the various ways computers can be used.

EVERYWHERE YOU TURN

It seems that everywhere you turn these days, there is a computer—in stores, cars, homes, offices, hospitals, banks. What are some of the traits of computers that make them so useful?

The Value of Computers

The computer is a workhorse. It is generally capable of laboring 24 hours a day, does not ask for raises or coffee breaks, and will do the ten-thousandth task exactly the same way it did the first one—and without complaining of boredom.

There are six key reasons why computers have become an indispensable part of our lives. The first three are inherent to computers; the last three are much-valued by-products:

- **Speed.** By now it is second nature to be resentful if service is not fast. But it is "computer nature" that provides that fast service. Thus, unless we are prepared to do a lot more waiting—for paychecks, grades, telephone calls, travel reservations, bank balances, and many other things—we need the split-second processing of the computer. The speed of the computer also makes the machine ideal for processing large amounts of data, as in accounting systems and scientific applications.

- **Reliability.** Computers are extremely reliable. Of course, you might not think this from the way stories about "computer errors" are handled in the press. Unfortunately, what these stories almost never bring out is that the mistakes are not the fault of the computers themselves. True, there are sometimes equipment failures, but most errors supposedly made by computers are really human errors. Although the phrase *computer error* is quite common, the blame usually lies elsewhere.

- **Storage capability.** Computer systems are able to store tremendous amounts of data, which can then be retrieved quickly and efficiently. This storage capability is especially important in an information age.

PERSONAL COMPUTERS IN ACTION

Off to Sea with Computers

The Holland-America Line, based in Seattle, is one of the five largest cruise companies in the United States. It is one of the oldest, too. The business has grown and prospered—and turned to modern technology to run the company. Holland-America has long used large computers for its principal business operations, such as accounting. The company was also one of the first to make personal computers a major part of its business operations. But the most interesting of Holland-America's personal computer applications takes place on board ship, where computers keep track of passenger needs. The shipboard computers track ship supplies and organize tours for passengers at ports of call. All this, of course, is done behind the scenes; all the passengers luxuriating on the deck know is that their every need is met.

- **Productivity.** Computers are able to perform dangerous, boring, routine jobs, such as punching holes in metal or monitoring water levels. Granted, computers will eliminate some jobs, but computers free human beings for other work. Most workers will probably notice increased productivity in offices where individuals are using computers to do their jobs better and faster.

- **Decision making.** Because of expanding technology, communications, and the interdependency of people, we suffer from an information deluge. Although this is in part brought on by the computer, it is also the computer that will help solve it. To make essential business and governmental decisions, managers need to take into account a variety of financial, geographical, logistical, and other factors. Using problem-solving techniques originally developed by humans, the computer helps decision makers sort through and organize this vast amount of information and make better choices.

- **Reduction in costs.** Finally, because it enhances productivity and the decision-making process, the computer helps reduce duplication of effort and hold down costs for labor and energy. Thus, computers help reduce the costs of goods and services.

With all these wonderful traits to its credit, it is no wonder that the computer has made its way into almost every facet of our lives. Let us look at some of the ways computers are being used to make our workdays more productive and our personal lives more rewarding.

The Uses of Computers

The jobs that computers do are as varied as we can imagine, but the following are some of the principal uses:

- **Graphics.** There is no better place to get a sense of the computer's impact than in the area of computer graphics, computer-produced visual images. The computer as artist is evidenced in medicine,

▶

Figure 1-2   Computer-generated action art.
Computers give artists a new creative tool. Computer artist David Brickley won a $10,000 prize for his rendition called *Divers,* pictured here, which he created with software called CorelDraw.

▲

Figure 1-3   Computer-generated still life.
This photo-like illustration, used on the cover of *Macworld* magazine, was developed using software whose long name includes the term *PhotoRealistic.* It could indeed be mistaken for a real photo.

where brain scanners produce color-enhanced "maps" to help diagnose mental illness. Biochemists use computers to model, in three dimensions, the structure of molecules. Architects use computer-animated graphics to give clients visual walk-throughs of proposed buildings, to show possible exteriors, and to subject buildings to hypothetical earthquakes.

Business executives play artist, making bar graphs and pie charts out of tedious figures and using color to convey information with far more impact than numbers alone can do. Finally, a whole new kind of artist has emerged who uses computers to create cartoon animation, landscapes, television logos, action sketches, and still lifes (Figures 1-2, 1-3).

- **Commerce.** Products from meats to magazines are now packaged with zebra-striped symbols that can be read by scanners at supermarket checkout stands to determine the price of the products. The stripes, the Universal Product Code, are part of one of the highly visible uses of computers in commerce; however, there are numerous others. Modern-day warehousing and inventory management could not exist without computers. Take your copy of this book, for instance. From printer to warehouse to bookstore, its movement was tracked with the help of computers.

- **Energy.** Energy companies use computers and geological data to locate oil, coal, natural gas, and uranium. Meter-readers use handheld computers to record how much energy is used each month in homes and businesses. The utility companies also use computers to monitor and analyze their vast power networks. In addition, computers can analyze the efficiency of the insulation in your home or office and the fuel consumption in your car.

- **Transportation.** Computers are used to help run rapid transit systems, load containerships, keep track of what railroad cars have been sent where (and send them rolling home again), fly and land airplanes and keep them from colliding, schedule airline reservations, and monitor traffic (Figure 1-4).

- **Paperwork.** There is no doubt that our society runs on paper. Though in some ways the computer contributes to this problem—as in adding to the amount of junk mail you find in your mailbox—in many other ways it cuts down paper handling. The techniques of word processing, for example, let you prepare documents in draft form and place them in computer storage. If the document needs to be changed, it can be retrieved, edited, and saved again or printed without retyping. Even Supreme Court justices use word processing, storing their opinions in draft form for future reference. Computerized bookkeeping, record keeping, and document sending have also made paperwork more efficient.

- **Money.** Computers have revolutionized the way money is handled, and nowhere is this more obvious than in banking (Figure 1-5). Once upon a time it was possible to write a check for the rent on Tuesday and cover it with a deposit on Thursday, knowing it would take a few days for the bank to process the rent check and debit it against the account. With computers, however, the recording of deposits and withdrawals is done more quickly. Computers have also brought us the age of do-it-yourself banking, with automated teller machines (ATMs) available for simple transactions. Computers have helped fuel the cashless economy, enabling the widespread use of credit cards and instant credit checks by banks, department stores, and other retailers. Some oil companies are now using credit card–activated, self-service gasoline pumps. And

▲
Figure 1-4   Fighting traffic.
This computer-enhanced satellite data map shows vegetation (red), city (blue), and white lines (new development).

◀
Figure 1-5   Computers where you expect them: in banks.
Louisiana's Hibernia National Bank can concentrate its time and attention on the business of banking. This bank has contracted with IBM for a service agreement to manage the bank's computing resources.

TALKING TO YOUR CAR

You have probably heard that some new car models come equipped with a computer. What you have probably not heard is that soon all cars will come with not one but dozens of computers. In fact, engineers are taking a new look at cars, trying to improve every function by using on-board computers.

Some of these computers are out of sight and mind, busily regulating aspects like the air-fuel mix fed to the cylinders. But the visible car computers promise to captivate us in new ways. Computer screens on the dashboard can give you maps for your destination or flash "oil change" if needed. But even those features seem routine compared with the car that listens to its master's voice.

Imagine walking up to the car and saying something like, "This is me." The car recognizes your voice. The door opens, the seat and steering wheel automatically adjust for you, and the radio tunes to your favorite station. What else could you and your car talk about? Well, you could talk to the computer as you drive and have it flash stock-market quotes on the dashboard screen. Or most anything else. The key question is this one: Is it worth it?

in many grocery stores, you can use your ATM card to transfer money from your account to pay for your groceries—with no cash changing hands.

- **Communications.** Any computer has the potential of linking up with other computers through a communications system such as the telephone lines. Most businesses use computer communications systems to send memos and reports, transfer computer data files, and even have "meetings" among people in dispersed locations.

- **Agriculture.** High tech down on the farm? Absolutely. Farming is big business, and computers can help with billing, crop information, cost per acre, feed combinations, automatic irrigation, and so on. A Mississippi cotton grower, for example, boosted his annual profit 50% by using a computer to determine the best time to fertilize. Cattle breeders use computers to generate information about livestock breeding and performance. Sheep ranchers shear their sheep by using a computerized robotic shearing arm. The arm is guided by sensors; the dimensions of a typical sheep are stored in the computer's memory.

- **Government.** The federal government is the largest single user of computers. The Social Security Administration, for example, produces millions of benefit checks each month, with the help of computers. Computers are also used for forecasting weather (Figure 1-6), for admitting vacationers to parks, for processing immigrants, for meting out justice, and—yes—for collecting taxes. The FBI keeps track of suspected criminals by compiling separate bits of information into elaborate dossiers, including computer-produced mug shots, that have already helped put several organized crime lords behind bars. A veteran can walk into a local Veterans Administration office and get a rundown of benefits in seconds. As one bureaucrat said, the only way you can survive in government is to learn to use computers.

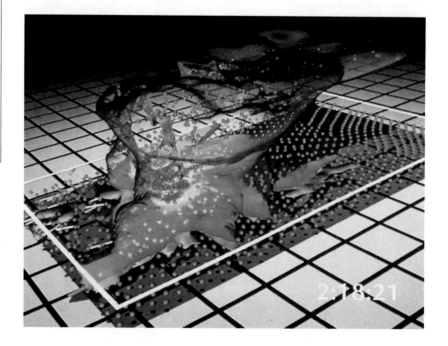

▶

Figure 1-6   When will the storm get here?   To improve the science of weather forecasting, researchers program various weather conditions into a computerized global weather model. In this graphic, different colors represent different water densities.

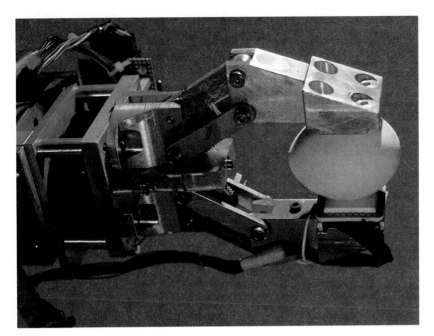

Figure 1-7   The tactile robot.
Robot chores do not usually require the delicate maneuvers required of this gripper, which can pick up an egg without crushing it.

- **Robotics.** With the age of the computer has arrived the age of the robot (Figure 1-7). Robots are information machines with the manual dexterity to perform tasks too unpleasant, too dangerous, or too critical to assign to human beings. Examples are pattern-cutting robots in the garment industry, which are able to get the most apparel out of bolts of cloth; robots used in defense to perform underwater military missions; robots used by fruit growers to pick fruit; and even robots that patrol jail corridors at night and report any persons encountered. Especially controversial are the robots that do tedious jobs better than human beings do, jobs such as welding or paint-spraying in factories. Clearly, these robots signal the end of jobs for many factory workers—a troublesome social problem.

- **Health and medicine.** Computers are used on the business side of medicine, for record keeping, and also in the diagnostic and healing process. For instance, computers are used to produce cross-sectional views of the body, to provide ultrasound pictures, and to help pharmacists test patients' medications for drug compatibility. In fact, it is estimated that computers make disease diagnoses with 85% accuracy. (The doctor, of course, makes the final diagnosis.) If you are one of the thousands who suffer one miserable cold after another, you will welcome the news that computers have been able to map, in exquisite atomic detail, the structure of a human cold virus; this is a big step on the way to a cure for the common cold (Figure 1-8). Computers are also being used for health maintenance, in everything from weight-loss programs to recording heart rates.

Figure 1-8   Cold virus.
This computer-produced model of a cold virus raises hope that a cure for the common cold may be possible after all. With the aid of a computer, the final set of calculations for the model took one month to complete. Researchers estimate that, without the computer, the calculations would have required ten years of manual effort.

- **Education.** Computers have been used behind the scenes for years in colleges and school districts for record-keeping and accounting purposes. Now, of course, they are rapidly coming into the classroom—elementary, secondary, and college. Many parents and teachers feel that computer education is a necessity, not a novelty.

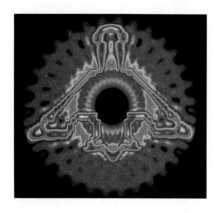

▲
Figure 1-9   Airplane design.
The precise design of this plane has yet to be
determined, but this computer-generated image
of a delta-wing craft suggests one possible
shape.

Parents want to be sure their children are not left behind in the
computer age. The pressure is on school districts to acquire computers and train teachers and students in their uses.

- **The home.** Are you willing to welcome the computer into your
home? Many people already have, often by justifying it as an educational tool for their children. But that is only the beginning.
Adults often keep records, write letters, prepare budgets, draw pictures, prepare newsletters for volunteer organizations, and communicate with other computers—all with their own computers at
home. The adventurous make their homes "smart" by using computers to control heating and air-conditioning, turn lights on and
off, "watch" for burglars, and so on.

- **The sciences.** Computers are used extensively in the sciences. For
example, the Food and Drug Administration uses a computer to
replace live subjects, such as mice, in experiments. Computers are
also used to generate models of DNA, the molecule that houses
the genetic instructions that determine the specific characteristics
of organisms. Aerospace engineers use computers to design and
test airplane parts (Figure 1-9). In England researchers have used
computers to invent a "bionic nose" that can distinguish subtle
differences in fragrance—an invention that could have major benefits for the food, perfume, and distilling industries.

- **Training.** Computers are being used as training devices in industry and government. It is much cheaper (and, of course, safer), for
instance, to teach aspiring sea captains to navigate in computerized
training simulators, than in real ships (Figure 1-10). Likewise, novice engineers or pilots can get the experience of running a train or
flying a plane with the help of a computerized device.

- **The human connection.** Are computers cold and impersonal?
Look again. The disabled don't think so. Neither do other people
who use computers in very personal ways. Computers can be used
to assist humans in areas in which we are most human. Can the
disabled walk again? Some can, with the help of computers. Can

▶
Figure 1-10   Pilot training.
These pilots practice ship handling in a
computer-controlled simulator. The view over
the port bow is actually a set of computer-
produced screens that are affected by the action
on the computer-connected pilot controls.

COMPUTING HIGHLIGHTS

The Cutting Edge

A s we approach the turn of the century, it seems like a good time for prognostications. Making predictions is a foolhardy business, but that has never stopped the experts—or us—from doing it. However, there is a bit of a safety net: New technology usually takes about a decade from lab to practical product, and the items described here are already in the labs or just entering them. These predictions relate to technology that may affect the way you work and live:

- Computers will lose their boxy shapes and, in fact, become all but unrecognizable by today's standards. Some experts talk of wristwatch-size computers that understand human speech. Others suggest book-size computers that contain entire libraries of information in what appears to be a slim volume of poetry.

- Keyboards will be replaced by handwriting screens that look like flat blotters on desks. The computer will translate hand-writing into type. Those of us with wretched handwriting will have to mend our ways just a bit.

- Communications networks will explode—soon any computer will be able to communicate almost instantly with any other computer. Voice, data, and video will be transmitted with equal ease.

- Your doctor will check your condition by having you walk through a computerized diagnostic machine that will make science-fiction writers want to take up another trade. Body-scanning technologies will open the interior of the body to a new view, so doctors will be able to diagnose problems in minutes.

- You will stop attending meetings in person and will participate electronically instead. To communicate with people, you will use a computer screen with several partitions, one per person, and you will call participants by using voice commands to arrange the conference.

Researchers are exploring the next generation of user interfaces. This screen reflects a room layout fed to the computer by a mounted camera, which can also capture user actions such as grasping, moving, and throwing.

- Last, and perhaps best, will be the continuing progress toward genuine ease of use. Using a computer will be like dialing a phone. Everyone will know how.

Technology has made astonishing leaps in just the last few years. The prevailing sentiment is why stop now?

dancers and athletes improve their performance? Maybe they can, by using computers to monitor and analyze their movements. Can we learn more about our ethnic backgrounds and our cultural history with the aid of computers? Indeed we can.

Now let us move to an early literacy check. You know more than you think you do. Even though you may not know a lot about computers yet, you have been exposed to computer hype, computer advertisements and discussions, and magazine articles and newspaper headlines about computers. You have interacted with computers in the various activities of your life—at the grocery store, your school, the library, and more. The beginnings of your computer literacy are already apparent.

Most careers involve computers in some way. This book will provide you with the foundation you need in computer literacy. If the computer is to help us rather than confuse us or threaten us, we must assume some responsibility for understanding it.

CHAPTER REVIEW

SUMMARY AND KEY TERMS

- Most people believe that computers make life easier and better, and they are optimistic about computers.
- Like the Industrial Revolution, the Computer Revolution is making massive changes in society. However, the Computer Revolution is happening more quickly than the Industrial Revolution did.
- Land, labor, capital, and information are the cornerstones of our economy. We are changing from an industrial society to an information society.
- Personal computers can be used in business and in the home for a variety of purposes.
- **Computer literacy** includes (1) an awareness of computers, (2) knowledge about computers, and (3) interaction with computers. To use a computer, however, you do not need to be able to write the instructions that tell a computer what to do.
- There are three key characteristics that make computers an indispensable part of our lives: speed, reliability, and storage capacity. By-products of these characteristics include increased productivity, enhanced decision making, and reduced costs.
- Computers are used in many areas, including graphics, commerce, energy, transportation, paperwork, money, agriculture, government, education, the home, health and medicine, robotics, the sciences, training, and helping people lead more satisfying lives.

SELF-TEST

Review Questions

1. In what ways are the Industrial Revolution and the Computer Revolution similar? In what ways are they different?
2. What are the four cornerstones of today's economy?
3. List four uses of personal computers in the home.
4. List four uses of personal computers in business.
5. What are the three components of computer literacy?
6. List three characteristics that make computers indispensable.
7. Name one use of computers in each of the following areas: graphics, commerce, energy, transportation, paperwork, money, agriculture, government, education, the home, health and medicine, robotics, the sciences, and training.

Discussion Questions

1. Do you believe that computers make life easier and better? Explain.
2. Why are you taking this class? What do you expect to learn from this class?

True/False

T F 1. The Computer Revolution will take about the same amount of time as the Industrial Revolution.

T F 2. The Computer Revolution is almost complete.

T F 3. Jobs assigned to robots are those that are too unpleasant, dangerous, or critical for humans to do.

T F 4. Computers have had a significant impact on cutting down on junk mail.

T F 5. Computer literacy means being able to give instructions to tell the computer what to do.

T F 6. The federal government is the largest single user of computers.

T F 7. Three key reasons why computers have become indispensable are speed, reliability, and storage capability.

T F 8. A "computer error" is usually the result of a breakdown in the computer.

T F 9. Computers are being distributed equally through the nation's schools.

T F 10. Computers help reduce waste and hold down costs.

Fill-In

1. Four cornerstones of today's economy are: _____, _____, _____, and _____.

2. The three components of computer literacy include: _____, _____, and _____.

3. The Computer Revolution is happening more quickly than the: _____.

4. Computers are used in the home to: _____, _____, _____, and _____.

5. Three much-valued by-products of computers are: _____, _____, and _____.

Answers

True/False: 1. F, 3. T, 5. F, 7. T, 9. F

Fill-In: 1. land, labor, capital, information; 3. Industrial Revolution; 5. productivity, decision making, reduction in costs.

CHAPTER 2

OVERVIEW

OVERVIEW OF A COMPUTER SYSTEM
HARDWARE, SOFTWARE, AND YOU

or 15 years Adele Brancolini had been the division office manager. The company's staff, from the division's general manager to the entry-level clerks, openly acknowledged that Adele "knew everything." However, when Adele learned that the company was planning to automate its offices to improve work output, she was a bit apprehensive. Computers might be a familiar part of everyday life to her teenage children, but to Adele they were still a mystery.

When the hardware and software began arriving, the loading dock was crowded with computer components to check in. As far as Adele was concerned, the product names on the invoices might as well have been in a foreign language. Calls from the consultants hired to set up the system were nearly impossible for her to answer. "Have all the CPUs arrived? What about the disk drives? We cannot begin installation until everything has come in." For once, Adele did not know everything, but she was determined to learn.

At last all the components were on hand. Off the desk went the typewriters. Up came the carpet as wires were strung everywhere. There was a constant chatter among the technicians about adapters and disks and cables and connectors. In the midst of the pandemonium, Adele's phone rang. Cindy Steiner, the training consultant with the firm doing the computer installation, was calling to ask Adele to set up a meeting with the office managers to discuss the new equipment. Adele agreed to arrange the training session and planned to attend herself.

Over coffee the next morning, Cindy explained the functions of the new computers in terms of office equipment the staff was already familiar with. Each computer, she explained, took on the role of several old systems. Word processing software let the computers and printers behave as typewriters. Spreadsheet software turned the computer into a flexible general ledger. Database software made the computer's disk into a super-convenient filing cabinet. And the wires that linked all the computers let them exchange electronic mail, eliminating most paper memos and solving the company's problem with "telephone tag."

Hearing the new system explained in familiar terms, Adele began to feel optimistic. She saw that her role in the division would not change. Instead, she would have a new set of tools to help her do her job. In a short time, Adele joined the ranks of millions who cannot imagine how they ever got along without computers. □

THE COMPUTER AS A TOOL

When most people think of tools, they think of hand tools such as hammers and saws, or perhaps lug wrenches and screwdrivers. But think of a tool in a broader sense, as anything used to do a job. This expands the horizon to include stethoscopes, baseball bats, kettles, typewriters, and—yes—computers.

The computer is a sophisticated tool, but a tool nonetheless. Who would use such a tool? Carrying our analogy further, would you buy a baseball bat if you had no intention of hitting a ball? Probably not. You probably would not purchase a computer either, or learn how to use it, unless you had some use in mind. Business people are not interested in buying useless tools. Instead, they have a plan in mind. Businesses purchase computers because they have a problem—or perhaps a set of problems—to solve.

STARTING OUT: WHAT YOU NEED TO KNOW

Knowing just a few basic concepts will prepare you for meeting a computer for the first time, whether at school or at home or on the job. If you are a beginner, you probably have heard of hardware and software, but you may have only a vague notion of what they are. The computer and its associated equipment are called **hardware.** The instructions that tell a computer what you want it to do are called **software.** The term **packaged software,** also called commercial software, refers to software that is literally packaged in a container of some sort—usually a box or folder—and is sold in stores. Most packaged software is **applications software,** software that is *applied*—or put to use—to solve a particular problem. There is a great assortment of software to help you with a variety of tasks—writing papers, preparing budgets, drawing graphs, playing games, and so forth. The wonderful array of software available is what makes computers so useful.

Software is also referred to as programs. To be more specific, a **program** is a set of step-by-step instructions that directs the computer to do the tasks you want it to do and produce the results you want. A **computer programmer** is a person who writes programs. But most of us do not write programs—we *use* programs written by someone else. This means we are **users**—people who use computer software. In business, users are sometimes called **end-users** because they are at the end of the "computer line," actually making use of the computer's information. We will emphasize the connection between computers and computer users throughout this chapter and, indeed, throughout this book.

As we continue the chapter now, we will first examine hardware, followed by software. Along the way we will note how these components work together to turn data into information. Finally, we will devote a separate section to computers and people. As the title of this chapter indicates, what follows is an overview, a look at the "big picture" of a computer system. Thus, many of the terms introduced in this chapter are defined only briefly. In subsequent chapters we will discuss the various parts of a computer system in greater detail.

HARDWARE

What is a computer? A six-year-old called a computer "radio, movies, and television combined!" A ten-year-old described a computer as "a television set you can talk to." That's getting closer, but the definition still does not recognize the computer as a machine that has the power to make changes. A **computer** is a machine that can be programmed to accept raw data (input) and process it into useful information (output). For example, a computer in a company's Payroll Department could be programmed to accept input data about an employee's rate of pay and hours worked and process it to create the employee's paycheck. The processing is directed by the software but performed by the hardware, which we will examine in this section.

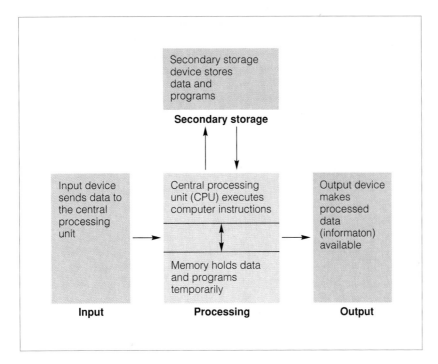

◀

Figure 2-1   The four primary components of a computer system.
To function, a computer system requires input, processing, output, and storage.

To function, a computer system requires four main areas of data handling: input, processing, output, and storage (Figure 2-1). The hardware responsible for these four areas operates as follows:

- **Input devices** accept data in a form that the computer can use and send the data to the computer's processing unit. These devices allow you to get data into the computer.

- The **central processing unit (CPU)** has the electronic circuitry that manipulates input data into the information wanted. The central processing unit actually executes computer instructions. **Memory** is associated with the central processing unit. Memory consists of the electronic circuitry that temporarily stores the data and instructions (programs) needed by the central processing unit.

- **Output devices** show you the processed data—information—in a form that is useful to you.

- **Secondary storage devices,** such as disks, can store additional data and programs permanently. These devices, which may or may not be physically attached to the computer, supplement memory.

Now let us consider the equipment making up these four parts in terms of what you would find on a personal computer.

Your Personal Computer Hardware

Suppose you want to do word processing on a personal computer, using the hardware shown in Figure 2-2. Word processing software allows you to input data such as an essay, save it, revise and resave it, and print it whenever you wish. The *input device*, in this case, is a keyboard, which you use to type, or key in, the original essay and any changes you want to make to it. All computers, large and small, must

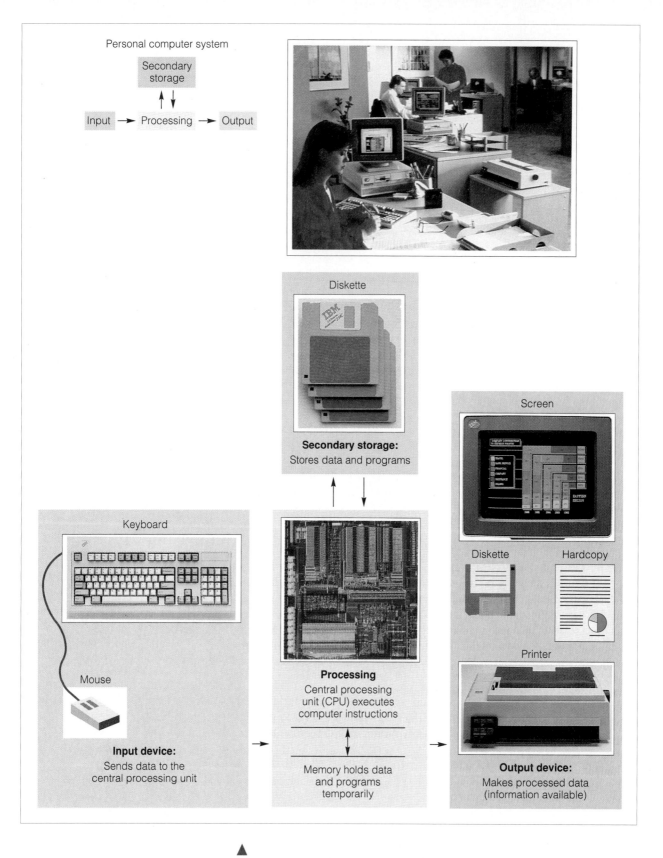

Personal computer system

Secondary storage

Input → Processing → Output

Diskette

Secondary storage:
Stores data and programs

Keyboard

Mouse

Input device:
Sends data to the central processing unit

Processing
Central processing unit (CPU) executes computer instructions

Memory holds data and programs temporarily

Screen

Diskette   Hardcopy

Printer

Output device:
Makes processed data (information available)

▲
Figure 2-2   A personal computer system.
In this IBM PS/2 personal computer system, the input devices are both a keyboard and a mouse, which feed data to the central processing unit. The central processing unit is an array of electronic circuits on a piece of silicon in the computer housing. The two output devices in this example are the screen and the printer. Secondary storage is on both $3\frac{1}{2}$-inch diskettes and hard disk. These four components of the system operate together to make the computer work for you.

have a *central processing unit*, so yours does too—it is within the personal computer housing. The central processing unit uses the word processing software to accept the data you input through the keyboard. Processed data from your personal computer is usually *output* in two forms, on a screen and a printer. As you enter the essay on the keyboard, it appears on the screen in front of you. After you examine the essay on the screen, make changes, and determine that the new version is acceptable, you can print the essay on a printer. Your *secondary storage device* in this situation could be a diskette, a magnetic medium that stores the essay until it is needed again.

Now we will take a general tour of the hardware needed for input, processing, output, and storage. All computer systems—whether small, medium, or large—are composed of these same components. In this discussion we will try to emphasize the types of hardware you are likely to see in your own environment. These topics will be covered in more detail in subsequent chapters.

Input: What Goes In

Input is the data put into the computer system for processing. Some of the most common ways of feeding input data into the system are by:

- Typing on a **keyboard.** The layout of a computer keyboard is similar to that of an electric typewriter keyboard, except that the computer responds to what you enter; that is, it "talks back" to you by displaying on the screen what you type (Figure 2-3a).

- Moving a **mouse** over a flat surface. As the ball on its underside rotates, the mouse movement causes corresponding movement on the computer screen. Buttons on the mouse let the user invoke commands (Figure 2-3a).

- Reading with a **wand reader,** which can be used to scan the special letters and numbers on price tags in retail stores (Figure 2-3b). Wand readers can read data directly from the source, such as a price tag, into the computer. Thus, they significantly reduce the cost and potential error associated with manually entering data on a keyboard.

- Moving a product over a **bar code reader,** which scans **bar codes,** the zebra-striped symbols now carried on nearly all products (Figure 2-3c). Like wand readers, bar code readers collect data at the source, reducing errors and costs.

An input device may be part of a **terminal** that is connected to a large computer. A terminal includes (1) an input device—a keyboard, wand reader, or bar code reader, for instance; (2) an output device—usually a television-like **screen;** and (3) a connection to the main computer. The screen displays the data that has been input. After the computer processes this data, the screen displays the results of the processing—the information wanted. In a store, for instance, the terminal screen displays the individual prices (the data) and the total price (the desired information).

The Central Processing Unit and Memory: Data Manipulation

The **central processing unit,** or **CPU,** is the computer's center of activity. The central processing unit consists of electronic circuits that

(a)

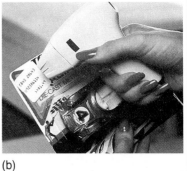
(b)

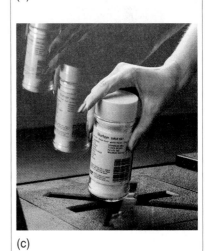
(c)

▲
Figure 2-3 Input.
(a) The most widely used input device is the keyboard. The mouse, however, is a common substitute for some keyboard functions. Movement of the mouse on a flat surface causes corresponding movement of a pointer on the screen. (b) To input data, this wand reader scans special letters and numbers on price tags. Wand readers are often found in department stores. (c) Bar code readers are used in supermarkets to input the bar codes found on product labels.

interpret and execute program instructions as well as communicate with the input, output, and storage devices.

It is the central processing unit that, using software, actually transforms data into information. **Data** is the raw material to be processed by a computer. Such material can be letters, numbers, or facts—such as grades in a class, baseball batting averages, or light and dark areas in a photograph. Processed data becomes **information**—data that is organized, meaningful, and useful. Data that is very uninteresting to one person may become very interesting information to another. The raw facts—the *data*—of births, eating habits, and growth rates of calves, for instance, may mean nothing to most people. But the computer-produced relationships among feed, growth, and beef quality are critical *information* to a cattle breeder.

The computer's **memory,** which is also known as **primary storage,** is closely associated with the central processing unit but separate from it. Memory holds the data after it is input to the system but before it is processed. It also holds the data after it has been processed but before it has been released to the output device. In addition, memory holds the programs (computer instructions) needed by the central processing unit. Memory consists of electronic circuits, just as the CPU does. Memory electronically stores letters, numbers, special characters (such as dollar signs and decimal points), and even graphic images.

Output: What Comes Out

The results produced by the central processing unit are, of course, a computer's whole reason for being; **output** is usable information. That is, raw input data has been processed by the computer into information that is relevant and useful to the user. Some ingenious forms of output have been devised, such as music and synthetic speech, but the most common forms are words, numbers, and graphics. Words, for example, may be the letters and memos prepared by office workers using word processing software. Other workers may be more interested in numbers, such as those found in formulas, schedules, and budgets. As we will see, numbers can often be understood more easily when they are output in the form of computer graphics.

Two common output devices are screens and printers. You already read about screens when you read the description of input. Screens can show lines of text, a numerical display, or color graphics (Figure 2-4a).

Printers are machines that produce printed documents at the instruction of a computer program (Figure 2-4b). Some printers form typed images on paper as typewriters do; they strike a character against a ribbon, which makes an image on the paper. Other printers form characters or graphics by using lasers, photography, or sprays of ink.

Secondary Storage

Secondary storage is additional storage that can hold data and programs permanently. Secondary storage has several advantages. For instance, it would be unwise for a college registrar to try to house student records in the computer's memory; if this were done, the computer probably would not have room to store anything else. Also, memory

(a)

(b)

▲
Figure 2-4   Output.
Screens and printers are two types of output devices. (a) The graphics displayed on this screen are one form of output. (b) This laser printer produces output in the form of printed documents.

holds data and programs only temporarily—hence the need for permanent secondary storage.

The two most common secondary storage media are magnetic disk and magnetic tape. A **magnetic disk** is a flat, oxide-coated disk on which data is recorded as magnetic spots. A disk can be a diskette or a hard disk. A **diskette,** used with a personal computer, looks something like a small stereo record. A diskette $5\frac{1}{4}$ inches in diameter is called a **floppy disk,** because it is somewhat flexible. The floppy disk used to be the most common. Now, however, the $3\frac{1}{2}$-inch disk, a flexible disk in a plastic jacket, is becoming the standard (Figure 2-5a). A **hard disk** is inflexible and is often in a sealed module. **Hard disks,** which are used by both small and large computers, hold more data and can be accessed faster than diskettes.

Disk data is read by **disk drives.** We have already considered personal computer disk drives that can read diskettes. Most personal computers also have hard disk drives. On some larger computer systems, the disk packs can be removed from the drives (Figure 2-5b). This permits the use of interchangeable packs, resulting in practically unlimited storage capacity.

Magnetic tape, which comes on a reel or in a cartridge, is similar to tape that is played on a tape recorder. Magnetic tape reels are

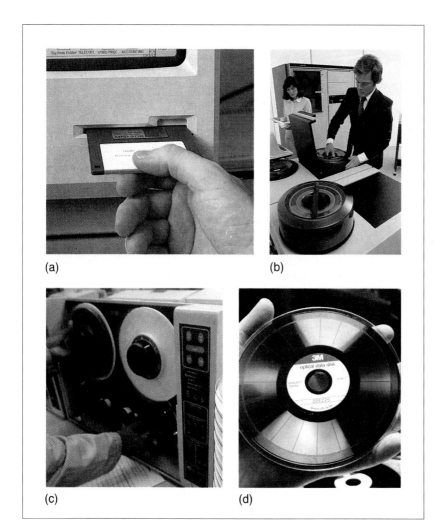

(a)

(b)

(c)

(d)

◄

Figure 2-5   Secondary storage.
(a) A $3\frac{1}{2}$-inch diskette is being inserted into a disk drive. (b) Hard disks are contained within the round disk pack shown on the top of the cabinets, which contain the disk drives. When it is to be used, a disk pack is lowered into the open compartment. (c) Magnetic tape, shown here being mounted on a tape drive, travels off one reel and onto another. (d) Optical disk technology uses a laser beam to store large volumes of data.

How well can you take care of yourself, computerwise? If you are a computer novice, you may think the answer for you is "not at all." If so, you may need to reconsider. Although you may think you are unfamiliar with computers, you probably use one often. For example, most people have used an automated teller machine (ATM), the money-dispensing machine on the outside of the bank's wall. In fact, they use it routinely, without giving a thought to the computer technology that supports it. The success of the ATM in the banking industry has inspired other service organizations to follow suit. That is, soon you are going to be seeing a variety of easy-instruction machines and receiving the opportunity to take care of yourself. Computer-based self-service options coming your way include self-ticketing airline flights, self-purchased insurance policies, and attendantless gas stations. With all these self-service machines in common use, you will be able to take

care of your own needs quickly and easily—with a little help from a computer.

mounted on **tape drives** when the data on them needs to be read by the computer system or when new data is to be written on the tape (Figure 2-5c). Magnetic tape is usually used for backup purposes—for "data insurance"—chiefly because tape is inexpensive.

The most recent storage technology, however, is **optical disk,** which uses a laser beam to store large volumes of data at low cost (Figure 2-5d).

The Complete Hardware System

The hardware devices attached to the computer are called **peripheral equipment.** Peripheral equipment includes all input, output, and secondary storage devices. In the case of personal computers, some of the input, output, and storage devices are built into the same physical unit. In the personal computer we saw in Figure 2-2, for instance, the CPU and disk drive are contained in the same housing; the keyboard and screen are separate.

In larger computer systems, however, the input, processing, output, and storage functions may be in separate rooms, separate buildings, or even separate countries. For example, data may be input on terminals at a branch bank, then transmitted to the central processing unit at the bank's headquarters. The information produced by the central processing unit may then be transmitted to the bank's international offices, where it is printed out. Meanwhile, disks with stored data may be kept in the bank's headquarters, and duplicate data may be kept on disk or tape for safekeeping in a warehouse across town.

Although the equipment may vary widely, from the simplest computer to the most powerful, by and large the four elements of a computer system remain the same: input, processing, output, and storage. Now let us look at the various ways computers are classified.

Classifications: Computers Big and Small

Computers come in sizes from tiny to monstrous, in both appearance and power. The size of a computer that a person or an organization needs depends on the computing requirements. The National Weather Service, keeping watch on the weather fronts of many continents, has different requirements from those of a car dealer's service department that is trying to keep track of its parts inventory. And the requirements of both of them are different from the needs of a salesperson using a laptop computer to record client orders on a sales trip.

Mainframes and Supercomputers

In the jargon of the computer trade, large computers are called **mainframes** (Figure 2-6a). Mainframes are capable of processing data at very fast speeds—several million program instructions per second, for example—and they have access to billions of characters of data. The price of a mainframe varies from several hundred thousand to many millions of dollars. With that kind of price tag, you will not buy a mainframe for just any purpose. The principal use of such a powerful computer is for processing vast amounts of data quickly. You will be most likely to use a mainframe if you work for a bank, an insurance company, a government agency, or a manufacturer. However, this list

▼
Figure 2-6 Computer classifications.
(a) Despite the sterile look of this staged photo, it does show that a mainframe computer has many components. Shown here is the IBM mainframe called Sierra. (b) The Cray-2 supercomputer has been nicknamed Bubbles because of its bubbling, shimmering coolant liquids. You can own it for a mere $17.6 million. (c) The VAX, a popular minicomputer made by Digital Equipment Corporation (DEC). (d) This personal computer is made by Hewlett-Packard.

(a)

(b)

(c)

(d)

is not all-inclusive; you could also use such a computer if you worked for a large mail-order house, an airline with a sophisticated reservations system, an aerospace company doing complex aircraft design, or the like.

The mightiest computers—and, of course, the most expensive—are known as **supercomputers** (Figure 2-6b). Supercomputers process *billions* of instructions per second. If you ever work for the federal government in an area such as worldwide weather forecasting, oil exploration, and weapons research, you will probably use a supercomputer. Supercomputers are now moving toward the mainstream, for activities as varied as creating special effects for movies and analyzing muscle structures. Supercomputers can also produce super graphics (Figure 2-7).

Minicomputers

The next step down from mainframe computers are **minicomputers** (Figure 2-6c). Minicomputers are generally slower than mainframes and are less costly. In fact, when minicomputers first appeared on the market, their lower price fell within the range of many small businesses, greatly expanding the potential computer market.

▼
Figure 2-7 Super supercomputers.
These graphics represent (a) mathematical shapes, (b) a simulation of the evolution of the universe, (c) human muscle, and (d) density flow patterns of a jet engine.

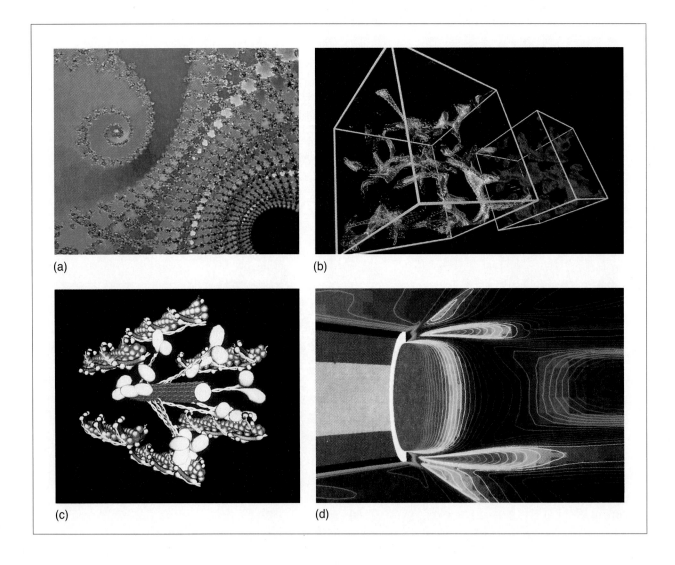

(a)

(b)

(c)

(d)

Minicomputers were originally intended to be small and serve some special purpose. However, in a fairly short time, they have become more powerful and more versatile, and the line between minicomputer and mainframe has blurred. In fact, the appellation *mini* no longer seems to fit very well. The term **supermini** has been coined to describe minis at the top of the size-price scale. If you will work in a retail business, a college, or a state or city agency, you are likely to use a minicomputer. However, the minicomputer market is diminishing somewhat as buyers choose computers that are less expensive: microcomputers.

Microcomputers

The smallest computers are called **microcomputers** (Figure 2-6d). Microcomputers are often called by other names, such as desktop or home or personal computers; we will use the common name **personal computer (PC)** in this book. For many years, the computer industry was on a quest for the biggest computer; the search was always for more power and greater capacity. Prognosticators who timidly suggested a niche for a smaller computer were subject to ridicule by people who, as it turned out, could not have been more wrong. Now, for a few hundred dollars, anyone can have a small computer. (Most people, however, are more likely to choose a computer that costs a few *thousand* dollars.)

Microcomputers—personal computers—are so important that we will return to them again in later chapters. You will probably also be interested in the Buyer's Guide, which describes how to buy a personal computer.

Data Communications: Processing Here or There

Suppose your job includes processing insurance policies for the San Francisco branch of a large insurance company that has branches throughout the United States and a headquarters office in Denver. Your training would certainly include how to access the computer and how to use the records stored in the computer system. But just where is the computer and where are the records? Is everything nearby, in one place, or is it more practical to have the hardware and the files spread around?

In the early days, computer hardware was kept in one place; that is, it was **centralized** in one room. Though this is still sometimes the case, more and more computer systems are **decentralized.** That is, the computer itself and some storage devices may be in one place, but the devices to access the computer—terminals or even other computers— are scattered among the users. These devices are usually connected to the computer by telephone lines. The subject of decentralization is intimately tied to **data communications,** the process of exchanging data over communications facilities. In the case of the insurance company, the computer and storage that contain the policy records could be at company headquarters; the terminals could be in branch offices all over the country, so an agent anywhere could access the records.

However, suppose this insurance company has gone a step further, placing both computers and storage devices in dispersed locations. This arrangement is known as **distributed data processing** because

PERSONAL COMPUTERS IN ACTION

But What Would I Use It For?

In addition to the general categories we have mentioned in the text, there are some very specific—and idiosyncratic—software packages that find their way into home computers. See if any of the offerings in this sampler appeal to you.

- **Jigsaw.** Slide a piece into place. And then another and another. But do not plan to do anything else for a while, because it is hard to abandon this electronic jigsaw puzzle until it is complete. Several scenes, including landscapes, are included in the program. (Britannica Software)
- **Action Planner.** This program offers computer power for your appointment book: Organize schedule, notes, and lists automatically. Print everything on prepunched paper, and enclose it in a genuine leather binder (included). (Power Up!)
- **VCR Companion.** Turn your home videos into major motion pictures! Well, the ad may overstate the case just a bit, but you can create your own title, credits, and graphics, then transfer them directly to videotape. (Broderbund)
- **Mastering the SAT.** The claim is straightforward: This program can dramatically improve your score on the Scholastic Aptitude Test (SAT) to get you into the college or university of your choice. In addition to teaching and testing, the program aims at improving test-taking strategies and reducing anxiety. (CBS Software)
- **Print Shop.** Design cards, posters, banners, or invitations that use a built-in art library of ready-made pictures and symbols and a dozen backgrounds and borders. Choose type style and size, all with optional outline and three-dimensional effects. You cannot produce cards that are as nice looking as those you buy in a store, but you can say, "Look, Mom, I made it myself." (Broderbund)
- **The Running Program.** Take just a few minutes each day to input your running data so that the program can produce graphs of how you performed over different distances at different paces. It also has screens full of advice—from warm-up exercises, including graphic demonstrations; to remedies for knee pains; to what you should wear. About the only thing it does not do is get you out of bed in the morning. (MECA Software)
- **World Atlas.** It's an atlas, an almanac, and a fact book all in one. The screen maps are especially useful with a mouse: Just point and click on a country, state, or city and be supplied with facts such as population and an array of climatic information. (Power Up!)

ing these problems is limited too. Thus, the problems and the software solutions fall, for the most part, into just a few categories. These categories of problems and their solutions can be found in most business environments (Figure 2-10). These major categories are word processing (including desktop publishing), spreadsheets, database management, graphics, and communications. We will present a brief description of each category here.

Word Processing

The most widely used software is for **word processing**. This software lets you create, edit, format, store, and print text. From this definition, it is the three words in the middle—"edit, format, and store"—that

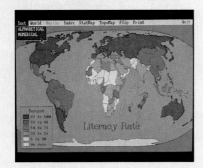

- **HouseCall.** The advertisements for this "computerized home medical advisor" say it was written by physicians. HouseCall offers 400 diagnoses in a program that is touted as fast, easy, and fun to use. (Rocky Mountain Medical Software)

- **Business Simulator.** Tired of games that test your reflexes? Ready to flex your mind? As this game begins, you start your own robotics company. You have $500,000 in seed money and access to robotics technology. As you play the game, you need to make all kinds of choices: choices about prices, number of units to build, marketing strategies, and when to offer new products.

Make the wrong choices and—just as in the real world—you lose. (Reality Development)

- **Heart-to-Heart.** No therapists are needed—so they say—if you have this software package, aimed at mending broken hearts and lesser problems. Described as a "communication session for couples to help improve and expand their relationships," the program should at least get the computer-junkie partner talking—even if it is through the computer. (Interactive Software)

- **Roots.** If you have studied your family's history, you know how much fun—and how confusing—it can be. Easy enough for ama-

teurs but powerful enough for professionals, Roots provides an organizational framework to help you untangle the family data. Its searching and sorting capabilities let you note relationships among newly discovered ancestors. You can look up family members by name, date, location, and more. (Commsoft)

- **Flight Simulator.** Climb into the cockpit of a Cessna 182 and get ready for almost anything in a flight simulation so realistic that even licensed pilots have their hands full with it. More than a game, this approaches training and is a real challenge. (Microsoft)

make word processing different from plain typing. Since you can store on disk the memo or document you type, you can retrieve it another time, change it, reformat it, or reprint it. The timesaving factor is that the unchanged parts of the saved document do not need to be retyped, and the whole document can be reprinted as if new. Businesses use word processing for every conceivable type of document—in fact, for everything that used to be typed.

Desktop publishing lets users employ software and a high-quality printer to produce printed materials that combine graphics with text. The resulting professional-looking newsletters, reports, and brochures can improve communication and help organizations make a better impression on the outside world (Figure 2-11). Although sophisticated users invoke software specifically designed for desktop publishing, many users produce similar results with the desktop publishing fea-

▶

Figure 2-10   Problem-solving software.
Decision makers in offices large and small rely on personal computers to help them solve problems. With the computers they use software for word processing, desktop publishing, spreadsheet, database management, graphics, and communications.

tures inherent in their word processing software. Since publishing in one form or another typically consumes up to 10% of a company's gross revenues, desktop publishing has been given a warm welcome by business. However, home users are becoming just as captivated by this technology, as evidenced by the improved look of club newsletters and the like.

Spreadsheets

Used to organize and analyze business data, a **spreadsheet** is a worksheet divided into columns and rows. For example, the simple expense

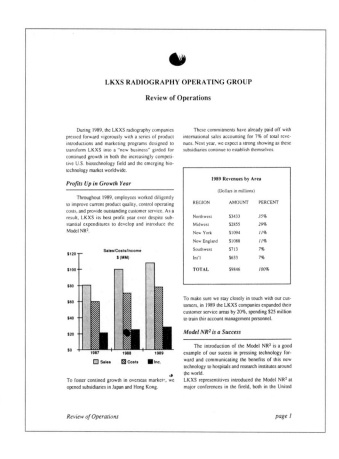

▶

Figure 2-11   Desktop publishing.
Desktop publishing software lets users produce attractive output that combines text and graphics.

spreadsheet in Figure 2-12a shows time periods (months) as columns and various categories (rent, phone, and so forth) as rows. Notice that figures in the rightmost column and in the last row are the result of calculations. Manual spreadsheets have been used as business tools for centuries. But a spreadsheet can be tedious to prepare by hand, and when there are changes a considerable amount of work may need to be redone. An **electronic spreadsheet** (Figure 2-12b) is still a spreadsheet, but the computer does much of the work. In particular, spreadsheet software automatically recalculates the results when a number is changed. The ability to automatically recalculate lets businesses experiment with numbers based on different forecasts or predictions—this kind of experimentation is called "What-if . . . ?" analysis—and obtain the results quickly. Many spreadsheet programs will also convert the spreadsheet into a graph or chart (Figure 2-12c).

Database Management

Software used for **database management**—the management of a collection of interrelated information—handles data in several ways. The software can store data, update it, manipulate it, and create reports in a

▼

Figure 2-12 A simple expense spreadsheet.

(a) This expense sheet is a typical spreadsheet of rows and columns. Note the calculations needed to generate the values in the rightmost column and the bottom row. (b) This spreadsheet summarizes the same information, but now the computer is doing the calculations. (c) The same information made into a simple pie-chart graphic.

EXPENSES	JAN	FEB	MARCH	APRIL	TOTAL
RENT	425.00	425.00	425.00	425.00	1700.00
PHONE	22.50	31.25	17.00	35.75	106.00
CLOTHES	110.00	135.00	156.00	91.00	492.00
FOOD	280.00	250.00	250.00	300.00	1080.00
HEAT	80.00	50.00	24.00	95.00	249.00
ELECTRICITY	35.75	40.50	45.00	36.50	157.75
WATER	10.00	11.00	11.00	10.50	42.50
CAR INSURANCE	75.00	75.00	75.00	75.00	300.00
ENTERTAINMENT	150.00	125.00	140.00	175.00	590.00
TOTAL	1188.25	1142.75	1143.00	1243.75	4717.75

(a)

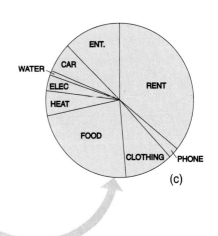

```
           A          B        C        D        E        F        G
  1   ████████████
  2                  JAN      FEB      MAR      APR     TOTAL
  3
  4   EXPENSES
  5   RENT          425.00   425.00   425.00   425.00  1700.00
  6   PHONE          22.50    31.25    17.00    35.75   106.50
  7   CLOTHES       110.00   135.00   156.00    91.00   492.00
  8   FOOD          280.00   250.00   250.00   300.00  1080.00
  9   HEAT           80.00    50.00    24.00    95.00   249.00
 10   ELECTRICITY    35.75    40.50    45.00    36.50   157.75
 11   WATER          10.00    11.00    11.00    10.50    42.50
 12   CAR INSURANCE  75.00    75.00    75.00    75.00   300.00
 13   ENTERTAINMENT 150.00   125.00   140.00   175.00   590.00
 14
 15
 16   TOTAL        1188.25  1142.75  1143.00  1243.75  4717.75
 17
 18
 19
 20
 09-FEB-92   02:39 PM
```

(b)

(c)

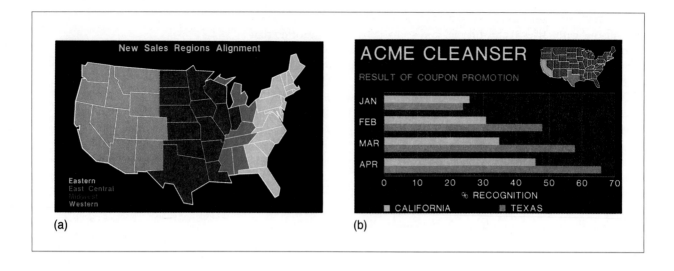

▲
Figure 2-13   Business graphics.
These colorful computer-generated graphics can help people compare data and spot trends.

variety of forms. A concert promoter, for example, can store and change data about upcoming concert dates, seating, ticket prices, and sales. The promoter can then use the software to retrieve information such as the number of tickets sold in each price range or the percentage of tickets sold the day before the concert. Database software can be useful for anyone who must keep track of and examine large amounts of information.

Graphics

It might seem wasteful to show business people **graphics**—pictorial representations of data—when it would be less expensive to use the numbers in standard computer printouts. However, maps, charts, and the like can help people compare data and spot trends more easily and make decisions more quickly (Figure 2-13). Six pages of numeric confusion can be made into a single chart that anyone can pick up and understand.

Communications

We have already described data communications in a general way. From the viewpoint of a worker with a personal computer, data communications means—in simple terms—that he or she can hook up the computer with the phone system or some other network and send data to or receive data from a computer in another location. Business users send memos, exchange project data, leave messages, send data to the headquarters office, access stock quotes, and on and on. Home users send greetings to friends and family who have computers, make bank funds transfers, order products, and so forth. There are few limitations once a computer is hooked up to a communications system.

PEOPLE AND COMPUTERS
• • • • • • • • • • • • • • • • • •

We have talked about hardware, software, and data, but the most important element in a computer system is people. Anyone nervous about a takeover by computers will be relieved to know that computers will never amount to much without people—the people who help make the system work and the people for whom the work is done.

Computers and You, the User

As we noted earlier, computer users have come to be called just *users*, a nickname that has persisted for years. Whereas once computer users were an elite breed—high-powered Ph.D.s, research-and-development engineers, government planners—the population of users has broadened considerably. This expansion is due partly to user-friendly software for both work and personal use and partly to the availability of small, low-cost computers.

The most elementary user is the novice, the person with minimal training on computers. He or she may be familiar with a software package or two, such as word processing, but uses just a few of the features available. Or, a novice may be an employee trained well enough to make the inquiries required for customer service, banking, or airline reservations.

A more experienced user has probably mastered several programs. Above this level are sophisticated users who use the computer as an integral part of their business or professional lives. Finally, a few advanced users have written some computer programs, understand computer jargon, and are well equipped to deal with computer professionals in the organization.

Computer People

Another way to think about people and computers is within the context of an organization. In an organization that uses large computers, the computer department may be called **Management Information Systems (MIS)** or **Computing Services** or—more commonly—**Information Services.** The department is the group of people responsible for the computer resources of an organization. Whether the department is within a university, a government bureau, or a corporation, this organization may well be the institution's most important asset. Most of the knowledge of that institution is contained in its computer files: research data, engineering drawings, marketing strategy, accounts receivable, accounts payable, sales information, manufacturing specifications, transportation plans, warehousing data—the list goes on and on. The guardians of this information are the same people who provide service to the users: the computer professionals. Let us touch on the essential personnel required to run computer systems.

Data entry operators prepare data for processing, usually by keying it, so it is in a machine-readable format. **Computer operators** monitor the computer, review procedures, and keep peripheral equipment running. **Librarians** catalog the processed disks and tapes and keep them secure.

Computer programmers design, write, test, and implement the programs that process data on the computer system. Furthermore, they maintain and update the programs as needed, an ongoing process. **Systems analysts** are knowledgeable in the programming area but have broader responsibilities: They plan and design not just individual programs, but entire computer systems. Systems analysts work closely with users to plan and revise systems to meet the users' needs. The department director, often called the **chief information officer (CIO),** must understand more than just computer technology. This person must understand the goals and operations of the entire organization.

Whether the organization is large or small, it will include staff to manage personal computers. Some organizations also need many people to train and support personal computer users, as well as oversee the related hardware and software. Small companies, especially those using personal computers exclusively, sometimes get by with a jack-of-all-trades employee who handles all these functions.

▲   ▲   ▲

In this chapter we have painted the computer industry with a broad brush, touching on hardware, software, data, and people. We now move on to the first chapter that explains the important role of personal computers in this scheme.

CHAPTER REVIEW

SUMMARY AND KEY TERMS

- The machines in a computer system are called **hardware.** The **programs,** or step-by-step instructions that run the machines, are called **software.** Software sold in stores, and usually contained in a box or folder, is called **packaged software.** Most packaged software is **applications software,** software that is applied to solve a particular problem. **Computer programmers** write programs for **users,** or **end-users**—that is, people who use computer software.

- A **computer** is a machine that can be programmed to process data (input) into useful information (output). A computer system comprises three main categories of data handling—input, processing, and output—and includes a fourth, storage.

- **Input** is data put into the computer. Common **input devices** include a **keyboard**; a **mouse;** a **wand reader,** which scans special letters and numbers such as those on specially printed price tags in retail stores; and a **bar code reader,** which scans the zebra-striped **bar codes** on store products. The wand reader and bar code reader read data directly from an original document, thus reducing the cost and human error associated with manual input.

- A **terminal** includes an input device, such as a keyboard or wand reader; an **output device,** usually a television-like **screen;** and a connection to the main computer. A screen displays both the input data and the processed information.

- The **central processing unit (CPU)** uses software to organize raw **data** into meaningful, useful **information.** It interprets and executes program instructions and communicates with the input, output, and storage devices. **Memory,** or **primary storage,** is associated with the central processing unit but is separate from it. Memory holds the input data before processing and after processing, until the data is released to the output device.

- **Output,** raw data processed into usable information, is usually in the form of words, numbers, and graphics. Users can see output displayed on screens and use **printers** to display output on paper.

- The computer's memory is limited and temporary. Therefore, **secondary storage** is needed, most commonly in the form of magnetic disks and magnetic tape. **Magnetic disks** can be diskettes or hard disks. **Diskettes,** or floppy disks, may be $5\frac{1}{4}$ inches or $3\frac{1}{2}$ inches in diameter. **Hard disks,** often contained in disk packs, hold more data than a diskette. Disk data is read by **disk drives. Magnetic tape** comes on reels that are mounted on **tape drives** when the data is to be read by the computer. **Optical disk** technology uses a laser beam to store large volumes of data relatively inexpensively.

- **Peripheral equipment** includes all the input, output, and secondary storage devices attached to a computer.

- Computers can be loosely categorized according to their capacity for processing data. Large computers called **mainframes** are used by such customers as banks, airlines, and large manufacturers to process very large amounts of data quickly. The most powerful and expensive computers are called **supercomputers. Minicomputers,** which are widely used by colleges and retail businesses, were originally intended to be small but have become increasingly similar to mainframes in capacity. Therefore, the largest and most expensive minicomputers are now called **superminis.** The smallest computers are called **microcomputers** or **personal computers (PCs).**

- A **centralized** computer system does all processing in one location. In a **decentralized** system, the computer itself and some storage devices are in one place, but the devices to access the computer are somewhere else. Such a system requires **data communications**—the exchange of data over communications facilities. In a **distributed data processing** system, a local office usually uses its own small computer for processing local data but is connected to the larger organization's central computer for other purposes.

- Often organizations use a **network** of personal computers, which allows users to operate their personal computers independently or in cooperation with other computers to exchange data and share resources.

- Software is accompanied by an instruction manual, also called **documentation.** Software that is easy to use is considered **user friendly.**

- Problem-solving software falls, for the most part, into just a few categories: **word processing, desktop publishing, spreadsheet, database management, graphics,** and **communications.**

- Computer users range from novices with no training to advanced users and computer professionals.

- People are vital to any computer system. In an organization that uses large computers, the computer resources department is often called **Management Information Systems (MIS)** or **Computing Services** or **Information Services.** This department includes **data entry operators** (who prepare data for processing), **computer operators** (who monitor and run the equipment), **librarians** (who catalog disks and tapes), **computer programmers** (who design, write, test, and implement programs), **systems analysts** (who plan entire systems of programs), and a **chief information officer** (who coordinates the department). Some organizations also need many people to train and support personal computer users as well as to oversee related personal computer hardware and software.

SELF-TEST

True/False

T F 1. The processor is also called the central processing unit, or CPU.
T F 2. Secondary storage units contain the instructions and data to be used immediately by the processor.
T F 3. Desktop publishing software is used to store and retrieve information.
T F 4. Processed data that is organized, meaningful, and useful is called information.
T F 5. *User-friendly* refers to a special kind of terminal.
T F 6. To use a computer, you need not know its internal functions.
T F 7. The people who write software are called computer operators.
T F 8. Computer hardware is always kept in one large room.
T F 9. These computer categories are listed from smallest to largest: microcomputers, minicomputers, mainframes.
T F 10. Computer users must be highly skilled and well trained.

Matching

_____ 1. spreadsheet   a. documentation

_____ 2. processor   b. disk pack

_____ 3. instruction manual   c. printer

_____ 4. secondary storage   d. data

_____ 5. input device   e. columns and rows

_____ 6. word processing   f. supercomputers

_____ 7. primary storage   g. CPU

_____ 8. raw facts   h. wand

_____ 9. output device   i. key, store, edit

_____ 10. most powerful computers   j. memory

Fill-In

1. After it is input but before it is processed, data is held in:

   _____

2. The input, output, and secondary storage devices attached to a computer are called: _____

3. Large computers are called: _____

4. The term describing a system whereby computers and data storage are placed in geographically separate locations: _____

5. Software to help people compare data and spot trends quickly is called:

   _____

6. The exchange of data over communication facilities is called:

   _____

7. Software that is easy to use is said to be: _____

8. The people who plan and design systems of programs are called:

   _____

9. The planned step-by-step instructions required to turn data into information are:

   _____

10. The most powerful computers are called: _____

Answers

True/False: 1. T, 3. F, 5. F, 7. F, 9. T

Matching: 1. e, 3. a, 5. h, 7. j, 9. c

Fill-In: 1. memory, 3. mainframes, 5. graphics, 7. user friendly, 9. software (or program)

CHAPTER 3

OVERVIEW

PERSONAL COMPUTERS
AN INTRODUCTION

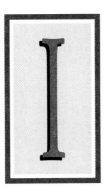 n the early 1980s, when personal computers began appearing on the desks of corporate managers, Jim Young, a veteran of the early days of computing, remained steadfastly wed to his mainframe. Jim's position as manager of the data processing department for a large insurance company was the result of a long-term perspective on computing. His mainframe system managed the company's thousands of accounts, supported the planning and forecasting that kept the company's assets growing, and served the internal administrative needs of the company's several hundred employees. Jim argued, quite correctly, that it took a big computer to do these big jobs. They were well beyond the capability of "toy computers," as Jim called personal computers.

Jim's department-level computing needs were smaller, though. While others around him had moved to personal computers to fulfill these needs, however, Jim had continued to base his own computing on the mainframe. Interestingly, it was one of the firm's newest employees who finally changed Jim's thinking about personal computers.

Ellen Chi, recently hired by the company's publications office, needed some data from Jim's department to produce a section of the company's annual report. Jim told her where on the mainframe she could find the figures she needed. He was surprised when she returned only an hour later with beautiful, three-dimensional color graphs of his data.

Ellen's secret was her personal computer. She had electronically transferred Jim's data to her own computer. Then, with the help of a data analysis software package, and a few keystrokes and clicks of the mouse, she was able to print polished graphs on her department's color laser printer. Although Jim had produced dozens of attractive reports and graphs over the years on the mainframe, Ellen had been able to create the same graphs in a fraction of the time.

Jim was finally convinced. A few weeks later, he had his own personal computer and a connection to the publications department printer. ∎

THE COMPLETE PERSONAL COMPUTER

Just how complete your personal computer system will be is a matter of personal taste, interest, and budget. You can scale way down to get by with the bare minimum, or you can start with top-of-the-line equipment and all the trimmings. Or, like most people, you can start out with a moderate investment and build on it.

The Basic Components

Let us begin by considering what is inside a personal computer. It is really pretty easy to have a look inside most personal computers; you may not even need a screwdriver. (Caution: Some manufacturers are *not* interested in having you peer under the hood, and doing so will void your warranty. Check your documentation—your instruction manual—first.) You will find an impressive array of electronic gear (Figure 3-1). Part of what you see before you is related to hardware we described in Chapter 2: the central processing unit and memory.

A miniaturized central processing unit can be etched on a chip smaller than a thumbtack (Figure 3-2), hence the term *computer on a chip.* A central processing unit on a chip is called a **microprocessor.** The type of microprocessor in your personal computer depends on the computer purchased. In addition to the microprocessor, a personal computer has two kinds of memory chips: **random-access memory (RAM)** and **read-only memory (ROM).** These terms are actually a

▼

Figure 3-1   Inside a personal computer. This drawing shows what you would see if you removed the cover from an IBM PS/2. A typical PS/2 probably has some of the expansion slots filled with a memory board and an internal modem.

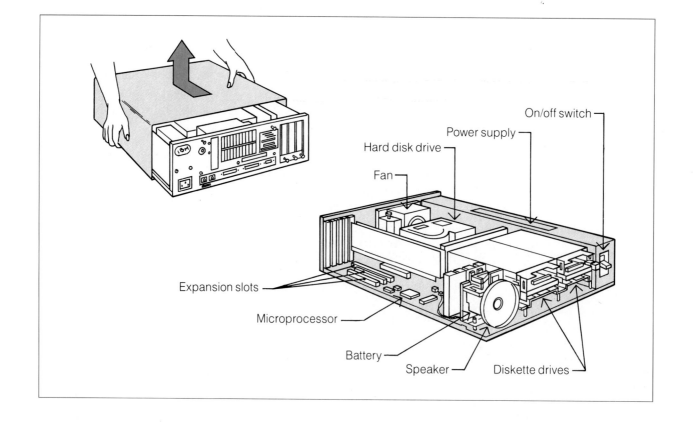

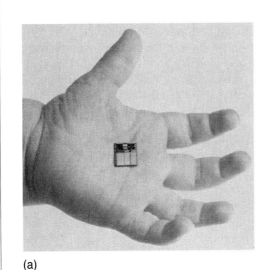 

(a)   (b)

▲
Figure 3-2   Computer on a chip.
(a) Microprocessors are small enough to fit on the palm of a baby's hand—with room to spare. (b) This is the Intel 80486 chip. Although the circuitry is complex, the entire chip is smaller than your thumbnail.

little misleading, since every chip, RAM or ROM, provides random-access storage. That is, the computer has access to all locations on each type of chip.

RAM is sometimes called the computer's "scratch pad" because it keeps the instructions and data for whatever programs you happen to be using. The data can be accessed in an easy and speedy manner. RAM is usually **volatile**—that is, its contents are lost once the power is shut off. RAM can be erased or written over at will by the computer software.

ROM contains programs and data that are permanently recorded into this type of memory at the factory; they can be read and used, but they cannot be changed by the user. ROM chips are used to store programs, sometimes called **firmware,** that cannot be altered. For example, a personal computer probably has a program for calculating square roots in ROM. ROM is nonvolatile—its contents do not disappear when the power is turned off.

Memory usually can be expanded, so you have the option of purchasing more. In general, the more memory, the more (and bigger) tasks the computer can do. External computer components vary. You need a keyboard, of course, so you can interact with the computer. Also, you need a video screen to display input and output. Most personal computers have a separate screen (or monitor) and a detached keyboard, so the positions of these components can be adjusted for individual comfort.

For secondary storage purposes, you need a disk drive to read and write on diskettes and, in particular, to load software into the computer. In addition, hard disks are available for most personal computers.

Special Attention to Printers

Basic personal computer hardware consists of memory, central processing unit, keyboard, screen, and storage device. In addition, most

(a)

(b)

(c)

Figure 3-3 Printed output for personal computers.
(a) Inexpensive dot-matrix printers are the most popular. (b) Laser printers are more expensive but are fast, quiet, and produce high-quality output. (c) Plotters for personal computers produce surprisingly good pictures.

systems have a printer. Personal computer users often want a printer quite soon after they have purchased the basic hardware; paper is a communication medium that is hard to do without. The printers most often used with personal computers are dot-matrix and laser printers (Figure 3-3).

Dot-matrix printers, which print characters as combinations of tiny dots, have traditionally been considered fast and adequate for most purposes. The latest dot-matrix models feature high-quality text, fast printing, and a variety of graphics capabilities. The key to the versatility of the new dot-matrix printers is a 24-pin printhead, which forms characters with more and smaller dots, thus producing printing known as **near letter quality.**

Laser printers, which form characters by using a technology based on light, have impressed personal computer users with their speed, their first-rate print quality, and their quiet operation. Note the comparison of printer outputs in Figure 3-4.

Picking the best printer from among the hundreds available might seem a difficult task. But once you narrow down your needs, the choices narrow as well. You can pay as little as a few hundred dollars for a serviceable printer or as much as several thousand for a printer with all the options. However, most users who buy personal computers for home use still settle on the versatile dot-matrix printer, somewhere in the $200 range. This type of printer produces standard copy quickly but can print correspondence using the near-letter-quality option.

We will examine printer purchases again in the Buyer's Guide.

Additional Equipment

You have seen people buy every kind of gadget for their boat or car or camper. For computer users, the story is no different. In this discussion *add-ons* refers loosely to any device that attaches to the computer so that it can participate in the computer's work. An example is an extra disk drive. *Accessories* are convenience items—such as dustcovers, lockup cables, and diskette trays—that are not directly related to the computer's work. Finally, *supplies* are necessary consumable goods, such as printer paper and diskettes.

Is "the box" expandable or not? That is the heart of the personal computer add-on discussion. An expandable computer is designed so that users can buy additional circuit boards and insert them in **expansion slots** (slots inside the computer) to support add-ons (Figure 3-5). If the machine is not expandable, add-ons are limited to those that can be plugged into the back of the computer. If you have an expandable machine, there is a host of add-ons you might like to consider: more memory; a hard disk; a color monitor; a modem to access data communications systems; a video camera; and input devices, such as a joy stick, light pen, or mouse.

Accessories and supplies are readily available and often not dependent on computer brand or model. Dozens of catalogs advertise computer supplies, and most items are also sold in computer or office-supply stores. Accessories and supplies are many and diverse (Figure 3-6). Check your local store to see what fits your needs.

Software to Go

Would you buy a fine sound system if no tapes or compact disks were available to play on it? Of course not. Unless you are determined to write all your own software—an unlikely scenario—a computer is only as good as the software available for it. Software for the personal computer is abundant. In fact, your software purchases may rapidly exceed the cost of the computer itself. Software can be very tempting: The range is dazzling, the power dizzying, and the ease of use enticing. Part 4 includes a description of the variety of software packages available and explains how some common software packages are used.

PERSONAL COMPUTERS IN THE HOME

Do you really need a computer at home? Advertisements would have you believe that a personal computer is indispensable. However, there is an opposing point of view. Arguments for the other side might sound something like this: "If you have serious business or education needs, then purchase an appropriate computer. If you want to play games, buy an inexpensive computer. But if you just want to file recipes or balance your checkbook, then use a recipe box or a calculator." Such thoughts can be persuasive, but let us look further before reaching any firm conclusions.

Home Computers for Ordinary People

There are always people who, for one reason or another, pursue the latest emerging technology. But these people are not a sufficient base for an industry; to be successful, home computers must be useful and easy to use for large numbers of consumers. The big market lies not with those who want to be computer experts but with customers who want machines to do things for them without a lot of fuss. So there it is: Let's have a machine that can do something for plain folks without making them stand on their heads.

What would make a computer indispensable? That would be like asking Thomas Edison what people were going to use electricity for. The personal computer does not yet seem indispensable. That time will come. For now, we can say that it can be a convenience in a number of ways.

Communications

Home computer users find many reasons to connect their personal computers to the rest of the world. Some people telecommute—that is, they work at home and use their machines as a link to the office or to customers. But most people have more mundane applications. A popular activity is hooking up to information services that offer, for a fee, an astounding variety of services: stock prices; foreign-language drills; tax assistance; airline and hotel reservations services; consumer guidance; home buying and selling information; daily horoscopes;

A dot-matrix printer in draft mode can print fast. However, type is less readable than output from other printers or from a dot-matrix printer in near letter quality mode.

This is an example of near letter quality output. A dot-matrix printer prints each character twice or uses a more dense array of dots for improved quality.

Laser printers are fast and they produce high quality output, as shown here. They are useful for desktop publishing, which often combines text and graphics in one document. Generally, laser printers are more expensive than most other printers.

▲
Figure 3-4 Comparisons of printer output.

▲
Figure 3-5 Extra circuitry.
This add-on circuit board is being inserted into an expansion slot of an IBM PS/2 computer.

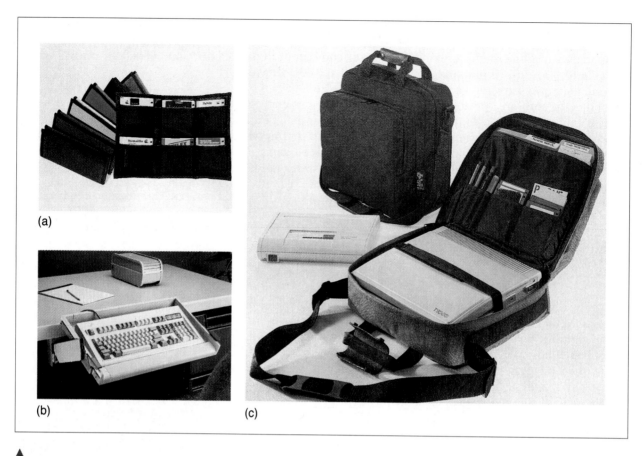

(a)

(b)

(c)

▲
Figure 3-6 Personal computer accessories.
(a) Diskette wallets, shown here in a variety of colors, are convenient for workers who need to carry software or data diskettes with them.
(b) Workers use this hidden drawer to slide the keyboard out of sight when it is not in use.
(c) This convenient carrying case holds a laptop computer as well as the usual supplies for workers who travel.

gourmet recipes; sports news; and much, much more. Other people use their computer networking capabilities to contact friends or collaborate with colleagues through their computers, or they use their machines as remote devices to shop or bank or pay bills.

Education

One mistake that many parents make is thinking that placing a computer in front of a child will automatically create a whiz kid. Another is equating the playing of video games with learning. That is like saying, "I think my little girl is going to grow up to be a television electronics expert. She watches TV all the time." A home computer and the right software can, however, create an entertaining environment for learning. Educational software often includes color animation, flashing lights, sounds, and music that give positive reinforcement and can make learning a great deal of fun.

A computer is a patient and consistent tutor for students of all ages. One warning, however: When left to their own devices, most children are more likely to play zap-'em games than to learn grammar or arithmetic. At the college level, computers are used for everything from writing plays to plotting business takeovers (Figure 3-7). However, education is not just for those in school. Adults can learn typing, foreign languages, and even how to play musical instruments on a computer. But perhaps you would like something a little more offbeat: There is educational software to help you study Morse code, survival skills, driving safety, stress management, resume writing, or how to predict the eruption of a volcano!

The Home Office

Let us begin with word processing. Other factors being equal, which report will get the higher grade, the typed one covered with smudges and white-out or the neatly presented paper prepared on a word processor? Let's face it: Neatness counts. And, with word processing, even children can achieve it. Children as young as nine or ten are impressing their teachers with word-processed essays and reports prepared at home. And, yes, for the most part, they prepare the reports themselves. Word processing is really not much of a trick (we will look at it in detail in Chapter 12), and the rudiments can be learned easily by any family member of at least school age. Word processing is also a key application for adults who want to do office work at home.

Entertainment

You have seen the ads: The whole family—even the dog—is gathered merrily around the computer. The message is clear: The computer brings the family together. However, family computing does not exist, at least not in the way that it is usually portrayed. The home computer is not a shared commodity; it is a device used by one individual at a time to perform specific tasks. Having said all that, however, we can note that entertainment is a possible exception, because family members can take turns on the keyboard, or they can use two joy sticks or hand-held computer games (Figure 3-8).

Some people scoff at the idea of buying a computer for entertainment. But many people consider entertainment a perfectly valid use. In fact, surveys consistently show that most people use their personal computers for entertainment at least some of the time. Programs can range from the purely recreational, such as PC versions of popular video-arcade action games, to the more subtle games of knowing trivia or psychoanalyzing your friends. There are several challenging software offerings for chess, backgammon, solitaire, and bridge. Sophisticated sports-action games provide hands-on versions of pro football, baseball, and basketball. Scanning the flashy software packaging on the computer store's game rack can keep you amused for some time.

Are all these reasons, collectively, enough to make you rush out to buy your first computer? Possibly not. So what will it take?

Computers to Support a Life-Style

Personal computers are entering the home in unprecedented numbers. The key reason seems to be changes in life-style. The shift to two-income families and the increase in single-parent households, plus long workdays and long commutes, are putting pressure on workers. The solution for many workers is to buy a home computer to match the computer at work. Workers can come home at a reasonable time, spend some time with the family, and then put in a couple more hours of work on the computer. It is estimated that over half the owners of home personal computers bought them for work-related purposes.

Even with the purchase trend just described, how many households have computers? Would you guess 50%? 30%? The answer is less than 25%. But more of us will be buying soon. Just what will it take to saturate the market?

The answer is becoming clearer each day: low cost. Cost is certainly the key limiting factor for the mass market today. Would you

▲
Figure 3-7 College student.
College students in every type of major are learning to put computers to use in their studies.

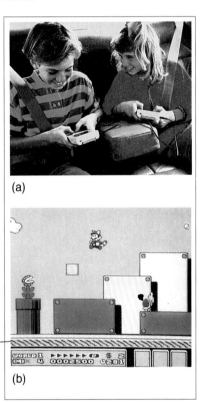

(a)

(b)

▲
Figure 3-8 The computer as entertainer.
The personal computer first made inroads into the home as an entertainment device. Now, with the help of miniaturization, (a) children are taking Game Boy with them wherever they go. (b) A typical screen for the popular Super Mario, one of the most popular Game Boy offerings.

▲
Figure 3-9   Computers in education.
IBM's Writing to Read software is based on the idea that children can write what they can say and can read what they can write. The Writing to Read software uses silly sentences to teach children vocabulary. For example, one screen says "Did you ever see a horse in a house?" The horse and the house are shown as pictures—graphics—beside the sentence. The introductory Writing to Read program uses sounds, letters, and words to build reading awareness.

buy a typewriter that cost $1000? When you look at what the average person buys that costs more than a thousand dollars, you find two things: a house and a car. Those with higher salaries may buy a camper or a boat. But for an item to be a mass-market commodity like a VCR or a microwave oven, it must cost less than $500. Computers are getting closer to being mass-market items. A useful personal computer system can now be purchased for under $1000.

PERSONAL COMPUTERS IN SCHOOLS

During the last few years, most U.S. schools, often spurred on by anxious parents, have been trying hard to work personal computers into their curriculums. Some have implemented exciting new programs, but, for some, computers have been an expensive distraction.

Not all schools know what to do with computers. Some, for instance, have used them exclusively to teach programming, almost always at the high-school level. Others rely on computers to provide extensive drills and practice exercises. High schools and elementary schools need to broaden their approach to computer education. Possible directions could include word processing and database accessing, so that early hands-on experiences are more like what the students will encounter in their first jobs.

Although some people worry that computers may depersonalize education, there is little evidence that this will happen. Many administrators have resisted introducing computers as substitutes for teachers; these educators recognize that computers are tools, not teachers. Few now expect the classroom of the future to look like a wired cubicle containing student and machine. The classroom, in fact, will look very much as it does today: teacher, students, blackboard, papers, books—and some computers on hand to help out (Figure 3-9).

PERSONAL COMPUTERS IN BUSINESS

The personal computer market has been enriched—some people would say driven—by the continuing flood of new uses found in business. Perhaps the most important development is that computers are no longer confined behind the fortress walls of the Data Processing Department's computer room. They appear on the desks and even in the briefcases of ordinary business people. Personal computers are used in business for accounting, inventory, business planning, financial analysis, word processing, and many more functions (Figure 3-10).

There is some sentiment in the computer industry that, in business, a personal computer is just that: personal, one-on-one, even private. Are personal computers really personal? That notion is being swept aside as businesses press to the outer edges of usefulness. Personal computers are being hooked together in networks, personal computers are accessing mainframes, and personal computers themselves are being used as multiuser devices. The impact of business on

Figure 3-10 Computers in a business setting.
Applying the phrase *computers in business* to personal computers often suggests an executive image, but computers are used routinely by almost everyone in this realty office.

computers and vice versa carries major implications for business and home use—implications we will examine in detail in Chapter 9.

PERSONAL COMPUTER MANUFACTURERS
. . . .

Since the one constant element in the personal computer industry is change, the players in the personal computer manufacturing game are sure to shift over time. We will look first at some of the early participants and then discuss a few of the most important companies operating in the personal computer market today.

From the Beginning: A Little Bit of History

The personal computer boom began in 1975, when the MITS Altair was offered as a kit to computer hobbyists. Building your own computer was considered an eccentric pastime. Then Apple came along to bring a small computer, the Apple II, to the people. Tandy started selling TRS-80 computers to everyday people in Radio Shack stores. Commodore enticed school administrators to let children try the company's PET computer. These three—Apple, Tandy, and Commodore—led the market from about 1977 to 1982. But there was a significant entry in 1981: IBM announced its own contender, the IBM PC,

---

ELECTRONIC PERKS

Standard big-shot perks—short for *perquisites*—have historically been company cars, membership in the country club, and the like. But there is a new perk in town: the opportunity to buy a computer at discount prices. And the perk recipient is not necessarily near the top of the corporate ladder; he or she can be any employee in a computer-conscious company. The most common arrangement is simply for a computer retailer to offer better prices to customers who identify themselves as the favored company's employees. In some cases, the company makes up the difference in price. However, the retailer may offer a good price because the manufacturer makes up the difference for employees of a favored company.

Companies making such arrangements usually emphasize that employees are not expected to buy a computer to take work home. The corporate thinking is that if employees simply become more familiar with computers, that will be of sufficient benefit to the company.

and nothing has been the same since. In a mere 18 months, IBM out-distanced them all.

Along the way there have been other manufacturers of personal computers, up to 200 at one point. Many tried and many failed. We are still in the period referred to as the Big Shakeout. At this point it is difficult to speak with confidence about any firm, but we are putting our money on IBM and Apple. We will discuss manufacturers in the order of their appearance, then give some attention to other key players.

Apple Leads the Way

Apple Computer, Inc. was formed in 1977 by Steven Jobs and Stephen Wozniak, who were working in what is now known as Silicon Valley in California. Apple was the first to replace the complicated switches-and-lights front panels, used at the time on personal computers, with easy-to-use typewriter keyboards. They were an immediate success. The popular Apple II, later updated to the IIe (Figure 3-11a), was followed by less successful variations.

In 1984, Apple introduced the innovative Macintosh, whose graphics and pull-down menus created a superb user interface. Figure

▼
Figure 3-11 Three Apples.
(a) The Apple IIe. (b) The Apple Macintosh.
(c) The Mac IIcx offers a color screen.

(a)
(b)
(c)

 ## MACINTOSH

The Serious Macintosh

The Apple Macintosh started out as a clever toy, overpriced and underpowered. Its outstanding graphics interface and ease of use, however, marked it as a machine that was user friendly. The Macintosh won instant friends in the home market and some educational markets.

Business was another matter. Apple tried to promote the Macintosh as a serious contender in offices, but many corporations resisted the machine in favor of IBM computers and machines like them. But now the Mac is making inroads. It is used for everything from word processing and desktop publishing to spreadsheets and communications in such heavyweight companies as The Bank of America and the accounting firm of Peat, Marwick, Mitchell & Company.

Why the turnaround? There are several reasons, including expanded software selection, a versatile network to hook the Macs together, and—finally—the option of compatibility with IBM. Furthermore, in a get-it-in-the-door strategy, Apple early-on offered Macs to corporations as loans or even gifts; in most cases the result was a significant sale.

3-11b shows the all-in-one, compact, boxy shape of this machine. The Macintosh has attracted a devoted following. Although particularly appealing to beginners, the Macintosh is also often the choice of the most demanding users. Apple departed from the traditional Macintosh look with its Macintosh II series, which was the first Mac to offer a color monitor and sound (Figure 3-11c).

The IBM Standard

IBM introduced its personal computer in the summer of 1981 (Figure 3-12a). The computer giant's IBM PC soon zoomed to the top in personal computer sales. Other versions—featuring more power, more memory, and hard disk—soon followed. IBM's most recent power entry is a family of computers called the Personal System/2—PS/2 for short (Figure 3-12b). The PS/2 comes in several different models, with power increasing with the model number.

The acceptance of this product—and the IBM name—cultivated the ground for others to produce software and peripherals. IBM set the standard with the IBM PC, and many other manufacturers climbed aboard. With the release of the PS/2 models, IBM abandoned its old standard and introduced a new one known as micro-channel architecture. Although it is beyond the scope of this book to describe the differences in these products, the key issue is that some manufacturers flocked to the new standard, but the old one is still going strong without IBM's blessing.

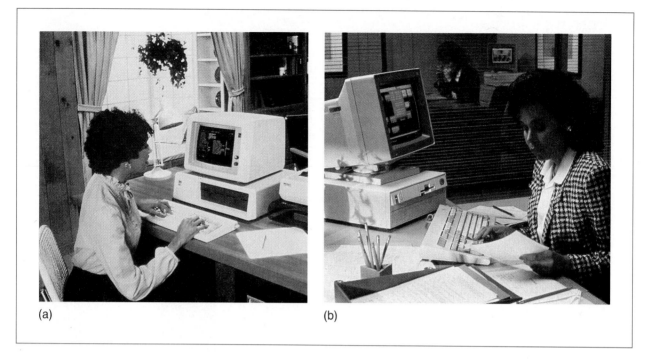

(a)   (b)

▲
Figure 3-12   IBM PC.
(a) From the time of its introduction in August 1981, the IBM PC took only 18 months to lead the competition. (b) The IBM PS/2 Model 502, shown here, is popular with business users.

Supermicros: The Top of the Line

They have been called the new wave of machines—the second generation of personal computers. **Supermicros,** more commonly called **workstations,** have a high-speed microprocessor and significantly increased memory and hard-disk storage capacity (Figure 3-13). In particular, the supermicros are **multiuser** (they can be shared by several users at the same time) and **multitasking** (they can run more than one applications package per user).

Workstations have been called desktop mainframes, a rather glamorous title that distances them from their more mundane personal

▶
Figure 3-13   Supermicros.
This powerful Sun workstation is both multiuser and multitasking, providing a higher level of personal computing.

COMPUTING HIGHLIGHTS

My Go-Everywhere Computer

It has become fashionable, especially with the millennium just a few years away, to imagine the personal computer of the future. In fact, Apple Computer sponsored a contest in this vein. The winners, a group of college students, proposed a go-everywhere tablet-size computer that you could write on with a stylus; other features included credit card–size file memories that could be traded as easily as baseball cards, icons to represent functions such as a telephone or calendar, and extraordinary communicating capabilities.

Other people have come up with their own wish lists. Voice data input is usually high on any list—many people would love to get rid of all that typing. Others yearn for inexpensive, super high-quality laser printers that also print in color and can even produce three-dimensional holograms. The personal computer of the future will require no assembly or setup time; you will simply take it out of the box and plug it in or insert the batteries. Many futurists envision an entertainment center that combines video, television, and computers. Others picture a separate personal computer that will

come with the purchase of a new house, much the way kitchen appliances do today; this computer will control heating, electrical systems, and security.

From the user's point of view, the key item is transparent use—the ability to use a system without being aware of the underlying software, much less having to learn how to use it. And, of course, the software itself will be several orders of magnitude "smarter" than today's software. Software will be used transparently by everyone to manage routine daily affairs.

computer cousins. However, users do not always find workstations glamorous to use; workstation software is not noted for being user-friendly. But new easy-to-use software is now on the market, and more is sure to follow.

Who needs all that power? Engineers and scientists were early supermicro users. However, now that software for workstations is friendlier, more and more business users are switching to supermicros.

Laptops: Small but Mighty

A computer that fits in a briefcase? A computer that weighs less than a newborn baby? A computer you do not have to plug in? A computer to use on your lap on an airplane? A computer that is "cute"? Yes, to all these questions. Laptop computers are rapidly gaining popularity with business travelers, as well as others who need a computer that can go with them.

It all began with the first portable computer from Osborne, which looked and carried like a sewing machine. It was portable in that you could take it with you in one piece (the keyboard snapped onto the computer to form a cover), but you would not want to lug its 25 to 40 pounds through an airport. **Laptop computers** are wonderfully portable, sleek, and functional (Figure 3-14). They often weigh under 10 pounds. Several laptops come with key software packages, such as word processing, right in the computer—that is, in the ROM chips. And, almost without exception, they are compatible with software that runs on IBM machines. Many have small screens (16 lines), but others come with full-size screens (25 lines); some screens even have color capabil-

(a)   (b)

▲
Figure 3-14 Laptops.
(a) The convenient Macintosh portable is every bit as powerful as its stay–at–home counterpart. (b) The Compaq LTE weighs only 7 pounds and comes with its own carrying case.

ity. Many models accept diskettes, so it is especially easy to move data from one machine to another. Although not commonly done, printers can be attached to laptops. Laptops are not as inexpensive as their size might suggest; many carry a price tag equivalent to a sophisticated personal computer for business.

The primary laptop customers have been journalists, who prepare copy on their computers right at the site of the story. But traveling executives, sales representatives, insurance auditors, and writers are also good candidates. In addition, lawyers frequently use portable computers in courtrooms. Then, of course, there is the Internal Revenue Service, whose agents use 15,000 laptops—the better to monitor their customers.

COMPUTER FITNESS AND SAFETY

Computers are a hardy lot, primarily because they have so few moving parts. Given proper care, your computer will probably last longer than you want it—that is, you will have your eye on the latest new machine long before your current machine wears out. Still, your computer's well-being cannot be taken completely for granted. It needs proper care.

Proper Care

Here are some tips for keeping your printer, disk, keyboard, and screen in good working order. The first and best advice is a preventive tip: Keep your computer and printer covered when not in use. Even so, vacuum the printer periodically and wipe surface areas with a cloth sprayed with an all-purpose cleaner. Do not lubricate the printer; oil will only collect dust, which practically guarantees failure.

PERSONAL COMPUTERS IN ACTION

Laptops Under the Big Top

L aptops are the computers made for people on the road. You probably picture computer-carrying travelers as wearing business suits and hefting briefcases. Other business people travel, however, and they wear suits of a different kind: clown suits. Although the circus is fun, to those running it the circus is definitely a business. And, of course, the circus business people are constantly on the road.

The Ringling Bros. and Barnum & Bailey Circus, a thriving conglomerate, has put laptop computers in the hands of just about all its employees short of the animal trainers. The laptop keepers use their computers for the usual applications—everything from payroll to tracking props, whose locations are listed in a database. The laptops

have probably had the biggest effect on the tour managers, who use the computers for on-site applications, such as scheduling, and to keep in touch with the headquarters office. All this computerized scurrying is necessary to put on The Greatest Show On Earth.

To keep the diskette drive read/write heads clean, use an approved head-cleaning kit occasionally. (A hard disk drive, of course, is sealed in an airtight container and does not need to be handled by anyone.) To keep the disk head properly aligned with the disk, avoid sudden jolts to the drive. Diskettes must be properly stored, since dirt is the single most common cause of disk error.

A keyboard can be ruined by soda pop, coffee, or anything crumbly; keep such things away from your computer. If a spill does occur, immediately take the keyboard to a service center for a thorough cleaning. The surface areas of the keys can be cleaned with any mild cleansing agent, but the place where dirt and grime really love to gather is between and under the keys. A can of compressed air (with a narrow nozzle) effectively blows out all that residue.

With the monitor turned off, occasionally wipe your screen clean with a mild cleaner. You may also wish to apply an antistatic solution to keep the screen from acting as a "dust magnet."

Environmental factors can have a significant influence on computer performance. Your computer should not sit near an open window, in direct sunlight, or near a heater. Computers work best in cool temperatures—below 80° Fahrenheit (27° Celsius). Also, smoking can be hazardous to your computer's health. Smoking adds tar and particulate matter to the air, where they then find their way into the computer.

The rewards for your diligence are largely invisible. Your computer will look a little nicer, of course, but—more important—it will
run smoothly for long stretches before it needs servicing.

Computer Security

When people talk about computer security, they are usually thinking
of corporate thieves, government secrets, or teenage hackers. But for
you and your personal computer, it is simpler: Will the machine still be
there when you get home? Burglars pick items that can be easily re-
sold. VCRs and TVs have always been favorites, but now personal
computers top the list. In addition to the usual precautions, you may
want to consider physical lockups for your computer—devices that
attach the computer to a desk or some other large piece of furniture.

One more note. Check your household insurance policy—there is
a good chance that personal computers are specifically excluded. It is a
good idea to buy separate insurance if your investment in your computer is substantial. Insurance companies now offer special packages
for this purpose for a nominal annual fee. We will address the subject
of security in detail in Chapter 10.

▲ ▲ ▲

What could possibly be next? The future is already in sight. In just a
few years, workers of all kinds will wonder how today's mute, passive
boxes were ever called computers. Say it again—*in just a few years*—
personal computers will talk and listen and display full-color, life-like
images. No computer will be an island: They will talk easily to one
another, taking calls and writing memos. Computers will shuffle the
electronic equivalent of paperwork between your computer and those
of your business associates and friends. Computers will provide easy
guidance through vast storehouses of information—encyclopedias,
huge databases, newspapers, films, stockholder reports, and much
more.

Access to all this stored information will be readily available in
public places. Banks of public-access computers, rather like today's
groups of pay phones, will be found in libraries, airports, hotels, shopping malls, and public meeting places. People who cannot leave their
computers at home will take them along. The newer, tiny portables
will be called, appropriately, credit card–size computers.

Other computers may disappear altogether, fading into the furniture to become part of the desk, the cabinet, the blackboard. It is the
fate of the computer to move into the background—and to be everywhere.

CHAPTER REVIEW

SUMMARY AND KEY TERMS

- The main components of a personal computer are the microprocessor, random-access memory (RAM), and read-only memory (ROM). A keyboard is used for inputting data, and a video screen displays input and output. A disk drive is used for reading and writing diskettes.

- A **microprocessor,** also called a computer on a chip, contains the computer's central processing unit. **Random-access memory (RAM)** chips, which are **volatile,** hold the data and instructions currently being used. **Read-only memory (ROM),** sometimes called **firmware,** stores programs that cannot be altered by the user; ROM is nonvolatile.

- Personal computer users usually choose a **dot-matrix printer** (which forms characters from dots) or a **laser printer** (which, using a light beam, produces fast, high-quality printing). The latest dot-matrix models produce **near-letter-quality** printing.

- *Add-ons* refers to devices that attach to the computer so that they can participate in the computer's work. *Accessories* are convenience items that are not directly related to the computer's work. *Supplies* are necessary consumable goods, such as printer paper.

- Expandable computers allow users to insert additional circuit boards into **expansion slots** inside the computers. Nonexpandable computers limit add-ons to those that can be plugged into the back of the computers.

- A broadly successful integration of computers into elementary- and high-school curriculums requires relevant software and emphasis on practical applications rather than just drills and exercises.

- Some business applications include accounting, inventory, planning, financial analysis, and word processing.

- Personal computer manufacturing, which began in 1975 with the MITS Altair, was dominated by three companies—Apple, Tandy, and Commodore—until IBM entered the market in 1981. IBM came to dominate the market with the original IBM PC and later models.

- **Supermicros,** also called **workstations,** are **multiuser, multitasking** personal computers that have a high-speed microprocessor, significantly increased memory, and hard-disk storage capacity.

- The first **portable computers** weighed between 25 and 40 pounds. **Laptop computers,** which often weigh under 10 pounds, are especially convenient for journalists and traveling businesspeople.

- Proper computer care includes such precautions as vacuuming the printer, storing disks properly, keeping food and drink away, cleaning the screen, and preventing exposure to cigarette smoke and excessive heat.

- For personal-computer owners, computer security may involve specially designed security kits or cabinets and perhaps a separate insurance policy.

SELF-TEST

True/False

T F   1. Early portable computers weighed about 10 pounds.
T F   2. Dot-matrix printers are fast, expensive, and quiet.
T F   3. Random-access memory is nonvolatile.
T F   4. An expandable computer can be expanded only by plugging devices into the back of the computer.
T F   5. The best care for a printer is vacuuming.
T F   6. ROM is also known as firmware.
T F   7. Laser printer technology is based on a light beam.
T F   8. Since its first personal computer in 1981, IBM has dominated the market.
T F   9. The central processing unit for a personal computer is on a chip.
T F 10. Laptops are multiuser and multitasking.

Matching

_____ 1. supplies   a. volatile
_____ 2. ROM   b. expandable
_____ 3. microprocessor   c. firmware
_____ 4. near letter quality   d. first personal computer kit
_____ 5. RAM   e. computer on a chip
_____ 6. expansion slot   f. consumable goods
_____ 7. laser printer   g. workstation
_____ 8. supermicro   h. highly portable
_____ 9. MITS Altair   i. best dot matrix
_____ 10. laptop   j. light beam

Fill-In

1. In an expandable computer, circuit boards can be inserted in:

   _____

2. Another name for workstation: _____

3. The memory that cannot be altered by the user is:

   _____

4. Apple Computer, Inc. was formed by Steve Jobs and:

   _____

5. The IBM PC first appeared in the year: _____

6. A computer that can accomplish several tasks at once is called:

   _____

7. The key ingredient for the success of computers in the schools is

   relevant: _____

8. The contents of RAM are destroyed when the power is turned off; thus,

   RAM is said to be: _____

9. The central processing unit on a chip is called:

   _____

10. A device that can be attached to the computer:

   _____

Answers

True/False: 1. F, 3. F, 5. T, 7. T, 9. T

Matching: 1. f, 3. e, 5. a, 7. j, 9. d

Fill-In: 1. expansion slots, 3. ROM, 5. 1981, 7. software, 9. microprocessor

PART TWO

INTERVIEW: Susan Yoachum—The *San Francisco Chronicle*

ell us a bit about your career in journalism. What kinds of stories do you cover for the *San Francisco Chronicle?*

I've been in journalism for about 15 years. Currently, I am the political writer for the *San Francisco Chronicle.* The stories I cover run the gamut from the San Francisco mayor's race, to the race for the United States Senate, to abortion, to how people are feeling about the city. It's a very broad-based beat. Before the *Chronicle,* I was with the *San Jose Mercury News* for about 12 years. Prior to that I was briefly with the *Marin Independent Journal* and before that the *Dallas Morning News.* So, I've had a bit of a checkerboard career.

In what ways do you use computers in your job? How has the use of computers changed during your career as a reporter?

When I began my career, I started with a Royal typewriter. I used to work out of a bureau—a satellite office—and transmit my stories to the main office over a modem that was incredibly slow. Now, in the main office, I work on a terminal that is hooked up to a mainframe computer. I can type my story directly into the computer and then transmit it to another terminal for editing. We also have access to an electronic mail (e-mail) system—it's one of the best things about having a computer on your desk. It allows you to transmit information quickly and efficiently to other people within the main office, and it's fun, too.

▲

Susan Yoachum is political writer for the San Francisco Chronicle. *Here she talks with us about how advances in computer hardware and communications technology have changed the way reporters cover breaking news stories.*

Also, I have a personal computer and a modem at home, which allow me a lot of flexibility. But my laptop computer is the computer that has really revolutionized the way I do business. When I am following a political campaign, traveling on a plane or a bus or in a car, I need to write my story while I'm on the road—I've often filed stories from an airport waiting room. When I'm ready to send the story, I simply find a telephone and transmit the story from my computer over the phone lines to the main office.

Without the portable computer, I would have to write out my story by hand and dictate it to someone over the telephone, which is a very time-consuming task. With the laptop, I have much more control over the story. It's efficient for me; it's efficient for my editors. It has really changed the way that newspaper reporters can cover breaking events.

Do you find that there are any disadvantages to using a computer?

It's funny, but one disadvantage to using the laptop is that people are so interested in it. In airport waiting rooms, I've had people come up and ask questions about the computer while I'm working. It's hardest when kids want to know what I'm doing. I would really like to teach kids about computers; I think that's important. But when I have a deadline, I have to walk the line between being rude and turning the kids off to computers and encouraging them so much that they won't go away. I will say to adults who try to engage me in conversation, 'I'm sorry, but I'm

EXPLORING HARDWARE AND SOFTWARE

working on a deadline right now.' And that's certainly respected. It's amazing how much attention a laptop computer still gets.

Another disadvantage for those of us who look at a computer screen all day is that people can develop blurred vision. People can also develop ergonomic problems—problems related to the physical design of the machines. The repetitive movements of keyboarding in certain positions can strain arms and hands, for example.

That's the downside to computers. But I am still one of their biggest boosters. For me, they make it possible to access whole new worlds. For example, I can tap into the *Los Angeles Times* database and get a *Times* story I need in an instant. To me, that's wonderful. That's just one of many things that I can do with the computer that I couldn't have done before, or that I could have done but it would have taken a long, long time. So, I've become a big computer enthusiast. At first, I didn't like the idea of computers; they were an invasion into my regular routine. Now I wonder, why was it so hard to give up the Royal typewriter?

Can you give us an example of an assignment you have worked on that has benefited from the use of computers?

One example comes to mind. On an election night, reporters deal with a great amount of information that comes in over wire services, which we access by computer. During the last presidential election, I was dealing with the *New York Times* and the *Washington Post* wire ser-

vices, and I had an amazing number of stories coming in on my terminal. My computer has the ability to show a split screen. So, I had the stories from the wires coming up on one side of my screen, and on the other side I was putting together the story that readers were going to see the next day. If I hadn't had that ability to split my screen and pick up blocks of type from the wire

> *Now I wonder, why was it so hard to give up the Royal typewriter?*

stories, fit them in, and rewrite them, I think I would have had a much more difficult time meeting my deadline.

Another example was back in '84, when I was with Walter Mondale in Minnesota for his concession speech. As he was talking, I was typing in his quotes on my laptop computer and fashioning the story. Then I rushed out to file the story before my West-coast deadline. That's something that I could never have done before computers.

How do you envision the news media's use of computers changing in the next five to ten years?

That is a hard question. Laptops are getting smaller, more compact, and lighter—which means I can pack another pair of shoes! They are also developing screens that are much easier on your eyes and much easier to work with. What I'm less certain of, because it's a little bit out of my field, is what's going to happen with the computers that are hooked up to a mainframe system. Are they going to get faster? Will they be smaller? That would be my guess.

I do have to say that the biggest change for me has been seeing how computers can help me do my job. I was so opposed to computers when I first learned about them 15 years ago, and now I couldn't do my job as well without them. Now I'm a cheerleader for computers. ☐

CHAPTER 4

OVERVIEW

CONVERTING INPUT TO OUTPUT

HOW IT HAPPENS

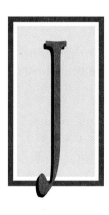

ust how are input, processing, and output related in a computer system? How do you "get in" to a computer system? Or, more formally, how do you provide your own input in a way that the computer can accept? And, if you can figure that much out, how do you get something back from the computer? And what might the output from the computer be, considering what you gave it as input? There are many possible answers to these questions, but Paul Yen's experience is fairly typical.

Paul did not have computers in mind as he thumbed through the catalog for Lands' End, a mail-order firm in Wisconsin that offers quality classic dress and sports clothing. Paul wanted to order a turtleneck shirt. He decided on a shirt and a leather belt, and he wrote these items on the order form. Paul's action, whether he knew it or not, started the computer action rolling.

The items on the order form became the input data to the computer system. In this example, input is the data related to the customer order—customer name, address, and (possibly) charge-card number—and data about each item—catalog number, quantity, description, and price. If this input data is handwritten on an order form, it is keyed into the system as soon as it arrives in the mail; if the order is received on the company's toll-free phone line, the Lands' End operator keys the data as the customer speaks the order. This data is placed on customer and order files to be used with files containing inventory data and other related data.

The computer can process this data into a variety of outputs, as shown in Box 4-1. Some outputs are for individual customers, and some show information combined from several orders: warehouse orders, shipping labels (to send the shirt and belt), back-order notices, inventory reports, supply reorder reports, charge-card reports, demographic reports (showing which merchandise sells best where), and so forth. And—to keep the whole process going—Lands' End also computer-prints Paul's name and address on the next catalog. ∎

Input and Output: The User Connection
• • • • • • • • • • • • • • • • • • •

We have already alluded to the fact that the central processing unit is the unseen part of a computer system. But users are very much aware—and in control—of the input data given to the computer. They submit data to the computer to get processed information, the output. Output is what makes the computer useful to human beings.

Sometimes the output is an instant reaction to the input. Consider these examples:

- Zebra-striped bar codes on supermarket items provide input that permits instant retrieval of outputs, price and item name, right at the checkout counter.

- You use a joy stick, a kind of hand-controlled lever, to input data to guide the little airplane or rabbit—or whatever—on the screen, and the output result is that the on-screen object moves according to your wishes.

- A bank teller queries the computer through the small terminal at the teller window by giving a customer's account number as input; the teller immediately receives the customer's account balance as output on that same screen.

- A forklift operator speaks to a computer directly through a microphone. Words like *left*, *right*, and *lift* are the actual input data. The output is the computer's instant response, which causes the forklift to operate as requested.

- In an innovative restaurant, input is your finger touching the listing of the item of your choice on a computer screen. The output is the order that appears immediately on the kitchen screen, where employees get to work on your Chili Hamburger Deluxe.

Some of these input/output examples may seem a bit frivolous, but all are possible. The concepts underlying them have practical applications.

Input and output are sometimes separated by time, or distance, or both. Some examples:

- Factory workers input data by using their plastic employee cards to punch in on a time clock as they go from task to task. The outputs, produced biweekly, are their paychecks and management reports that summarize hours per project and other information.

- Data from the checks we write is used as input to the bank's computer and eventually processed to prepare a bank statement once a month.

- Charge-card transactions in a retail store provide input data that is processed at month's end to produce customer bills.

- Water-sample data is determined at lake and river sites, keyed in at the environmental agency office, and used to produce reports that show patterns of water quality.

The examples in this section have shown the diversity of computer applications, but in all cases the litany is the same: input-processing-output.

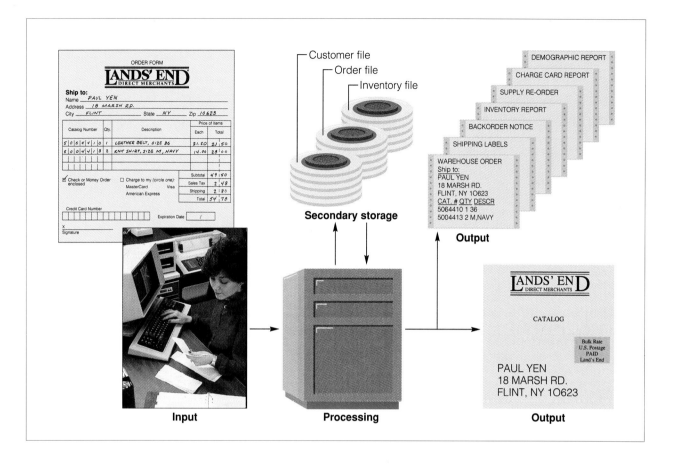

Input

Processing

Output

INPUT: HOW YOU GET DATA INTO THE COMPUTER

• • • • • • • • • • • • • • • •

Some input data can go directly to the computer for processing, as in reading bar codes, or speaking, or pointing. However, sometimes input data must go through a great deal of intermediate handling, such as when it is handwritten on a **source document** (jargon for the original written data) and then translated to a medium that a machine can read, such as magnetic disk. In either case the task is to gather data to be processed by the computer—sometimes called *raw data*—and convert it into some form the computer can understand. The evolution of input devices is toward equipment that is easier to use, faster, and more accurate.

Keyboard Entry

The most common input device is the keyboard. A computer keyboard, which is usually similar to a typewriter, may be part of a personal computer or part of a terminal connected to a computer somewhere else (Figure 4-1a). Not all keyboards are traditional, however. A fast-food franchise like McDonald's, for example, uses keyboards whose keys each represent an item, such as large fries or a Big Mac (Figure 4-1b).

▲

Box 4-1   Lands' End.
At this mail-order house, customer order data is input, processed, and used to produce a variety of outputs.

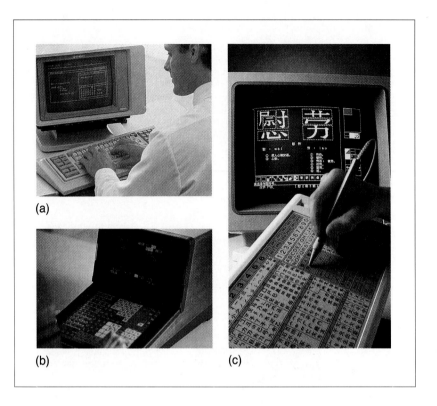

▶

Figure 4-1   Keyboards.
(a) A traditional computer keyboard.
(b) Workers at McDonald's press a key for each
item ordered. The amount of the order is
totaled by the computer system, then displayed
on a small screen so the customer can see the
amount owed. (c) Chinese characters are
significantly more complicated than the letters
and digits found on a standard keyboard. To
enter Chinese characters into the computer
system, a person uses a stylus on this special
keyboard to select the character wanted. A
graphics interpretation of the character can be
displayed on the computer screen.

(a)

(b)

(c)

The Mouse

A **mouse,** popularized by the Macintosh computer, is a computer
input device that actually looks a little bit like a mouse (Figure 4-2).
The mouse, which has a ball on its underside, is rolled on a flat surface,
usually the desk on which your computer sits. The rolling movement
that results when you push the mouse causes the related output, a
corresponding movement on the screen. Moving the mouse allows you
to reposition the **pointer,** or **cursor,** an indicator on the screen that
shows where the next interaction with the computer will take place.
The cursor can also be moved by pushing various keyboard keys. In
addition, you can communicate with the computer by pressing the
button on top of the mouse. Many users turn to the mouse as a quick
substitute for the keyboard.

Source Data Automation: Collecting Data Where It Starts

The key to productive data entry is clear: Cut down the number of
intermediate steps required between the data input and data processing. The best way to do this is by **source data automation**—by using
special equipment to collect data at the source and send it directly to
the computer. Source data automation is an enticing alternative to
keyboarding input, because it eliminates the intermediate keying function; therefore, source data automation reduces both costs and opportunities for human-introduced mistakes. Since data about a transaction
is collected when and where the transaction takes place, source data
automation also improves the speed of the input operation.

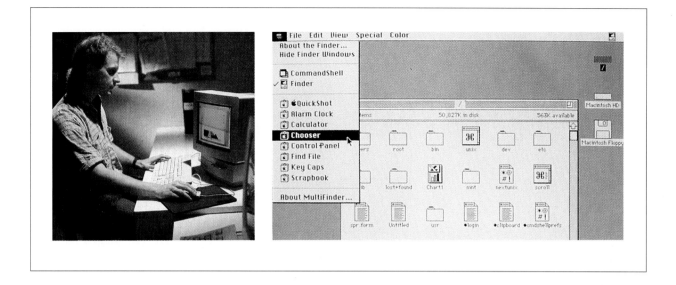

▲
Figure 4-2   Mouse.
As the ball on the underside of the mouse moves over a smooth surface such as a desktop, the pointer on the screen makes a corresponding movement. Once the pointer is in position, a user can select an option from a list of choices by pressing the button on the mouse.

For convenience we will divide the discussion of source data automation into four areas: magnetic-ink character recognition, optical recognition, data collection devices, and voice input. Let us consider each of these in turn.

Magnetic-Ink Character Recognition

Magnetic-ink character recognition (MICR) is a method of machine-reading characters made of magnetized particles. The most familiar example of magnetic characters is the array of numbers on the bottom of your personal check. Figure 4-3 shows what some of these numbers represent.

The MICR process is, in fact, used mainly by banks for processing checks. Checks are read by a machine called a **MICR reader/sorter,** which sorts them into different compartments and sends electronic signals—read from the magnetic ink on the check—to the computer.

Optical Recognition

Optical-recognition systems read numbers, letters, special characters, and marks. An electronic scanning device converts the data into electrical signals and sends the signals to the computer for processing. Various optical-recognition devices can read these types of input:

- Optical marks
- Optical characters
- Handwritten characters
- Bar codes

The first type of system, **optical-mark recognition (OMR),** is sometimes called mark sensing because a machine senses marks on a piece of paper. As a student, you may immediately recognize this approach as a technique used to score certain tests. Using a pencil, you make a mark in a specified box or space that corresponds to your answer. The answer sheet is then graded by a device that uses a light beam to detect the marks and convert them to electrical signals, which are sent to the computer for processing.

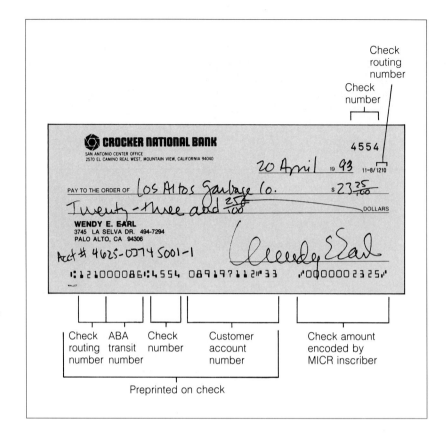

▶ **Figure 4-3   The symbols on your check.**
Magnetic-ink numbers and symbols run along the bottom of a check. The symbols on the left are preprinted; the MICR characters in the lower-righthand corner of a cashed check are entered by the bank that receives it. Note that these latter numbers should correspond to the amount of the check.

▲
Figure 4-4   OCR-A typeface.
This is a common standard font for optical-character recognition.

Optical-character recognition (OCR) devices also use a light source to read special characters and convert them into electrical signals to be sent to the computer. The characters—letters, numbers, and symbols—can be read by both humans and machines. They are often found on sales tags in department stores or imprinted on credit-card slips in gas stations after the sale has been written up. A standard typeface for optical characters, called **OCR-A,** has been established by the American National Standards Institute (Figure 4-4). The hand-held **wand reader** is a popular input device for reading OCR-A. In retail stores the wand reader is connected to a **point-of-sale (POS) terminal.** This terminal is like a cash register in many ways, but it performs many more functions. When a clerk passes the wand reader over the price tag, both the price and the merchandise number are entered into the computer system. Given the merchandise number, the computer can retrieve a description of the item from a file. This description is displayed on the screen of the POS terminal along with the price. (Some systems, by the way, input only the merchandise number and retrieve both price and description.) A small printer produces a customer receipt that also shows both the item description and the price. The computer calculates the subtotal, the sales tax, and the total. This information is displayed on the screen and printed on the receipt. The raw purchase data becomes valuable information when it is summarized by the computer system. This information can be used by a business's accounting department to keep track of how much money is taken in each day, by buyers to determine what merchandise should be reordered, and by the marketing department to analyze the effective-

	Good	Bad
1. Make your letters big	*TAPLEY*	*TAPLEY*
2. Use simple shapes	*25370*	*25370*
3. Use block printing	*STAN*	*STAN*
4. Connect lines	*B5T*	*135T*
5. Close loops	*9068*	*9068*
6. Do not link characters	*LOOP*	*LOOP*

◄ **Figure 4-5   Handwritten characters.**
Legibility is important in making handwritten characters readable by optical recognition.

ness of its ad campaigns. Thus, capturing data at the time of the sale provides many benefits beyond giving the customer a fancy computerized receipt.

Machines that can read **handwritten characters** are yet another means of reducing the number of intermediate steps between capturing data and processing it. There are many instances where it is preferable to write the data and immediately have it available for processing rather than having it keyed in later by data entry operators. However, not just any kind of handwritten scrawl will do; the rules as to the size, completeness, and legibility of the handwriting are fairly rigid (Figure 4-5).

Each product on your store shelf has its own unique number, which is part of the **Universal Product Code (UPC).** This code number is represented on the product's label by a pattern of vertical marks, or bars, called **bar codes.** These zebra stripes can be sensed and read by a **bar code reader,** a photoelectric scanner that reads the code by means of reflected light (lasers). As with the wand reader in retail stores, the bar code reader in grocery stores is part of a point-of-sale terminal. When you buy a container of, say, chocolate milk mix in a supermarket, the checker moves the container past the scanner that reads the bar code (Figure 4-6a). The bar code merely identifies the product to the store's computer; the code does not contain the price, which may vary. The price is stored in a file that can be accessed by the computer. (Obviously, it is easier to change the price once in the computer than to have to repeatedly restamp the price on each container of chocolate milk mix.) The computer automatically tells the point-of-sale terminal what the price is, and a printer prints the item description and price on a paper tape for the customer.

Although bar codes were once found primarily in the supermarket, there are a variety of other interesting applications. Bar coding has been described as an inexpensive and remarkably reliable way to get data into a computer. It is no wonder that virtually every industry has found a niche for bar codes. In Brisbane, Australia, bar codes help the Red Cross manage its blood bank inventory (Figure 4-6b). Also consider the case of Federal Express, whose management attributes a large part of the corporation's success to the bar-coding system they use to track packages. As each package wends its way through the transportation system, its unique bar code is read at each point, and the bar-code

 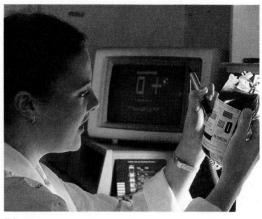

(a)   (b)

▲

Figure 4-6   Bar codes.
(a) This photoelectric bar code scanner, often seen at supermarket checkout counters, reads the product's zebra-striped bar code. The bar code identifies the product to the store's computer, which retrieves price information. The price is then automatically rung up on the point-of-sale terminal. (b) The Australian Red Cross combines personal computers and hand-held bar code readers to verify blood type labels.

number is fed to a central computer. An employee can use a computer terminal to check the location of a given shipment at any time; the sender can request a status report on a package and receive a response within 30 minutes.

Data Collection Devices

Another direct source of data entry is a **data collection device,** which may be in the warehouse or factory or wherever the activity that is generating the data is. Using such a device eliminates intermediate steps that endanger accuracy. An example of this type of device was noted earlier in the chapter: Factory employees who use a plastic card to punch job data directly into a time clock are using a data collection device.

Such devices must be sturdy, trouble-free, and easy to use, since they are often in dusty, humid, or hot or cold locations. They are used by people such as warehouse workers, packers, forklift operators, and others whose primary work is not clerical. Examples of remote data collection devices are machines for taking inventory, reading shipping labels, and recording job costs.

Voice Input

Have you talked to your computer recently? Has it talked to you? Both feats are possible with current technology, even though there are some limitations. We will examine both "speakers"—you and the computer. Since we are discussing input here, we will begin with you, as you talk to your computer. What method of input could be more direct than speaking?

Voice input is the process of presenting input data to the computer through the spoken word. Voice input can be about twice as fast as keyed input entered by a skilled typist. **Speech recognition devices** accept the spoken word through a microphone and convert it into digital code that can be understood by the computer. There are a great many uses for this process, quite apart from its being an aid to those who hate to type. In fact, voice input has created new uses for computers. Typical users are those with "busy hands" or hands that are too dirty for the keyboard or hands that must remain cleaner than using a keyboard would permit. Among current uses are:

- Controlling inventory in an auto junkyard
- Reporting analyses of pathology slides that are under a microscope
- Making phone calls from a car
- Calculating a correct anesthetic dosage for a patient in surgery
- Performing nonflight control jobs such as changing radio frequencies in airplane cockpits
- Asking for stock quotations over the phone
- Sorting packages
- Inspecting items moving along a factory assembly line
- Acting on commands from physically disabled users
- Commanding a car to start the motor, lock the doors, or turn on the windshield wipers

In each of these cases, the speech recognition system "learns" the voice of the user, who speaks isolated words repeatedly. The voiced words the system "knows" are then recognizable in the future. The worker sorting packages, for instance, can speak digits representing zip codes. The factory inspector can voice the simple words "Good" or "Bad," or "Yes" or "No." A biologist can tell a microscope to scan up, down, right, and left.

Experts have tagged speech recognition as one of the most difficult things for a computer to do. Some of the world's largest companies, such as AT&T and IBM, have been developing speech technology for years without the hoped-for degree of success. But someday machines that recognize speech will be commonplace. People will routinely talk to their computers, toys, TV sets, refrigerators, ovens, automobiles, and door locks. And no one will stare at them when they do.

Computer Screens: Input/Output Devices

The relationship between input and output is an important one. Although some people naively think the computer wields magical power, the truth is that the output produced is directly related to the input given. Programmers have a slang phrase for this fact: *garbage in, garbage out*, abbreviated **GIGO.** That is, the quality of the information the computer produces can be no better than the quality and accuracy of the data given to it in the first place. That fact is most obvious when input and output devices are closely related. For instance, computer screens are involved in both input and output: When data is entered, it appears on the screen; the computer response to that data—the output—also appears on the screen. Thus, if a mistake is made in entering data or there is a problem with the computer program, the mistake shows up right away on the screen.

Types of Screens

Computer screens come in many different shapes, sizes, and colors. The most common type of screen is the **cathode ray tube,** or **CRT.**

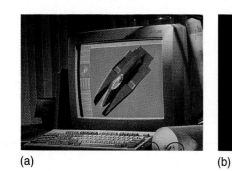
(a)

(b)

(c)

▲
Figure 4-7 A variety of screens.
(a) This high-resolution brilliance is available only on a color graphics display. (b) An amber screen. (c) Laptop computers use liquid crystal display (LCD) technology for their small, lightweight screens.

Color monitors are available for displaying color text and graphics (Figure 4-7a). Some screens are **monochrome,** meaning only one color appears on a black background. The most common monochrome screens display green letters and numbers on a dark background, but amber characters are also available and are thought to be easier on the eyes (Figure 4-7b). Another type of screen is the **liquid crystal display (LCD),** a flat display screen found on laptop computers (Figure 4-7c). These screens are much smaller and lighter than CRTs, but the quality suffers somewhat. Screen size can vary from large screens that can show two facing pages to small screens on some point-of-sale terminals, which are just large enough to display the item name and price.

Terminals

A screen may be the monitor of a self-contained personal computer, or it may be part of a terminal that is one of many terminals attached to a large computer. A **terminal** consists of an input device, an output device, and a communications link to the main computer. Most commonly, a terminal has a keyboard for an input device and a screen for an output device, although there are many variations on this theme. A terminal with a CRT screen is called a **video display terminal (VDT).**

So far, we have looked at types of input and at screens, which are input/output devices. Now it is time to examine how the input to the computer is processed.

PROCESSING: CHANGING INPUT TO OUTPUT

Gretchen Schumacher is an attorney in a corporate law office in Atlanta. Her work includes researching legal issues, which she can access from computer files via a terminal on her office desk. The input she gives the computer system varies from a subject name, such as "merger" or "shareholder," to the name of a particular case, such as "Piper v. Chris-Craft Industries, Inc." Gretchen can select the type of output that will be useful to her, such as a published article or a judge's opinion on the subject matter. She can also choose to have the output returned to her on her screen or on a nearby printer.

PERSONAL COMPUTERS IN ACTION

Now We Can See How It Works

When Wendy Colton first began teaching word processing at Beaumont Community College, she understood why her students were overwhelmed by the descriptions of some commands. For example, just to move a paragraph from one place to another in a letter, she had to rattle off something like this: "First move the cursor to the beginning of the paragraph, hold down the Alt key while pressing the F4 key, then move the cursor to the end of the paragraph, noticing that the paragraph is now highlighted in reverse video, and press Ctrl/F4, followed by pressing the 1 key twice." And all that was just to remove the para-

graph from its old position. Furthermore, she did not even mention the screen options presented by the word processing program.

Wendy tried to find textbooks that would show this kind of activity on a screen in small, progressive steps, but the books had serious limitations. The answer came to her in the form of something quite different: a hardware item called a projection panel. This device let her demonstrate the commands on a personal computer, whose screen was projected onto a full-size wall screen in front of the classroom. The equipment required consists of a personal computer, a standard

overhead projector, and the projection panel. The panel plugs into the computer and is placed on the top of the projector, operating much like a transparency master.

Instructors are using the new equipment for demonstrating everything from programming to graphics. Students appreciate expanding the use of their senses in the learning process. Instead of having their ears assaulted with technical mumbo-jumbo, they can watch commands and other instructions, and see the results each step of the way.

We have described the input and output devices Gretchen uses and the type of data offered and information received. But how does the input get translated to output? Like most users, Gretchen knows that her requests are processed by the computer's hardware and software. But—also like most users—she knows that she does not have to understand the details to put the computer to work.

In fact, most users know little about the actual processing, partly because they cannot see the operations. We will examine the processing operation briefly, beginning with the hardware that does the work, the central processing unit.

The Central Processing Unit

The human element in computing is involved with data input and information output, but the controlling activities of the computer lie in between. The **central processing unit (CPU)** is a highly complex, extensive set of electrical circuits. It executes the stored program instructions that accept the input, process the data, and produce the output. As Figure 4-8 shows, it consists of two parts:

- The control unit
- The arithmetic/logic unit

Let us consider each of these components of the central processing unit.

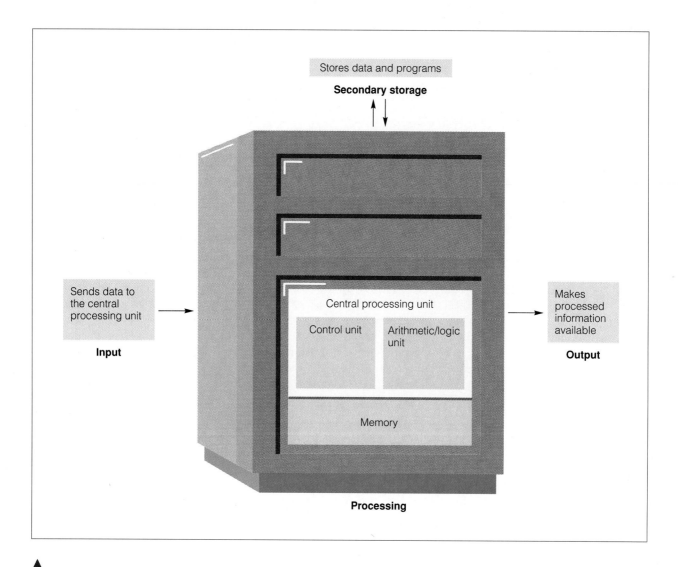

Stores data and programs

Secondary storage

Sends data to the central processing unit

Input

Central processing unit

Control unit

Arithmetic/logic unit

Memory

Makes processed information available

Output

Processing

▲
Figure 4-8   The central processing unit.
The two parts of the CPU are the control unit and the arithmetic/logic unit. Memory holds data and instructions temporarily at the time the program is being executed. The CPU interacts closely with memory, referring to it for both instructions and data.

The Control Unit

The **control unit** contains circuitry that uses electrical signals to direct and coordinate the entire computer system in carrying out, or executing, stored program instructions. Like an orchestra leader, the control unit does not execute the instructions itself; rather, it directs other parts of the system to do so. The control unit must communicate with both the arithmetic/logic unit and memory.

The Arithmetic/Logic Unit

The **arithmetic/logic unit (ALU)** contains the electronic circuitry that executes all **arithmetic operations,** such as addition and multiplication, and **logical operations,** which are usually comparing operations. The arithmetic/logic unit is able to compare numbers, letters, or special characters and take alternative courses of action. Comparing operations can determine whether one value is *equal to, less than,* or *greater than* another. This is a very important capability. It is by comparing that a computer is able to tell, for instance, whether there are unfilled seats on airplanes, whether charge-card customers have exceeded their credit limits, and whether one candidate for Congress has more votes than another.

Memory

Memory is also known as **primary storage, primary memory, main storage, internal storage,** and **main memory**—all these terms are used interchangeably. Memory is also called *random access memory,* or RAM, as we noted in the previous chapter on personal computers. Memory is the part of the computer that holds data and instructions for processing. Although closely associated with the central processing unit, memory is technically separate from it. (However, specific applications such as watches or microwave ovens may combine the CPU and memory on a single chip.) Memory is used only temporarily—it holds your program and data only as long as your program is in operation. For three reasons, it is not feasible to keep your program and data in memory when your program is not running:

- Most types of memory store data only while the computer is turned on—the data disappears when the machine is turned off.
- If you share your computer, other people will be using the computer and need the memory space.
- There may not be enough room in memory to hold your processed data.

Data and instructions from an input device are put into memory by the control unit. Data is then sent from memory to the arithmetic/logic unit, where an arithmetic operation or logical operation is performed. After being processed the information is sent to memory, where it is held until it is ready to be incorporated into other calculations or released to an output unit. The chief characteristic of memory is that it allows very fast access to data and instructions.

How the CPU Executes Program Instructions

Let us examine the way the central processing unit, in association with memory, executes a computer program. We will be looking at how just one instruction in the program is executed. In fact, most computers today can execute only one instruction at a time.

Before an instruction can be executed, program instructions and data must be placed into memory from an input device or a secondary storage device. In the legal search example, the program instructions tell the computer how to find particular information matching the input request and the data is what the user input, such as "merger." (Keep in mind that a user would not need to know anything about the program itself, only how to give it input.)

As Figure 4-9 shows, the central processing unit then performs the following four steps for each instruction:

1. The control unit "fetches" (gets) the instruction from memory.
2. The control unit decodes the instruction (decides what it means) and gives instructions for necessary data to be moved from memory to the arithmetic/logic unit. These first two steps are called instruction time, or **I-time.**

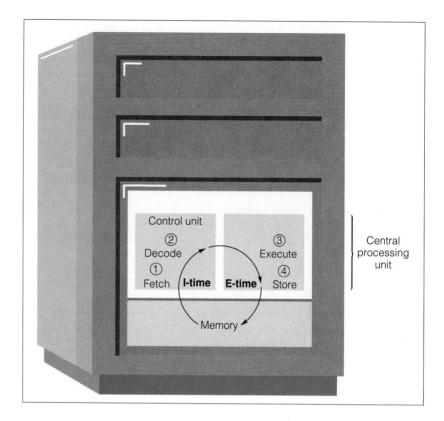

► **Figure 4-9 The machine cycle.**
Program instructions and data are brought into
memory from an external device, either an input
device or secondary storage. The machine
cycle executes instructions, one at a time, as
described in the text.

3. The arithmetic/logic unit executes arithmetic and logic instructions. That is, the ALU is given control and performs the actual operation on the data.

4. The result of this operation is stored in memory or in a temporary location called a register. Steps 3 and 4 are called execution time, or **E-time.**

After the appropriate instructions are executed, the control unit directs memory to release the results to an output device or a secondary storage device. The combination of I-time and E-time is called the **machine cycle.**

Data Representation: On/Off

We are accustomed to thinking of computers as complex mechanisms, but the fact is that these machines basically know only two things: on and off. This on/off, yes/no, two-state system is called a **binary system.** Using the two states—which can be represented by electricity turned on or off—the computer can construct sophisticated ways of representing data.

Let us look at one way the two states can be used to represent data. Whereas the decimal number system has a base of 10 (with the digits 0, 1, 2, 3, 4, 5, 6, 7, 8, and 9), the binary system has a base of 2. This means it contains only two digits, 0 and 1, which correspond to the two states off and on. Combinations of 0s and 1s are used to represent larger numbers.

Bits, Bytes, and Words

Each 0 or 1 in the binary system is called a **bit** (for *bi*nary dig*it*). The bit is the basic unit for storing data in computer memory—0 means off, 1 means on.

Since single bits by themselves cannot store all the numbers, letters, and special characters (such as $ and ?) that must be processed by a computer, the bits are put together in a group called a **byte.** Each byte usually represents one character of data—a letter, digit, or special character.

Computer manufacturers express the capacity of memory in terms of the number of bytes it can hold. The number of bytes is expressed as **kilobytes,** 2 to the tenth power (2^{10}), or 1024 bytes. *Kilobyte* is abbreviated **KB** or, simply, **K.** Thus, the memory of a 640K computer can store 640×1024, or 655,360 bytes. Memory capacity may also be expressed in terms of a **megabyte** (1024×1024), abbreviated **MB.** Megabyte means, roughly, one million bytes.

Coding Schemes

As we said, a byte—a collection of bits—represents a character of data. But just what particular set of bits is equivalent to which character? In theory we could each make up our own definitions, declaring certain bit patterns to represent certain characters. But this would be about as practical as each of us speaking our own special language. Since we need to communicate with the computer and with each other, it is appropriate that we use a common scheme for data representation. That is, we must agree on which groups of bits represent which characters.

The code called **ASCII** (pronounced "AS-key"), which stands for American Standard Code for Information Interchange, uses 7 bits for each character. For example, the letter *A* is represented by 1000001. The ASCII representation has been adopted as a standard by the U.S. government and is found in a variety of computers—particularly minicomputers and microcomputers. Figure 4-10 shows the ASCII codes.

Computer Processing Speeds

Although speed is basic to computer processing, speed is also an ever-changing facet. The characteristic of speed is universally associated with computers. Certainly all computers are fast, but there is a wide diversity of computer speeds. The execution of an instruction on a very slow computer may be measured in less than a **millisecond,** which is one-thousandth of a second (see Table 4-1). Most computers can exe-

Character	ASCII
A	100 0001
B	100 0010
C	100 0011
D	100 0100
E	100 0101
F	100 0110
G	100 0111
H	100 1000
I	100 1001
J	100 1010
K	100 1011
L	100 1100
M	100 1101
N	100 1110
O	100 1111
P	101 0000
Q	101 0001
R	101 0010
S	101 0011
T	101 0100
U	101 0101
V	101 0110
W	101 0111
X	101 1000
Y	101 1001
Z	101 1010
0	011 0000
1	011 0001
2	011 0010
3	011 0011
4	011 0100
5	011 0101
6	011 0110
7	011 0111
8	011 1000
9	011 1001

▲

Figure 4-10 The ASCII code.
Shown are binary representations for letters and numbers. The representation is in two columns to improve readability.

Table 4-1 Units of Time: How Fast Is *Fast?*

Unit of Time	Fraction of a Second	Mathematical Notation
Millisecond	Thousandth: 1/1000	10^{-3}
Microsecond	Millionth: 1/1,000,000	10^{-6}
Nanosecond	Billionth: 1/1,000,000,000	10^{-9}
Picosecond	Trillionth: 1/1,000,000,000,000	10^{-12}

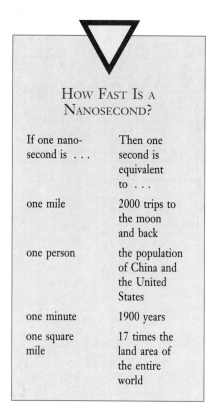

cute an instruction measured in **microseconds,** one-millionth of a second. Some modern computers have reached the **nanosecond** range—one-billionth of a second. Still to be broken is the **picosecond** barrier—one-trillionth of a second.

OUTPUT: HOW INFORMATION COMES BACK TO YOU

As we have already seen, output can take many forms, such as screen output, paper printouts, and voice. Other forms of output include overhead transparencies, 35mm slides, and microfilm. Even within the same organization there can be different kinds of output. You can see this the next time you go to a travel agency that uses a computer system. If you ask for airline flights to Toronto, Calgary, and Vancouver, say, the travel agent will probably make a few queries to the system and receive output on a screen: information about the availability of various flights. After the reservations have been confirmed, the agent can ask for printed output of three kinds: the tickets, the traveler's itinerary, and the invoice. In addition, for management purposes the agency may periodically receive printed reports and charts, such as monthly summaries of sales figures or pie charts of regional costs.

As you might already suspect, the printer is one of the principal devices used to produce computer output.

Printers

A **printer** is a device that produces printed paper output—known in the trade as **hard copy** because it is tangible and permanent (unlike **soft copy,** which is displayed on a screen). Some printers produce only letters and numbers, whereas others are also able to produce graphics.

Letters and numbers are formed by a printer either as solid characters or as dot-matrix characters. **Dot-matrix printers** create characters in the same way that individual lights in a pattern spell out words on a basketball scoreboard. These printers construct a character by activating a matrix of pins that produce the shape of the character. Figure 4-11 shows how this works. A typical matrix is 5 × 7—that is, five dots wide and seven dots high. These printers are sometimes called 9-pin printers, because they have two extra vertical dots for descenders on lowercase letters *g, j, p,* and *y.* The 24-pin dot-matrix printer, which uses a series of overlapping dots, is increasingly popular and will soon dominate the dot-matrix market. The more dots, the better the quality of the character produced. Some dot-matrix printers can produce color images.

There are two ways of making an image on paper: the impact method and the nonimpact method. Let us take a closer look at the difference.

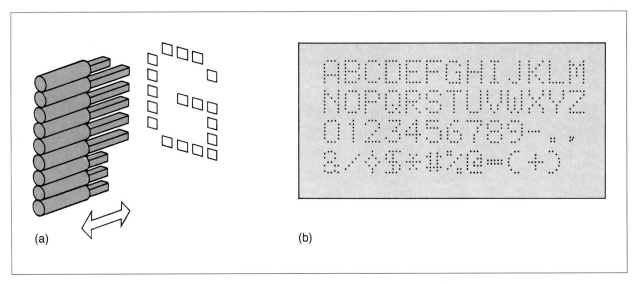

(a)   (b)

▲
Figure 4-11   Forming dot-matrix characters.
(a) This art shows the letter *G* being printed as a 5 by 7 dot-matrix character. The moving matrix head has nine vertical pins, which move in and out as necessary to form each letter.
(b) Letters, numbers, and special characters formed as 5 by 7 dot-matrix characters. Although not shown in this figure, dot-matrix printers can print lowercase letters too. The two lowest pins are used for the parts of the lowercase letters *g*, *j*, *p*, and *y* that go below the line.

Impact Printers

The term *impact* refers to the fact that **impact printers** use some sort of physical contact with the paper to produce an image, physically striking paper, ribbon, and print hammer together. The impact may be produced by a print hammer character like that of a typewriter striking a ribbon against the paper or by a print hammer hitting paper and ribbon against a character. High-quality impact printers print only one character at a time. However, users who are more concerned about high volume than high quality usually use line printers, impact printers that print an entire line at a time.

Nonimpact Printers

There are many advantages to **nonimpact printers,** but there are two major reasons for their growing popularity: They are faster and quieter. There is never physical contact between the printer and the paper. Other advantages of nonimpact printers over conventional mechanical printers are their ability to change typefaces automatically and their graphics capability.

The major technologies competing in the nonimpact market are laser and ink jet. Both use the dot-matrix concept to form characters. **Laser printers** use a light beam to help transfer images to paper, producing extremely high-quality results (Figure 4-12). Laser printers print a page at a time at record-breaking speeds. Initially very expensive, low-end laser printers can now be purchased for a few thousand dollars or even less.

The rush to laser printers has been influenced by the trend toward desktop publishing—using a personal computer, a laser printer, and special software to make professional-looking publications.

Ink-jet printers spray ink from jet nozzles and are up to ten times faster than impact printers. Ink-jet printers, by using multiple nozzles, can print in several different colors of ink to produce excellent graphics (Figure 4-13).

▲
Figure 4-12   Laser printer.
The high-quality print of the Hewlett-Packard LaserJet printers make them best-sellers.

Figure 4-13   Ink-jet printer.
Ink-jet printers are noted for high-quality graphics output.

Voice Output

We have already examined voice input. As you will see in this section, however, computers are frequently like people in the sense that they find it easier to talk than to listen. **Speech synthesis**—the process of enabling machines to talk to people—is much easier than speech recognition.

"The door is ajar," your car says to you in a human-like voice. But this is not a real human voice; it is the product of a **voice synthesizer** (also called a **voice-output device** or **audio-response unit**), which produces sounds understandable as speech to humans.

Those with speech impairments are often eager to try voice synthesizers. Several software packages exist that let people communicate on the phone by typing their messages, which are then converted to synthetic speech. For example: "Hello. I am not able to speak, but I am able to hear you, and my computer is doing the talking for me. Would you please tell me if you have tickets for the Beethoven concert on Friday the 18th?" This message can be keyed before the phone call. After the call is dialed and someone answers, the user pushes the speak button, and the message goes out over the phone.

Voice output has become common in such places as airline and bus terminals, banks, and brokerage houses. It is typically used when an inquiry is followed by a short reply (such as a bank balance or flight time). Many businesses have found other creative uses for voice output as it applies to the telephone. Automatic telephone voices ("Hello, this is a computer speaking . . . ") take surveys, inform customers that catalog orders are ready to pick up, and remind consumers that they have not paid their bills.

Now it is time to return to computer screens and consider everyone's favorite topic, computer graphics.

COMPUTER GRAPHICS

Computer output in the form of graphics has come into its own in a major—and sometimes spectacular—way. What reader of this book could possibly be unaware of the application of graphics to video games? Who has not seen TV commercials or movies that use computer-produced animated graphics? Computer graphics can also be found in education, computer art, science, sports, and more (Figure 4-14). But perhaps their most prevalent use today is in business.

Business Graphics

It might seem wasteful to display in color graphics what could more inexpensively be shown to managers as numbers in standard computer printouts. However, colorful graphics, maps, and charts can help managers compare data more easily, spot trends, and make decisions more quickly. Also, the use of color helps people get the picture—literally. Finally, although color graphs and charts have been used in business for years—usually to make presentations to higher management or outside clients—the computer allows them to be rendered quickly, before information becomes outdated. One user refers to business graphics as "computer-assisted insight."

◄
Figure 4-14   Computer graphics.
Both the world of science and the world of art benefit from the power of computer graphics.

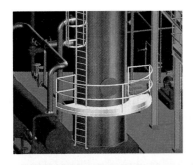
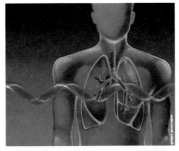

COMPUTING HIGHLIGHTS

Everyday Input and Output

One way or another, delivering input to a computer is a common activity in our daily lives. Input activities in which you may have engaged could include items on the list that follows. Have you:

- Bought an item whose price tag was scanned with a wand reader
- Filled out an application for a magazine subscription
- Purchased groceries whose bar codes were scanned
- Filled out registration forms
- Recorded test answers by using a pencil on an optical-mark recognition, OMR, sheet

Many other activities require us to provide input to a computer.

Over time, we may supply input in these circumstances: seeking credit, paying taxes, applying for a job, entering a contest, paying bills, entering the armed services, signing a petition, going to the doctor, joining an organization, applying for a scholarship or grant, seeking government assistance, giving charitable donations, ordering products through the mail, and on and on.

This data is supplied willingly, and most people give little thought to the route it will travel. Almost all the data will end up in computer files, to reside there indefinitely. What happens to those files is another topic; for now, be aware that it all starts with input.

At this point consider the computer output that is all around us. Sometimes it is obvious. You have received computer-produced bills and have doubtless learned to spot personalized computer junk mail. ("We can send this product right to your home at 6214 Second Avenue NW . . .") But some mail is fully automated and not at all obvious; it looks like a nicely typed letter and even has a "handwritten" signature.

Another place to watch for computer-produced output is on your TV screen. Many advertisements consist completely of computer graphics. In fact, just about anything that is not clearly film of human beings could be of computer origin.

Video Graphics

Unfettered by reality, video graphics can be as creative as an animated cartoon (Figure 4-15). Although they operate on the same principle as a moving picture or cartoon—one frame at a time in quick succession—**video graphics** are produced by computers. Video graphics have made their biggest splash on television, but many people do not realize they are watching the computer at work. The next time you watch television, skip the sandwich and pay special attention to the commercials. Unless there is a live human in the advertisement, there is a good chance that the moving objects you see, such as floating cars and bobbing electric razors, are computer output. Another fertile ground for

Figure 4-15 Video graphics.
This television commercial for LifeSavers Holes uses computer–generated video graphics to bring the playground scene to life.

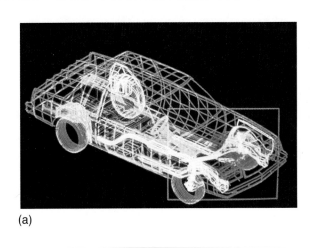
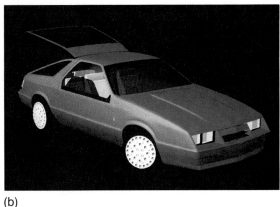

(a)   (b)

video graphics is the network's logo and theme. Accompanied by music and swooshing sounds, the network symbol spins and cavorts and turns itself inside out, all with the finesse that only a computer could supply.

Video graphics do not have to be commercial in nature, of course. Some video artists produce beauty for its own sake. In science, video graphics have helped produce moving models—such as a model of DNA molecules whose atoms, represented by gleaming spheres, twist and fold.

Computer-Aided Design/Computer-Aided Manufacturing

For more than a decade, computer graphics have also been part and parcel of a field known by the abbreviation **CAD/CAM**—short for **computer-aided design/computer-aided manufacturing.** In this area computers are used to create two- and three-dimensional pictures of everything from hand tools to tractors. CAD/CAM provides a bridge between design and manufacturing. As a manager at Chrysler said, "Many companies have design data and manufacturing data and the two are never the same. At Chrysler, we have only one set of data that everyone dips into." For one result of their efforts, see Figure 4-16.

Graphics Input Devices

There are many ways to produce and interact with screen graphics. We have already described the mouse; the following are some other common devices. Some of these devices can also be used for input not related to graphics.

Digitizer

An image—whether a drawing or a photo—can be scanned by a device called a **digitizer,** which converts the image into digital data that the computer can accept and represent on the screen. However, a **digitizing tablet** (Figure 4-17) lets you create your own images. This device has a special stylus that can be used to draw or trace images, which are then converted to digital data that can be processed by the computer.

Figure 4-16   CAD/CAM.
With computer-aided design and computer-aided manufacturing (CAD/CAM), the computer can keep track of all details, maintain designs of parts in memory, and combine parts electronically as required. (a) A computer-aided design wireframe used to study design possibilities. (b) A polygonal, shaded image used to evaluate the appearance—is it pleasing or not?—of a car's body design.

Figure 4-17   Digitizers.
This engineer is using a digitizing tablet to input his drawing to the computer.

Figure 4-18   Light pen.
When a pen with a light-sensitive cell at the end is placed against the screen of a graphics display terminal, it closes a photoelectric circuit, enabling the terminal to identify the point on the screen. This engineer is using a desktop mainframe computer with a light pen.

Figure 4-19   Touch screen.
A pointing finger interrupts light beams emitted from the edges of the screen. The computer translates the interruption into a point on the screen.

Light Pen

For direct interaction with your computer screen, few things beat a light pen. It is versatile enough to modify screen graphics or make a menu selection—that is, to choose from a list of activity choices on the screen. A **light pen** (Figure 4-18) has a light-sensitive cell at the end. When the light pen is placed against the screen, it closes a photoelectric circuit that pinpoints the spot the pen is touching. This tells the computer where to enter or modify pictures or data on the screen.

Joy Stick

Another well-known graphics input device is the **joy stick,** dear to the hearts of video game addicts. This device allows fingertip control of figures on a CRT screen.

Touch Screen

If you disdain pens and sticks and mice, perhaps you would prefer the direct human touch, your finger. **Touch screens** accept input data by letting you point at the screen to select your choice (Figure 4-19). Sensors on the edges of the screen pinpoint the touch location and cause a corresponding response on the screen.

Scanner

"You are about to witness something amazing." This sentence is part of a demonstration of a hand-held **scanner.** The demonstration *is* rather amazing. As you watch the scanner being moved over written text and pictures, the same text and pictures appear on the screen of the attached computer—and are stored in a disk file. Scanners come in both hand-held and desktop models (Figure 4-20). Although all scanners can scan images, they vary in their ability to scan text. Files cre-

(a)

(b)

ated by scanning can be used like any other file: edited, printed, and so forth.

Who would use such a device? Anyone who prefers scanning to typing. For example, teachers can scan text in books for use in classroom exercises. Lawyers can scan contracts. Publishers can save the cost of retyping manuscripts. In addition, a variety of users may wish to scan art to be manipulated by the computer.

▲
Figure 4-20 Scanner.
(a) As this hand-held scanner is held over a picture, the image appears on the computer screen. (b) With a desktop scanner, the picture is laid facedown on the scanner, which looks somewhat like a small copy machine. Once an image is scanned, it can be altered and it can be combined with text to produce a document complete with illustrations.

Graphics Output Devices

Just as there are many different ways to input graphics to the computer, there are many different ways to output graphics. Graphics are most commonly output on a screen or printed paper, which we have already discussed. Another popular graphics output device is the **plotter,** which can draw hard-copy graphics output in the form of maps, bar charts, engineering drawings, and even two- or three-dimensional illustrations (Figure 4-21). Plotters often come with a set of four pens in four different colors. Most plotters also offer shading features.

MULTIMEDIA: THE COMPUTER AS CENTERPIECE
. . . .

Photography, video, music, recorded voice—all these media have something to offer. Traditional media, however, are not normally interactive; they are not planned to produce results based on spontaneous requests. Now put these same devices under the control of a computer, and put the computer under the control of an individual. The result is **multimedia,** interactive computer control of multiple devices.

The California Academy of Sciences, a natural history museum, is famous for its dinosaur models. However, in a room next to the dinosaurs are a series of small booths that let visitors learn about evolution by using a computer-based system. The system is based on a videodisc containing photographs, charts and drawings—all enhanced with ani-

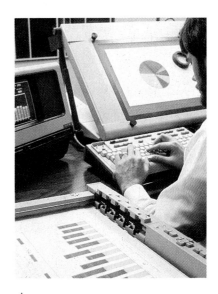

▲
Figure 4-21 A Plotter.
Designers of circuit boards, street maps, schematic diagrams, and similar applications can work in fine detail on a computer screen, then print the results on a plotter.

▶
Figure 4-22   Multimedia.
At the California Academy of Sciences, visitors use an interactive computer system called LifeMap to learn about evolution. This multimedia system uses a videodisc to give museum patron access to huge amounts of information, photographs, charts, and drawings. Users can decide for themselves what and how much they want to learn about the exhibit.

mation and recorded speech—that users can browse through with no special training. By pointing at the computer screen, a user can select any object in the collection; the screen will display the matching description (Figure 4-22).

Multimedia is making swift inroads into educational settings, where students can switch from Kennedy's inauguration speech to footage of Martin Luther King's marches to the first moon landing. The competition for students' interest is so lively and intense today that schools want to get every edge they can in attracting and holding it. Multimedia may be one component of success.

▲ ▲ ▲

New forms of computer input and output are announced regularly, with an array of benefits for human use. The effectiveness of the new forms, however, depends on two components that we have not yet discussed: storage and software. We will study the first of these in the next chapter.

CHAPTER REVIEW

SUMMARY AND KEY TERMS

- The keyboard is a common input device for personal computers, as well as for those who use computer terminals to enter data from **source documents.**

- A **cursor** is a flashing indicator on a screen. The cursor shows where the next interaction with the computer will take place.

- A **mouse** is an input device whose movement on a flat surface causes corresponding movement of the **pointer,** or **cursor,** on the screen.

- **Source data automation,** the use of special equipment to collect data and send it directly to the computer, is a more efficient method of data entry than keyboarding. Four means of source data automation are magnetic-ink character recognition, optical recognition, data collection devices, and voice input.

- **Magnetic-ink character recognition (MICR)** readers read characters made of magnetized particles, such as the preprinted characters on a personal check.

- **Optical-recognition** systems convert optical marks, optical characters, handwritten characters, and bar codes into electrical signals sent to the computer. **Optical-mark recognition (OMR)** devices use a light beam to recognize marks on paper. **Optical-character recognition (OCR)** devices use a light beam to read special characters, such as those on price tags. These characters are often in a standard typeface called **OCR-A.** A commonly used OCR device is the hand-held **wand reader,** which is often connected to a **point-of-sale (POS) terminal** in a retail store. Some optical scanners can read precise **handwritten** characters. A **bar code reader** is a stationary photoelectric scanner used to input a **bar code,** the pattern of vertical marks representing the **Universal Product Code (UPC)** that identifies a product.

- **Data collection devices** allow direct, accurate data entry. **Voice input** processes data to the computer through the spoken word. **Speech recognition devices** convert spoken words into a digital code for the computer.

- **GIGO** stands for *garbage in, garbage out,* which means that the quality of the output depends on the quality of the input.

- Some computer screens are **monochrome**—the characters appear in one color on a black background. Color screens display color text and graphics. The most common type of screen is the **cathode ray tube (CRT).** Another type is the **liquid crystal display (LCD),** a flat screen found on portable computers.

- A screen may be the monitor of a self-contained personal computer, or it may be part of a **terminal,** an input-output device linked to a main computer. A terminal with a CRT screen is called a **video display terminal (VDT).**

- The **central processing unit (CPU)** executes program instructions. It consists of a control unit and an arithmetic/logic unit.

- The **control unit** of the CPU coordinates the computer's execution of the program instructions by communicating with the arithmetic/logic unit—the part of the system that actually executes the program—and with memory.

- The **arithmetic/logic unit (ALU)** contains circuitry that executes **arithmetic operations** and **logical operations.** Logical operations determine if one value is *equal to, less than,* or *greater than* another.

- **Memory** is closely associated with the CPU but not part of it. Memory temporarily holds data and instructions before and after they are processed by the arithmetic/logic unit. Memory is also known as **primary storage, primary memory, main storage, internal storage,** and **main memory.**

- The central processing unit follows four main steps when executing an instruction: It (1) gets the instruction from memory, (2) decodes the instruction and directs the transfer of data from memory to the arithmetic/logic unit, (3) directs the ALU to perform the actual operation on the data, and (4) sends the result of the operation to memory or a register. The first two steps are called **I-time** (instruction time), and the last two steps are called **E-time** (execution time). A **machine cycle** is the combination of I-time and E-time.

- Since a computer can only recognize whether electricity is on or off, data is represented by an off/on **binary system.** In a binary system two digits, 0 and 1, correspond to the two states off and on. Combinations of 0s and 1s can represent numbers, digits, or special characters.

- Each 0 or 1 in the binary system is called a **bit** (*bi*nary dig*it*). A group of bits is called a **byte.** Each byte usually represents one character of data, such as a letter, digit, or special character. Memory capacity is expressed in **kilobytes (KB, or K),** which are equal to 1024 bytes, and **megabytes (MB),** which are millions of bytes.

- A common coding scheme for representing characters is **ASCII** (American Standard Code for Information Interchange), which uses 7-bit characters.

- Computer instruction speeds fall in various ranges, from a **millisecond,** which is one-thousandth of a second; to a **microsecond,** one-millionth of a second; to a **nanosecond,** one-billionth of a second. Still to be achieved is the **picosecond** range—one-trillionth of a second.

- **Printers** produce **hard copy,** or printed paper output. (**Soft copy** is displayed on a screen.) Some printers produce solid characters; **dot-matrix printers,** however, construct characters by producing closely spaced dots.

- Printers can also be classified as being either **impact printers,** which form characters by physically striking the paper, or **nonimpact printers,** which use a noncontact printing method. Nonimpact printers, which include **laser** and **ink-jet printers,** are faster and quieter than impact printers.

- Computer **speech synthesis** has been accomplished through **voice synthesizers** (also called **voice-output devices** or **audio-response units**).

- **Video graphics** are computer-produced animated pictures.

- In **computer-aided design/computer-aided manufacturing (CAD/CAM),** computers are used to create two- and three-dimensional pictures of manufactured products such as hand tools and vehicles.

- Common graphics input devices include the **mouse, light pen, digitizer, joy stick, touch screen** and **scanner..**

- Graphics output devices include screens, printers, and **plotters.**

- With **multimedia** a user has interactive computer control over more than one medium—video, music, and photography, for example.

SELF-TEST

True/False

T   F   1. The control unit consists of the CPU and the ALU.

T   F   2. Screen output is called soft copy.

T   F   3. A kilobyte (KB) is 1024 bytes.

T   F   4. Primary storage is part of the central processing unit.

T   F   5. A microsecond is briefer than a millisecond.

T   F   6. LCD stands for *liquid crystal display*.

T   F   7. Bar code scanning is an optical-recognition system.

T   F   8. A cursor is an indicator on a screen; the cursor shows where
the next computer interaction will take place.

T   F   9. Laser printers use a light beam to transfer images to paper.

Matching

_____ 1. fetch and decode	_____ 6. mouse	a. OCR-A	f. traces images
_____ 2. mark-sensing	_____ 7. flat screen	b. speech recognition	g. underside ball
_____ 3. one color	_____ 8. voice input	c. bar codes	h. LCD
_____ 4. data coding scheme	_____ 9. digitizing tablet	d. monochrome	i. OMR
_____ 5. standard typeface	_____ 10. Universal Product Code	e. I-time	j. ASCII

Fill-In

1. The combination of I-time and E-time: _____

2. GIGO stands for: _____

3. The use of special equipment to collect data at the source and send it to a computer: _____

4. The method is used mainly by banks for processing checks:

   _____

5. Screen output is called _____ and printed computer output is called: _____

6. This device scans a graphic image and converts the image into digital data:

   _____

Answers

True/False: 1. F, 3. T, 5. T, 7. T, 9. T

Matching: 1. e, 3. d, 5. a, 7. h, 9. f

Fill-In: 1. machine cycle, 3. source data automation, 5. soft copy, hard copy

CHAPTER 5

OVERVIEW

STORAGE DEVICES
WHERE YOU CAN KEEP YOUR RECORDS

ike Myers, an airline executive, bought a personal computer for his office. He had seen what several of his colleagues were able to do with their computers and was intrigued. Mike was, of course, a little concerned about starting out and making all the right equipment choices. But he knew that if computing was good for everyone else in the company, it would probably be good for him, too.

Mike took a little time to investigate personal computers. He wanted a machine that had growth potential. Working with a professional from the Information Systems Department, Mike decided on a midpriced model with ample speed and memory, a color monitor, and a laser printer.

Mike hesitated about the storage, however. The Information Systems consultant convinced him that having both a diskette drive and a hard drive would be a real advantage. (As we will see, this arrangement is timesaving and convenient.) But Mike had some misgivings about the capacity of the hard disk. Could he ever really use the 60-megabyte disk the consultant recommended? How could he possibly come up with 60 *million* characters of data? Mike chose instead a 30-megabyte disk, which seemed more than adequate to him at the time.

Mike's hard disk *was* adequate for its original purposes—storing notes, letters, outlines, documents, speeches, and position papers.

But Mike soon began branching out in other directions, using various types of software. He tracked names and phone numbers, analyzed financial data, and used his computer to produce business graphics. He even used the machine to file ideas that he could access instantaneously. All his computer activities used disk space, however, and Mike eventually found that his hard disk was getting crowded.

To prevent dilemmas like Mike's, computer professionals usually advise computer buyers to estimate disk needs generously and then double the estimate. But estimating future needs is rarely easy. Many users, therefore, make later adjustments. In this chapter, we will examine several storage options, including the hard disk Mike chose. ◻

WHY SECONDARY STORAGE?

Whether considering personal computer storage or the broader needs of a corporation or government agency, the choices can be complicated. Picture, if you can, how many filing-cabinet drawers would be required to hold the millions of files of, say, criminal records kept by the U.S. Justice Department or employee records kept by General Motors. The rooms to hold the filing cabinets would have to be enormous. Computer storage, which allows the storage of many records in extremely compressed form and quick access to them, is unquestionably one of the computer's most valuable assets.

Secondary storage, you will recall, is needed for two reasons. First, memory is limited in size, whereas secondary storage media can store as much information as necessary. Also, memory, or primary storage, can be used only temporarily; data disappears from memory when you turn most computers off. However, you probably want to store the data you have used or the information you have derived from processing.

Suppose, for example, you spend a long afternoon at the computer as part of your assignment as a management trainee. You have created and reworked a special report for the vice president of marketing to take on an upcoming sales trip. The report needs only another couple hours of polishing, which you can do the next morning. It is out of the question to begin again from scratch; you must save your work in computer storage so that you can retrieve it and carry on where you left off. Thus you need secondary storage, or **auxiliary storage.**

Personal computer users know that they need secondary storage as a place to keep the various files they create—letters, memos, reports, and even complex output such as financial calculations or graphics. Writing such files onto a personal computer output medium, usually a disk, is a relatively simple matter. A user needs only to learn the output commands associated with the software being used; the software package takes care of the details.

Working with business systems on large computers is another matter altogether. To begin with, business systems are usually concerned with records—possibly data about products or customers or employees. A user—probably a computer programmer—planning computer output needs to have a firm understanding of how data is organized and processed and of the storage medium that will hold the data. (Personal computer users can also keep these kinds of records.)

We begin by considering how data is organized and how it is processed. From there we will move on to storage media, first for large computers and then for personal computers.

DATA: GETTING ORGANIZED

To be processed by the computer, data—represented by characters— is organized into fields, records, files, and sometimes databases (Figure 5-1). We will start with the smallest element, the character.

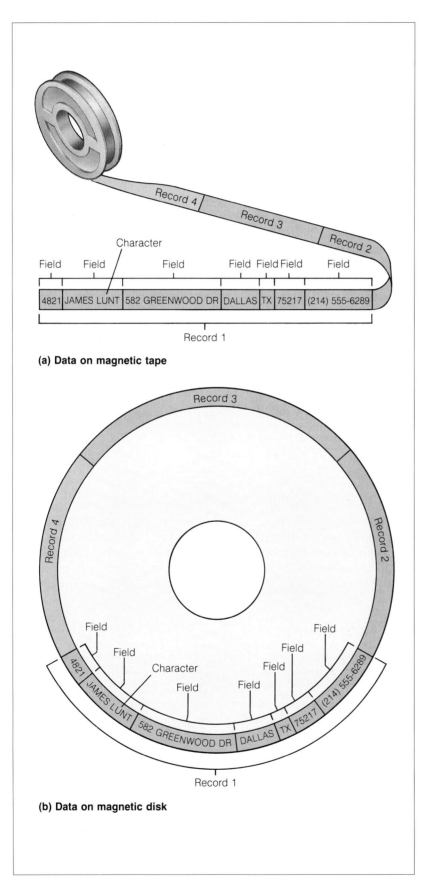

Figure 5-1   How data is organized.
Data, represented by characters, is organized
into fields, records, and files. A file is a
collection of related records.

- A **character** is a letter, number, or special character (such as $, ?, or *). One or more related characters constitute a field.
- A **field** contains a set of related characters. For example, suppose a health club is making address labels for a mailing. For each person it has a member-number field, a name field, a street-address field, a city field, a state field, a zip-code field, and a phone-number field.
- A **record** is a collection of related fields. Thus, on the health-club list, one person's member-number, name, address, city, state, zip code, and phone number constitute a record. (The fields are considered related because they are for the same person.)
- A file is a collection of related records. All the member records for the health club compose a membership file.
- A **database** is a collection of interrelated files stored together. (However, a file is not necessarily part of a database; many files exist independently.) In a database, specific data items can be retrieved for various applications. For instance, if the health club is opening a new outlet, it can pull out the names and addresses of all the people with specific zip codes that are near the new club. The club can then send a special announcement about opening day to those people.

PROCESSING DATA INTO INFORMATION: A USER PERSPECTIVE

There are several methods of processing data in a large computer network or mainframe system. The two main methods are batch processing (processing data transactions in groups) and transaction processing (processing the transactions one at a time as they occur). A combination of these two techniques may also be used. We will now look at these methods and give examples of their use.

Batch Processing

Batch processing is a technique in which transactions are collected into groups, or batches, to be processed. Let us suppose that we are going to update the health-club address-label file. The **master file,** a semi-permanent set of records, is, in this case, the records of all members of the health club, including their names, addresses, and so forth.

All changes to be made to the master file are compiled on a separate **transaction file.** Such changes can be of the following types:

- *Additions* are transactions to create new master records for new names added. If Sally Kelley is joining the club, a transaction containing the fields for Ms. Kelley—including member number, name, address, and so forth—will be prepared to add the new member record to the file.

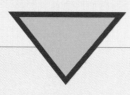

Just as people look at pictures first in a book, so they turn first to graphics in a computer publication. Graphics offer color, variety, and drama. Although some look like real-life photographs, all the graphics in this gallery were produced by a computer.

Realistic Art

(1) This computer illustration was inspired by Claude Monet's *Water Lilies Pool—Harmony in Green*. Monet used paint and canvas to create his masterpiece in 1899. Now, almost a century later, artists have a new tool for creativity—the computer.

(2-4) These computer-generated light-bulb images illustrate the evolution of realistic graphics. **(2)** In the late 1970s, curved surfaces appeared as a series of flat surfaces. **(3)** By the late 1980s, models could be produced with smooth, curved surfaces; this quality is now possible on some personal computers. **(4)** This realistic computer-generated model, with numerous textures and transparent surfaces, can be produced by powerful workstations.

1

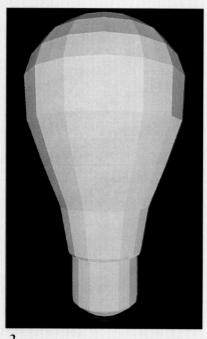

2

3

4

5

6

7

(5) This bright puppet, although simple in appearance, requires the considerable skills of a computer artist to create.

(6) This computer-generated image of a Japanese teacup is so realistic that we must make a disclaimer —it is not a photograph.

(7) A Macintosh computer was used to create this vivid image of the Golden Gate Bridge in California.

(8) This realistic bus scene was created to grace the cover of *Computer Graphics World* magazine. Note the snow effect on the bus and buildings.

8

ABSTRACT ART

(9) This fanciful image was created in Milan, Italy, as part of an advertising campaign for Alisarda Airlines.

(10) Even crayons have found new artistic life in this computer-generated piece entitled *Flying Colors II*.

(11) Sophisticated graphics such as the reflections on these spheres require considerable computing power.

(12-14) These three artistic renditions were all created by Steve Wilson, an art professor at California State University at Chico. Professor Wilson is a highly respected innovator in the field of computer graphic art.

9

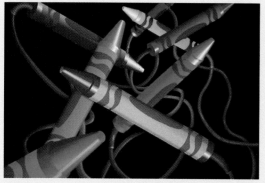

10

11

12

13

14

Virtual Reality

In virtual reality, you become immersed in an environment created by computer. This is made possible by sophisticated computers and optics that deliver to your eyes a three-dimensional scene in living color, complete with motion. By moving your body, you can interact with the virtual (artificial) world you see, and the computer-generated world responds to your actions. Sensors on your body translate your movements to the computer, which then adjusts the scene being sent to your eyes. As one virtual realist says, "We're building imaginary worlds, and we're helping put people in them." The examples shown here will take you on a guided tour of this fascinating new field of computer graphics.

(15) Playing virtual reality racquetball: Special goggles block out the player's view of the real world and replace it with a computer-generated view of a racquetball court, a ball, and a racquet. The player moves around an empty room, smashing an imaginary ball. Using this technology, a handicapped person could "fly" over the imaginary scene, competing with a player who is running; even people in different cities could play against each other on the same virtual racquetball court.

(16) Using this head-mounted display, a user can see a computer image and the reality in front of him at the same time. In the future, this technology may enable a doctor to have "x-ray vision"—to look at a patient and "see" inside the patient by linking medical imaging devices to virtual reality hardware and software.

(17) Just for fun, a computer translates video images of people into silhouettes and, reacting to certain motions, adds computer-generated images. For instance, if you point your fingers, sparks fly from your fingertips on the computer screen. This is part of an exhibit called *Video Place* at the Connecticut State Museum of Natural History in Storrs, Connecticut.

15

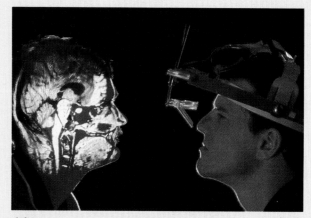

16

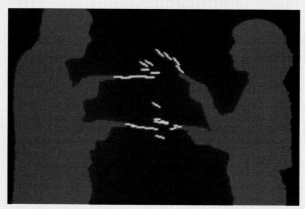

17

18

19

(18) Using a "magic wrist," scientists can now "feel" the atoms on a gold surface as they steer the tip of a microscope over a sample of gold. The specialized microscope maps the atoms on the surface, producing a color image such as the one shown in the background.

(19) In the future, air-traffic controllers may work like this: Micro-laser scanner glasses project computer-generated images of aircraft directly into the controller's eyes, immersing the controller in a three-dimensional scene showing all the aircraft in the area. To establish voice contact with the pilot of a plane, the controller merely touches the plane's image with a sensor-equipped glove.

(20) Using an electronic glove, M.I.T. musician–computer scientist–professor Todd Machover conducts computer-generated music in conjunction with live musicians.

20

THE DISCUS THROWER

Countering the computer's reputation as an unfeeling machine, a computer artist has created this image of inspiration.

- *Deletions* are transactions with instructions to remove master records of people who have resigned from the health club. For example, if Ha Dao resigns from the club, a transaction is prepared to remove her record from the file.

- *Revisions* are transactions to change fields such as street addresses or phone numbers on the master records. For example, if Benson Porter changes his address and phone number, a transaction is prepared to reflect these changes on his record in the master file.

At regular intervals, perhaps monthly in this example, the master file is **updated** with the changes called for on the separate transaction file. The result is a new, up-to-date master file. The new file in this example has a new record for Sally Kelley, no longer has a record for Ha Dao, and has a changed record for Benson Porter.

An advantage of batch processing is that it is usually less expensive than other types of processing because it is more efficient: A group of records is processed at the same time. A disadvantage of batch processing is that anyone interested in the outcome—customers or business users—has to wait. It does not matter that you want to know what the gasoline bill for your car is now; you have to wait until the end of the month, when all your credit-card gas purchases are processed together with those of other customers. Batch processing cannot give you a quick response to your question.

Transaction Processing

Transaction processing is a technique of processing transactions one at a time in random order—that is, in any order they occur. Transaction processing is handy for anyone who needs an immediate update or feedback from the computer: a contractor who needs to check a supplier's rates; an airline clerk making a reservation; a retailer who wants to confirm product inventory; and many, many others. In fact, transaction processing has become a staple in all kinds of service industries in which speedy service is a must.

Transaction processing is real-time processing. **Real-time processing** can obtain data from the computer system in time to affect the activity at hand. In other words, a transaction is processed fast enough for the results to come back and be acted upon right away. For example, a teller at a bank (or you at an automatic teller machine) can find out immediately what your bank balance is. You can then decide right away how much money you can afford to withdraw. For processing to be real-time, it must also be **on-line**—that is, the user's terminal must be directly connected to the computer.

The great leap forward that transaction processing represents was made possible by the development of magnetic disk as a means of storing data. With magnetic tape it is not efficient to go directly to the particular record you are looking for—the tape might have to be advanced several feet first. However, with disk you can go directly to one particular record. The invention of magnetic disk meant that data processing is more likely to be **interactive**, as is possible with the personal computer. The user can communicate directly with the computer, maintaining a dialogue back and forth. The direct access to data on disk dramatically increases the use of interactive computing.

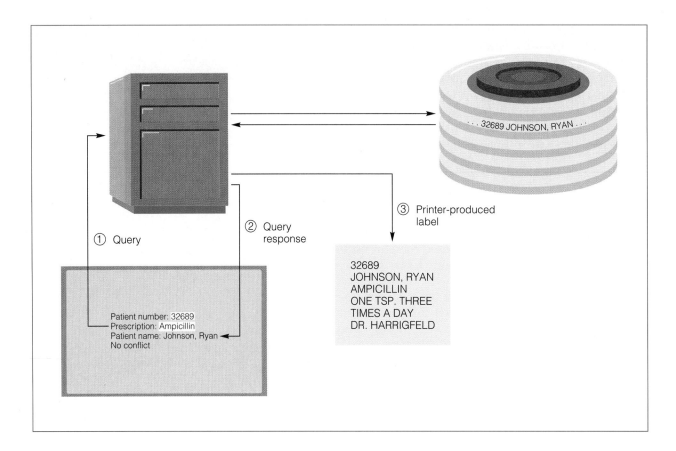

▲
Figure 5-2   How transaction processing works.

The purposes of this hospital-clinic pharmacy system are to verify that a patient's prescription is safe, produce a prescription label for the medication bottle, and update the patient's medical records. Because of the possibility of patients having the same name, the file is organized by patient number rather than by name. Here Ryan Johnson, patient number 32689, brings his prescription to the pharmacist. (1) Through a terminal, the pharmacist asks the computer system whether the ampicillin prescribed is apt to conflict with other medication the patient is taking. (2) The computer screen shows that 32689 is Ryan Johnson and displays the message "No conflict." The computer then updates Johnson's file so other physicians can see later that ampicillin was prescribed for him. (3) A printer attached to the computer system prints a prescription label that the pharmacist can place on the ampicillin bottle. All this is done while the patient is waiting.

There are several advantages to transaction processing. The first is that you do not need to wait. For instance, a department store salesclerk using a point-of-sale terminal can key in a customer's charge-card number and a code that asks the computer "Is this charge card acceptable?" and get an immediate reply. Immediacy is a distinct benefit, since everyone expects fast service these days. Second, the process permits continual updating of a customer's record. Thus the salesclerk can not only verify your credit but also record the sale in the computer, and you will eventually be billed through the computerized billing process.

Figure 5-2 provides an example of transaction processing, in which a patient submits a prescription.

Batch and Transaction Processing: Complementary

Numerous computer systems combine the best features of both of these methods of processing. A bank, for instance, may record your withdrawal transaction during the day at the teller window whenever you demand your cash. However, the deposit that you leave in an envelope in an "instant" deposit drop may be recorded during the night by means of batch processing.

Another common example of both batch and transaction processing is in retail sales. Using point-of-sale terminals, inventory data is captured as sales are made; this data is processed later in batches to produce inventory reports.

STORAGE MEDIA

• • • • • • • • • • • • • • • • • •

As we have mentioned, two primary media for storing data are magnetic tape and magnetic disk. Since these media have been the staples of the computer industry for three decades, we will begin with them.

Magnetic Tape Storage

Magnetic tape looks like the tape used in home tape recorders—plastic Mylar tape, usually $\frac{1}{2}$ inch wide and wound on a $10\frac{1}{2}$-inch-diameter reel (Figure 5-3). The tape has an iron-oxide coating that can be magnetized. Data is stored as extremely small magnetized spots, which can then be read by a tape unit into the computer's main storage.

Figure 5-4a shows a **magnetic tape unit** that is part of a large computer system. The purpose of the unit is to write and to read—that is, to record data on and retrieve data from—magnetic tape. This is done by a **read/write head** (Figure 5-4b). Reading is done by an electromagnet that senses the magnetized areas on the tape and converts them into electrical impulses, which are sent to the processor. The reverse is called writing. Before the machine writes on the tape, the **erase head** erases any previously recorded data.

Records are stored on tape sequentially—that is, in order by some identifier such as a social security number.

▲
Figure 5-3   Magnetic tape.
Magnetic tape on $10\frac{1}{2}$-inch-diameter reels has been the workhorse of data processing for years. However, a smaller tape cartridge (bottom left) has been introduced that can hold 20% more data in 75% less space.

▼
Figure 5-4   Magnetic tape units.
Tapes are always covered—in this case, by glass doors—to protect them from outside dust and dirt. (a) Magnetic tape on reels runs on these tape drives. (b) This diagram highlights the read/write head and the erase head found in magnetic tape units.

(a)

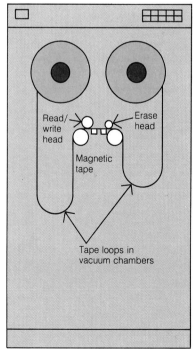

(b)

(a)

(b)

(c)

▲
Figure 5-5   Magnetic disks.
(a) Hard magnetic disks come in a variety of sizes, as shown by these three individual disks. Disk packs can vary in the number of disks they contain, as illustrated by the two disk packs shown here. (b) This 5¼-inch diskette is in a square protective thin plastic jacket. (c) This 3½-inch diskette is protected by a firm plastic exterior cover.

Magnetic Disk Storage

Magnetic disk storage is another common form of secondary storage. A **hard magnetic disk,** or **hard disk,** is a metal platter coated with magnetic oxide that looks something like a large brown compact disk. Hard disks come in a variety of sizes; 14, 5¼, and 3½ inches are typical diameters. Several disks of the same size are assembled together in a **disk pack** (Figure 5-5a). A disk pack looks like a stack of stereo records, except that daylight can be seen between the disks. There are different types of disk packs, with the number of platters varying by model. Each disk has a top and bottom surface on which to record data.

Another form of magnetic disk storage is the **diskette,** which is a round piece of plastic coated with magnetic oxide (Figure 5-5b, c). Diskettes and small hard disks are used with personal computers. We will discuss secondary storage for personal computers later in this chapter, but keep in mind that the principles of disk storage discussed here also apply to disk storage for personal computers.

How Data Is Stored on a Disk

As Figure 5-6 shows, the surface of each disk has tracks on it. Data is recorded as magnetic spots on the tracks. The number of tracks per

COMPUTING HIGHLIGHTS

The Computerized Hotel

Most major hotels offer computer amenities of some kind, often a separate room stocked with personal computers, printers, modems, phone jacks, and fax machines. But many hotels go much further, putting all that equipment in individual guest rooms. If you need a place to compute as well as to sleep, any major hotel chain can help you out.

But suppose you are going on vacation and do not want to go anywhere near computers? That may be a bit difficult, especially if you bunk at the Hotel Macklowe near Times Square in Manhattan. The Mack-

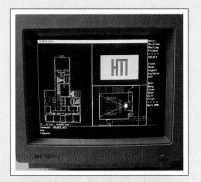

lowe is computerized from top to bottom. Each room at the Macklowe offers computer access so that guests can receive phone mail,

change airline reservations, purchase theater tickets, play computer games with guests in other rooms, or check out of the hotel.

surface varies with the particular type of disk. A track on a disk is a closed circle—any point on a particular track is always the same distance from the center. All tracks on one disk are concentric—that is, they are circles with the same center.

The same amount of data is stored on every track, from outermost (track 000) to innermost (track 399 of a 400-track disk), and it takes the same amount of time to read the data on the outer track as on the inner, even though the outer track moves faster.

A magnetic disk is a **direct-access storage device (DASD).** With such a device you can go directly to the record you want. With tape storage, on the other hand, you must read all preceding records in the file until you come to the desired record. Records can be stored either sequentially or randomly (in whatever order the records occur) on a direct-access storage device.

The Disk Drive

A **disk drive** is a device that allows data to be read from a disk or written on a disk. A diskette is inserted into a disk drive that is part of a personal computer. A disk pack, however, is mounted on a disk drive that is a separate unit connected to a large, shared computer. Some disks are permanently mounted inside a disk drive. Generally, these are used in personal computers or in cases where several users are sharing data. A typical example is a disk with files containing flight information that is used by several airline reservations agents.

The mechanism for reading or writing data on a disk is an **access arm** (Figure 5-7a). The access arm acts somewhat like the arm on a

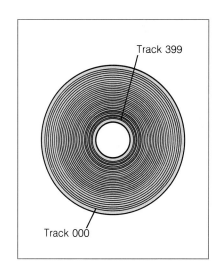

▲
Figure 5-6   Surface of a disk.
Note that each track is a closed circle, unlike the tracks on a stereo record. This drawing is only to illustrate the location of the tracks; you cannot actually see tracks on the disk surface.

stereo, although it does not actually touch the surface. A disk pack has a series of access arms, which slip in between the disks in the pack (Figure 5-7c). Two read/write heads are on each arm, one facing up for the surface above it, one facing down for the surface below it. However, only one read/write head can operate at any one time.

Winchester Disks

In some disk drives, the access arms can be retracted, then the disk pack can be removed from the drive. In other cases, however, the disks, access arms, and read/write heads are combined in a **sealed module** called a **Winchester disk.** Winchester disk assemblies are put together in clean rooms so even microscopic dust particles do not get on disk

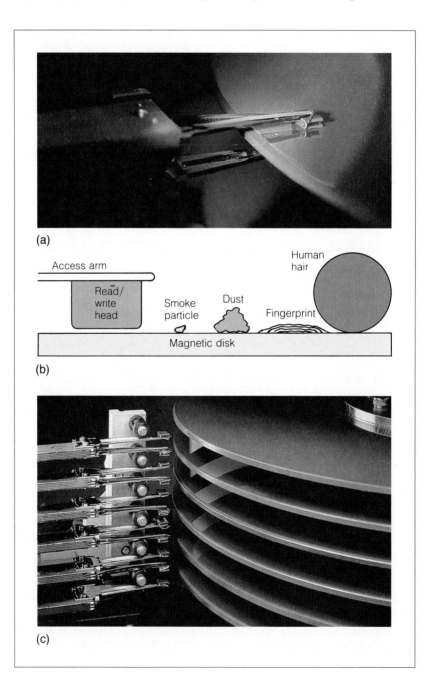

▶

Figure 5-7   Read/write heads and access arms.
(a) This photo shows a read/write head on the end of an access arm poised over a hard disk. (b) When in operation the read/write head comes very close to the disk surface. In fact, particles as small as smoke, dust, fingerprints, and a hair loom large when they are on a disk. If the read/write head crashes into a particle like one of these, data is destroyed and the disk damaged. You can see why it is important to keep disks and disk drives clean. (c) Note that there are two read/write heads on each access arm. Each arm slips between two disks in the pack. The access arms move simultaneously, but only one read/write head operates at any one time.

surfaces. Many Winchester disks are built-in, but some are removable in the sense that the entire module can be lifted from the drive. The removed module, however, remains sealed and contains the disks and access arms.

Winchester disks were originally 14 inches in diameter, but now smaller versions are made. Hard disks on personal computers—$5\frac{1}{4}$- and $3\frac{1}{2}$-inch disks—always employ Winchester technology. Until 1980 the most common type of high-speed storage consisted of removable disk packs. Since then that technology has been supplanted by Winchester disks; today around 85% of all disk storage units sold are of the fixed, Winchester variety. The principal reason is that, compared to removable disk packs, Winchester disks cost about half as much and go twice as long between failures. This increased reliability results because operators do not handle the Winchester disk at all and because the sealed module keeps the disks free from contamination.

Advantages of Disk Storage

As we have seen, disk storage has many advantages over tape storage. There are those in the industry who wonder why tape is still around at all. Disk does indeed seem the very model of an effective storage medium:

- Disk has high data-volume capacity and allows very fast access.
- Disk is reliable; barring a catastrophe, the data you put there will still be there when you want to retrieve it.
- Disk files permit immediate access to read or write any given record. This is the biggest advantage and is basic to real-time systems, such as those providing instant credit checks and airline reservations.

However, we can say a few words for tape, too. Although records cannot easily be processed directly on tape, tape has certain advantages that make it a viable storage medium. It is portable—a reel of tape can be carried or mailed. It is relatively inexpensive: A 2400-foot reel of tape costs less than $15. (Compare this with a full-size disk pack, which costs $300 or more.)

The chief use of magnetic tape today is as a backup medium for disk files. Although a hard disk is an extremely reliable device, the drive is subject to electromechanical failure. With any method of data storage, a **backup system**—a method of storing data in more than one place to protect it from damage or loss—is vital. Backup copies of disk files are made regularly on tape as insurance against disk failure and accidental file deletions.

PERSONAL COMPUTER STORAGE

The market for data storage devices is being profoundly affected by the surge in popularity of personal computers. Storage media are available in two basic forms: diskettes and hard disk. Let us consider each of these.

PERSONAL COMPUTERS IN ACTION

How to Handle Diskettes

Do not lock your diskette in the trunk of the car on a hot day, or leave it on the dashboard in the sun, or stick it to the door of your refrigerator with a magnet. Avoid smoking cigarettes around your computer, since smoke particles caught under the read/write head can scratch the disk surface.

These are only a few of the rules for taking care of diskettes. The main forces hostile to diskettes are dust, magnetic fields, liquids, vapors, and temperature extremes. Although 3½-inch diskettes have plastic jackets and are thus less fragile than 5¼-inch diskettes, both require care in handling.

1 Do not touch the disk surface. It is easily contaminated, which causes errors.

2 Do not use alcohol, thinners, or freon to clean the disk.

Alcohol   Thinner   Freon

3 Do not use magnets or magnetized objects near the disk. Data can be lost from a disk exposed to a magnetic field.

4 Do not bend or fold the disk.

5 Do not place heavy objects on the disk.

16 TON

6 Do not use rubber bands or paper clips on the disk.

7 Do not use erasers on the disk.

Eraser

8 Do not expose the disk to excessive heat or sunlight.

9 Apply the index label to the right of the manufacturer's label. Do not use labels in layers.

Manufacturer's label   Index label

10 Write on the index label with felt-tip pen only, not pencil or ball-point pen.

Manufacturer's label   Felt-tip pen   Index label

11 Insert carefully, by grasping upper edge of disk and placing it into the disk drive.

Disk drive

12 Keep disk in its protective envelope when not in use.

Floppy disk   Envelope

Diskettes

Diskettes, sometimes called *floppy disks*, are popular among personal computer users. Diskettes are transferable from one computer to another, provided the density—capacity—of the borrowed disk does not exceed what the disk drive can handle. Also, diskette drives are relatively inexpensive. The 5¼-inch diskette was popular in the 1980s;

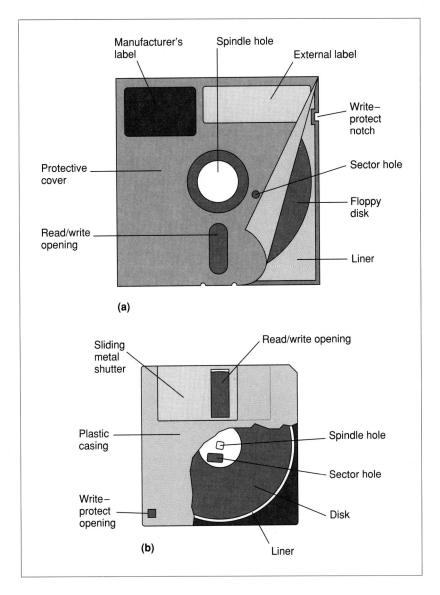

(a)

(b)

Figure 5-8   Diskettes.
(a) Cutaway view of 5¼-inch diskette.
(b) Cutaway view of 3½-inch diskette.

WHO WILL PAY FOR MY CAMPAIGN?

If you make a contribution to a political campaign, be assured that your name and address are stored safely in the campaign files, so that you can be solicited—again and again—in the future. High tech is a fixture on the campaign trail, and much of the technology is devoted to creating and using disk files of contributors. Computerized fund-raising lets campaigners reach more people more often, and on a more personalized basis. Files of potential contributors can be organized by sex, age, zip code, income, education, and other criteria; mailings can then be geared to a particular audience. For example, with help from the computer files, campaign workers can easily send to senior citizens a letter supporting additional social security benefits.

Although disk files of contributors are a key campaign factor, computers are useful in a variety of ways. They help with get-out-the-vote mailings, delegate counts, media buying, news releases, scheduling, financial reporting, cost control, voter trend tracking, research, and speech writing.

Some people feel that computers make a campaign seem impersonal. Computers, they argue, cannot walk the streets, pressing hands and kissing babies. Nevertheless, these days a tight race may be won by the candidate with the best computer operation.

however, the newer 3½-inch diskette, which can hold more data, is supplanting the 5¼-inch diskette (Figure 5-8).

The small disk is easier to store, and it fits handily into a shirt pocket or purse. Its hard plastic jacket provides better protection for the diskette than does the thin jacket of the larger disk. The higher capacity of the 3½-inch diskette lets users store many files on a disk, so users do not have to shuffle so many disks around. Finally, since the 3½-inch disk drive is small, manufacturers can make their computers smaller, so they take up less desk space.

Hard Disks

Personal computer **hard disks** are 5¼-inch or 3½-inch Winchester disks in sealed modules (Figure 5-9a). The cost of hard disks has come down substantially: A hard disk with a capacity of 30 megabytes of storage now costs only a few hundred dollars, down from several thousand dollars just a few years ago. Winchester disks are extremely reliable, since they are sealed against contamination by outside air or human hands.

Hard disks can save you time as well as space. Just the way the hard disk speeds up your computing can make it worthwhile, even if you do not need all the storage hard disk provides. Accessing files on hard disk is significantly faster than on diskettes—up to about 20 times faster. Furthermore, users find that accessing files from a hard disk is more convenient than handling diskettes.

Unlike a diskette, however, most hard disk units cannot be transported from one computer to another. For that reason most hard disk systems include at least one diskette drive to provide users with software and data portability.

RAM Disks

It is called a **RAM disk,** or an **electronic disk,** or a **phantom disk,** but it is not really a disk at all. A RAM disk is set up by software that fools your computer into regarding part of its memory as another disk drive that can be used to store programs and data. The advantage of a RAM disk is that it works much faster than a standard disk drive. A RAM disk is particularly helpful if a user is transferring data from one computer to another. Instead of waiting for the diskette or hard disk to send data, the data can be sent directly from the RAM disk.

So why not put all files on RAM disk and enjoy the speed? In addition to being much more expensive, RAM disk is volatile. Its contents are lost if the computer is turned off or there is a power failure. You can load your programs onto RAM disk for the day, but you must save new data in real disk files.

▼
Figure 5-9   Hard disks.
(a) Hard disks. (b) Innards of a hard disk. This drive stores about 20 million characters on a pair of 3½-inch disks.

(a)

(b)

MACINTOSH

Making Your Disk Space Count

Sooner or later it happens to most of us. No matter how inexhaustible we imagined our hard disks to be, the day arrives when we run out of storage space. Perhaps we first learn about it in the information available along the top of the Macintosh's screen: The message tells us we have less than a diskette's worth of storage left on our hard disk. Or maybe we try to copy a large file onto our hard disk and the computer beeps at us. A dialog box appears, saying "Not enough room on disk. . . ." Then we know it has happened: We have filled the hard disk—all 10, 20, 40 (or more) million bytes of it.

How did it happen? There are lots of ways. One is software gluttony. Most of us use only a few software applications regularly, and we may keep a couple more around for occasional odd chores. But software gluttons load up their hard disks with every software product they can find. At an average of 200 kilobytes per application package, these files add up to megabytes in no time.

With desktop publishing applications you can create reports, newsletters, brochures, even entire magazines on the Mac and store them on the hard disk. But beware: A sophisticated desktop publishing file can easily exceed a megabyte in size.

There are ways to fill a hard disk inadvertently, too. For example, some powerful word processing packages automatically save backup copies of your documents. Each time you edit a file, a copy of the current draft is made and given a new name. Unless you delete them, these backups accumulate on your hard disk, consuming a few thousand bytes at a time.

Here are some inexpensive storage solutions:

- If you are a software glutton, copy some of those unused or little-used applications onto diskettes and store them near your computer.

- If you are a desktop publisher, look into compression utilities. They let you make backup copies of your documents in a space-saving format. You can store these compressed files on diskettes until you need to unpack them for reuse.

- If someday you might need access to final versions of those word processing files, consider deleting the automatic backup files kept on your hard disk and, instead, saving duplicates of the final versions on diskettes.

If you really cannot get along without more space for your many favorite software applications and document files, you are going to have to buy additional storage capacity. One option for the Mac is the external hard disk—one that is enclosed in its own case and sits under or beside the machine. The Mac Plus and all subsequent models feature a connector into which you can plug an external hard disk. The Mac SE and the Mac II family have provisions for internally mounted hard disks. Installed by a computer shop technician, an internal disk saves space on your desk and generally works faster than the external models.

How much storage space is enough? These days a total of 20 megabytes of storage capacity should suffice for home use. If you are a real computer enthusiast or use your Mac for business purposes, you will probably find 40 megabytes less limiting in the long run and well worth the extra cost.

▲
Figure 5-10   Optical disk.
Optical disk technology provides greatly
increased storage capacity.

OPTICAL STORAGE

• • • • • • • • • • • • • • • • • • •

Would you like to have the *Encyclopaedia Britannica* at your fingertips—
all 30 volumes? Although it would require an astonishing 1250 standard diskettes to hold the entire encyclopedia, its contents fit nicely on a single 540-megabyte optical diskette. The explosive growth in storage needs compels the computer industry to provide storage devices that are increasingly higher in capacity, a demand tailor-made for the technology that is now upon us: the optical disk (Figure 5-10).

Optical storage works like this. A laser beam hits a layer of metallic material spread over the surface of the disk. When data is written to the disk, heat from the laser produces tiny spots on the disk's surface. To read the data, the laser scans the disk and a lens picks up different light reflections from the various spots.

Optical storage technology is categorized according to its read/write capability. Data is recorded on **read-only** media by the manufacturer and can be read from but not written to by the user (you can read it, but you cannot change it). This technology is sometimes referred to as **OROM,** for **optical read-only memory.** Obviously, you could not use an OROM disk to store your files, but manufacturers could use it to supply software. A current multiple-application, or integrated, package—a product that provides word processing, spreadsheets, graphics, and a database—sometimes takes as many as six diskettes; the contents could fit easily on one OROM disk.

Write once, read many media, also called **WORM,** may be written to once. When the WORM disk is filled, it becomes read-only media. A WORM disk is nonerasable. For applications demanding secure storage of original versions of valuable documents, such as wills or other legal papers, the primary advantage of nonerasability is clear: Once they are recorded, no one can erase or modify them.

A popular variation on optical technology is the **CD-ROM,** for **compact disk read-only memory.** CD-ROM has a major advantage over other optical disk designs: The disk format is identical to that of *audio* compact disks, so the same dust-free manufacturing plants that are now stamping out digital versions of Bach or Springsteen can easily convert to producing anything from software to the aforementioned *Encyclopaedia Britannica.* Since manufacturing CD-ROM disks is simply a matter of pressing out copies from a master disk, it is much more economical than traditional magnetic storage, which makes copies byte by byte.

Early optical disks could not be written on, but now that has changed. **Erasable optical disks** can indeed accept writing, and their future seems limitless.

▲   ▲   ▲

What is the future of storage? Whatever the technology, it seems likely that we will be seeing greater storage capabilities in the future. Such capabilities have awesome implications—think of the huge data files for law, medicine, science, education, and government.

To have access to all that data from any location, we need data communications. We now turn to this topic in the next chapter.

CHAPTER REVIEW

SUMMARY AND KEY TERMS

- **Secondary storage,** or **auxiliary storage,** is necessary because memory can be used only temporarily.

- To be processed by a computer, data represented by characters is organized into fields, records, files, and databases. A **character** is a letter, number, or special character (such as $). A **field** is a set of related characters, a **record** is a collection of related fields, a **file** is a collection of related records, and a **database** is a collection of interrelated files.

- The two main methods of large-scale data processing are **batch processing** (processing data transactions in groups) and **transaction processing** (processing data transactions one at a time).

- Batch processing involves a **master file,** which contains semi-permanent data, and a **transaction file,** which contains additions, deletions, and changes to be made to **update** the master file. An advantage of batch processing is the cost savings resulting from processing records in groups; the main disadvantage is the delay receiving output.

- In **transaction processing,** the transactions are processed in the order they occur. This is **real-time processing** because the results of the transaction are available quickly enough to affect the activity at hand. Real-time processing requires having the user's terminal **on-line**—directly connected to the computer. The development of disk storage permitted **interactive** processing—a computer/ user dialogue—by providing users with easier access to data.

- **Magnetic tape** is a plastic storage medium coated with iron oxide. A **magnetic tape unit** records and retrieves data by using a **read/write head,** an electromagnet that can convert magnetized areas into electrical impulses (to read) or reverse the process (to write). Before the machine writes, the **erase head** erases any previously recorded data.

- A **hard magnetic disk** is a metal platter coated with magnetic oxide. Several disks are assembled in a **disk pack.** A **diskette** is a round piece of plastic coated with magnetic oxide.

- The surface of a magnetic disk has tracks on which data is recorded as magnetic spots. All the tracks are closed circles having the same center, and the same amount of data is stored on each track.

- A disk storage device is a **direct-access storage device (DASD)** because the read/write head can locate a record on it directly.

- A **disk drive** rapidly rotates a disk or disk pack as an **access arm** moves a read/ write head that detects the magnetized data.

- A **Winchester disk** combines disks, access arms, and read/write heads in a sealed module.

- Disk storage provides high-volume data capacity and allows users to find and update records immediately. Tape storage can be used only for batch processing, but it is portable and less expensive than disk storage.

- A **backup system**—a method of storing data in more than one place to protect it from damage or loss—is vital. Backup copies of disk files are made regularly on tape as insurance against disk failure.

- Diskettes and hard disks are the most common storage media for personal computers. **Diskettes** are available in $5\frac{1}{4}$-inch and $3\frac{1}{2}$-inch sizes. A **hard disk** is more expensive than a diskette and usually cannot be moved from computer to computer, but it does provide more storage and faster processing.

- A **RAM disk,** also called an **electronic disk** or **phantom disk,** is software that fools the computer into regarding part of its memory as another disk drive for storing programs and data.

- In optical disk technology, a laser beam enters data by producing tiny spots on the optical disk's metallic surface. Data is read by having the laser scan the disk surface while a lens picks up different light reflections from the spots.

- Optical storage technology is categorized according to its read/write capability. The manufacturer records on **read-only media** through a technology sometimes called **optical read-only memory (OROM);** the user can read the recorded media but cannot change it. **Write once, read many (WORM)** media can be written to once; then it becomes read-only media. **CD-ROM** stands for **compact disk read-only memory.** CD-ROM disks have the same format as audio compact disks. An **erasable optical disk** allows data to be stored, moved, changed, and erased—just as on magnetic media.

SELF-TEST

True/False

T F 1. Real-time processing gives results fast enough to affect the computer user's next action.

T F 2. Processing data by groups of transactions is called batch processing.

T F 3. A transaction file contains records to update the master file.

T F 4. The quickest way to back up a hard disk is to use diskettes.

T F 5. Another name for OROM is RAM disk.

T F 6. Transaction processing systems are usually real-time systems.

T F 7. A drawback of magnetic tape storage is that it is very expensive.

T F 8. Optical disk can never be erased.

T F 9. A field is a set of related records.

T F 10. Auxiliary storage can be used only temporarily.

Matching

_____ 1. RAM disk   a. concentric

_____ 2. interactive   b. semi-permanent

_____ 3. magnetic disk   c. dialogue

_____ 4. sealed data module   d. transactions in groups

_____ 5. record   e. any order

_____ 6. master file   f. direct-access storage

_____ 7. disk tracks   g. Winchester technology

_____ 8. transaction processing   h. phantom disk

_____ 9. on-line   i. related fields

_____ 10. batch processing   j. direct computer connection

Fill-In

1. The two most common media for secondary storage are:

   _____ and _____

2. A technique for processing transactions in any order they occur:

   _____

3. Another name for a RAM disk is: _____

4. The communication when the user maintains a dialogue with the computer:

   _____

5. Optical storage technology is categorized according to this ability:

   _____

6. CD-ROM stands for: _____

7. The technology supporting a sealed disk module:

   _____

8. Records that can add, delete, or revise master file records are called:

   _____

9. A file is a group of related: _____

10. The smallest unit of data is: _____

Answers

True/False: 1. T, 3. T, 5. F, 7. F, 9. F

Matching: 1. h, 3. f, 5. i, 7. a, 9. j

Fill-In: 1. magnetic tape and magnetic disk, 3. electronic or phantom disk, 5. read/write, 7. Winchester, 9. records

CHAPTER 6

OVERVIEW

COMMUNICATIONS
COMPUTER CONNECTIONS

onday morning Ellen Carr began working through the stack of paperwork in her IN basket. As purchasing agent for Connor Medical Specialties, her job was to find the best vendors and prices for everything the small company bought. This made her an expert in a lot of areas and also put her in the middle of a lot of battles. Mondays were usually a pretty light day for the IN basket, but on this Monday she was flabbergasted to find there, neatly clipped together, 25 individual requests for high-priced laser printers. After checking her calendar to make sure it was not April Fools' Day, she got a cup of coffee and took another look at the orders.

Every personal computer user in the company had filled out an order form, asking for a personal printer. The point was not lost on Ellen. She knew how tired the staff had grown of taking their diskettes to one of the three secretaries in the plant who had printers, interrupting to ask that a file be printed out, and waiting around until the secretary could comply. Thinking about the impact this had on the secretaries, Ellen was pretty sure she could guess who had masterminded the great printer-order conspiracy.

Fortunately, Ellen had a solution in mind. Gail, one of the computer sales reps who called on Ellen regularly, had taken her to a seminar on networking. There Ellen had learned that, for the price of a couple of new printers, she could buy hardware and software that would connect all the personal computers in the plant to the three printers Connor Medical already owned.

Ellen called Gail later that morning. She learned that there was more she could do with a network than just printing. If she could afford to buy another personal computer or if one of the current 25 was not being used much, she could make it do double duty as a server. With a server, personal computer users who needed to share text or data files wouldn't have to trade diskettes any more.

She found, too, that a server could help her cut software costs. If she bought a single copy of a program and put it on the server, any of the personal computer users could run it. She would need to buy special licenses for the software, but they would be much less expensive than buying 25 separate copies.

Finally, she learned, another network benefit would be electronic mail. Companies with mainframe computers had had it for years and swore by it. But a personal computer network could give Connor Medical the same capability for a lot less than a mainframe would cost.

After putting some figures together, considering the cost of wiring, hardware and software installation, and user training, Ellen went to visit her boss. She was confident that she had the solution to the laser printer crisis. ∎

DATA COMMUNICATIONS NOW

Merging communications and computers can help you get full value from each technology. Possible benefits include access to services like computer banking and computer shopping and to other workers in a computer network. People who use computer communications technology are just as casual about linking up with a computer in another state or country as they are about using the telephone. The technology that makes it possible is called data communications.

Data communications systems—computer systems that transmit data over communications lines such as public telephone lines or private network cables—have been gradually evolving since the mid-1960s. When computers were still a novelty, users placed everything—all processing, hardware, software, and storage—in one central location, a scheme now called **centralized data processing.** Centralization, however, proved inconvenient. The next logical step was **teleprocessing,** connecting users to the central computer via telephone lines and terminals right in their own offices.

The most innovative scheme, however, is **distributed data processing (DDP),** which is similar to teleprocessing but accommodates both remote *access* and also remote *processing.* Processing and files are dispersed among several remote locations and can be handled by local computers—usually mini- or microcomputers—all hooked up to the central host computer and sometimes to each other as well. A typical application of a distributed data processing system is a business or organization with many locations, branch offices, or retail outlets.

The whole picture of distributed data processing has changed dramatically with the advent of networks of personal computers. By **network,** we mean a computer system that uses communications equipment to connect two or more computers and their resources. DDP systems are networks. We will examine networking in more detail in later sections of the chapter.

In the next section we will preview the components of a communications system to give you an overview of how these components work together.

THE COMPLETE COMMUNICATIONS SYSTEM: HOW IT ALL FITS TOGETHER

Suppose you work at a sporting goods store. You learn the first day that the store has a computer that is part of a network. The network is connected to the warehouse and to other stores so that you can exchange inventory and other information. What components are in place to help you do your job?

The basic configuration—how the components are put together—is straightforward, but the choices for each component vary and the technology is ever changing. Assume that you have some data—a message—to transmit from one place to another. The basic hardware components of a data communications system to transmit that message are (1) the sending device, (2) a communications link, and (3) the receiving device. In the sporting goods store, you might want to send a message to the warehouse to inquire about a Wilson tennis racquet, an item you need for a customer. In this case, the sending device is your terminal or personal computer at the store, the communications link is the phone line, and the receiving machine is the computer at the warehouse. As you will see, however, there are many other possibilities.

There is another often-needed component in this basic configuration, as you can see in Figure 6-1. This component is a modem, which is sometimes needed to convert computer data to signals that can be carried by the communications channel and vice versa.

Let us see how these components work together, beginning with how data is transmitted.

SENDING YOUR DATA: DATA TRANSMISSION

If you want to communicate with other computers, you must jump one important hurdle: the inherent incompatibility of computers with most communications links. A terminal or computer produces digital signals, which are simply the presence or absence of an electrical pulse. Some communications lines accept digital transmission directly. However, most communications go via telephone lines, which were built for voice transmission; voice transmission requires analog signals. We will look at these two types of transmissions, then consider modems, which translate between them.

Types of Transmission: Digital and Analog

Digital transmission sends data as distinct pulses, either on or off, and thus can accept computer-generated data directly. However, most communications media—such as telephone lines, coaxial cables, and

▼
Figure 6-1 Communications system components.
Data originating from (1) a sending device is (2) converted by a modem to data that can be carried over (3) a link and (4) reconverted by a modem at the receiving end before (5) being sent to the receiving computer.

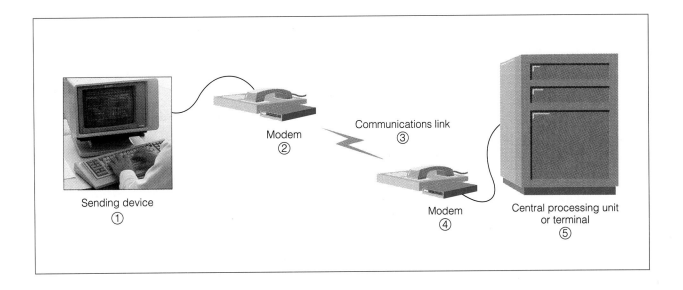

Sending device
①

Modem
②

Communications link
③

Modem
④

Central processing unit
or terminal
⑤

microwave circuits—are not digital. For most users, transmitting via one of these common means is more practical than establishing a means of digital transmission. And the common communications media have a common characteristic: They all use analog transmission.

Analog transmission uses a continuous electrical signal in the form of a wave. A digital signal must be converted to analog before it can be sent over analog lines. Conversion from digital to analog signals is called **modulation,** and the reverse process—reconstructing the original digital message at the other end of the transmission—is called **demodulation.** So we see that the marriage of computers to communications is not a perfect one. Instead of just "joining hands," a third party may be needed in between to make signal conversions. This extra device is called a modem.

Making the Switch: Modems

A **modem** is a device that converts a digital signal to an analog signal and vice versa (Figure 6-2a). *Modem* is short for *mo*dulator/*dem*odulator. Once a modem is attached to your computer, whether at home or in the office, you no longer need to be concerned about the translation of data from one type of signal to another. All you have to do is send the data; the modem will take care of the translation automatically.

▼
Figure 6-2 Modems.
(a) Modems convert—modulate—digital data signals to analog signals for traveling over communications links, then reverse the process—demodulate—at the other end. (b) This external modem rests under the telephone that hooks the computer to the outside world. (c) This internal modem slips into an expansion slot inside the computer. The phone cord plugs into a jack, accessible through the back of the computer.

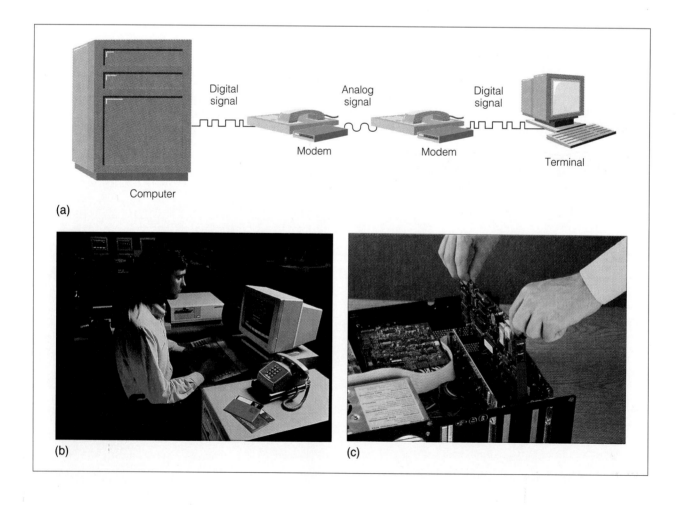

Modems vary in the way they connect to the telephone line. A **direct-connect modem** is directly connected to the telephone line by means of a telephone jack. An **external direct-connect modem** is separate from the computer (Figure 6-2b). Its main advantages are that it can be used with a variety of computers and that it is easy to install. However, personal computer users who regard a modem as one more item taking up desk space can buy an **internal modem,** a modem board that can be inserted in the computer (Figure 6-2c). Some new personal computers even have an internal modem built-in as part of the standard equipment.

A modem's speed of transmission is an important consideration. In general, modem users use normal telephone lines to connect their computers and pay telephone charges based on the time they are connected. Thus, there is a strong incentive to transmit as quickly as possible. Although traditional transmission speeds have been 300 bits per second (bps) and 1200 bps, a 2400-bps modem is common today and most manufacturers offer 9600-bps modems. At 2400 bps, a modem can transmit a 20-page single-spaced report in five minutes; the same report can be transmitted at 9600 bps in just over one minute. Now that we have discussed translating the data, let us turn to the media that transmit it.

CARRYING YOUR DATA: COMMUNICATIONS LINKS

What communications link will you choose to send your data? A communications **link** is the physical medium used for transmission. If your computer is at home, you will doubtless hook up to the telephone system. Large organizations, however, have more choices and must consider the cost factor. The cost for linking machines can be substantial (as much as one-third of the data processing budget), so it is worthwhile to examine the communications options.

Types of Communications Links

There are several kinds of communications links. Some may be familiar to you already.

Wire Pairs
Among the most common communications media are **wire pairs,** also known as **twisted pairs** (Figure 6-3a). Wire pairs are wires twisted together to form a cable, which is then insulated. Wire pairs are inexpensive and frequently used to transmit information over short distances, such as in a phone system within a metropolitan area.

Coaxial Cables
Known for contributing to high-quality transmission, **coaxial cables** are insulated wires within a shield enclosure (Figure 6-3b). These cables can be laid underground or undersea, and they can transmit data at rates much higher than telephone lines.

COMPUTING HIGHLIGHTS

What Happens When You Charge a Purchase

Say you have just decided to buy a wristwatch from a merchant in Ann Arbor, Michigan. You offer your Visa charge card to pay for the $160 purchase. While you idly chat with a friend or stare out the window, the salesclerk is checking your credit card. Is the card good? Do you really have $160 available in credit to pay for the watch? Only the computer knows for sure.

However, it is not just "the computer" at work here, but a series of machines, all linked together to relay the questions and answers.

Follow the trail: (1) The clerk passes your Visa card through a slot on a credit verification terminal and keys in data related to the sale. (2) The data travels by satellite or microwave to the regional computers of a data service clearinghouse in Cherry Hill, New Jersey. (3) From there, the credit inquiry travels to the data service's headquarters computers in Atlanta for processing. The transaction exceeds $50, so it needs a second opinion. The request is turned over to the Visa computers, which

(4) send the query to its mainframe computers in McLean, Virginia. (5) The Visa mainframe determines that the card is from a San Francisco bank and sends the transaction to the bank's computer, which checks to see if there is $160 available credit. The bank's OK retraces the path of the request in reverse order, working its way back to the store in Ann Arbor.

Total time elapsed? Approximately 15 seconds. And you hardly noticed.

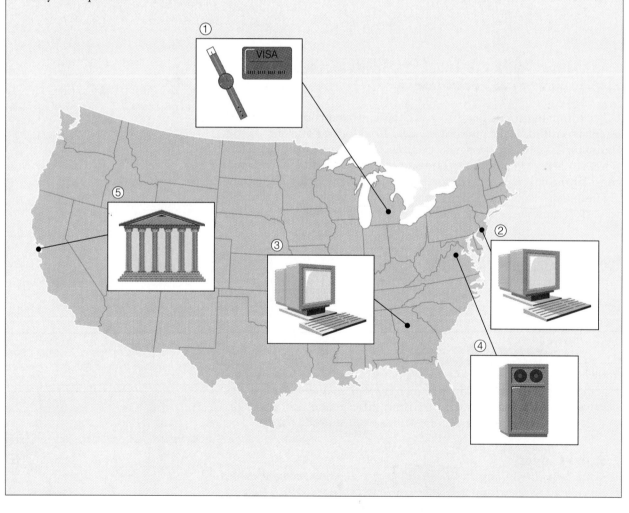

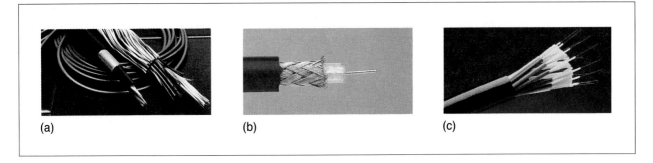

(a)   (b)   (c)

Fiber Optics

Traditionally, most phone lines have transmitted data electrically over wires made of metal, usually copper. These wires must be protected from water and other corrosive substances. **Fiber optics** technology was developed by Bell Laboratories to solve these and other problems (Figure 6-3c). Instead of using electricity to send data, fiber optics uses light. The cables are made of glass fibers, thinner than a human hair, that guide light beams for miles. Fiber optics can transmit data faster than some technologies, yet the materials are lighter and less expensive than wire cables.

Microwave Transmission

Also popular is **microwave transmission** (Figure 6-4a), which uses what is called line-of-sight transmission of data signals through the atmosphere. Since these signals cannot bend around the curvature of the earth, relay stations—usually antennas in high places such as the tops of mountains, towers, and buildings—are positioned at points approximately 30 miles apart to continue the transmission. Microwave transmission offers speed, cost-effectiveness, and ease of implementa-

Figure 6-3   Communications links.
(a) Wire pairs are twisted together to form a cable, which is then insulated. (b) A coaxial cable. (c) Fiber optics are hair-like glass fibers that carry voice, television, and data signals.

Figure 6-4   Microwave transmission.
(a) To relay microwave signals, dish-shaped antennas such as these are placed atop buildings, towers, and mountains. Microwave signals can follow only a line-of-sight path, so stations must relay this signal at regular intervals to avoid interference from the earth's curvature. (b) This satellite acts as a relay station and can transmit data signals from one earth station to another. A signal is sent from an earth station to the relay satellite in the sky, which changes the signal frequency before transmitting it to the next earth station.

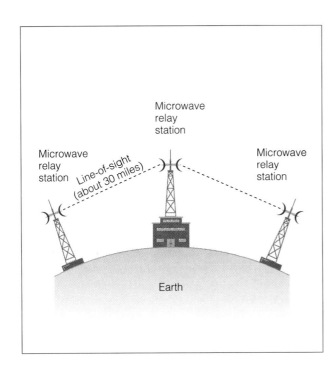

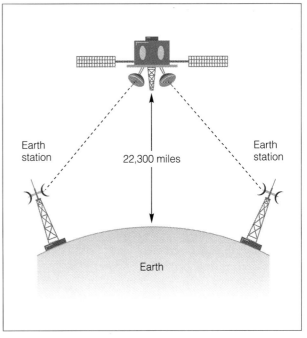

USA TODAY: NEWSPAPER
IN SPACE

"Without our satellite system, it would be impossible to produce the newspaper." The speaker is William Hider, who ought to know. He is in charge of data communications for *USA Today,* the "nation's newspaper." And around the nation it is, first thing every morning at homes, bus stops, hotels, and eateries from Maine to Oregon. This is obviously not a paper delivered in an ordinary way.

USA Today is faxed via satellite. Four-color graphics are sent in all directions by this sophisticated satellite network. The heart of the system is a dish antenna atop the passageway between two high-rise office buildings at the newspaper's headquarters near Washington, D.C. The dish sends newspaper data to its orbiting satellite which, in turn, relays the data to 31 printing plants scattered across the United States. Each plant is equipped with its own receiving dish.

tion. Unfortunately, there are some real problems with "traffic jams" in microwave transmission. In major metropolitan areas, for instance, there are difficulties because of electronic interference from intervening tall buildings.

Satellite Transmission

Communications satellites dangle in space 22,300 miles above the earth. The basic components of **satellite transmission** are the earth stations that send and receive signals and the satellite component, which is called a transponder. The **transponder** receives the transmission from earth, changes the signal, and retransmits the data to a receiving earth station (Figure 6-4b). (The signal is changed so that the weaker incoming signals will not be impaired by the stronger outgoing signals.) This entire process takes less than a second.

Line Configurations

There are two principal line configurations, or ways of connecting terminals with the computer: point to point and multipoint.

The **point-to-point line** is simply a direct connection between each terminal and the computer or from computer to computer (Figure 6-5a). The **multipoint line** contains several terminals connected on the same line to the computer, as Figure 6-5b shows. In many cases a point-to-point line is sufficient, but in other cases it is not efficient, convenient, or cost-effective. For instance, if the computer is at the head office in Dallas, but there are several branch offices with terminals in Houston, it does not make sense to connect each Houston terminal individually to the computer in Dallas. It is usually better to run one line between the two cities and hook all the terminals on it in a multipoint arrangement. On a multipoint line only one terminal can transmit at any one time, although more than one terminal can receive messages from the computer simultaneously.

HOOKING UP TO THE BIG COMPUTER: WIDE AREA NETWORKS

• • • • • • • • • • • • • • • • • •

As noted earlier, computers that are connected so they can communicate among themselves form a network. There are two kinds of networks: wide area networks and local area networks. Wide area networks send data over long distances. Most of these networks use the telephone system, though some companies have implemented their own microwave and satellite networks. Local area networks allow communication among computers linked together in one building or in buildings that are close together. Let us first consider wide area networks.

A **wide area network (WAN)** is a network of geographically distant computers and terminals. In business, a personal computer sending data any significant distance is probably sending it to a minicomputer or mainframe computer. Since these larger computers are

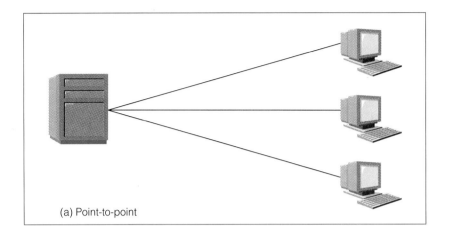

(a) Point-to-point

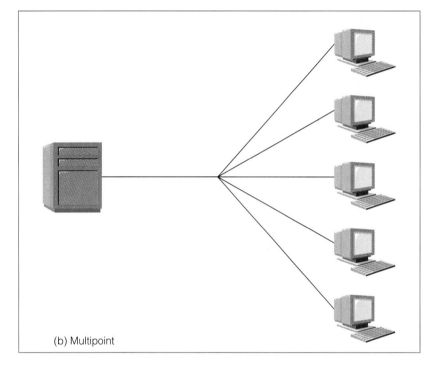

(b) Multipoint

◄

Figure 6-5   Point-to-point and multipoint lines.
(a) In point-to-point lines, each terminal is connected directly to the central computer.
(b) In multipoint lines, several terminals share a single line and only one terminal can transmit at a time.

designed to be accessed by terminals, a personal computer can access a minicomputer or a mainframe only if it uses special software to imitate a terminal. That is, the larger computer must consider the personal computer as just another user input/output communication device—a terminal.

The computer to which a "terminal" is attached is called the **host** computer. A user can use the terminal to type keystrokes to the host computer, and the host computer can send output for display on the terminal screen. Real terminals do not usually have their own disk drives or central processing units, so programs and data files are stored on the host computer's disk. Since terminals cannot store files, a personal computer masquerading as a terminal cannot send them. Likewise, a personal computer acting as a terminal can display a file sent to it by the host, but it cannot store the file. However, special software lets a user overcome these limitations. The software permits **downloading**—retrieving files from the host computer—or **uploading**—

sending files from a personal computer to the host computer. The trend in business is to replace the limited terminals with the more flexible personal computers.

An alternative network is a local area network, which can communicate information much faster than most wide area networks.

NETWORKING WITHIN THE OFFICE: LOCAL AREA NETWORKS

• • • • • • • • • • • • • • • • • •

A **local area network (LAN)** is a collection of computers, usually personal computers, that share hardware, software, and data. In simple terms, LANs hook personal computers together through communications media so the computers can share resources. Personal computers attached to a LAN are often referred to as **workstations.** All the devices—personal computers and other hardware—attached to the LAN are called **nodes** on the LAN. As the name implies, LANs cover short distances, usually one office or building.

How Users Use Local Area Networks

Here are some typical tasks for which LANs are especially suited:

- A personal computer can read data from a hard disk belonging to another personal computer as if the data were its own. This allows users who are working on the same projects to share word processing, spreadsheet, and database data.

- A personal computer may print one of its files on the printer of another personal computer. This second computer is usually used especially for printing. (Since few people need exclusive access to a high-quality printer, only a few of the expensive printers need be hooked to the LAN.)

- One copy of an applications program, when purchased with the proper license from the vendor of the program, can be used by all the personal computers on the LAN. This is less confusing and less expensive than purchasing a copy of the program for each user.

LAN usage goes beyond simple convenience; some applications require that the same data be shared by coworkers. Consider, for example, a company that sends catalogs to customers, who can then place orders over the telephone. Waiting at the other end of the phone line are customer-service representatives, who key the order data into the computer system as they are talking to customers.

The representatives use their own personal computers to enter orders but share common computer files that provide information on product availability and pricing. Having a separate set of files for each representative would lead to trouble because one representative would not know what others had sold. One representative, for example, could accept an order for 20 flannel shirts when, because of recent sales, only 5 shirts remain in stock.

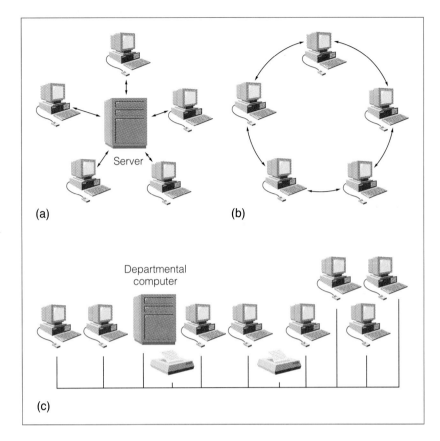

(a)   (b)

(c)

◄

Figure 6-6   LAN topologies.
(a) The star topology has a central host computer, a server, that runs the LAN. (b) The ring topology connects computers in a circular fashion. (c) The bus topology assigns a portion of network management to each computer but preserves the system if one computer fails.

In this kind of application workers must have access to one central master file that reflects the activities of other workers. LANs make such access possible.

How Local Area Networks Are Set Up

The physical layout of a local area network is called its **topology.** Local area networks come in three basic topologies: star, ring, and bus networks (Figure 6-6). A **star network** has a central computer that is responsible for managing the LAN. It is to this central computer—sometimes called a **server**—that the shared disks and printers are usually attached. All messages are routed through the server. A **ring network** links all nodes together in a circular manner without benefit of a server. Disks and printers are scattered throughout the system. A **bus network** assigns a portion of network management to each computer but preserves the system if one node fails.

THE NUTS AND BOLTS OF LOCAL AREA NETWORKS
• • • • • • • • • • • • • • • • • • •

We have heard about some of the uses of local area networks, and gotten an overview of how LANs are set up. Now let us take a closer look at the hardware and software that make up a LAN.

Table 6-1 Layers of a LAN

Layer	Functions
Application	Printer sharing File sharing Terminal imitation Electronic mail
Data communications	Control of data flow Error detection and correction
Physical	Wiring specifications Electrical specifications Network topology

Think of a LAN as being made up of layers. The International Standards Organization uses a seven-layer model to describe all the functions of a network, but we can describe the network more simply with three—the physical layer, the data communications layer, and the applications layer (Table 6-1).

The Physical Layer

As we have seen, there are several topologies for laying out a network. In each, cables connect the participating computers to one another or to a central server computer. Most modern networks use twisted-pair cable similar to that used in telephone installations. Most other networks use coaxial cable like that used to hook your home up to cable television.

In addition to wires, connecting a computer to a network requires electronic circuitry in each network node and server. This circuitry is built in to some computers; in others it must be added to one of the computer's expansion slots in the form of a **network interface card.**

One common type of hardware used to link IBM and IBM-style computers into LANS is called Ethernet. In Macintoshes, built-in LocalTalk hardware provides the physical layer for the AppleTalk network.

The Data Communications Layer

The data communications layer includes the software that controls the signals that travel over the network's physical layer. LAN software is generally termed network operating system software. Really an addition to the basic operating system of the personal computer, a network operating system packages the data for transmission over the network, receives and interprets incoming data and ensures that the data it receives has not been altered en route. Some common LAN software programs include Novell's NetWare and Apple's AppleShare.

MACINTOSH

AppleLink Lets Macintosh Users Branch Out

Tough questions about computers? Apple Computer, Inc. thinks AppleLink is the answer. Based on a mainframe computer at Apple headquarters in California, AppleLink is a system of electronic libraries, bulletin boards, and electronic mail services accessible by telephone. Armed with only a modem and the special AppleLink software, a Macintosh user in need can log into the AppleLink system and find a vast array of reference material.

The AppleLink on-line libraries are actually databases that the user can search for information related to a given problem. If the answer is not there, the user can send, via AppleLink, an electronic mail inquiry directly to an expert at Apple. If the problem is particularly thorny, perhaps involving products from several vendors, experts from many sources can be called in to collaborate on a solution through an AppleLink electronic conference.

Some support issues do not involve problems with hardware or software; they focus instead on which new or improved products should be purchased for a given task. Sales-related information—pricing, product descriptions, promotional offers, and so on—is available for items produced by Apple and by other developers.

AppleLink also provides demonstration versions of the latest software. Using the telephone lines, AppleLink users can transfer these programs to their own disks and then run the programs to get a feel for how they work.

One of the most useful features of the AppleLink environment is the user-to-user bulletin board. Mac support personnel from all over the world can listen to each other's problems and offer advice, encouragement, and—when those are not enough—sympathy.

AppleLink access is not free. There is a charge for each minute the user is logged in. But with the special software provided, users can prepare much of their work off-line and then upload it to the mainframe in seconds.

As desktop computers become more powerful and as telecommunications networks become faster and more reliable, a limitless variety of information services like AppleLink will become available to every home, office, and classroom.

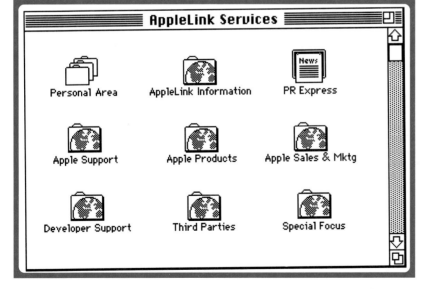

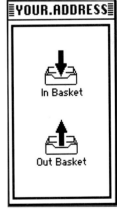

E-MAIL NO-NOS

Managers used to worry about getting their employees to accept electronic mail. Now their worries are quite different; they would like employees to back off a bit on e-mail use. Managers might ignore occasional personal messages or graphics cartoons sent by e-mail, but they are dismayed when electronic mail systems are clogged at holiday time because employees are sending holiday greetings via e-mail. The ultimate misuse, however, has been e-mail chain letters, which are—among other things—illegal. Employers emphasize that e-mail is a limited resource, reserved for business use.

The Applications Layer

Most network products come with software that provides basic services over the network. This software controls network functions such as file sharing, printer sharing, and electronic mail.

USING NETWORKS IN THE OFFICE AND HOME

Think of it: There are more than 500 million telephones installed throughout the world and, theoretically, you can call any one of them. Further, every one of these phones has the potential to be part of a computer network. Although we have discussed other communications media, it is still the telephone that is the basis for networking at home or in the office. Revolutionary changes are in full swing in both places, but particularly in the office.

Automation in the office is as variable as the offices themselves. As a general definition, however, **office automation** is the use of technology to help achieve the goals of the office. Much automated office innovation is based on communications technology. We begin this section with several important office technology topics—electronic mail, voice mail, teleconferencing, and facsimile.

Electronic Mail

Perhaps you have heard about "telephone tag." From your office you call Ms. Jones. She is not in, so you leave a message. You leave your office for a meeting, and when you return you find a message from Ms. Jones; she returned your call while you were out . . . and so it goes. Few of us, it seems, are sitting around waiting for the phone to ring. It is not unusual to make dozens of calls to set up a meeting among just a few people. **Electronic mail** is the process of sending messages directly from one computer to another. Electronic mail releases workers from the tyranny of the telephone.

Perhaps a company has employees who find communication difficult because they are geographically dispersed or are too active to be reached easily. Yet these may be employees who need to work together frequently, whose communication is valuable and important. These people are ideal candidates for electronic mail. Through a computer network a user can type messages to a colleague downstairs; a query across town to that person who is never available for phone calls; even memos simultaneously to regional sales managers in Cleveland, Raleigh, and San Antonio. The beauty of electronic mail, or **e-mail,** is that a user can send a message to someone and know that the person will receive it.

Electronic mail users shower the technology with praise. E-mail crosses time zones, can reach many people with the same message, reduces the paper flood, and does not interrupt meetings the way a ringing phone does. It has its limitations, however. The current problem is similar to the problem faced by telephone users a hundred years ago: It is not of much use if you have the only one. As use of electronic mail becomes more common, its usefulness will increase.

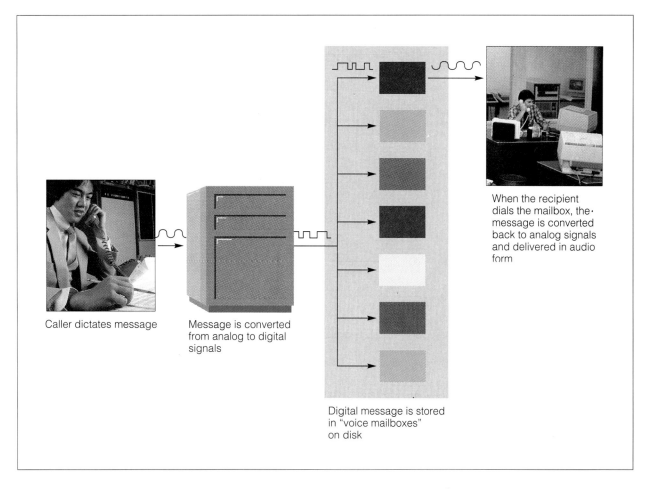

When the recipient dials the mailbox, the message is converted back to analog signals and delivered in audio form

Caller dictates message

Message is converted from analog to digital signals

Digital message is stored in "voice mailboxes" on disk

▲
Figure 6-7   A voice mail system.
The caller's message is stored in the recipient's voice mailbox on disk. Later, the recipient can check his mailbox to get the message.

Voice Mail

Here is how a typical **voice mail** system works. A user tries to complete a call by dialing the desired number in the normal way. If the recipient does not answer, the caller is then prompted to dictate his or her message into the system. The voice mail computer system translates the words into digital impulses and stores them in the recipient's "voice mailbox." Later, when the recipient dials his or her mailbox, the system delivers the message in audio form (Figure 6-7).

This may sound like a spoken version of electronic mail. There is one big difference between electronic mail and voice mail, however. To use electronic mail, you and the mail recipient must have compatible devices and a keyboard and be able to use them. In contrast, telephones are everywhere and everyone knows how to use them.

Teleconferencing

An office automation development with great promise is **teleconferencing,** a method of using technology to bring people and ideas "together" despite geographic barriers. The technology has been available for years, but the acceptance of it is quite recent. The purpose of teleconferencing is to let people interact with others in different geographic locations.

Figure 6-8   A videoconferencing system.
Geographically distant groups can hold a meeting with the help of videoconferencing. Note the camera in the upper-righthand corner; it captures images of the local participants for the benefit of distant viewers.

There are several varieties of teleconferencing. The simplest, computer conferencing, is a method of sending, receiving, and storing typed messages within a network of users. Computer conferences can be used to coordinate complex projects over great distances and for extended periods. Participants can communicate at the same time or in different time frames, at the users' convenience. Conferences can be set up for a limited period to discuss a particular problem, as in a traditional office gathering. Or they can be ongoing networks for weeks or months or even years.

A **computer conferencing** system is a single software package designed to organize communication. The conferencing software runs on a network's host computer, be it a micro, mini, or mainframe. In addition to access to the host computer and the conferencing software, each participant needs a personal computer or terminal, a telephone, a modem, and communications network software. Computer conferencing is a many-to-many arrangement; everyone is able to "talk" to anyone else. Messages may be sent to a specified individual or set of individuals or broadcast to all receivers. Recipients are automatically notified of incoming messages.

Would you like your picture broadcast live across the miles for meetings? Add cameras and audio to computer conferencing, and you have another form of teleconferencing called **videoconferencing** (Figure 6-8). The technology varies, but the pieces normally put in place are a large (possibly wall-size) screen, cameras, and a computer system to record communication among participants.

Although this setup is expensive to rent and even more expensive to own, the costs seem trivial when compared to travel expenses for in-person meetings.

Facsimile Technology

Figure 6-9   Faxing it.
This facsimile machine can send text and graphics long distance.

One alternative to meetings is to use computers and data communications technology to transmit drawings and documents from one location to another. **Facsimile technology**, operating something like a copy machine connected to a telephone, uses computer technology to send graphics, charts, text, and even signatures almost anywhere in the world. In fact, facsimile technology has evolved into a speedy alternative mail service. The drawing—or whatever—is placed in the facsimile machine at one end (as shown in Figure 6-9), where it is digitized. Those digits are transmitted across the miles and then reassembled at the other end into the original picture. All this takes only minutes—or less. Facsimile is not only faster than overnight letter services, it is less expensive too. Facsimile is abbreviated **fax,** as in "I sent a fax" and "I faxed the report to the Chicago office." Faxing has become common in many businesses and some home offices.

A variation on the fax machine is the **fax board,** which fits inside a personal computer, thus facilitating transmission of computer-generated text and graphics. (If the document to be sent is on paper, it must be scanned by a scanner and stored in the computer first.) When a fax comes in, it can be reviewed on the computer screen and printed out.

One problem with owning a facsimile machine is "junk faxes," unordered faxes that come to your machine—advertisements sent from another computer, for example. It is bad enough that junk faxes tie up your machine; to add insult to injury, you must pay for the paper to print them. This kind of abuse is already being outlawed in some states.

Electronic Fund Transfers: Instant Banking

You may already be handling some financial transactions electronically instead of using checks. In **electronic fund transfers (EFTs),** people pay for goods and services by having funds transferred from various checking and savings accounts electronically, using computer technology. One of the most visible manifestations of EFT is the ATM—the automated teller machine.

Incidentally, over 650 million social security checks have been disbursed by the government directly into the recipients' checking accounts via EFT rather than by mail. Unlike those sent via U.S. mail, such payments are unlikely to be lost. Moreover, EFT payments are traceable—again, unlike the ordinary mail. A more recent trend is electronic transfer of salaries from businesses to employees' bank accounts. No more extra trips to the bank on payday!

Bulletin Boards

Person-to-person data communications is one of the more exhilarating ways of using your personal computer, and its popularity is increasing at breakneck speed. A **bulletin board system (BBS)** uses data communications to link personal computers to provide public access to messages.

Electronic bulletin boards are somewhat like the bulletin boards you see in Laundromats or employee lounges. Somebody leaves a message, but the person who picks it up does not have to know the person who left it. To get access to a bulletin board on someone else's computer, all you really have to know is that bulletin board's phone number. You can use any kind of computer, but you need a modem so you can communicate over the phone lines. Anyone who has a personal

YOUR TWO OFFICES

No, these offices are not at the opposite ends of your far-flung east-west empire, and they are not your official and hideaway offices in the building where you work. Your two offices are in the two places you spend the most time: one in the workplace and one at home.

The proliferation of such dual offices, connected by communications systems, is upon us. If you think about it, it had to come—not just for telecommuters, but for people whose job is, theoretically, 100% at the office. First of all, many workers take work home; it makes sense that they can continue their computer work at home, too.

The most likely two-office workers are single-parent families or two-parent working families. These parents cannot linger at the office; they must pick up their children at day care. So they pop a few diskettes and supporting paperwork into their briefcases and head home, to work in their home offices later. Another scenario familiar to working parents is leaving work at midday to care for a sick child. The doctor can take care of the child, and the home computer can take care of the interrupted work activity, perhaps with the parent sending messages to the office from home.

PERSONAL COMPUTERS IN ACTION

Computers at the Store

Computers in sales are not found just in stores that sell computers. Computers are hidden—or not so hidden—in most retail stores. The most obvious sign of a computer presence is at the cash register, where scanning systems tote up your purchases. But there are many other computer activities in the store, some of which relate directly to the customer. Some examples:

- The average shopper may not notice, but customer traffic flows smoothly down the aisles in the Nordstrom store in Seattle. What is more, products have been placed within easy reach of the customer. These features were planned using a computerized floor-plan layout system.

- Customers in the Florsheim Shoe Store in San Francisco can let their fingers do the shopping, using an in-store computer to order shoes electronically. Customers can view the shoe on the screen and, if it is not in stock, order it to be delivered to a home address.

- Toys R Us uses a distributed network to connect its 300 stores nationwide. The network is the key to managing inventory. If a doll is back-ordered in one store, for example, excess dolls in another store can be sent to the undersupplied store.

- The computer-customer relationship does not end as the customer exits the store. Stores want to gather information to draw the customer back to the store. In fact, the amount of information stores accumulate is rather astonishing: how often the customer shops at the store, how often he or she uses checks or credit cards, and what types of items he or she likes to buy. Sears, Roebuck and Co. is developing a single database containing such customer profiles.

- Touch screens in shopping malls respond to shoppers' requests for information 24 hours a day, seven days a week.

computer can set up a bulletin board: It takes a computer, a phone line, a couple of disk drives, and free or inexpensive software. You just tell a few people about your board, and you are in business.

Bulletin boards perform a real service. For example, a message can give advice about a particular vendor's product, post a notice to buy or sell a computer, or even announce a new business venture.

Data Communications Retailing

One of the newest forms of retailing is interactive, two-way cable **videotex**—data communications merchandising. Using videotex, participating retailers can offer products or services directly to the consumer in the home or office (Figure 6-10). After the retailer's computer receives the order, the retailer assembles the goods from a fully

▲
Figure 6-10   Catalog retailing.
Computer users can make purchases or just "window-shop" from the comfort of their offices or homes. The three screens shown here are from Prodigy, an on-line service that, among other things, offers shopping from Sears, J.C. Penney, Spiegel, and others.

automated warehouse. Simultaneously, funds are transferred from the customer's to the retailer's bank account, or perhaps the cost is charged to a charge card. Customers choose between picking up the order at a nearby distribution point or having it delivered.

Commercial Communications Services

We have talked about specific services, but some companies offer a wide range of services. Users can connect their personal computers to commercial, consumer-oriented communications systems via telephone lines. These services—known as **information utilities**—are widely used by both home and business customers. Two examples of information utilities are CompuServe Information Service and Prodigy.

CompuServe offers program packages, text editors, encyclopedia reference, games, a software exchange, and a number of programming languages. CompuServe services include travel reservations, home shopping, banking, weather reports, and even medical and legal advice. Of particular interest to business users are investment information, world news, and professional forums—enough to keep any communications junkie busy.

Prodigy is newer and much more user friendly, mainly because of its splashy graphics screens and its clear directions. Prodigy offers many of the same services as CompuServe, from news and weather to airlines schedules and financial information. But Prodigy is also family-oriented, offering services such as meal-planning advice and children's educational games. But perhaps the most interesting aspect of Prodigy is its fixed monthly rate—there is no extra charge for the amount of time you are connected to the service. This low price is made possible by Prodigy's advertising support: There is a sales pitch on almost every screen. But Prodigy users happily tolerate the ads because they know they keep the cost down.

Computer Commuting

A logical outcome of computer networks is **telecommuting,** the substitution of data communications and computers for the commute to work. Many in the work force are information workers; if they do not

- A **local area network (LAN)** is a collection of personal computers that share hardware, software, and information. Personal computers attached to a LAN are referred to as **workstations.** All the devices—personal computers and other hardware—attached to the LAN are called **nodes** on the LAN. The physical layout of a local area network is called its **topology.** A **star network** has a central computer that is responsible for managing the LAN; it is to this central computer—sometimes called a **server**—that the shared disks and printers are usually attached. A **ring network** links all nodes together in a circular manner. A **bus network** assigns a portion of network management to each computer but preserves the system if one node fails.

- To connect to a LAN, some computers need the addition of a **network interface card.**

- A LAN is made up of three layers: physical, data communications, and application. Ethernet and AppleTalk are different types of hardware used in LANS.

- **Office automation** is the use of technology to help achieve the goals of the office. **Electronic mail (e-mail)** and **voice mail** allow workers to transmit messages to the computer files of other workers. **Teleconferencing** includes **computer conferencing**—in which typed messages are shared among many users—and **videoconferencing**—computer conferencing combined with cameras and screens. **Facsimile technology (fax)** can transmit graphics, charts, and signatures. **Fax boards** can be inserted inside computers. In **electronic fund transfers (EFTs),** people pay for goods and services by having funds transferred from various checking and savings accounts electronically, using computer technology. Retailers can offer products to the office or home using **videotex,** a video display catalog.

- A **bulletin board system (BBS)** uses data communications systems to link personal computers to provide public-access message systems.

- *CompuServe* and *Prodigy* are two major commercial communications services, or **information utilities.**

- **Telecommuting** is the substitution of data communications and computers for the commute to work.

SELF-TEST

True/False

T F 1. Teleprocessing allows a user to query a central computer a thousand miles away.

T F 2. An internal modem is normally used with a variety of computers.

T F 3. A modem can be used for either modulation or demodulation.

T F 4. Microwave uses line-of-sight transmission.

T F 5. Fiber optics is a cheaper form of communications link than wire cables.

T F 6. The majority of LANs use a ring structure.

T F 7. Fax and videotex are identical technologies.

T F 8. A ring network has no central host computer.

T F 9. Fax boards can be inserted into computers.

T F 10. Telecommuting is a form of information utility.

Matching

_____ 1. modulation
_____ 2. fiber optics
_____ 3. facsimile
_____ 4. common communications media
_____ 5. demodulation
_____ 6. DDP
_____ 7. teleconferencing
_____ 8. ring network
_____ 9. teleprocessing
_____ 10. wire pairs

a. fax
b. twisted
c. remote processing
d. analog to digital
e. remote access
f. communications link
g. digital to analog
h. computerized meetings
i. no central host computer
j. approved organizations

Fill-In

1. Most telephone lines require which kind of signal:

   _____

2. A device that converts a digital signal to an analog signal or vice versa:

   _____

3. Prodigy and CompuServe are examples of: _____

4. The general term for the use of technology in the office:

   _____

5. The line configuration that describes a direct connection between each terminal and the central computer: _____

6. A network that links distant computers and terminals:

   _____

7. The physical medium used for transmission is called:

   _____

8. The term for computer networks that share resources in a limited geographical location: _____

9. A video display catalog used to shop at home: _____

10. BBS stands for: _____

Answers

True/False: 1. T, 3. T, 5. T, 7. F, 9. T

Matching: 1. g, 3. a, 5. d, 7. h, 9. e

Fill-In: 1. analog, 3. information utilities, 5. point-to-point line, 7. communications link, 9. videotex

CHAPTER 7

OVERVIEW

Programming and Languages
A Glimpse of What Programmers Do

AutoInfo is well known in the Midwest as the best software for running an automobile repair shop. The program is easy to use and runs on inexpensive equipment. For two years Ed Embree used it in his three repair shops and was a satisfied AutoInfo buyer.

Ed's business was changing, however. His new accountant needed more information than AutoInfo tracked, and stiff new environmental laws increased the paperwork Ed had to provide on certain types of repair. Ed called Andrea Weiss, his representative at AutoInfo, to talk about getting some changes made to his copies of the software. Andrea agreed to prepare an estimate. Ed was flabbergasted to find that the modifications would cost $4500. That was nearly twice the price he had paid for three copies!

The next conversations Ed and Andrea had were strained. Ed did not understand the high cost of the work he had proposed, and Andrea had trouble explaining over the phone the complexities of customizing Ed's software. Finally, Andrea convinced Ed to visit the AutoInfo office to see what was involved.

Andrea let Ed look over the long listing of computer instructions that made up the AutoInfo program. Ed had always thought of AutoInfo as a set of menus that somehow knew how to manage his business. Looking at the listing, he found that behind each option offered on the menu screens there were hundreds, sometimes thousands, of lines of computer program instructions. Some instructions displayed a menu option, some detected the keystrokes with which the user responded, and others stored the responses in memory. Other instructions examined each of the user's commands, checked its appropriateness, and called up other instructions to fulfill the user's wish. These instructions gathered data from the disk, sorted it, arranged it in the machine's memory, and manipulated it in the ways needed to do the job.

Andrea outlined the work needed to modify the program to meet Ed's new needs and ensure that the modified software would continue to work reliably. She explained that volume sales made the cost of the standard program relatively low, but that customization such as Ed had in mind was expensive.

With a new perspective on computer software, Ed thanked Andrea for her help. Eventually, he decided not to customize the software. For $4500 his accountant could adapt to the standard version, and Ed could do the environmental paperwork by hand.

A year later, Andrea called Ed. Several other repair shops had asked for changes similar to those Ed had proposed. AutoInfo had created a new version that included the changes and was offering it to current customers at a low upgrade price. Andrea wanted Ed to be the first to know; he placed his order that day. ◻

WHY PROGRAMMING?

You may already have used commercial software to solve problems. But perhaps now you are ready to learn something about how software is written. As we noted earlier, a **program** is a set of step-by-step instructions that directs the computer to do the tasks you want it to do and produce the results you want. This chapter introduces you to the programming process and what programmers do.

WHAT PROGRAMMERS DO

Suppose you manage an urban entertainment complex that features movies and various live performances. You need to plan a year in advance, considering the availability of performers, the time of year, and the need to present a balanced selection. Several factors vary with the type of act and must be considered in the early planning stages, including local props, special lighting effects, union extras, work permits, and so forth. The set of tasks is complex and difficult to coordinate. You need to enlist the aid of a computer because you have work that requires computer power.

The easiest way to get the computer's help is to use an existing commercial software package—a package you can buy off the shelf or from a vendor. Using existing software is also the fastest and least expensive way if the software fits your needs. Commercial scheduling software may solve some of your problems in the scheduling example. But, after consulting with a computer professional, it seems clear that most of your problems are too complicated and too company-specific for commercial software. You need a customized program and someone to write it: a programmer.

In general, the programmer's job is to convert a problem solution, such as a scheme for handling the entertainment complex problems just described, into instructions for the computer. That is, the programmer prepares the instructions of a computer program and runs, tests, and corrects the program. The programmer also documents the way the program works. These activities are all done for the purpose of helping a user fill a need—to manage a business, pay employees, bill customers, admit students to college, and so forth. Programmers help the user develop new programs to solve problems, weed out errors in existing programs, or make changes to programs as a result of new requirements (such as a change in a payroll program to make automatic union dues deductions).

A programmer typically interacts with a variety of people. For example, if a program is part of a system of several programs, the programmer probably coordinates with a systems analyst and other programmers to make sure that the programs operate well together.

Let us turn now from programmers to programming.

THE PROGRAMMING PROCESS

Developing a program requires five steps:

1. Defining the problem
2. Planning the solution
3. Coding the program
4. Testing the program
5. Documenting the program

Let us discuss each of these in turn.

Defining the Problem

Suppose you are a programmer. Users consult with you because they need your services. You meet with users from a client organization to analyze a problem, or you meet with a systems analyst who outlines a project. Eventually, you produce a written agreement that, among other things, specifies the kind of input, processing, and output required. This is not a simple process. It is closely related to the process of systems analysis, which we will discuss in Chapter 9.

Planning the Solution

Two common ways of planning the solution to a programming problem are to draw a flowchart or write pseudocode. Essentially, a **flowchart** is a symbolic diagram of an orderly step-by-step solution to a problem. It is a map of what your program is going to do and how it is going to do it. **Pseudocode** is an English-like language that you can use to state your solution with more precision than you can in plain English but with less precision than is required when using a formal programming language. We will discuss flowcharts and pseudocode in greater detail later in this chapter.

Coding the Program

As the programmer, your next step is to code the program—that is, to express your solution in a programming language. You will translate the logic from the flowchart or pseudocode—or some other tool—to a programming language. There are many programming languages: BASIC, COBOL, Pascal, FORTRAN, and C are common examples. These languages operate grammatically, somewhat like a simple version of the English language, but they are much more precise. To get your program to work, you have to follow exactly the rules—**syntax**—of the language you are using. Of course, using the language correctly is no guarantee that your program will work, any more than speaking grammatically correct English means you will actually communicate. The point is that correct use of the language is the required first step. Then your coded program must be keyed, often at a terminal, in a form the computer can understand.

PROGRAMMERS IN THE SCHEME OF THINGS

What kind of people become programmers? What training do they need? What companies do they work for? And, finally, do they like being programmers?

People who become programmers are usually people with logical minds, often the same ones who are good at math and who like to solve puzzles. Programmers need some credentials, most often a two- or four-year degree in computer information systems or computer science. Jobs vary by organization and region, but it is fair to say that many business programmers work for medium-size to large business organizations such as banks, insurance companies, and retailers. The programmers who write software for personal computers often have a degree in computer science.

As for whether they like being programmers, surveys of programmers consistently report a high level of job satisfaction. There are several reasons for this contentment. One is the challenge—most jobs in the computer industry are not routine. Another is security, since established computer professionals can usually find work. And that work pays well—you will probably not be rich, but you should be comfortable.

One more note here. An experienced programmer can often write code for simple programs directly at a terminal or personal computer, skipping the coding-on-paper step. However, even experienced programmers can get into trouble and waste a lot of time when they do not define the problem and plan the solution carefully before beginning to code.

We will discuss programming languages in more detail later in the chapter.

Testing the Program

Some experts support the notion that a well-designed program can be written correctly the first time. However, the imperfections of the world are still with us, so most programmers get used to the idea that there will be a few errors in the early versions of their programs.

After coding and keying the program, you test it to find the mistakes. Many programmers use these phases: desk-checking, translating, and debugging.

Desk-Checking

In **desk-checking,** you simply sit down and mentally trace, or check, the logic and the syntax of the individual instructions of the program to ensure that the program is error-free and workable. This phase, similar to proofreading, may uncover several errors and possibly save several computer runs. In businesses that account for every second of computer time, this is especially important.

Translating

A **translator** is a program that translates your program into language the computer can understand. A by-product of the process is that the translator tells you if you have improperly used the programming language in some way. The types of mistakes a translator catches are **syntax errors.** The translator produces descriptive error messages. For instance, if in FORTRAN you mistakenly write N = 2*(I + J))— which has two closing parentheses instead of one—you will get a message something like "UNMATCHED PARENTHESES." Programs are most commonly translated by a compiler or an interpreter. A **compiler** translates your entire program at one time, giving you all the syntax error messages—called **diagnostics**—at once. The compiler usually places these diagnostics in context in a **source program listing,** a list of the program as written by the programmer, which can be used to make any corrections necessary to the program. An **interpreter,** often used for the BASIC language, translates your program one line at a time.

As shown in Figure 7-1, the original program, called a **source module,** is translated to an **object module,** to which prewritten programs may be added during the **link/load phase** to create a load module. The **load module** can then be executed by the computer.

Debugging

A term used extensively in programming, **debugging** is detecting, locating, and correcting bugs (mistakes) by running the program. These bugs are **logic errors,** such as telling a computer to repeat an opera-

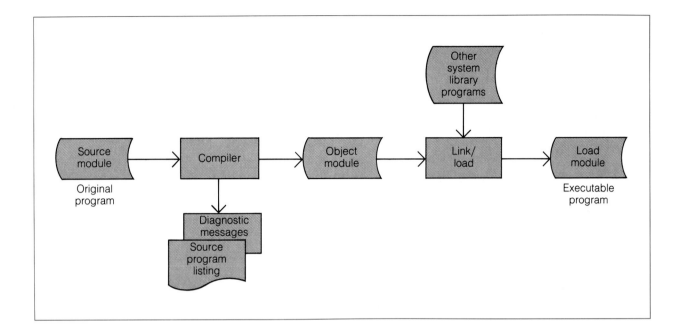

▲
Figure 7-1   Preparing your program for execution.
Your original program, the source module, is translated by the compiler into an object module, which represents the program in machine language that the computer can understand. The compiler may produce diagnostic messages, indicating syntax errors. A listing of the source program may also be output from the compiler. After the program successfully compiles, the object module is linked in the link-load phase with system library programs as needed, and the result is a load module, or executable program.

tion but not telling it how to stop repeating. In this phase you run the program against test data, which you devise. You must plan the test data carefully to make sure you test every part of the program.

Documenting the Program

Documentation is a written detailed description of the programming cycle and specific facts about the program. Documenting is an ongoing process needed to supplement human memory and to help organize program planning. Also, documentation is critical to communication with others who have an interest in the program. Typical program documentation materials include the origin and nature of the problem, a brief narrative description of the program, logic tools such as flowcharts and pseudocode, data descriptions, program listings, and testing results. Comments embedded in the program itself are also considered an essential part of documentation.

In a broader sense, program documentation could be part of the documentation for an entire system.

PLANNING THE SOLUTION: A CLOSER LOOK AT FLOWCHARTS AND PSEUDOCODE

· · · · · · · · · · · · · · · · · ·

We have described the five steps of the programming process in a general way. We noted that the first step, defining the problem, is related to the larger arena of systems analysis and design. The last three steps—coding, testing, and documenting the program—are done in the context of a particular programming language.

We will study the second step, planning the solution, in this section. This discussion will help you understand how program logic is

Computing Highlights

Can They Absolutely Positively Guarantee That It Works?

Does the software you use really work? Are you sure? Did the programmer who wrote it guarantee that it would never have a glitch that would ruin your work?

Some jobs have little room for error or second guessing—the job must be done right the first time. An air traffic controller has such a job; for example, directing a plane to the wrong altitude could have fatal consequences. Programmers, on the other hand, have many opportunities to ponder, to test, to rethink. Given those opportunities, it seems reasonable to hope that the completed software will have a high degree of reliability. In fact, some people think that a programmer should indeed be able to absolutely positively guarantee that the software works as it is supposed to.

However, reliability has not been the hallmark of computer software. There are several reasons for this. One is the inherent complexity of most software. The most vexing is that, despite heroic efforts by the programmer or programmers, the nature of the desired software often changes as it is developed, causing time and budget crunches. Finally, as in every field, there are some incompetent people writing computer programs.

Although software may be less

than perfect when first tested, programmers usually work out the kinks until it is acceptable. Sometimes, however, unreliable software is inadvertently released to an organization or to the public. So let the user beware.

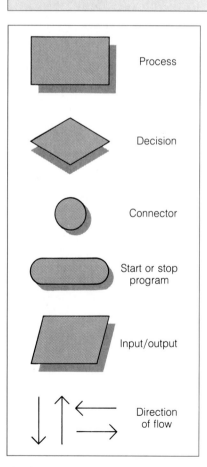

Figure 7-2 ANSI flowchart symbols.

Process

Decision

Connector

Start or stop program

Input/output

Direction of flow

developed. The following sections in this chapter offer an introduction to flowcharting and pseudocode.

Some standard flowchart symbols have been established and are accepted by most programmers. These symbols, shown in Figure 7-2, are called ANSI flowchart symbols. (**ANSI** stands for American National Standards Institute.) The most common symbols a programmer uses represent process, decision, connector, start/stop, input/output, and direction of flow.

Pseudocode is easy to maintain. Since pseudocode is just words, it can be kept on a computer file and changed easily, using text editing or word processing. Although pseudocode is not a visual tool, it is nevertheless an effective vehicle for stating and following program logic. For these reasons, flowcharts have fallen out of favor among professionals and pseudocode has become popular. But flowcharting is still useful for beginners and in complex programming situations, so we include them here.

Example: Preparing a Letter

Figure 7-3 shows how you might diagram the steps of preparing a letter for mailing. There is usually more than one correct way to design a flowchart; this becomes obvious with more complicated examples.

The rectangular **process boxes** indicate actions to be taken—"Address envelope," "Fold letter," "Place letter in envelope." Sometimes the order in which actions appear is important, sometimes not.

In this case the letter must be folded before it can be placed in the envelope.

The diamond-shaped box ("Have stamp?") is a **decision box.** The decision box asks a question that requires a yes-or-no answer. It has two **paths,** or **branches**—one path represents the response yes; the other, no. Note that the decision box is the only box that allows a choice; no other box has more than one exit. Whether you do have a stamp or do not, you take a path that comes back to a circle that puts you on a path to the end. The circle is called a **connector** because it connects the paths. Notice that the flowchart begins and ends with the oval **start/stop** symbol.

This example suggests how you can take almost any activity and diagram it in flowchart form—assuming, that is, that you can always express your decisions as choices between yes and no, or something equally specific, such as true or false. Now let us use flowcharting for an example related to computer programming.

Example: Summing Numbers from 1 through 100

Figure 7-4 shows how you might flowchart a program to find the sum of all numbers from 1 through 100. You should observe several things about this flowchart.

First, the program uses two locations in the computer's memory as storage locations, or places to keep intermediate results. In one location is a counter, which might be like a car odometer: Every time a mile passes, the quantity 1 is added to the counter. In the other location is a sum—that is, a running total of the numbers counted. The sum location will eventually contain the sum of all numbers from 1 through 100: $1 + 2 + 3 + 4 + 5 + \cdots + 100$.

Second, note that we must initialize the counter and the sum. When you **initialize,** you set the starting values of certain storage locations, called **variables,** usually as program execution begins. We will initialize the sum to 0 and the counter to 1.

Third, note the looping. You add the quantity stored in the counter to the sum and add a 1 to the counter, then come to the decision diamond, which asks if the counter is greater than 100. If the answer is no, the computer loops back around and repeats the process. The decision box contains a **compare operation;** the computer compares two numbers and performs alternative operations based on the comparison. If the result of the comparison is yes, the computer produces the sum as output, as indicated by the print instruction. Notice that the parallelogram-shaped symbol is used for printing the sum because it represents an output process.

A **loop** is the heart of computer programming. The beauty of the loop, which may be defined as instructions causing the repetition of actions under certain conditions, is that you, as the programmer, have to describe certain actions only once rather than describing them repeatedly. One trip around the loop is called an **iteration.** Once the programmer has established the loop pattern and the conditions for concluding (exiting from) the loop, the computer begins looping and exits as it has been instructed to do. Notice that the flowchart can be modified easily to sum the numbers from 1 to 1000 or from 500 to 700 or any other variation.

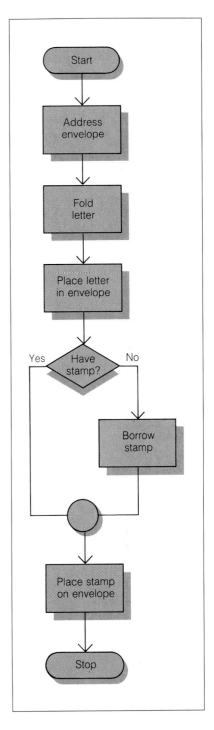

▲
Figure 7-3 A simple flowchart.
This flowchart shows how to prepare a letter for mailing.

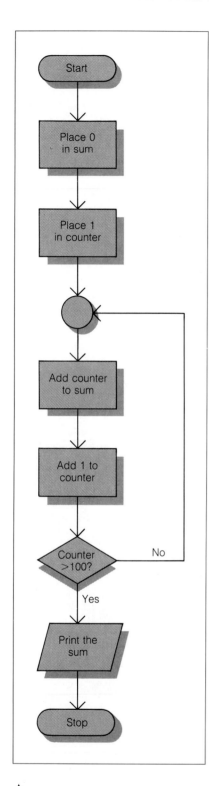

Figure 7-4   Loop example.
This flowchart uses a loop to find the sum of numbers from 1 through 100.

Example: Counting Salaries

Let us now consider a more complex example. Suppose you have been named manager of a personnel agency that has 50 employees, and you need some salary information about them. To take a simple case, let us say you want to know how many people make over $20,000 a year, between $10,000 and $20,000 a year, and under $10,000 a year. Figure 7-5 shows a solution to your problem. The solution is shown in both flowchart and pseudocode form.

Example: Student Grades

Now let us see how a flowchart or pseudocode is translated into a program. You could enter this program directly into your computer. The computer would deliver back to you, on the monitor or in print-out form, the answers you seek.

The problem is, first, to compute the student grades (ranging from 0 through 100) for six students, and, second, to count the number of students whose scores are lower than 60. The grade points are based on student performance on two tests, on a midterm exam, and on a final exam, the scores of which have been weighted in a certain way.

Figure 7-6 shows the flowchart, pseudocode, program, and output. The program is written in the programming language called BASIC. There are several dialects of the BASIC language, but we have chosen for this example a version called Microsoft BASIC.

In Figure 7-6c, the numbers in the far left column are called statement numbers. REM stands for *remark statement*. These statements simply document the program, providing a brief description of what the program is supposed to do and a list of all variable names—symbolic names of locations in memory. The PRINT statement tells the computer what message or data to print out, the READ statement reads the data to be processed, the GOTO (go to) statement tells which statement the computer is to go to, and DATA statements list the data to be read by the computer.

BASIC is similar to English in many ways, so you can probably follow the program in a general way, even with no knowledge of BASIC. The following section introduces other languages.

PROGRAMMING LANGUAGES

. . . .

What language will a programmer use to communicate with the computer? Surely not the English language, which—like any human language—can be ambiguous and is full of colloquialisms, slang, variations, and complexities. And, of course, the English language is constantly changing. A programming language is needed. A **programming language**—a set of rules that provides a way of telling the computer what operations to perform—is anything but loose and ambiguous.

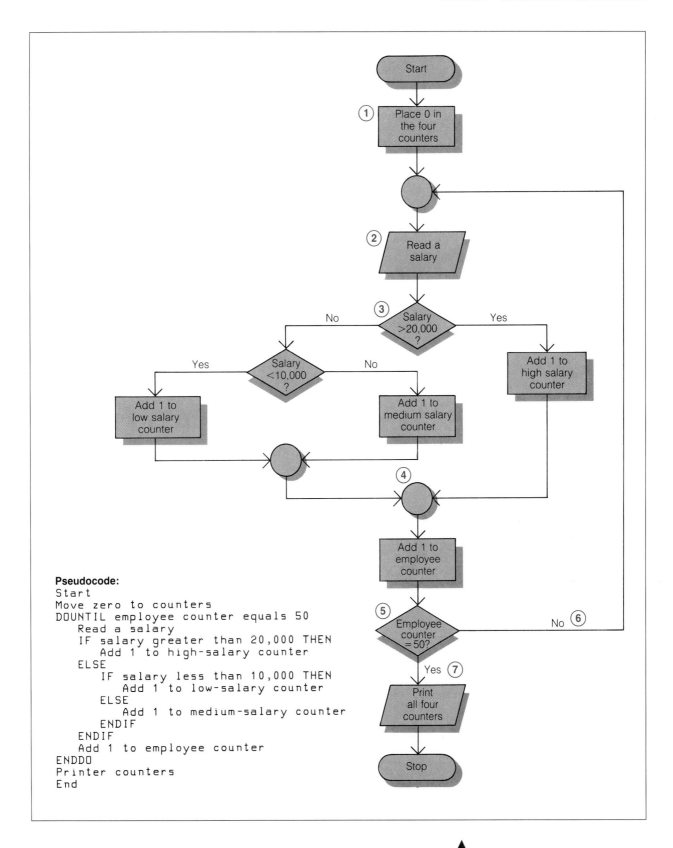

Pseudocode:
```
Start
Move zero to counters
DOUNTIL employee counter equals 50
    Read a salary
    IF salary greater than 20,000 THEN
        Add 1 to high-salary counter
    ELSE
        IF salary less than 10,000 THEN
            Add 1 to low-salary counter
        ELSE
            Add 1 to medium-salary counter
        ENDIF
    ENDIF
    Add 1 to employee counter
ENDDO
Printer counters
End
```

▲
Figure 7-5 Counting salaries.

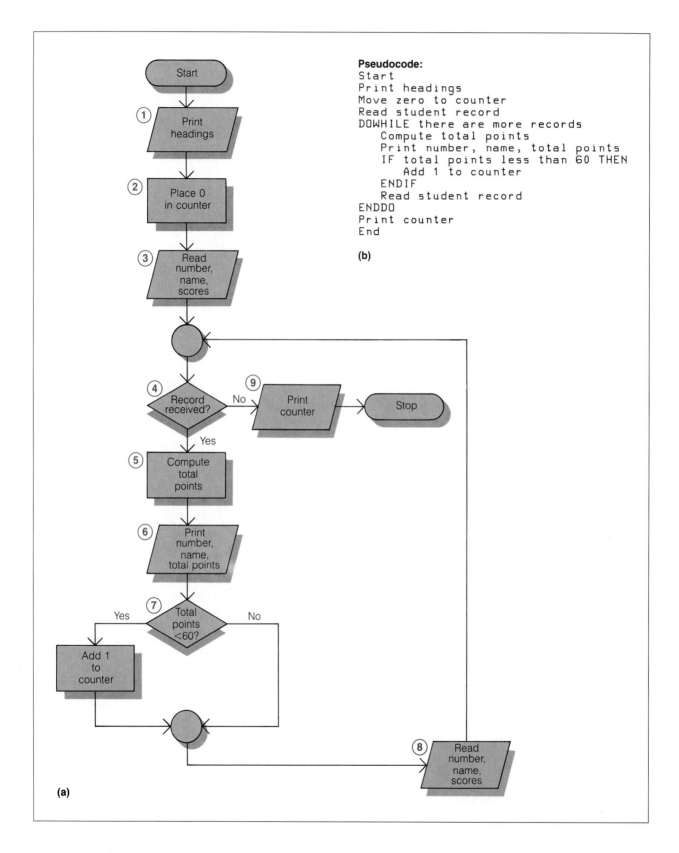

Pseudocode:
```
Start
Print headings
Move zero to counter
Read student record
DOWHILE there are more records
    Compute total points
    Print number, name, total points
    IF total points less than 60 THEN
        Add 1 to counter
    ENDIF
    Read student record
ENDDO
Print counter
End
```

(b)

(a)

```
10   REM PROGRAM TO COMPUTE STUDENT POINTS
20   REM
30   REM THIS PROGRAM READS, FOR EACH STUDENT,
40   REM    STUDENT NUMBER, STUDENT NAME, AND
50   REM    4 TEST SCORES. THE SCORES ARE TO
60   REM    BE WEIGHTED AS FOLLOWS:
70   REM
80   REM       TEST 1: 20 PERCENT
90   REM       TEST 2: 20 PERCENT
100  REM       MIDTERM: 25 PERCENT
110  REM       FINAL: 35 PERCENT
120  REM
130  REM VARIABLE NAMES USED:
140  REM
150  REM    COUNT   COUNT OF STUDENTS SCORING LESS THAN 60
160  REM    NUM     STUDENT NUMBER
170  REM    NAM$    STUDENT NAME
180  REM    S1      SCORE FOR TEST 1
190  REM    S2      SCORE FOR TEST 2
200  REM    S3      SCORE FOR MIDTERM
210  REM    S4      SCORE FOR FINAL
220  REM    TOTAL   TOTAL STUDENT POINTS
230  REM
240  PRINT
250  PRINT "     STUDENT GRADE REPORT"
260  PRINT
270  PRINT "STUDENT","STUDENT","TOTAL"
280  PRINT "NUMBER","NAME","POINTS"
290  PRINT
300  PRINT
310  LET COUNT = 0
320  READ NUM,NAM$,S1,S2,S3,S4
330  IF NUM = -9999 THEN 390
340  LET TOTAL = .20*S1+.20*S2+.25*S3+.35*S4
350  PRINT NUM,NAM$,TOTAL
360  IF TOTAL < 60 THEN COUNT = COUNT+1
370  READ NUM,NAM$,S1,S2,S3,S4
380  GOTO 330
390  PRINT
400  PRINT "NUMBER OF STUDENTS WITH POINTS < 60:";COUNT
410  STOP
420  DATA 2164,ALLEN SCHAAB,60,64,73,78
430  DATA 2644,MARTIN CHAN,80,78,85,90
440  DATA 3171,CHRISTY BURNER,91,95,90,88
450  DATA 5725,CRAIG BARNES,61,41,70,53
460  DATA 6994,RAOUL GARCIA,95,96,90,92
470  DATA 7001,KAY MITCHELL,55,60,58,55
480  DATA -9999,XXX,0,0,0,0
490  END
```

(c)

```
        STUDENT GRADE REPORT

STUDENT        STUDENT              TOTAL
NUMBER         NAME                 POINTS


  2164         ALLEN SCHAAB          70.4
  2644         MARTIN CHAN           84.4
  3171         CHRISTY BURNER        90.5
  5725         CRAIG BARNES          56.5
  6994         RAOUL GARCIA          92.9
  7001         KAY MITCHELL          56.8

NUMBER OF STUDENTS WITH POINTS < 60: 2
```

(d)

Figure 7-6 Student grades.
The (a) flowchart and (b) pseudocode for (c) the program that produces (d) a student grade report.

A programming language, the key to communicating with the computer, has certain definite characteristics. It has a limited vocabulary. Each "word" in it has precise meaning. Even though a programming language has limitations, it can still be used in a step-by-step fashion to solve complex problems. There is not, however, just one programming language; there are many.

At present there are over 200 programming languages—and these are just the ones that are still being used. Where did all these languages come from? Initially, programming languages were created by various people in universities or in government and were devised for special functions. However, it soon became clear that some standardization was needed. As we will see, the languages in use today tend to meet some need, such as programming for scientific or business applications. Before we turn to the discussion of specific languages, however, we need to discuss levels of language.

LEVELS OF LANGUAGE

Programming languages are said to be lower or higher, depending on whether they are closer to the language the computer itself uses (0s and 1s—low) or to the language people use (more English-like—high). We will consider five levels of language. They are numbered 1 through 5 to correspond to what are called the generations of programming languages. Each generation has improved on the ease of use and capabilities of its predecessors. The five generations of languages are:

1. Machine language
2. Assembly languages
3. High-level languages
4. Very high-level languages
5. Natural languages

Note the time line for the language generations in Figure 7-7. Let us look at each of these categories.

Old and Difficult: Machine Language and Assembly Languages

Humans do not like to deal in numbers alone—we prefer letters and words. But, strictly speaking, numbers are what machine language is. This lowest level of language, **machine language,** represents information as 1s and 0s—binary digits corresponding to the on and off electrical states in the computer. Each type of computer has its own machine language.

In the early days of computing, programmers had rudimentary systems for combining numbers to represent instructions such as add or compare. Primitive by today's standards, the programs were not at all convenient for people to read and use. The computer industry moved to develop assembly languages.

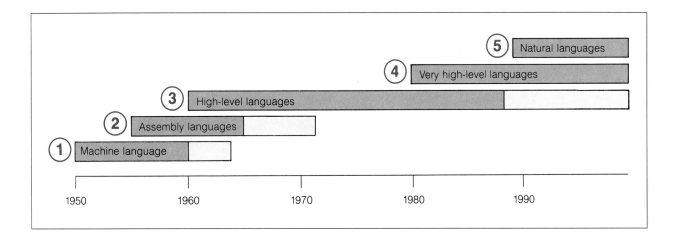

▲
Figure 7-7   Language generations on a time line.
The darker shading indicates the period of greater use by applications programmers; the lighter shading indicates the time during which a generation faded from popular use.

Today **assembly languages** are considered very low level—that is, they are not as convenient for people to use as more recent languages. At the time they were developed, however, they were considered a great leap forward. Rather than using simply 1s and 0s, assembly languages use abbreviations or mnemonic codes as substitutes for machine language: A for Add, C for Compare, MP for Multiply, and so on. Although these codes were not English words, they were still—from the standpoint of human convenience—preferable to numbers alone.

The programmer who uses an assembly language requires a translator, called an **assembler program,** to convert his or her assembly-language program into machine language. A translator is needed because machine language is the only language the computer can actually execute. A programmer need not worry about the translating aspect; the translation is taken care of by the computer system.

Although assembly languages represent a step forward, they still have the disadvantage of requiring the programmer to describe in excruciating detail every small step involved in the program.

Readable: High-Level Languages

The first widespread use of **high-level languages** in the early 1960s transformed programming into something quite different from what it had been. The harried programmer working on the nitty-gritty details of mnemonic codes became a programmer who could pay more attention to solving the client's problems. Programs in high-level languages could still solve very complex problems. At the same time they were written in an English-like manner, thus making them more convenient to use. As a result of these changes, the programmer could accomplish more with less effort.

Of course, a translator was needed to translate the symbolic statements of a high-level language into computer-executable machine language; this translator is usually a **compiler.**

Some languages are created to serve a specific purpose, such as controlling industrial robots or creating graphics. Many languages, however, are extraordinarily flexible and are considered to be general-purpose. In the past, the majority of programming applications were written in FORTRAN, COBOL, or BASIC—all general-purpose languages. In addition to these three, other popular high-level languages today are Pascal and C, among others. We will examine these languages later in the chapter.

More Like English: Very High-Level Languages

Languages called **very high-level languages** are often known by their generation number. That is, they are called **fourth-generation languages** or, more simply, **4GLs.** But if the name is easy, the definition is not.

Definition

There is no consensus about what constitutes a fourth-generation language. The 4GLs are essentially shorthand programming languages. An operation that requires hundreds of lines in a third-generation language such as COBOL typically requires only five to ten lines in a 4GL. However, beyond the basic criterion of conciseness, 4GLs are difficult to describe.

Characteristics

Fourth-generation languages share some characteristics. The first is that they make a true break with the prior generation. Also, they are basically nonprocedural. A **procedural language** tells the computer *how* a task is done: add this, compare that, do this if something is true, and so forth—a very specific step-by-step process. The first three generations of languages are all procedural. In a **nonprocedural language,** the concept changes. Here, users define only *what* they want the computer to do; the user does not provide the details of just how it is to be done. Obviously, it is a lot easier and faster to just say what you want rather than explain how to get it. This leads us to the issue of productivity, a key characteristic of fourth-generation languages.

Productivity

Most experts say the average productivity improvement factor is about 10—that is, you can be ten times more productive in a fourth-generation language than in a third-generation language. Consider this task: Produce a report showing the total units sold for each product, by customer, in each month and year, and with a subtotal for each customer. In addition, each new customer must start on a new page. The 4GL request looks something like this:

```
TABLE FILE SALES
SUM UNITS BY MONTH BY CUSTOMER BY PRODUCT
ON CUSTOMER SUBTOTAL PAGE BREAK
END
```

Even though some training is required to do even this much, you can see that it is pretty simple. The third-generation language COBOL, however, would typically require over 500 statements to fulfill the same request. If we define productivity as producing equivalent results in less time, then fourth-generation languages clearly increase productivity.

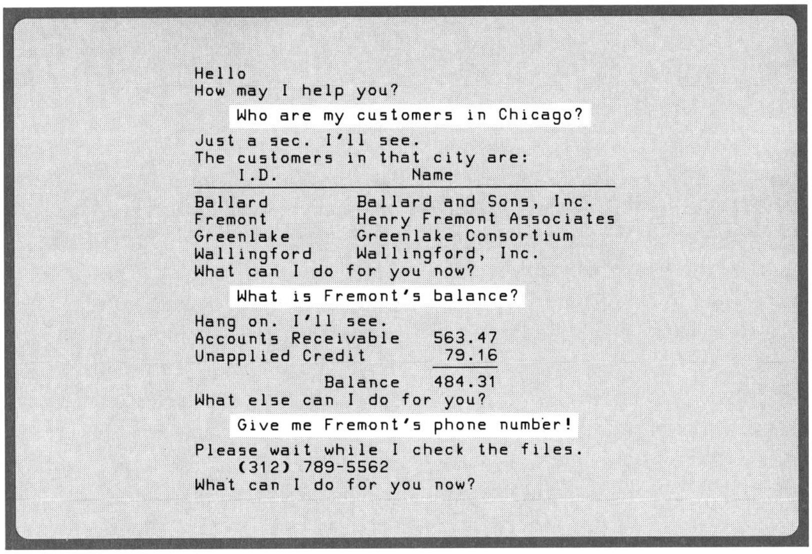

```
Hello
How may I help you?
    Who are my customers in Chicago?
Just a sec. I'll see.
The customers in that city are:
    I.D.              Name
Ballard          Ballard and Sons, Inc.
Fremont          Henry Fremont Associates
Greenlake        Greenlake Consortium
Wallingford      Wallingford, Inc.
What can I do for you now?
    What is Fremont's balance?
Hang on. I'll see.
Accounts Receivable    563.47
Unapplied Credit        79.16
           Balance     484.31
What else can I do for you?
    Give me Fremont's phone number!
Please wait while I check the files.
    (312) 789-5562
What can I do for you now?
```

◀

Figure 7-8 A natural language.
This package, called Cash Management System, uses a language that is so "natural" that some might think it is a little too cute, as in "Just a sec."

Everyday Speech: Natural Languages

The word *natural* has become almost as popular in computing circles as it has in the supermarket. But fifth-generation languages are, as you may guess, even harder to define than fourth-generation languages. Those in the fifth generation are most often called **natural languages** because of their resemblance to the "natural" spoken English language. Instead of being forced to key correct commands and data names in correct order, a manager (programmers are not needed) tells the computer what to do by keying in his or her own words. Figure 7-8 illustrates a natural language.

A manager can say the same thing any number of ways. For example, "Get me tennis racket sales for January" works just as well as "I want January tennis racket revenues." Such a request may contain misspelled words, lack articles and verbs, and even use slang. The natural language translates human instructions—bad grammar, slang, and all—into code the computer understands. If it is not sure what the user has in mind, it politely asks for further explanation.

Consider this request that could be given in the 4GL called Focus: "SUM ORDERS BY DATE BY REGION." If we alter the request and, still in Focus, say something like "Give me the dates and the regions after you've added up the orders," the computer will spit back the user-friendly version of "You've got to be kidding" and give up. But some natural languages could handle such a request. Users can relax the structure of their requests and increase the freedom of their interaction with the data.

SOME POPULAR LANGUAGES

• • • • • • • • • • • • • • • • • •

How does a programmer choose the language in which to write a program? Perhaps a particular language is the standard at the programmer's place of business. Perhaps the manager decrees that everyone on a project will use a certain language.

PERSONAL COMPUTERS IN ACTION

Home Sweet Home

Maybe programmers should work at home. The idea is not new, but new factors are affecting the decision to work at home or in the office. The first is the freedom derived from the personal computer and the second is the newly acknowledged influence of environment on productivity.

First the personal computer. Many programmers in the office still work on terminals that interact with a large mainframe computer. The response time from the mainframe is either uniformly awful or so unpredictable that it becomes difficult to plan work effectively. In contrast, a single-user personal computer provides relatively instant and uniform response times for most programming tasks. A programmer working with a personal computer at home can sit right down and get to business.

Now, what about the environment? Recent studies have shown that a programmer's physical work environment influences his or her productivity more profoundly than managers had suspected. Although programming productivity has long been known to vary dramatically from one individual to another, these variances have usually been attributed to differences in experience and ability. But Tom DeMarco of Atlantic Systems Guild reports that his studies suggest something quite different. When he compared groups of people in different environments, he found that productivity is improved by such environmental factors as desk size, noise levels, and privacy.

The direction seems clear. Get a personal computer for home use, place it on a large desk in a quiet room, and lock yourself in. Your productivity should soar. Well, it is hardly that simple, but the findings are worthy of consideration by all who want to work at home.

A sensible approach is to pick the language that is most suitable for the particular program application. The following sections on individual languages provide an overview of the languages in common use. We describe these languages: FORTRAN, COBOL, BASIC, Pascal, and C—all third-generation languages in common use today. Special features of each language are noted, including the types of applications for which they are often used. Table 7-1 summarizes the important features of these languages.

To accompany our discussion of particular languages, we will show a program and its output to give you a sense of what the language looks like. All these programs are designed to average numbers; in our sam-

Table 7-1 Applications of some important programming languages

Language	Application
FORTRAN FORmula TRANslator (1954)	Scientific
COBOL COmmon Business-Oriented Language (1959)	Business
BASIC Beginners' All-purpose Symbolic Instruction Code (1965)	Education, Business
Pascal named after French inventor Blaise Pascal (1971)	Education, systems programming
C invented at Bell Labs (1972)	Systems programming, general use

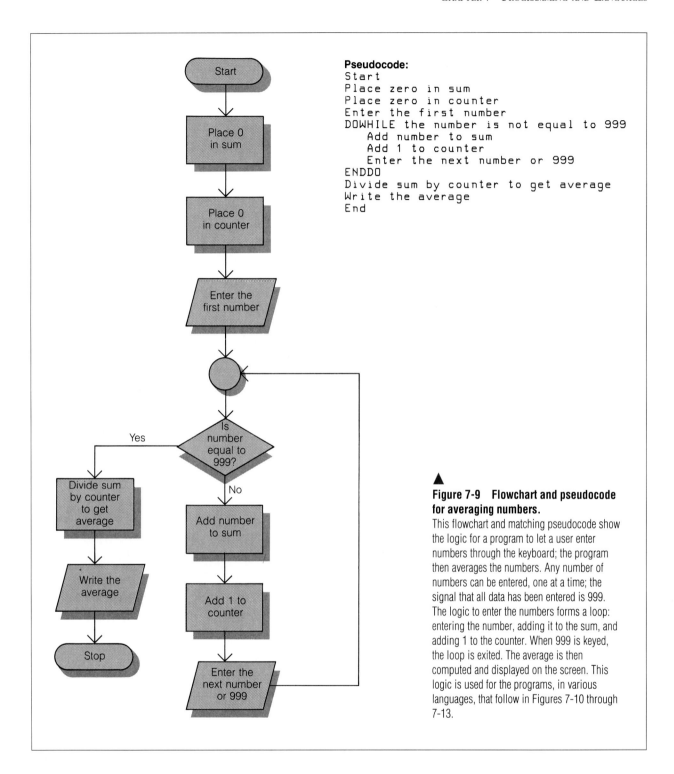

Pseudocode:
```
Start
Place zero in sum
Place zero in counter
Enter the first number
DOWHILE the number is not equal to 999
    Add number to sum
    Add 1 to counter
    Enter the next number or 999
ENDDO
Divide sum by counter to get average
Write the average
End
```

▲
Figure 7-9 Flowchart and pseudocode for averaging numbers.
This flowchart and matching pseudocode show the logic for a program to let a user enter numbers through the keyboard; the program then averages the numbers. Any number of numbers can be entered, one at a time; the signal that all data has been entered is 999. The logic to enter the numbers forms a loop: entering the number, adding it to the sum, and adding 1 to the counter. When 999 is keyed, the loop is exited. The average is then computed and displayed on the screen. This logic is used for the programs, in various languages, that follow in Figures 7-10 through 7-13.

ple output, we find the average of three numbers. Since we are performing the same task in each program, you will see some of the differences and similarities between the languages. We do not expect you to understand each line of these programs; they are here merely as illustrations. Figure 7-9 provides a flowchart and pseudocode for the task of averaging numbers.

Figure 7-10   A FORTRAN program and sample output for averaging numbers. This program is interactive, prompting the user to supply data. (a) The first two lines are comments, as they are in the other programs in this chapter. The WRITE statements send output to the screen in the format matching the number in the WRITE parentheses. The READ statements accept data from the user and place it in location NUMBER, where it can be added to the accumulated SUM. The IF statement checks for number 999 and, when it is received, diverts the program logic to statement 2, where the average is computed. The average is then displayed. (b) This screen display shows the interaction between program and user.

```
C          FORTRAN PROGRAM
C          AVERAGING INTEGERS ENTERED THROUGH THE KEYBOARD
           WRITE (6,10)
           SUM = 0
           COUNTER = 0
           WRITE (6,60)
           READ (5,40) NUMBER
     1     IF (NUMBER .EQ. 999) GOTO 2
           SUM = SUM + NUMBER
           COUNTER = COUNTER + 1
           WRITE (6,70)
           READ (5,40) NUMBER
           GO TO 1
     2     AVERAGE = SUM / COUNTER
           WRITE (6,80) AVERAGE
    10     FORMAT (1X, 'THIS PROGRAM WILL FIND THE AVERAGE OF ',
       *   'INTEGERS YOU ENTER ',/1X, 'THROUGH THE ',
       *   'KEYBOARD. TYPE 999 TO INDICATE END OF DATA.',/)
    40     FORMAT (I3)
    60     FORMAT (1X, 'PLEASE ENTER A NUMBER   ')
    70     FORMAT (1X, 'PLEASE ENTER THE NEXT NUMBER   ')
    80     FORMAT (1X, 'THE AVERAGE OF THE NUMBERS IS ',F6.2)
           STOP
           END
```

(a)

```
THIS PROGRAM WILL FIND THE AVERAGE OF INTEGERS YOU ENTER
THROUGH THE KEYBOARD. TYPE 999 TO INDICATE END OF DATA.
PLEASE ENTER A NUMBER      6
PLEASE ENTER THE NEXT NUMBER     4
PLEASE ENTER THE NEXT NUMBER     11
PLEASE ENTER THE NEXT NUMBER     999
THE AVERAGE OF THE NUMBERS IS    7.00
```

(b)

FORTRAN: The First High-Level Language

Developed by IBM and introduced in 1954, **FORTRAN**—for FORmula TRANslator—was the first high-level language. FORTRAN is a scientifically oriented language—in the early days use of the computer was primarily associated with engineering, mathematical, and scientific research tasks. FORTRAN is still the most widely used language in the scientific community. A FORTRAN program is shown in Figure 7-10.

COBOL: The Language of Business

In the 1950s FORTRAN had been developed, but there was still no accepted high-level programming language appropriate for business.

The U.S. Department of Defense was interested in creating such a standardized language, and so it called together representatives from government and various industries, including the computer industry, to come up with such a language. This language, called **COBOL,** for COmmon Business-Oriented Language, was introduced in 1959. The principal feature of COBOL is that it is English-like—far more so than FORTRAN or BASIC. Even if you know nothing about programming, you can still read a COBOL program and understand its general purpose.

COBOL can be used for just about any task related to business programming; indeed, it is especially suited to processing alphanumeric data such as street addresses, purchased items, and dollar amounts—the data of business. A COBOL program is shown in Figure 7-11.

BASIC: For Beginners and Others

We have already shown **BASIC**—Beginners' All-purpose Symbolic Instruction Code—earlier in the chapter (Figure 7-6c). BASIC was developed at Dartmouth College by John Kemeny and Thomas Kurtz in 1965. BASIC was originally intended for use by students in an academic environment. In the late 1960s it became widely used in universities and colleges. The use of BASIC has extended to business and personal mini- and microcomputer systems. The primary advantage of BASIC is one that may be of interest to many readers of this book: BASIC is easy to learn, even for a person who has never programmed before.

Pascal: The Language of Simplicity

Named for Blaise Pascal, the seventeenth-century French mathematician, **Pascal** was developed as a teaching language by a Swiss computer scientist, Niklaus Wirth, and first became available in 1971. Since that time it has become quite popular, first in Europe and now in the United States, particularly in universities and colleges offering computer-science programs.

The foremost feature of Pascal is that it is simpler than other languages—it has fewer features and is less wordy than most. Because of its limited input/output capabilities, however, it is unlikely to have a serious impact on the business community in its present form. Pascal is making large strides in the personal computer market as a simple yet sophisticated alternative to BASIC. Figure 7-12 presents an example of a Pascal program.

C: A Sophisticated Language

A language that lends itself to sophisticated programming as well as to more mundane programming tasks, C was invented by Dennis Ritchie at Bell Labs in 1972. Its unromantic name evolved from earlier versions called A and B. C produces code that approaches assembly language in efficiency while still offering high-level language features.

```
**************************************************************
 IDENTIFICATION DIVISION.
**************************************************************
 PROGRAM-ID.  AVERAGE.
* COBOL PROGRAM
* AVERAGING INTEGERS ENTERED THROUGH THE KEYBOARD.
**************************************************************
 ENVIRONMENT DIVISION.
**************************************************************
 CONFIGURATION SECTION.
 SOURCE-COMPUTER.         H-P 3000.
 OBJECT-COMPUTER.         H-P 3000.
**************************************************************
 DATA DIVISION.
**************************************************************
 FILE SECTION.
 WORKING-STORAGE SECTION.
 01 AVERAGE          PIC ---9.99.
 01 COUNTER          PIC 9(02)       VALUE ZERO.
 01 NUMBER-ITEM      PIC S9(03).
 01 SUM-ITEM         PIC S9(06)      VALUE ZERO.
 01 BLANK-LINE       PIC X(80)       VALUE SPACES.
**************************************************************
 PROCEDURE DIVISION.
**************************************************************
 100-CONTROL-ROUTINE.
     PERFORM 200-DISPLAY-INSTRUCTIONS.
     PERFORM 300-INITIALIZATION-ROUTINE.
     PERFORM 400-ENTER-AND-ADD
             UNTIL NUMBER-ITEM = 999.
     PERFORM 500-CALCULATE-AVERAGE.
     PERFORM 600-DISPLAY-RESULTS.
     STOP RUN.
 200-DISPLAY-INSTRUCTIONS.
     DISPLAY
        "THIS PROGRAM WILL FIND THE AVERAGE OF INTEGERS YOU ENTER".
     DISPLAY
        "THROUGH THE KEYBOARD. TYPE 999 TO INDICATE END OF DATA.".
     DISPLAY BLANK-LINE.
 300-INITIALIZATION-ROUTINE.
     DISPLAY "PLEASE ENTER A NUMBER".
     ACCEPT NUMBER-ITEM.
 400-ENTER-AND-ADD.
     ADD NUMBER-ITEM TO SUM-ITEM.
     ADD 1 TO COUNTER.
     DISPLAY "PLEASE ENTER THE NEXT NUMBER".
     ACCEPT NUMBER-ITEM.
 500-CALCULATE-AVERAGE.
     DIVIDE SUM-ITEM BY COUNTER GIVING AVERAGE.
 600-DISPLAY-RESULTS.
     DISPLAY "THE AVERAGE OF THE NUMBERS IS ",AVERAGE.
```

(a)

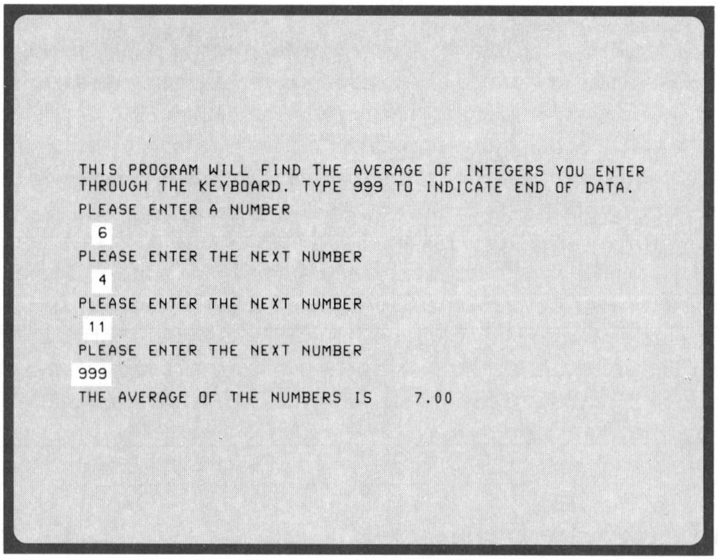

```
      THIS PROGRAM WILL FIND THE AVERAGE OF INTEGERS YOU ENTER
      THROUGH THE KEYBOARD. TYPE 999 TO INDICATE END OF DATA.
      PLEASE ENTER A NUMBER
       6
      PLEASE ENTER THE NEXT NUMBER
       4
      PLEASE ENTER THE NEXT NUMBER
       11
      PLEASE ENTER THE NEXT NUMBER
      999
      THE AVERAGE OF THE NUMBERS IS     7.00
```

(b)

► **Figure 7-11 A COBOL program and sample output for averaging numbers.**
The purpose of this program and its results are the same as those of the FORTRAN program in Figure 7-10, but the look of the COBOL program is very different. (a) Note the four divisions. In particular, note that the logic in the procedure division uses a series of PERFORM statements, diverting logic flow to other places in the program. After a section has been performed, logic flow returns to the statement after the one that called the PERFORM. DISPLAY writes to the screen, and ACCEPT takes the user input. (b) This screen display shows the interaction between program and user.

```
PROGRAM AVERAGE (INPUT, OUTPUT);
(* PASCAL PROGRAM *)
(* AVERAGING INTEGERS ENTERED THROUGH THE KEYBOARD *)
VAR
    COUNTER, NUMBER, SUM : INTEGER;
    AVERAGE : REAL;
BEGIN
WRITELN ('THIS PROGRAM WILL FIND THE AVERAGE OF INTEGERS YOU ENTER');
WRITELN ('THROUGH THE KEYBOARD. TYPE 999 TO INDICATE END OF DATA.');
WRITELN;
SUM := 0;
COUNTER := 0;
WRITELN ('PLEASE ENTER A NUMBER');
READ (NUMBER);
WHILE NUMBER <> 999 DO
    BEGIN
    SUM := SUM + NUMBER;
    COUNTER := COUNTER + 1;
    WRITELN ('PLEASE ENTER THE NEXT NUMBER');
    READ (NUMBER);
    END;
AVERAGE := SUM / COUNTER;
WRITELN ('THE AVERAGE OF THE NUMBERS IS',AVERAGE :6:2);
END.
```
(a)

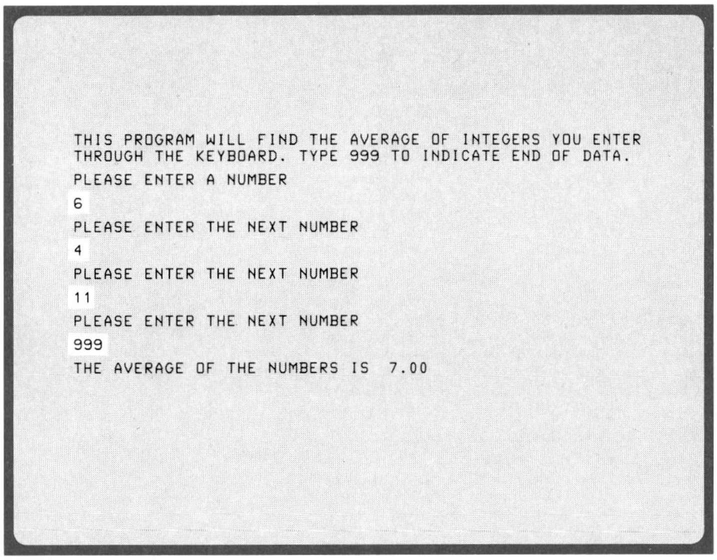

```
THIS PROGRAM WILL FIND THE AVERAGE OF INTEGERS YOU ENTER
THROUGH THE KEYBOARD. TYPE 999 TO INDICATE END OF DATA.
PLEASE ENTER A NUMBER
6
PLEASE ENTER THE NEXT NUMBER
4
PLEASE ENTER THE NEXT NUMBER
11
PLEASE ENTER THE NEXT NUMBER
999
THE AVERAGE OF THE NUMBERS IS  7.00
```
(b)

▲
Figure 7-12   A Pascal program and sample output for averaging numbers. Comments are from (* to *). Each variable name must be declared. The symbol := assigns a value to the variable on the left; the symbol < > means not equal to. WRITELN by itself puts a blank line on the screen. (b) This screen display shows the interaction between program and user.

```
/* C PROGRAM */
/* AVERAGING INTEGERS ENTERED THROUGH THE KEYBOARD */
main()
{ float average;
  int counter = 0; number; sum = 0;
  printf("THIS PROGRAM WILL FIND THE AVERAGE OF INTEGERS YOU ENTER\n");
  printf("THROUGH THE KEYBOARD. TYPE 999 TO INDICATE END OF DATA.\n\n");
  printf("PLEASE ENTER A NUMBER");
  scanf("%d",&number);
  while (number != 999)
    {
        sum = sum + number;
        counter ++ ;
        printf("PLEASE ENTER THE NEXT NUMBER");
        scanf("%d",&number);
    }
  average = sum / counter;
  printf("THE AVERAGE OF THE NUMBERS IS %F ",AVERAGE);
}
```

(a)

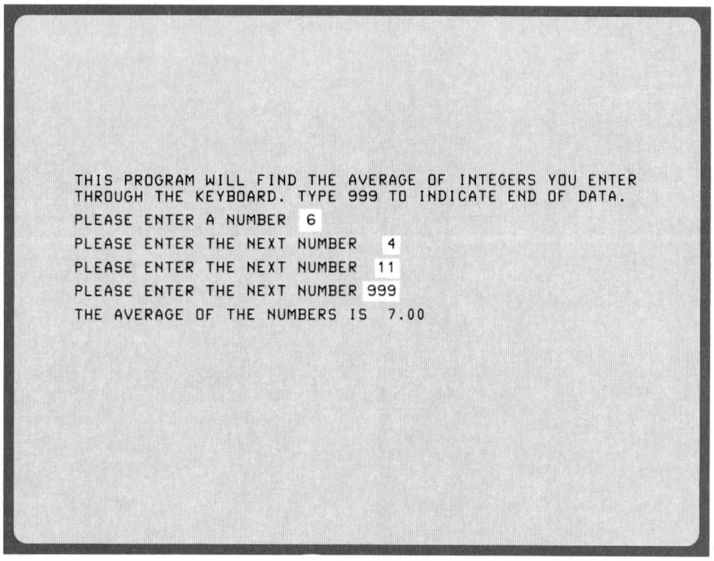

```
THIS PROGRAM WILL FIND THE AVERAGE OF INTEGERS YOU ENTER
THROUGH THE KEYBOARD. TYPE 999 TO INDICATE END OF DATA.
PLEASE ENTER A NUMBER  6
PLEASE ENTER THE NEXT NUMBER   4
PLEASE ENTER THE NEXT NUMBER  11
PLEASE ENTER THE NEXT NUMBER 999
THE AVERAGE OF THE NUMBERS IS  7.00
```

(b)

▲

Figure 7-13   A C program and sample output for averaging numbers.
(a) Comments are between /* and */. The command printf sends output to the screen and scanf accepts data from the user. (b) This screen display shows the interaction between program and user.

Although C is simple and elegant, it is not simple to learn. It was developed for gifted programmers, and the learning curve is steep indeed. Straightforward tasks may be solved easily in C, but complex problems require mastery of the language. Figure 7-13 shows an example of a C program and sample output.

▲   ▲   ▲

In this chapter we have glimpsed the habits of mind and care required to write programs and looked at the direction of language development. We now turn to one special set of programs—the operating system.

CHAPTER REVIEW

SUMMARY AND KEY TERMS

- A programmer converts solutions to the user's problems into a **program,** or instructions for the computer, by defining the problem, planning the solution, coding the program, testing the program, and documenting the program.

- Defining the problem means discussing it with the users to determine the necessary input, processing, and output.

- Planning can be done by using a **flowchart,** which is a pictorial representation of the step-by-step solution, and by using **pseudocode,** which is an English-like language.

- Coding the program means expressing the solution in a programming language.

- Testing the program consists of desk-checking, translating, and debugging. The rules of a programming language are referred to as its **syntax. Desk-checking** is a mental checking or proofreading of the program before it is run. In translating, a **translator program** converts the program into language the computer can understand and in the process detects programming language errors, which are called **syntax errors.** Two types of translators are **compilers,** which translate the entire program at one time and give all the error messages (**diagnostics**) at once, and **interpreters,** which translate the program one line at a time. The compiler also produces a **source program listing.** The original program, called a **source module,** is translated to an **object module,** to which prewritten programs may be added during the **link/load phase** to create an executable **load module. Debugging** is running the program to detect, locate, and correct mistakes—**logic errors.**

- **Documentation** is a detailed written description of the program and the test results.

- The standard symbols used in flowcharting are called **ANSI** (American National Standards Institute) symbols. The rectangular **process box** shows an action to be taken. The diamond-shaped **decision box**—with two **paths,** or **branches**—is the only symbol that allows a choice. The **connector** is a circle that connects paths. The oval **start/stop symbol** is used at the beginning and end of a flowchart.

- To **initialize** is to set the starting values of certain storage locations, or **variables,** before running a program.

- A **loop** is a set of instructions causing the repetition of actions under certain conditions. An **iteration** is one trip through the loop. The computer can recognize these conditions by performing a **compare operation.**

- **Pseudocode** allows a programmer to plan a program, without being concerned about the rules of a specific programming language.

- A **programming language** is a set of rules for instructing the computer what operations to perform.

- **Machine language,** the lowest level, represents information as 1s and 0s.
- **Assembly languages** use letters as abbreviations or mnemonic codes to replace the 0s and 1s of machine language. An **assembler program** translates assembly language into machine language.
- **High-level languages** consist of English-like words. A **compiler** translates high-level languages into machine language.
- **Very high-level languages,** also called fourth-generation languages or **4GLs,** are basically nonprocedural. A **nonprocedural language** only defines *what* the computer should do, without detailing the procedure. A **procedural language** tells the computer specifically *how* to do the task.
- Fifth-generation languages are often called **natural languages** because they resemble natural human language.
- The first high-level language, **FORTRAN** (FORmula TRANslator), is a scientifically oriented language that was introduced by IBM in 1954.
- **COBOL** (COmmon Business-Oriented Language) was introduced in 1959 as a standard programming language for business.
- When introduced, **BASIC** (Beginners' All-purpose Symbolic Instruction Code) was intended for instruction, but its uses now include business and personal-computer systems.
- **Pascal,** first available in 1971, is popular in college computer courses.
- Invented by Bell Labs in 1974, **C** offers high-level language features while producing efficient code.

SELF-TEST

True/False

T F 1. Process boxes in flowcharting have two exits called paths.
T F 2. Lower-level languages are closer to the language the computer uses than are higher-level languages.
T F 3. A flowchart is an example of pseudocode.
T F 4. Desk-checking is the first phase of testing a program.
T F 5. A translator is hardware that translates a program into language the computer can understand.
T F 6. The highest-level languages are called, simply, high-level languages.
T F 7. Debugging is the process of locating program errors.
T F 8. Expressing a problem solution in Pascal is an example of coding a program.
T F 9. An advantage of pseudocode is that it can be used both to plan and execute a program.
T F 10. A 4GL increases clarity but reduces productivity.

Matching

_____ 1. diagnostics	a. BASIC
_____ 2. for beginners	b. ANSI symbol
_____ 3. debugging	c. desk-checking
_____ 4. connector	d. FORTRAN
_____ 5. machine language	e. planning the solution
_____ 6. pseudocode	f. compiler
_____ 7. steep learning curve	g. program listing
_____ 8. scientific	h. lowest level
_____ 9. documentation	i. C
_____ 10. proofreading	j. logic errors

Fill-In

1. A translator that translates high-level languages into machine language:

   _____

2. Two common methods of planning the solution to a problem are:

   _____ , _____

3. A language written by Niklaus Wirth: _____

4. A language specifically designed to write systems software:

   _____

5. The standard symbols used in flowcharting are called:

   _____

6. A kind of language that tells the computer *what* needs to be done, as opposed to *how*: _____

7. Languages that resemble spoken languages are called:

   _____

8. The first high-level language: _____

9. The error messages a translator provides are: _____

10. One trip through a loop: _____

Answers

True/False: 1. F, 3. F, 5. F, 7. T, 9. F

Matching: 1. f, 3. j, 5. h, 7. i, 9. g

Fill-In: 1. compiler, 3. Pascal, 5. ANSI symbols, 7. natural, 9. diagnostics

CHAPTER 8

OVERVIEW

OPERATING SYSTEMS
THE UNDERLYING SOFTWARE

All the scientists and technicians at Ollis Biomedical Products used computers for their research. Walt Tokuda was an Ollis executive, and he too found his desktop computer useful. He used it to share electronic mail with the research staff, monitor the departmental budget, and draft an occasional confidential memo.

Eventually, Walt found his computer so indispensable that he decided to buy one for home use. He bought a personal computer just like the one on his desk at work, and he bought all the same software he used there.

When he got it home, Walt had no trouble putting the computer together. The instructions were simple: Plug in a few cords, insert a diskette, flip a switch. The computer started up. But that was as far as he got. His office computer always greeted him with a menu of options—electronic mail, budget software, word processing. This computer just displayed "A>." He went back to the manual, but there he found only a lot of talk about formatting and partitioning and other mysterious topics.

Walt was not sure what was wrong, but he knew the person to call. He phoned Rick Pettay, Ollis Biomedical's personal computer manager. Rick explained that the menus Walt worked with at the office were based on special software—called EZ-ACCESS—that simplified his use of the operating system. He told Walt that he could buy EZ-ACCESS, and

Rick volunteered to do the initial setup of Walt's machine, just as he had done with Walt's office computer. But, Rick cautioned, doing so would limit the flexibility of Walt's home machine.

Rick advised Walt to learn to use the operating system without menus. Doing so, he said, would make Walt more self-sufficient. If he learned to prepare his own diskettes, install his own software, copy files from one disk to another, and so on, he could then experiment with new software, play computer games, work on his taxes, and dial in to computer conferences and bulletin boards.

In a few lessons Rick taught Walt how to pilot the operating system directly. With the help of his manuals and Rick's lessons, Walt found he had no trouble adapting to the Spartan environment of the operating system. In fact, he found that working without the menus gave him control he never knew he could have when his only contact with his computer had been through the EZ-ACCESS software. ◻

OPERATING SYSTEMS: POWERFUL SOFTWARE IN THE BACKGROUND

. . . .

An **operating system** is a set of programs that allows the computer to control and manage its own resources, such as the central processing unit, memory, and secondary storage. Figure 8-1 gives a conceptual picture of operating system software as an intermediary between the hardware and applications programs, such as word processing and database programs. Much of the work of an operating system is hidden from the user; many necessary tasks are performed behind the scenes. In other words, whether or not you are aware of it, using any software application requires that you invoke—call into action—the operating system as well. As a user, you must be able to interact with an operating system at some level, however rudimentary.

Operating systems for mainframe and other large computers are complex indeed, since they must keep track of several programs running at the same time. Although some personal computer operating systems also can support concurrent programs, most are concerned only with a single user running a single program at a given time. This chapter concentrates on the interaction between a user and a personal computer operating system.

OPERATING SYSTEMS FOR PERSONAL COMPUTERS

. . . .

If you peruse software offerings at a retail store, you will generally find the software grouped according to the computer, probably IBM or

▶

Figure 8-1   A conceptual diagram of an operating system.
On the outer rim, closest to the user, are applications programs—software that helps a user compute a payroll or play a game or calculate the trajectory of a rocket. The operating system is the set of programs between the applications programs and the hardware.

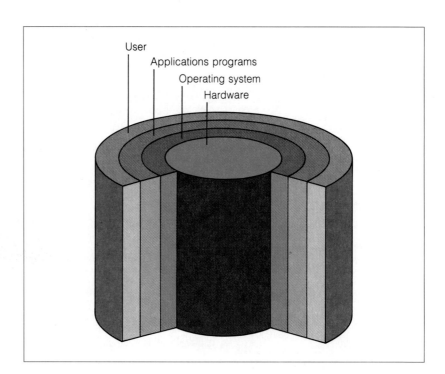

Macintosh, with which the software can be used. But the distinction is actually finer than the differences between computers: the applications software is really divided by the operating system on which the software can run.

Generally, an application program can run on just one operating system. Just as you cannot place a Nissan engine in a Ford, you cannot take a version of WordPerfect designed to run on an IBM machine and run it on an Apple Macintosh. This is because IBM personal computers and others like them use one operating system (Microsoft's MS-DOS—DOS stands for *disk operating system*) and Macintoshes use an entirely different operating system (called Macintosh and produced by Apple). Although some computers can run more than one kind of operating system, most personal computers are limited to one of these two.

Software makers must decide for which operating system to write a software package. Obviously, software makers want to sell as many copies of their product as they can. Since MS-DOS now has more than 80% of the personal computer market, there is more software written for this operating system than for any other.

Users do not set out to buy operating systems; they want computers and the applications software to make them useful. However, since the operating system determines what software is available for a given computer, many users observe the high volume of software available for MS-DOS machines and make their computer purchases accordingly. However, others prefer the user-friendly style of the Macintosh operating system and choose Macs for that reason.

Although operating systems differ, many of their basic functions are similar. We will show some of the basic functions of operating systems by examining MS-DOS.

GETTING STARTED WITH MS-DOS

Some software packages hide the operating system interface by including the operating system on the application disk. However, at some point you will probably need to use your own copy of the operating system. Loading the operating system into the computer's memory is called bootstrapping, or **booting,** the system. The word *booting* is used because, figuratively speaking, the operating system pulls itself up by its own bootstraps. When the computer is switched on, a small program (in ROM—read-only memory) automatically pulls up the basic components of the operating system from a diskette or hard disk.

The net observable result of booting MS-DOS is that the characters A>, or C> if you are using the hard disk drive, appear on the screen. The A or C refers to the disk drive; the > is a **prompt,** a signal that the system is *prompting* you to do something. At this point you must give some instruction to the computer. Perhaps all you need to do is insert a commercial software disk, then type certain characters to make the application software take the lead. But it could be more complicated than that because A> or C> is actually a signal for direct communication between the user and the operating system.

GARY WASN'T HOME, BUT BILL WAS

The first person to have some success promoting an operating system standard for personal computers was Gary Kildall, who wrote and marketed CP/M through his company, Digital Research. He was the fellow IBM turned to when the company needed an operating system for its own personal computer; IBM representatives set up an appointment with him. On the fateful day, the IBM contingent showed up, only to learn that Kildall was out.

Kildall's lawyer was on the premises, the story goes, and was reluctant to sign IBM's standard pretalk nondisclosure agreement. Kildall later tried to telephone one of his visitors but did not succeed. Two weeks later Kildall's contact at IBM left the project, and Kildall could not reach the new project leaders.

He never did, because they were in contact with Bill Gates, the young president of Microsoft. Gates delivered MS-DOS (which IBM calls PC-DOS—the two programs are almost identical) for the IBM PC, and the rest is history. Microsoft has since diversified to include software applications, and the company is now the leading independent software house.

Personal computers in action

How to Use MS-DOS

In the first section in this box, you will find directions for loading MS-DOS in a typical IBM PC system. The next two sections present directions for using MS-DOS to accomplish two common tasks: formatting a blank disk (which means preparing it for holding data files) and copying files from one disk to another. The instructions here assume you are using a computer with two diskette drives, drive A and drive B. If you are using a different system—with diskette drive A and hard drive C, for example—ask your instructor how to revise the instructions.

Loading MS-DOS

As you read these steps, follow along on the drawing. (Note: If your computer has hard drive C, then the operating system is automatically loaded when you turn on the computer; no action is required from you.)

1. Insert the MS-DOS disk in the lefthand disk drive (drive A) and shut the disk drive door.

2. Turn the computer on. The red light in drive A goes on, and the drive whirs for a few seconds. Then the red light goes off.

3. When the screen requests the date, you can either enter the new date (month-day-year; for example, 10-13-92) and press Enter or simply press Enter without entering the new date.

4. When the screen requests the time, you can either enter the new time (24-hour clock time; for example, 14:30) and press Enter or simply press Enter without entering the new time.

5. When the A> appears on the screen, MS-DOS is loaded.

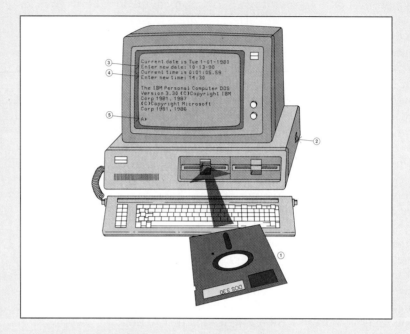

Formatting a Blank Disk

Caution: If your computer has hard drive C, *never* format the disk in drive C. Formatting destroys all data on a disk.

1. Load MS-DOS as previously described. Now insert a DOS system disk that contains external files, specifically FORMAT.COM, in drive A.

2. Insert the blank disk in drive B.

3. After A> type:

    FORMAT B:

4. Press Enter.

5. Press any key.

6. When the red light in drive B goes off, the disk has been formatted and is ready to use.

Copying Files

1. Load MS-DOS as previously described. Remove the disk.

2. Insert the original disk (the one to be copied) in drive A.

3. Insert the formatted disk (the one to be copied to) in drive B.

4. a. To copy a specific file on the disk in drive A to the disk in drive B, after A> type:

    COPY A:FILENAME B:

    For example, if the file name is PAYROLL, the screen should read:

    A>COPY A:PAYROLL B:

    b. To copy *all* the files on the disk in drive A to the disk in drive B, after A> type:

    COPY A:*.* B:

5. Press Enter.

6. When the light in drive B goes off, the computer has completed the copying.

Booting the system using MS-DOS. The numerals in the drawing refer to steps in the section called "Loading MS-DOS."

Although the prompt is the only visible result of booting the system, MS-DOS also provides the basic software that coordinates the computer's hardware components and a set of programs that lets you perform the many computer system chores you need to do.

USING MS-DOS

• • • • • • • • • • • • • • • • • •

We will now refer to MS-DOS by its abbreviated name, DOS, pronounced to rhyme with "boss." DOS is stored on one or more diskettes, which were probably purchased with the computer. If your computer has a hard disk drive, DOS is probably stored there also. DOS programs are executed by issuing a **command,** a name that invokes an operating system program. Whole books have been written about DOS commands, but we will consider only the commands you need to use applications software. These commands let you:

• Access files using DOS commands

• Prepare (format) new diskettes for use

• List the files on a disk

• Change the names of files on a disk

• Copy files from one disk to another

• Erase files from a disk

Table 8-1 shows the commands for performing these and a few other tasks.

Table 8-1   Some MS-DOS commands.   Here are some simple operating system commands, which you enter after the A> or C> prompt, and a description of what each command does. Although part of MS-DOS, these commands represent the kinds of things all operating systems are designed to help you do.

Command	Use
CHKDSK	Check disk. Display information about the status of a disk, including number of files, number of bytes used in files, and number of bytes available for use.
CLS	Clear the screen.
COPY	Make another copy of a file.
DATE	Enter the current date.
DEL or ERASE	Delete a file.
DIR	Directory. List all files on a disk.
DISKCOPY	Copy all files on a disk to another disk.
FORMAT	Prepare a disk for use.
RENAME	Give a file a new name.
TIME	Enter the current time.
TYPE	Display a file on the screen.

COMPUTING HIGHLIGHTS

The Commands You Will Use Most

Your principal connection with an operating system is likely to be the operating system commands you use in conjunction with applications software such as a word processing or spreadsheet package. The operating system commands you need to learn are not difficult. Let us consider the MS-DOS commands you might need.

FORMAT (Prepare a disk for use). Whether the data you are producing is a document, spreadsheet, database, or graph, you must have some place to keep it. Unless you are fortunate enough to have a hard disk, the place to keep your data is on a diskette. However, a diskette fresh from the store must be format-

ted before it can be used, and that is the purpose of this command.

COPY (Make a copy of a file). One important reason to copy a file is to produce a backup, a copy that you can use if the original is damaged. Protecting your investment in software by making backups is common. It is also a good idea to back up any important file and keep the copy and original on different disks.

DIR (Directory). In no time at all, most computer users have lots of files on lots of disks; forgetting where files are is easy. DIR produces an on-screen list of file names along with the file sizes in bytes and the date the files were last modified.

DATE (Enter the current date). Some systems are sophisti-

cated enough to keep track of the correct date and time. However, if your system asks you to input the current date and time when you boot the operating system, it is wise to do so. That way, you can glance at a listing of your files (see DIR) and know exactly what date and time a given file was created or last revised.

DEL (Delete a file). When your disk gets cluttered with files you no longer want, it is time to clean house. Use DEL with the name of each file you want to delete.

RENAME (Give a file a new name). If you decide you did not name a file properly, RENAME takes care of the problem easily.

A Brief Disk Discussion

Since many DOS commands involve files on disk, we are particularly concerned about disk drives in this chapter.

Disk Drive Configuration
There are two kinds of disk drives associated with a personal computer: diskette drives and hard disk drives, or hard drives. If you have two diskette drives, they are called drives A and B. A hard drive is called drive C. (Occasionally, there is a second hard drive, called drive D.) Configurations vary, but the three most common are shown in Figure 8-2.

The Default Drive
Consider the MS-DOS command DIR, which displays a list of files. How does DOS know which drive to look at when you type DIR? If you do not specify a particular drive, DOS will look at the default drive.

The **default drive,** also called the **current drive,** is the drive that the computer is currently using. Only one disk drive at a time can be the default drive. If your computer does not have a hard disk, DOS will always begin with drive A as the default drive. If you do have a hard disk, then the hard disk drive—drive C—is usually the default drive.

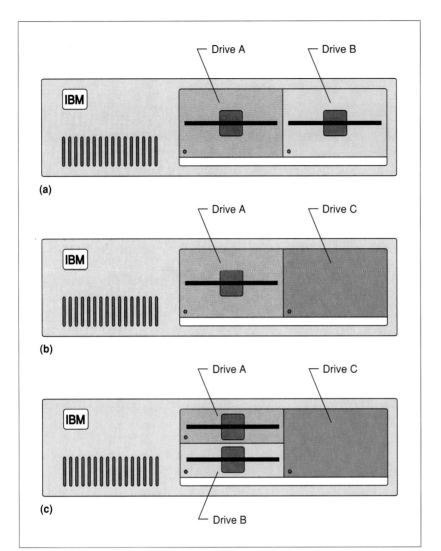

◀

Figure 8-2 Disk drive configurations.
As you use different computers, you may see several different types of disk drive combinations. The following are common. (a) Diskette drive A on the left, diskette drive B on the right. (b) Diskette drive A on the left; hard drive C on the right. (c) Diskette drives A and B stacked on the left, hard drive C on the right.

DOS uses the prompt to remind you which drive is currently the default drive. If you see A>, then the default drive is A. Similarly, C> means the default drive is C.

You can change the default to another drive if you wish. After the prompt, type the letter of the desired drive, type a colon, and then press Enter. Suppose, for example, that the default drive is currently drive A (as you can see from "A>" on the screen), but you want to access files on hard-disk drive C. To change the default drive to C, type C: (C followed by a colon) and then press Enter. (You can, by the way, type either an upper- or lowercase C—DOS recognizes both.) Now the screen should show C>.

Types of Diskettes

The three types of diskettes—disks—you may use are (1) DOS system disks, (2) applications software disks, and (3) data disks. What do these three have in common? All contain files. DOS system disks contain files of the operating system programs. Applications software disks contain files of the applications software, such as a word processing program. Data disks contain files of the data that is related to applications software.

When are these three types of disks used? The DOS system disk may be used to start the computer system and, as you proceed, to provide services and control of software and files. Applications software disks are used after DOS has been loaded into memory. (Sometimes DOS and applications software are on the same disk.) Data disks are used concurrently with applications software, either to supply input data or, more likely, to store the files you create. (Keep in mind that we are discussing diskettes here; for convenience, all kinds of files are stored on hard disks.)

Data files are different from DOS system and applications software files. To begin with, the DOS and applications software may belong to your school or company and may be used by several people. Data disks, on the other hand, are usually purchased by you, are used only by you, and contain data created by you.

When you first purchase a data disk, it contains no files—that is, the disk is empty. To prepare a disk to receive the files you will create, you must use the FORMAT command (see the box "How to Use MS-DOS"). In contrast, DOS and applications software disks that you purchase already have files on them, have been formatted, and should not be formatted again.

When you create a file for your data disk, using applications software, you must choose a name for the file. When there are several files on the disk, you may want to see a list of all the file names. You may want to copy files from one data disk to another so you can have a backup copy. You may want to erase files you no longer need. To do these things, you need to know how to use the appropriate DOS commands.

Internal DOS Commands

Certain DOS programs must be in your computer's memory before you can use the computer. These essential DOS programs are usually referred to as **internal** DOS programs. They are placed into your computer's memory when you boot the operating system. If your computer has a hard drive, then the programs for the internal DOS commands are loaded automatically from the hard disk when you turn the computer on.

However, if your computer has only diskette drives, the internal DOS programs are loaded when you boot the system from a DOS system disk in drive A. Once the internal DOS programs are in the computer's memory, you can remove the DOS disk and still use the DOS internal commands.

When you want to use the internal DOS programs, you ask—command—DOS to execute the programs by typing in the names of the programs. These programs execute immediately because they are already in memory. (In contrast, external programs, which we will discuss next, reside on disk as program files and must be read from disk before they can be executed.) An example of an important internal command is COPY, which lets you make copies of files.

External DOS Commands

Running most applications programs requires a lot of computer memory. Therefore, to save memory, only internal DOS programs, which are necessary to support the work of applications programs, are loaded into memory when the system is booted. The other DOS programs, which reside on the DOS disk, are called **external** DOS programs. The computer retrieves and executes a specific external program when you type the corresponding external DOS command.

Usually, in terms of DOS commands, all you will need are the internal commands; you will not use the external commands that often. The point of this discussion is that you must have access to the external DOS programs before you can use them. Therefore, to effect external DOS commands, you must have a diskette containing the programs in the proper disk drive or have the programs accessible on a hard disk. An example of an important external command is FORMAT, which prepares a disk so that it is capable of accepting files.

OPERATING ENVIRONMENTS: THE SHELL GAME

Figure 8-3 tells the story at a glance: Another layer has been added to separate the operating system and the user. This layer is often called a **shell** because it forms a "coating" for the user. More formally, this layer is called an **operating environment** because it creates a new environment—one more palatable to many users than the A> or C> prompt.

The Shell Interface

When using an operating environment, you see pictures and/or simply worded choices instead of the A> or some other prompt. Instead of having to *know* some command to type, you have only to make a selection from the choices available on the screen. Apple's Macintosh paved the way for simple interfaces between users and the operating system, and now various manufacturers are battling over future operating environment standards for DOS-based computers.

Microsoft Windows

Of many operating environments available, a key product is *Microsoft® Windows™* graphical environment—Windows, for short—a colorful graphics interface that, among other things, eases access to the operating system (Figure 8-4). Although earlier versions of Windows were not especially successful, Windows 3.0, introduced in 1990, received a warm welcome. The new version offered many improvements, including sophisticated screen graphics and faster operation. Almost immediately, many businesses large and small made plans to convert their personal computer systems to Windows. Will Windows become a new

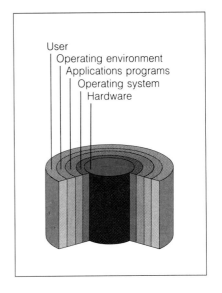

User
Operating environment
Applications programs
Operating system
Hardware

▲
Figure 8-3   An operating environment.
This illustration is identical to Figure 8-1, except that an environment layer has been added to shield the user from having to know commands of the operating system.

Figure 8-4 Microsoft Windows.
The operating environment provided by Windows, a Microsoft product, can run several programs concurrently and let users follow their progress on a screen divided into windows. Windows offers easy-to-use menu systems as well as user-friendly access to the operating system.

Figure 8-5 Microsoft Windows in Action.

These screens vividly illustrate the Windows graphical user interface. (a) The icons along the lefthand side represent available software tools, several of which are displayed in overlapping windows on the screen. (b) Windows provides users access to several applications programs at one time. The icons at the bottom of the screen represent additional applications.

corporate standard? Some computer industry watchers say that Windows signals the beginning of a new era for the DOS-based personal computer. So, what is so special about Windows?

The Look and Feel

When it comes to providing an easy-to-use interface, the Macintosh beat DOS-based computers hands down—until Windows. The feature that makes Windows so easy to use is a **graphical user interface (GUI),** in which users work more with on-screen pictures called **icons** and with **pull-down menus** rather than with keyed-in commands (Figure 8-5a). Furthermore, icons and menus encourage pointing and clicking with a mouse, an approach that can make computer use both faster and easier.

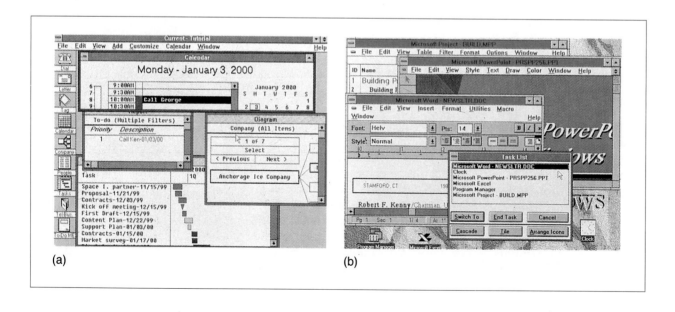

(a) (b)

 WINDOWS

Doing More Than One Task at a Time

Microsoft Windows brings an easy-to-use graphical user interface to DOS-based personal computers. Although nearly all DOS-based software can be made to work in the Windows operating environment, it is with applications that were written specifically for this environment that Windows really shines. Manufacturers of most major DOS applications have now introduced special versions of their products for Windows.

A major advantage of the Windows operating environment is that it allows many applications to run at the same time. This is called multitasking. In separate windows on the screen, you can run a spreadsheet program, a word processing program, and an electronic mail session. Depending on the amount of memory installed in the computer, as many as 20 applications can be active at a time. By contrast, only one application at a time can run on a computer that uses standard DOS only.

The advantages of multitasking become clear when you consider that the way people think and work is a form of multitasking. For instance, if you are writing a memo at the office and the phone rings, you normally would not put your writing materials in a drawer before answering. If a coworker walks in while you are on the phone, you would not hang up before you ask your visitor to come back later. Humans do multitasking naturally—with Windows, now your computer can too.

The name *Windows* refers to the fact that various software tools can be accessed and displayed on the screen in overlapping rectangles that look like windows. In fact, one application can be used when you are right in the middle of another (Figure 8-5b). To give a simple example, you can be using a word processing software package and invoke a computer file calendar to record an appointment just made over the phone; the calendar window pops up on the screen on command and then disappears just as fast when no longer needed, leaving the screen just as it was before you invoked the calendar.

To enhance ease of use, Windows is usually set up so that the attractive Windows display is the first thing a user sees when the computer is turned on. The user points and clicks among a series of narrowing choices until arriving at the software of choice.

Software Applications with Windows

Just what will Windows do for your favorite software application? Although you can tell Windows to access your existing software, you will not get the full benefits of Windows unless you use a software version especially designed for use with Windows. Anticipating the popularity of Windows, dozens of software manufacturers have done and are doing just that.

Reality Check

There are two serious impediments to Windows use: speed and memory. Evaluators argue that, although Windows 3.0 is cosmetically more attractive than earlier versions, decent performance requires a computer with a speedy microprocessor—at least the 80386—and at least 2 megabytes of memory. Many serious users, especially business users, already have such a system in place; those who do not should expect slow going with Windows.

MACINTOSH

The Macintosh Applications Interface

Computers based on the MS-DOS operating system, such as the IBM PC and PS/2 families, are fundamentally different from Macintosh computers. The first difference that catches the personal computer user's eye is the Macintosh's graphical user interface (GUI). The Mac uses a rich mixture of pictures and words to give the user information about the system: what software is available, what disks are available, where files are on those disks, and so forth.

Microsoft Windows gives DOS-based computers many of the features of a GUI, but even Windows users notice a difference when they use a Mac.

The second, more subtle difference takes personal computer users a bit longer to notice: the Macintosh applications interface. Unlike most personal computer applications, no two of which work the same way, Macintosh applications are all written to conform consistently to the

Mac's GUI. This means that each Macintosh application has the same "look and feel" as all other Mac programs.

No matter what application is being used—from Finder, the main operating system program, to the most elaborate desktop publishing package—the user knows that across the top of the screen will be the same list of menu items, beginning with "File" and "Edit." And the user knows that a click of the

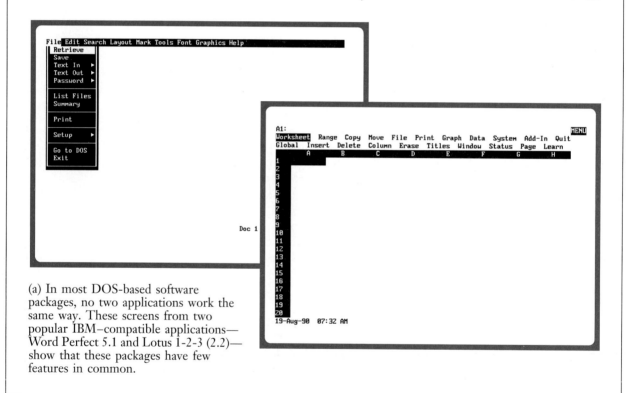

(a) In most DOS-based software packages, no two applications work the same way. These screens from two popular IBM–compatible applications—Word Perfect 5.1 and Lotus 1-2-3 (2.2)—show that these packages have few features in common.

▲ ▲ ▲

Do I really need to know all this? The answer to that question depends on how you expect to use a computer. If you use a computer primarily as a tool to complete a specific type of work, then you may have minimum interaction with an operating system. In that case, whether you are using a personal computer or a mainframe, you will learn to access the software of choice very quickly.

mouse will offer a predictable set of services. This gives the impression, quite falsely, that all Macintosh software is produced by a single manufacturer. In fact, there are hundreds of Mac software companies, and competition among them is hot. But they have all agreed on one thing: They all use the Macintosh applications interface.

This kind of cooperation did not happen by accident. A frequent complaint in the DOS world con-

cerned the expense of training office staff to use different software packages, all of which worked differently. Apple took note of this complaint and, long before the first Mac was sold, actively encouraged software developers to conform to the Mac's well-publicized standard. Apple took a major step toward encouraging this conformity when it included in each Mac the set of operating system programs needed to manage the mouse, the pull-down

menus, the icons, and the other features that are now familiar in all Mac software.

DOS-based software manufacturers that create programs for the Windows environment are conforming to a standard similar to the Mac applications interface. Thanks to a standard applications interface, the day is near when a little bit of training will suffice for users of both Mac and DOS-based computers.

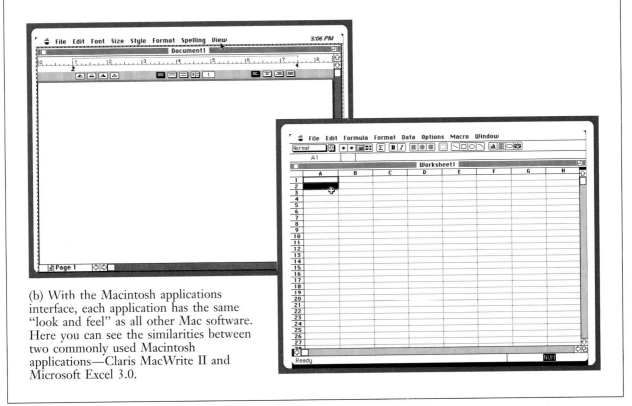

(b) With the Macintosh applications interface, each application has the same "look and feel" as all other Mac software. Here you can see the similarities between two commonly used Macintosh applications—Claris MacWrite II and Microsoft Excel 3.0.

But there are other ways to use a computer. In fact, there are far more options than we are able to present in this introductory chapter. Those who want or need to put the computer to its highest and best use will take direct command of the operating system because doing so increases their effectiveness and flexibility. You can learn your way around the operating system of any computer through on-the-job training or manuals that accompany the software.

CHAPTER REVIEW

SUMMARY AND KEY TERMS

- An **operating system** is a set of programs through which the computer manages its own resources, such as the CPU, memory, secondary storage devices, and input/output devices.

- In general, an application program can run on just one operating system.

- Since MS-DOS now has more than 80% of the personal computer market, there is more software written for this operating system than for any other.

- Loading the operating system into memory is called **booting** the system.

- In the on-screen A> and C> prompts, the A or C refers to the disk drive. A **prompt** is a signal that the system is waiting for you to do something.

- The **default drive,** also called the **current drive,** is the drive that the computer is currently using.

- MS-DOS programs are executed by issuing a **command,** a name that invokes the corresponding program. **Internal** DOS programs are placed into your computer's memory when you boot the operating system. The other DOS programs, which reside on disk, are called **external** DOS programs.

- Diskettes may hold DOS files, applications software files, or data files.

- Some operating systems provide pictures and/or simply worded choices instead of giving a prompt. In effect, these pictures and choices form a user-friendly "coating," or **shell.** They create a comfortable **operating environment** for the user, who does not have to remember or look up the appropriate commands.

- A key shell product is *Microsoft Windows 3.0*, software with a colorful **graphical user interface (GUI).** Windows offers on-screen pictures called **icons** and **pull-down menus,** both of which encourage pointing and clicking with a mouse, an approach that can make computer use faster and easier. The name *Windows* refers to the fact that various software tools can be accessed simultaneously and displayed on the screen in overlapping rectangles that look like windows.

- Although software makers are designing products especially for use with Windows, decent performance with Windows requires a fast computer and at least 2 megabytes of memory.

SELF-TEST

True/False

T F 1. The key feature of Microsoft Windows is user-keyboard interaction.
T F 2. FORMAT is an example of an internal DOS command.
T F 3. "C>" on the screen means that C is the current drive.
T F 4. The default drive is the current drive.

T   F   5. If you boot with a DOS disk in drive A, the default drive will be A.
T   F   6. A GUI uses icons.
T   F   7. Windows runs well on any computer.
T   F   8. An operating system is not needed if a shell is used.
T   F   9. The name *Windows* refers to circular drawings on the screen.
T   F   10. A diskette may hold applications software files.

Matching

_____ 1. prompt   a. mouse
_____ 2. COPY   b. load memory
_____ 3. shell   c. external command
_____ 4. Microsoft   d. manage computer resources
_____ 5. FORMAT   e. internal command
_____ 6. icon selector   f. now type a command
_____ 7. operating system   g. Windows
_____ 8. internal DOS files h. reside on disk
_____ 9. boot   i. operating environment
_____ 10. external DOS files j. booted into memory

Fill-In

1. When the computer is waiting for you to issue a command, it displays a:

   _____

2. If your computer has a hard drive, the initial default drive is:

   _____

3. Another name for an operating environment: _____

4. GUI stands for: _____

5. Loading the operating system is called: _____

6. Another name for the current drive: _____

7. The DOS command to list files: _____

8. The DOS command to get a disk ready to accept files:

   _____

9. The DOS command to move a file to another disk:

   _____

10. The DOS command to erase a file: _____

Answers

True/False: 1. F, 3. T, 5. T, 7. F, 9. F

Matching: 1. f, 3. i, 5. c, 7. d, 9. b

Fill-In: 1. prompt, 3. shell, 5. booting, 7. DIR, 9. COPY

PART THREE

INTERVIEW: David Kimball, California Pacific Medical Center

ell us about your current position. What are your primary job responsibilities?

As vice president for information services, I'm responsible for all the automated systems used in the medical center, running the gamut from systems for patient care to all of the different systems that a business needs, such as general ledger, payroll, billing, accounts receivable, purchasing, the storeroom—the whole works. My responsibilities include acquiring, installing, and maintaining those systems.

What kind of training have you had to prepare you for this position?

My academic training is in industrial engineering and operations research, which in a way is the liberal arts degree of engineering. I also have a master's degree in business administration. So, my training is primarily in management.

How has the medical center's use of computers changed in the time you have been here?

When I came here in 1983, all of the financial systems and the clinical laboratory were automated, and that was it. Since then, entirely new financial systems have been installed. We have brought in an information system in the Cardiology Department that assists with the processing of electrocardiograms, and we are in the middle of installing a large Patient Care Information System (PCIS). It will eventually have terminals and printers in all the nursing units and in all the support departments. Medical orders can be written directly into the terminal, and clinical lab results, x-ray reports, and so forth can be sent back to the nursing unit. In addition, nurses can chart the administration of medications, vital signs, and nurse's notes on the system, and all of that information can be printed out at the nursing station to be put in the patient's medical record.

How would patients see this system in use?

Up until now the nurses have been using handwritten patient-care plans. The new system gives them detailed printouts that tell them hour by hour what medications are due to which patient, and so on. A patient would see that as a more organized medical and nursing staff.

Are you finding any resistance to the process of automation?

There is some. However, I think one of the fundamental ground rules is that you have to let the system be the user's system. You have to be willing to educate users and let the decisions

▲
David Kimball is vice president for Information Services at California Pacific Medical Center. In this interview, he gives us some insight into how advances in information systems technology are changing the business of health care.

COMPUTERS AND BUSINESS

about how the screens look and so forth be the end-users' decisions, not the Information Systems Department's decisions. People who work in information systems should view themselves as staff support to the areas of the business that are delivering the goods, so to speak.

How do you feel that computers have been changing the business of health care?

A lot. For example, one of the reasons that we bought the particular system we did is that, once it is fully installed, we will be able to set up what is called a permanent patient record. That means that each time a patient is in the medical center, literally from birth to death, all of the data on that patient is recorded and stored on-line. Most medical centers have a different medical record for inpatients and different ones in the different outpatient departments. Now those records can be brought together in one common record, and that record is as close as a terminal.

Do people have concerns about security or privacy issues related to this record system?

Absolutely. Obviously, by making this information available, there's a great gain, particularly to the medical staff. But along with that goes the risk of making the chart more accessible. In our system, users are assigned a secret code that only they and two other people in the Information Systems Department know. We have established a policy that if you give out your user code intentionally, it is grounds for immediate

dismissal. Another concern is that the system is set up so that doctors can see the record for *any* patient, not just their own. Of course, any doctor can walk onto any nursing unit and look at a chart. But there is a psychological barrier to doing that on a unit where the doctor doesn't normally practice—and now that barrier doesn't exist. It really steps up the kind of professional ethics that we all have to follow.

> *One of the fundamental ground rules is that you have to let the system be the user's system.*

What other changes do you see happening in the future?

Down the road, I think we'll see patients carrying a type of credit card with a magnetic strip on the back that contains their medical record. That technology is available today. The limiting factor is that every medical center in the country would have to have a standard way of reading and writing such information onto the magnetic strip,

CALIFORNIA PACIFIC MEDICAL CENTER

and that standard is a good 10 to 15 years away. Once we have standard patient records, however, it would be very easy to set up an 800 telephone number so that if, for example, a cancer patient or a transplant patient shows up at the emergency room in Seattle, the emergency room can call the 800 number. The operator can print out a particular piece of documentation and fax the information to different areas of the country or, really, the world.

In addition, we are now looking at a CD-ROM system that we could network with terminals placed in key locations to allow the staff to do very focused literature searches. And I don't want to stop with just giving that to the medical staff. I want to see patients have access to it as well, because I think the highest-quality and most cost-effective medicine is going to occur when doctors and patients are real partners in patient care. ☐

CHAPTER 9

OVERVIEW

PERSONAL COMPUTERS ON THE JOB
FOR INFORMATION SYSTEMS MANAGERS AND EVERYONE ELSE

hen Sally Kelley was studying for her degree in accounting, she took on computers too. She knew she had to master spreadsheet software so she could propose "What if . . . ?" scenarios to her clients. Furthermore, she was convinced that word processing would be useful for memos and reports. When she was hired by a major bank, she anticipated that she would use a personal computer on a fairly regular basis. What she did not anticipate was that the computer would be the major tool on her desk and that she would use it constantly for everything she did.

On a typical work morning, Sally turns on the personal computer, which is part of a network of office computers, as soon as she walks into her office. While she removes her coat and unpacks her briefcase, the computer is displaying a list of options. She selects "Today's Calendar," and the screen displays "10:30 AM--Carston meeting re new trust" and "1:00 PM--lunch with T. Morales, Lakeside Cafe." The meeting notice reminds her to ask accountant Amy McKenna to bring the latest Carston reports to the meeting. She uses word processing to compose a memo quickly, then sends it to Amy via the office computer network. Next, she selects the option "Read Mail" from the screen and checks the list of incoming messages. Sally decides that the memo from her boss needs immediate attention and displays it on the screen. She sees

that he is calling for an emergency meeting in the conference room at 9 o'clock. Sally stores the other messages so she can read them later, and she heads for her first meeting of the day.

As the day moves on, Sally uses the computer to fetch client data from her database, to retrieve information about a company via a data communications system, and to plot client strategies by using spreadsheet software. She prints reports on the laser printer. And, finally, she takes home diskettes of office data to work with that evening on her computer at home. Sally has learned to use all this technology as casually as she uses the telephone or the copy machine. Sally is a prime example of a personal computer user on the job. ◻

PERSONAL COMPUTERS IN THE WORKPLACE: WHERE ARE THEY?

• • • • • • • • • • • • • • • • • •

Rather than ask where computers are in the workplace, it would be easier to ask where personal computers are *excluded* from the workplace. The list of areas in which computers are used, however, is instructive: retailing, finance, insurance, real estate, health care, education, government, legal services, sports, politics, publishing, transportation, manufacturing, agriculture, construction, and on and on (Figure 9-1).

Asked how her company used personal computers, a staffer replied, "You might as well ask how we use telephones. The computers are everywhere. We use them for everything." It was not always that way.

Evolution of Personal Computer Use

The evolution of personal computers on the job seems to fall into three phases. Personal computers were first used in business by individual users to transform work tasks. The constantly retyped document, for example, became the quickly modified word-processed document. Similarly, the much-erased manual spreadsheet became the automatically recalculated electronic spreadsheet, and overflowing file drawers were transformed into automated databases. This individual productivity boost could be considered the first phase of on-the-job personal computer acceptance. Many organizations are still in phase 1.

Many more organizations have entered the second phase—that is, they have gone beyond the individual, using personal computers to transform a working group or department. This department-oriented phase probably embraces a network and may also include personal computer access to mainframe computers. This phase requires planning and structure.

▼
Figure 9-1   Personal computer users.
Personal computers support business people in a variety of ways. (a) Architects use the computer's graphics abilities to render and revise their drawings. (b) This scuba gear vendor uses a computerized database to check inventory.

(a)

(b)

The third phase in the evolution of personal computer use in business is the most dramatic, calling for the transformation of the entire business. Practically speaking, however, phase 3 is really just an extension of the earlier phases: Each individual and each department uses computers to enhance the company as a whole. Few companies have fully entered phase 3. This three-stage transformation—individual, department, and business—broadly describes the progress a company has made in blending computers into the achievement of its business goals.

The Impact of Personal Computers

In the decades to come, personal computers will continue to alter the business world radically, much as the automobile did. For more than 50 years, the automobile fueled the economy, spawning dozens of industries from oil companies to supermarkets. Other industries, like real estate and restaurants, were transformed by the mobility the car provided. Personal computers will have a similar effect for two reasons: (1) Computers are now cost-effective at a level affordable to most businesses, and (2) few businesses without computers can provide the levels of service their computerized competitors provide.

Now that computers are here, let us consider who really needs to use them in business.

Where Personal Computers Are Almost a Job Requirement

Who absolutely positively must know how to use a personal computer to perform some part of a job? Someday the answer may be everyone. But we are not close to that landmark yet. Even if you can see that your intended job is in the must-know category, it is likely that you can receive some on-the-job training. Let us browse through a list of some probable could-need-computer jobs and the computer skills they require. Notice that many of the job titles mentioned can be listed with more than one skill:

- Real estate broker, attorney, doctor, auto mechanic: search for information in a variety of ways

- Accountant, tax planner, medical researcher, farmer, psychologist, budget manager, financial planner, stockbroker: analyze data

- Advertising copy writer, secretary, author, teacher, legislator: write and change documents

- Designer, editor, nurse, military personnel, retail sales manager: share data with other workers

- Project leader, construction manager, reservations agent, trucker, factory supervisor: keep track of schedules

- Insurance salesperson, fitness consultant, political candidate, sports manager: give a compare-the-results sales pitch

This list may have made you pause; you may not have seen computers in some of these roles. But there is no question that computers are changing the way we work.

TOGETHER AT LAST

There was a time when little Apple Computer nipped at the heels of big IBM. When IBM introduced its first personal computer in 1981, Apple placed a full page ad in the trade press, saying: "WELCOME, IBM. SERIOUSLY!" Apple felt that the IBM name would add luster to the concept of a small computer—a concept upon which IBM had built its company. Even so, Apple took up the habit of needling the corporate behemoth in public statements and advertisements. IBM did not bother to respond.

The chasm deepened as IBM's Personal Computer quickly outdistanced Apple products and became the standard for the computer industry. Eventually, the buying public was faced with the choice of the IBM standard or the easy-to-use Apple Macintosh. The dividing line was clear and, apparently, uncrossable.

But wait. In 1991, IBM and Apple announced a joint venture that stunned the industry. Why the sudden switch? IBM has been losing market shares to clones—computers that conform to the IBM standard but are made by someone else. Furthermore, both companies are frustrated by the dominance of Microsoft. Although IBM lifted Microsoft out of obscurity when it awarded the tiny company the contract to develop the operating system for the first IBM PC, Microsoft has since developed software that threatens both IBM and Apple.

So far, other than an increase in frayed nerves, the unlikely alliance has had little effect on the industry. The world waits.

PERSONAL COMPUTERS IN ACTION

A Sampler of Computers in Business

Computers are in businesses big and small. Here is a cross section of some computer applications.

- **Hotel management.** The Hilton Hotel chain uses a micro-to-mainframe link to connect its hotels to the main headquarters system. The system gives hotels two-way communication; the reservations system, for example, can both send and receive information.

- **Newspaper reporting.** The *Dallas Morning News* has over 100 laptop computers assigned to reporters, who take them everywhere from ballparks to inaugurations. In the office, other computers are used for the extensive graphics imagery the paper needs on each page.

- **In-Store shopping.** Bloomingdale's, the New York department store, offers a touch-screen computer system that lets customers select a category and then see pictures, prices, and other information about items for sale. However, the customer still needs to find a salesperson to make a purchase.

- **Shelf stocking.** Frito-Lay employees use hand-held computers to monitor the movement of snack-food products. The data gathered helps the company justify assigning ever-scarcer shelf space to Frito-Lay products.

- **Baseball records.** The Baseball Hall of Fame in Cooperstown, New York—yes, it is a business—features an interactive computer. Visitors can spend hours comparing their heroes' baseball statistics.

- **Car manufacturing.** The Ford Motor Company uses computers for every aspect of making a new car—engineering, manufacturing, assembling, and testing. Personal computers are used by people in all parts of the company to access data.

- **Stock trading.** Many brokerage houses let customers use their own computers to call up instant information. To gain access to these services, a customer needs only a personal computer and a modem to link up the system. Software is provided by the brokerage firm.

- **Door-to-Door selling.** Amway distributors—who sell cosmetics, detergents, and other household products nationwide—now have personal computers that they can use to place orders directly to the headquarters office in Michigan.

- **Restaurant management.** Las Casuelas Terraza, a restaurant in Palm Springs that seats 200 people, uses computers to automate cashiering, keep track of food inventory, design and print menus, monitor employee comings and goings, and keep track of employee tips.

How Computers Change the Way We Work

Computers are changing the way individuals and organizations work. By providing timely access to data, computers let us spend less time checking and rechecking data and more time getting work done. In addition to increasing overall productivity, computers have had a fundamental impact on the way some people approach their jobs.

Executives were among the first to notice the change. An oil company executive noted that her secretary is no longer the keeper of all knowledge, because many documents now get prepared without the secretary even seeing them. In fact, a lot of professionals use their computers in lieu of yellow pads. The net result is that work is done much more effectively (Figure 9-2).

Many business executives have opted for a do-it-yourself approach, buying their own personal computers and packaged software. A pharmaceutical executive, for instance, wanted direct access to data about company finances and sales. With some assistance from a computer specialist within the company, he purchased personal computers for himself and his staff. They took classes in spreadsheet software, which let them examine business strategy issues such as the level of sales discounts and advertising support needed to reach company sales targets. Before the computers arrived strategic planning was fairly informal; planners just eyeballed the numbers and made their best guesses. Now all that has changed in favor of computer-supported strategy.

People who dismiss the impact of the personal computer sometimes say, "It's just another tool." But what a tool! The personal computer is making profound changes even in the work lives of business people who seem unaware of what is going on.

Regional business manager Susan Swann, for example, once thought that the computer had not changed her life. But now she acknowledges that changes are apparent. Some time ago she began using her personal computer to draw up a budget and design a compensation package for the 80 people under her supervision. Later, she added hardware and software to hook up to computers in other regions. She also used her computer to write memos and reports. Susan eventually succumbed to a second personal computer, which she uses at home to do office work in the evening. She found it easier to carry diskettes to and from work than to lug a briefcase full of paper. That is a lot of change.

The Portable Worker

Many workers attribute their success to plain hard work—and they want to be able to take their work with them wherever they go. These days, taking work along means taking the computer along.

The Tools of Portability

The ideal set of machines a worker needs for portability include a personal computer, a laptop computer, and a laser printer. Keep in mind that it is the worker who is "portable," not all these machines. Most of the machines are in the office, though some workers, especially managers, have them at home also or carry laptops while traveling (Figure 9-3). Ideally, all computers are able to communicate with

▲
Figure 9-2   Professionals and executives often use computers heavily.

▲
Figure 9-3   Portable worker.
Workers can carry laptop computers wherever their jobs take them.

MACINTOSH

Office Publishing Is Easier than Ever

If there is one application that sets the Macintosh apart from other computers in the office, it is desktop publishing. Combining a page layout program with a laser printer lets office workers—or anyone, for that matter—create attractive publications, from brochures to newsletters to full-size books. Since you can easily move text and graphics around on the screen, Macintosh software simulates what graphic artists do when they cut and paste on a drafting table.

But buying desktop publishing software does not turn a person into a graphic designer. In fact, it is much easier to use the software than to produce a page that is attractive. Although many of us pick up a little something about drawing and mixing colors during our school days, design literacy is not a hot topic on the national education agenda. Thus, most people do not know where to begin when laying out a publication.

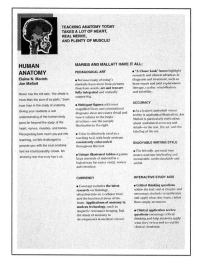

Fortunately, you do not have to begin laying out pages from scratch. To help desktop publishers who lack design experience, some software companies offer computer-produced templates, professionally created page layouts that can be used with your own text and graphics. For example, the software package PageMaker from Aldus comes with a set of designs for a brochure, newsletter, calendar, and directory. Aldus also markets a collection of templates, such as a portfolio of 21 newsletter designs and a package for businesses that features designs for proposals, reports, memos, overhead transparencies, and so on.

Learning to design pages with a personal computer takes time, even for professional graphic artists. Although the process can be frustrating at times, the results are gratifying. When the final version rolls off the laser printer, you can show it off with justifiable pride.

other computers. Regardless of place, appropriate software allows a worker to do whatever tasks are necessary, from writing reports to comparing financial options for a possible merger. Workers can use technology to transmit messages to other computers, to be read at the recipient's convenience. A report prepared at home or on the road can be sent via communications devices to the office, where it is printed by a laser printer. These electronic tools are catching on rapidly, and they are spreading beyond the traditional office.

The New Convenience

Some say the new technology goes beyond convenience—that a better word is *liberation*. Liberation from the confines of the office. Liberation from the 9-to-5 day with a commute on each end. Liberation from "telephone tag." Liberation from time-zone barriers. But the liberation being described here is not a pattern of being at home—it is the lack of a pattern. Workers can, for all practical purposes, stay in touch with the office and the action where and when they choose—24 hours a day, seven days a week—from almost any location.

THE INFORMATION SYSTEMS MANAGER

An **information system (IS)** may be defined as a set of business systems designed to provide information for an organization. Whether or not such a system is officially called an information system, every company has one. Even managers who make hunch-based decisions are operating with some sort of information system—one based on their experience. However, today the term *information system* usually means a system that includes at least one computer as its major component. Information serves no purpose unless it gets to its users in a timely way; the computer can act quickly to produce information.

An information system uses computer technology to solve problems for an entire organization, instead of attacking them piecemeal. Although in many companies a complete information system is still only an idea, the scope of information systems is expanding rapidly in many organizations.

The **information systems manager** runs the Information Systems Department. This position has been called information resource manager, director of information services, chief information officer, and a variety of other titles. In any case, the person who serves in this capacity should be comfortable with both computer technology and the organization's business.

Turf Wars

Is the information systems manager responsible for the whole company? Not really, but sometimes it seems that way. If computers are everywhere—and they will be—what does the future hold for the Information Systems Department? Through the 1960s and 1970s, anyone who needed computer services made a formal request to the computer professionals. That is, employees had to present their needs to the official keepers of automated power, where information was dispensed. A great deal of power, both computer and political, was concentrated in one place. However, as access to computers has been spread around, so has the power that goes with it.

The Distribution of Power

Distribution of power has come in a variety of ways. For example, placing minicomputers in remote locations, such as branch offices, gave computer users better access and more control. But the biggest change was made by placing personal computers directly in the hands of users.

In some ways, however, this distribution of power is an illusion. Users are sometimes constrained by their need for the corporate data, and that data is still firmly in the hands of the Information Systems

Department. Many personal computers are plugged into networks that the department must control and monitor. Also, users rely heavily on information centers, which help them with computer-related problems. It certainly seems that a lot of power still rests with the Information Systems Department.

In many companies, the role of those in the Information Systems Department is changing. They used to be caretakers of large computers; now they are becoming supporters of personal computers. And their support is offered right in the user's environment. Some companies choose to spin off a new department, usually called something like User Computing Support, to focus on personal computer use. Whatever the company's structure, information systems managers can no longer hide—as some did—behind the protective cloak of technical mystery, because their users have become more sophisticated. In effect, even the management style of the information systems manager is changing to meet the challenges of personal computers.

MANAGING PERSONAL COMPUTERS

Personal computers burst on the business scene in the early 1980s, with little warning and less planning. The experience of the Rayer International Paper Company is typical. One day a personal computer appeared on the desk of engineer Ruben Garcia—he had brought in his machine from home. Then accountants Sandy Dean and Mike Molyneaux got a pair of machines—they had squeezed the money for them out of the overhead budget. Keith Wong, the personnel manager, got personal computers for himself and his three assistants in the company's branch offices. And so it went, with personal computers popping up all over the company. Managers realized that the trigger for runaway purchases was that personal computers were so affordable: Most departments could pay for them out of existing budgets, so the purchasers did not have to ask anyone's permission.

Managers, at first, were tolerant. There were no provisions for managing the purchase or use of personal computers, and there certainly was no policy *against* them. It was soon apparent that the computers were more than toys; pioneer users had no trouble justifying their purchases with increased productivity. In many cases, managers began to see that personal computers were providing workers with the computer power the Information Systems Department was not. In this sense, dissatisfaction with the department boosted personal computer use. By mastering software for word processing, spreadsheets, and database access, many users were able to declare their independence from the Information Systems Department.

Soon, however, managers were faced with several problems. The first was incompatibility. The new computers came in an assortment of brands and models that did not mesh well. Software that worked on one machine did not necessarily work on another. In addition, users were not as independent of the Information Systems Department as they had thought—they needed assistance in a variety of ways. In particular, they needed data from the Information Systems Department,

WINDOWS

Keeping Track of Changes

Historically, one of the biggest problems in managing information has been updating a fact or figure in all the places it has been used. Microsoft Windows provides a feature called dynamic data exchange that makes updating a snap.

Imagine a business spreadsheet. In it are hundreds of entries, representing a company's expenditures and income. Imagine further that this is an electronic spreadsheet, stored in a file on a personal computer disk. Now imagine a week in which the company's business manager incorporates this information in a chart for the annual report to stockholders, in a table in a letter to a banker, and in the written plan for next year's budget. What happens

when the company's accountant identifies an error in the electronic spreadsheet? With a traditional computer system, the business manager would have to make the change to the original spreadsheet, then make corresponding changes to each of the three other documents in which the data had been used. With luck, none would be overlooked.

With Windows applications supporting dynamic data interchange however, errors can be corrected or new information added much more easily. The computer keeps track of every instance in which data from one text or data file was "pasted" into another. When a fact or figure in the original file is changed, corre-

sponding changes are made to every other file containing that fact.

The concept of dynamic data exchange is not new. "Live" links between software data files have been an intriguing prospect for many years, and a number of software products have offered such a feature for their own data files. But Windows is a clear leader in the linking of files among different applications. With over 50 million DOS-based computers in the world, and millions of them now using Windows, Microsoft's dynamic data exchange feature promises to have a great impact on the way information is managed.

and they needed it in formats compatible with their personal computers. And, finally, no one person was in charge of the headlong plunge into personal computers. Many organizations solved these management problems in these ways:

- They addressed the compatibility problem by establishing hardware and software acquisition standards and policies.
- They solved the assistance problem by creating information centers that provided, among other things, in-house training.
- They corrected the management problem by creating a new position often called personal computer manager.

Let us examine each of these solutions.

Personal Computer Acquisition 获得

In an office environment managers know they must control the acquisition and use of personal computers. As we noted, workers initially purchased personal computers before any companywide or officewide policies had been set. The resulting incompatibility meant that they could not communicate easily or share data with each other or the corporate mainframe. Consider this example: A user's budget process may call for certain data that resides in the files of another worker's personal computer or perhaps output incorporating the figures produced by yet a third person. If the software and machines these work-

ers use are different, accessing or outputting the data may become a major problem. Some companies have solved this problem by starting over: They purchased uniform hardware and software in volume and, most probably, hooked the computers together in a network. Other companies have taken other approaches:

- **Standards.** Some companies have simply established standards for personal computers, for the software that will run on them, and for data communications. Commonly, users must stay within established standards so they can tie in to corporate resources.

- **Limited manufacturers.** Some companies limit the number of hardware and software manufacturers from which they allow purchases. Personal computer managers have discovered they can prevent most user complaints about incompatibility by allowing products from just a handful of producers.

- **Limited support.** An Information Systems Department generally controls a company's purchases by specifying which hardware and software products the department will support.

As you can see, these methods overlap. But all of them, in one form or another, give the Information Systems Department control. In other words, users are being told, "If you want to do it some other way, then you're on your own."

The Information Center

If personal computer users compared notes, they would probably find that their experiences are similar. The experience of budget analyst Marissa Kallman is typical. She convinced her boss to let her have her own personal computer so she could analyze financial data. She learned to use a popular spreadsheet program. She soon thought about branching out with other products. She wanted a statistics software package, but was not sure which one was appropriate. She thought a modem for data communications would be useful, but she did not feel qualified to make a hardware decision. And, most of all, she felt her productivity would increase significantly if she could access the data in the corporate data files.

The company **information center** is the solution to these kinds of needs. Although no two are alike, information centers are devoted exclusively to giving users service. Best of all, user assistance is often immediate, with little or no red tape.

Information centers often offer the following services:

- **Software selection.** Information center staff members help users determine which software packages suit their needs.

- **Data access.** If appropriate, the staff helps users get data, in formats compatible with the users' own computers, from the large corporate computer systems.

- **Training.** Education is a principal reason for an information center's existence. Classes are usually small, frequent, and on a variety of topics.

- **Technical assistance.** Information center staff members are ready to assist in any way possible, short of actually doing the users' work for them. That help includes aiding in the selection and use of software, finding errors, helping submit formal requests to the Information Systems Department, and so forth (Figure 9-4).

To be successful, the information center must be placed in an easily accessible location. The center should be equipped with personal computers and terminals, a stockpile of software packages, and perhaps a library. It should be staffed with people who have a technical background but whose explanations feature plain English. Their mandate must be that the user comes first.

The Personal Computer Manager

The benefits of personal computers for individual users have been clear almost from the beginning: increased productivity, worker enthusiasm, and easier access to information. But once personal computers move beyond entry status, standard corporate accountability becomes a factor; large companies are spending millions of dollars on personal computers, and top-level managers want to know where all this money is going. Company auditors begin worrying about data security. The company legal department begins to worry about workers illegally copying software. Before long, everyone is involved, and it is clear that someone must be placed in charge of personal computer use. That person is the **personal computer manager,** also known as the **microcomputer manager.**

There are four key areas that need the attention of the personal computer manager:

Figure 9-4 The information center.
Classes are often held in the company information center to teach employees how to use the company computers.

- **Technology overload.** The personal computer manager must maintain a clear vision of company goals so that users are not overwhelmed by the massive and conflicting claims of aggressive vendors. Users engulfed by phrases like *network topologies* or *file gateways* or a jumble of acronyms can turn to the personal computer manager for guidance with their purchases.

- **Cost control.** Many people who work with personal computers believe the initial costs are paid back rapidly, and they think that should satisfy managers who hound them about expenses. But the real costs entail training, support, hardware and software extras, and communications networks—much more than just the cost of the computer itself. The personal computer manager's role includes monitoring *all* the expenses.

- **Data security and integrity.** Access to corporate data is a touchy issue. Many personal computer users find they want to download data from the corporate mainframe to their own machines, and this presents an array of problems. Are they entitled to the data? Will they manipulate the data in new ways, then present it as the official version? Will they expect the Information Systems Department to take the data back after they have done who-knows-what with it? The answers to these perplexing questions are not always clear-cut, but at least the personal computer manager will be tuned in to the issues.

- **Computer junkies.** And what about the employees feverish with the new power and freedom of the computer? These user-abusers

COMPUTING HIGHLIGHTS

Growing Pains

hen it comes to placing personal computers in the office, it is clear that the good outweighs the bad. Computerization is not without growing pains, however. Now that the excitement of computerization has subsided, it is possible to view the process objectively. Consider these problems.

Personnel Problems

Fear tops the list: fear of looking stupid, fear of diminished power, fear of job loss. All these fears have some basis; all are possibilities. But a manager should anticipate these problems and alleviate them with thorough training. There is also some worry about health problems, including eyestrain and back and wrist injury.

Hidden Costs

Placing computers in the office may involve hidden costs. The obvious costs are hardware, software, and supplies. Additional costs may include connection to a network of office computers and access to shared long-distance communication, database management systems, and mainframes—not to mention the cost of troubleshooting all these activities. Also, computerization may call for changes in the office environment, such as redesigning lighting, rewiring the site for additional electric power, increasing the amount of air-conditioning, and improving acoustics to reduce the noise generated by the new equipment. Startup costs for training are obvious, but hidden startup costs may include inefficiencies in serving customers by new and unfamiliar means, time spent converting existing files to computer-readable form, job interruptions due to unfamiliar procedures, and time spent in meetings to negotiate changes in handling the work.

Mixing and Matching

Equipment for personal computers in the office is rarely acquired in one gigantic purchase. This benefits cash flow, but it can produce large headaches in terms of compatibility—in many cases, separately purchased machines cannot communicate or exchange data.

Security

Personal computers in the office present a new variety of security problem. Office systems and home systems have much in common, and both well-intentioned users and system abusers find that this compatibility leads to the migration of software to home computer systems. Another costly problem is that office workers are finding it easy to steal keyboards, software, diskettes, and supplies. Creative fixes are on the market. One, for example, sounds a piercing alarm if a component is disconnected. This does not do much, however, about the software-laden diskettes going out the door in briefcases.

Office systems are particularly vulnerable to security lapses because they use data that is in fairly finished form. In contrast to the masses of raw data that mainframes manipulate, office systems accumulate correspondence and summary information—just the sort of thing that the unscrupulous find useful.

are often called junkies because their fascination with the computer seems like an addiction. Unable to resist the allure of the machine, they overuse it and neglect their other work. Personal computer managers usually respond to this problem by setting down guidelines for computer use.

The person selected to be the personal computer manager is usually from the information systems area. Ideally, he or she has a broad technical background, understands both the potential and limitations of personal computers, and is well known to a diverse group of users. In small companies, the personal computer manager may be a jack-of-all-trades, as long as the "trade" is computers. That is, in addition to the duties listed here, the personal computer manager may handle computer acquisitions and fill the functions normally assumed by information center personnel.

B UYER'S GUIDE

How to Buy Your Own Personal Computer

We cannot choose your new computer system for you any more than we might select a new car for you. But we can tell you to look for or avoid various features. We do not mean that we can lead you to a particular brand and model—so many new products are introduced every month that doing so would be impossible. If you are just starting out, however, we can help you define your needs and ask the right questions.

Where Do You Start?

Maybe you have already done some thinking and have decided that a personal computer offers advantages. Now what? You can start by talking to other personal computer owners about how they got started and how to avoid pitfalls. Or you can read some computer magazines, especially ones with evaluations and ratings, to get a feel for what is available. Next visit several dealers. Don't be afraid to ask questions. You are considering a major purchase, so plan to shop around.

Analyze Your Wants and Needs

Begin with a wants-needs analysis. Why do you want a computer? Be realistic: Will it probably wind up being used for games most of the time or for business applications? People use personal computers for a variety of reasons. Prioritize your needs; don't plan to do everything at once. At some point you will have to establish a budget ceiling. After you have examined your needs, you can select the best hardware-software combination for the money.

An Early Consideration

Although there are many brands of computers available, the business standard is an IBM or IBM-compatible machine; these computers account for approximately 75% of the market. If you will be using your computer for business applications and, in particular, if you need to exchange files with others in a business environment, consider sticking with the standard. However, the

▲ **The complete personal computer system.** A complete personal computer system has a central processing unit and memory, monitor, keyboard, a drive for a storage device, and a printer.

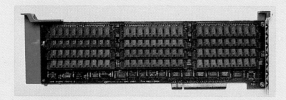

▲ **Adding memory.** This add-on memory board gives an IBM PS/2 an additional 12 million bytes of memory.

Apple Macintosh, with approximately 10% of the market, is an attractive alternative. The Macintosh is noted for ease of use, especially for beginners.

WHAT TO LOOK FOR IN HARDWARE

The basic personal computer system consists of a central processing unit (CPU) and memory, a monitor, a keyboard, a drive for a storage device (a 5 1/4- or 3 1/2-inch diskette or hard disk), and a printer. Unless you know someone who can help you out with technical expertise, the best advice is probably to look for a packaged system—that is, one in which the preceding components (with the exception of the printer) are assembled and packaged by the same manufacturer. This gives you some assurance that the various components will work together.

Central Processing Unit

Today, most manufacturers make machines with 16-bit or 32-bit processors. More bits mean more power, faster processing, and more memory. If you plan to purchase an IBM or compatible machine, many software packages run most efficiently on computers using an 80386—a "386"—microprocessor.

Memory

Memory is measured in bytes. The amount of memory you need in your computer is determined by the amount of memory required by the applications programs (like word processing or spreadsheets) that you want to use. A minimum of 640 kilobytes is suggested for personal computers used for business applications, although many have a million bytes or more of memory. Most machines have expandable memory, so you can add more later if you need it.

Monitor

Sometimes called a video display screen, the monitor is a very important part of your computer system—you will spend all your computer time looking at it. Before you buy any monitor, test it by using it to run some of the applications programs you intend to buy.

Color or Monochrome. Monochrome (green, amber, white on a black background or black on a white background) monitors are best when a computer will be used mostly for simple word processing applications. However, if you want to create graphics on your screen or if you plan to run entertainment programs on your computer, you will probably want to buy a color monitor. Many programs are written to be run solely on computers with color monitors. Most users prefer a color monitor.

Screen Width. Although some Macintosh computers have a 9-inch screen, most monitors have a screen display of between 12 and 14 inches. Generally, a larger screen provides a display that is easier to read, so you will probably want at least a 12-inch screen. For most purposes, a screen that displays 25 lines of 80 characters each is standard.

Screen Readability. Be sure to compare the readability of different monitors. First, make certain that the screen is bright and has minimum flicker. Next, check the shape of the characters. Some screens are difficult to read because they chop off the descenders—the tails that fall below the line—of the lowercase letters *g*, *p*, *q*, and *y*. In addition, if characters appear crowded on the screen, they will be difficult to read. Glare is another major consideration. Harsh lighting nearby can cause glare to bounce off the screen, and some screens seem more susceptible to glare than others.

A key factor affecting screen quality is resolution, a measure of the number of dots, or pixels, that can appear on the screen. The higher the resolution—that is, the more dots—the more solid the text characters appear. For graphics, more pixels means sharper images. But do not be tempted to pay a higher price for the best resolution unless your applications need it.

Graphics Adapter Boards. If you want to use an applications program with graphics and the computer you are considering does not come with the ability to display them, you will need to buy a graphics adapter board (sometimes called a graphics card) to insert into the computer. There are several different standards for graphics adapter boards, such as Enhanced Graphics Array (EGA) or Video Graphics Array (VGA). Monitors designed for use with one type of card may not be capable of "understanding" the signals from a different type. Check carefully that you have the right monitor–graphics board combination.

Ergonomic Considerations. Can the monitor swivel and tilt? If so, this will eliminate your need to sit in one position for a long period. The ability to adjust the position of the monitor becomes an important consideration when several users share the same computer. Another possibility is the purchase of add-on equipment that allows you to reposition the monitor.

Keyboard

Keyboards vary in quality. To find what suits you best, sit down in the store and type. Consider how the keys feel. Assess the color and layout of the keyboard, and find out whether it is detachable. You may be surprised by the real differences in the feel of keyboards. Make sure the keys are not cramped together; you will find that your typing is error-prone if your fingers are constantly overlapping more than one key. Ideally, keys should be gray with a matte finish. The dull finish reduces glare.

Most keyboards follow the standard QWERTY layout of typewriter keyboards. However, some have a separate numeric keypad. In addition, most keyboards have separate function keys, which simplify applications program commands.

A detachable keyboard—one that can be held on your lap, for example—is desirable. You can move a detachable keyboard around to suit your comfort. This feature becomes indispensable when a computer is used by people of different sizes, such as large adults and small children.

Secondary Storage

You will need one or more disk drives to read programs into your computer and to store any programs or data that you wish to keep.

Diskettes. Most personal computer software today comes on disks. Modern diskettes are 3 1/2 inches across. Many systems have at least one disk drive built into the computer. Although not necessary, you may find it helpful to have a 5 1/4-inch disk drive to use the larger diskettes.

◄ **Monitor displays.** (Top) Color monitors let you see your graphic displays and text in a multitude of colors. (Bottom) High-resolution mono-chrome monitors are highly readable.

▲ **Ergonomic considerations.** This monitor stand tilts and swivels so your neck does not have to.

▲ **Typewriter-style keyboard.** Many keyboards now have 12 function keys along the top of the board, a numeric keypad on the right, plus an extra cursor movement pad.

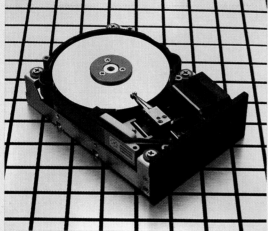

▲ **Secondary storage.** (Top) The 3 1/2-inch diskettes are standard on most IBM and IBM-compatible Macintosh computers. A diskette of this size is enclosed in a plastic case, which helps protect the disk. The 5 1/4-inch floppy diskette is still used on older IBM personal computers and compatibles and newer machines with the disk drives to accommodate the larger size. (Bottom) The inside of this hard disk drive shows the access arm hovering over the disk.

Hard Disks. Although more expensive than diskettes, hard disks are fast and reliable and hold more data. These features make the hard disk an increasingly attractive option for personal computer buyers. Computers are available with a built-in hard disk with a storage capacity of 30 million bytes—characters—of data; greater capacities are available if you can afford them. You may choose to purchase a hard disk after your initial computer purchase.

Printers

A printer is probably the most expensive piece of peripheral equipment you will buy. Although some inexpensive models are available, you will find that those costing $400 and up are the most useful. When choosing a printer, consider speed, quality, and cost. Verify that the printer will work with the applications software you intend to use. For example, will it print graphs created with Lotus 1-2-3?

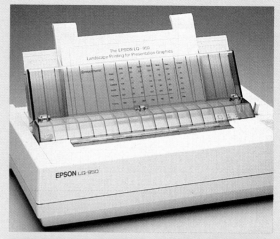

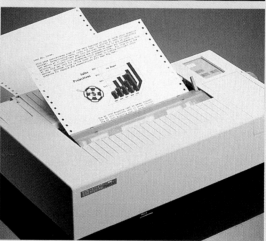

▲ **Printers.** (Top) The 24-pin dot-matrix printers, such as this one, can produce results of near letter quality.
(Middle) Laser printers are often used with desktop publishing software.
(Bottom) Ink-jet printers can produce colorful graphic output.

For everyday printing, a **dot-matrix printer**, capable of printing 250 characters per second, will do very nicely. Each character is formed out of a grid of dots in the same way the lights on a temperature sign or stadium scoreboard spell out messages. Dot-matrix printers can also be used for printing computer-generated graphics. Near-letter-quality printers are dot-matrix printers that make a second pass at the characters or use a more dense array of dots to make the letters more fully formed.

Letter-quality printers use a daisy wheel, a device that can be removed (like a typewriter element) and replaced with a wheel that has a different type font on it. The disadvantage of this equipment is that it is relatively slow. These printers cannot print computer-generated graphics, but they do produce the sharp characters needed for business correspondence.

Although relatively slow, **ink-jet printers** can produce text and graphics whose color range and density usually surpass the color graphics of dot-matrix printers.

Laser printers are the top-of-the-line printers for quality and speed. They are also the most expensive. Laser printers are used by desktop publishers to produce text and graphics on the same page.

Plotters draw hard-copy graphics: maps, bar charts, engineering drawings, overhead transparencies, and even two- or three-dimensional illustrations. Plotters often come with a set of six pens in different colors.

Portability

Do you plan to let your computer grow roots after you install it, or will you be moving it around? Do you want a large video display or will the smaller versions on laptop computers do? Portable computers have found a significant niche in the market, mainly because they are packaged to travel easily. A laptop computer is lightweight (often under 10 pounds) and small enough to fit in a briefcase. There are trade-offs, however, such as screen readability and the amount of internal power available.

Other Hardware Options

There are a great many hardware variations; we will mention a few here.

Communications Connections. If you wish to connect your computer via telephone lines to electronic bulletin boards, mainframe computers, or information utilities such as CompuServe or Prodigy, you will need a modem. This device converts computer data into signals that can be transmitted over telephone lines. The Hayes Smartmodem family of products has become the industry standard; most new modems claim some degree of Hayes compatibility.

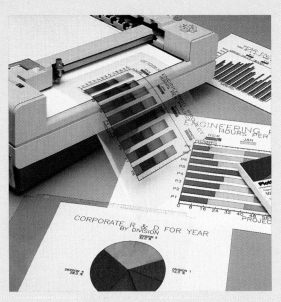

▲ **A plotter.** Plotters for personal computers can produce high-quality graphic output.

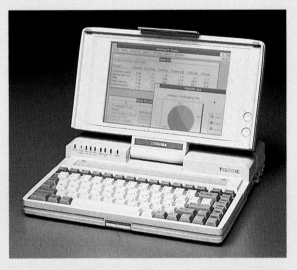

▲ **A laptop computer.** These small computers, which often include built-in software, are an attractive option for users who travel.

Other Input Devices. If you are interested in games, you may wish to acquire a **joy stick**, which looks like the stick shift on a car. A joy stick allows you to manipulate a cursor on the screen. A more sophisticated device is a **mouse**, a gadget that you roll on a tabletop to move the cursor on the screen to make selections. Many software packages are designed to let you work most efficiently if your computer has a mouse attached. A **scanner** is useful if you need to store pictures and typed documents in your computer. Scanners are frequently purchased by people who want to use their computers for desktop publishing.

Surge Protectors. These devices protect against the electrical ups and downs that can affect the operation of your computer. Some of the more expensive models provide up to 10 minutes of full power to your computer if the electric power in your home or office is knocked out. This gives you time to save your work on disk (so that the work won't be lost if the power fails) or to print out a report you need immediately. If lightning storms or power fluctuations occur in your area, you would be well advised to purchase a surge protector.

What to Look for in Software

The current standard for operating systems is MS-DOS, made popular by IBM. Many applications programs that will do what you want to do are available for DOS-based computers. There are also many excellent programs written to run on the Apple Macintosh. Now, let us consider hardware requirements, brand names, demonstrations, and languages.

Hardware Requirements for Software

Identify the type of hardware required before you buy software. Usually, the salesperson can advise you on hardware requirements for any software you purchase.

Brand Names

In general, publishers of well-known software offer better support than lesser-known companies. Support may be in the form of tutorials, classes by the vendor or others, and the all-important hot-line assistance. In addition, brand-name software usually offers superior documentation and upgrades to new and better versions of the product.

SYSTEM REQUIREMENTS

Operating Systems
MS-DOS (2.0 or higher for single user).

Hardware Requirements
IBM Models and compatibles.
Hard disk required.

Main Memory
Minimum of 1M bytes of RAM required.

Printer
Any IBM compatible printer.

▲ **Read the directions.** Make sure your hardware works with the software you are buying by reading the fine print on the software package.

QUESTIONS TO ASK THE SALESPERSON AT THE COMPUTER STORE

➤ Is the machine popular enough to have a user's group in my area?

➤ Is there anyone I can call about problems?

➤ Does the store offer classes on how to use this computer and software?

➤ Do you offer a maintenance contract for this machine?

➤ Can I expand the capabilities of the machine later?

Software Demonstrations

Always ask for a demonstration before you buy. However, if you purchase your software through the mail from advertisements in computer magazines, you will not have an opportunity for a demonstration. In some cases, you can rely on a friend's recommendation, or you can consult the software reviews found in trade publications such as *InfoWorld*, *PC Magazine*, or *Macworld*.

Languages

You may purchase languages on disk if you wish to write your own applications programs. BASIC is the most popular language for personal computers, but some personal computers can use FORTRAN, Pascal, C, and other languages.

Shopping Around: Where to Buy

Where you buy is important, and usually the trade-off is between price and service—but not necessarily.

The Dealer

Remember that you are buying a relationship with the dealer as well as purchasing a computer. In a sense, you are also paying for your dealer's expertise. Answers to your questions, both now and later, may be the single most important part of your purchase. Vendors like IBM, Apple, and Hewlett-Packard have established nationwide organizations of authorized dealers. A vendor-authorized dealer is usually a well-established business with recognized expertise in the product it sells.

You might also decide to purchase a personal computer from a computer store, a discount house, or a bookstore. If you work for a large company or educational

▲ **Dealer support.** Some dealers provide software demonstrations so you can try before you buy.

▲ **Repair.** If your computer breaks down, you will probably need to take it to a repair center.

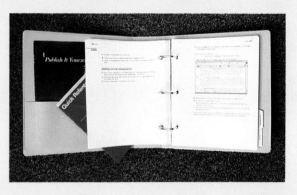

▲ **Documentation**. Clear, easy-to-follow documentation is one of the most important features of a software package.

institution, ask whether your employer has made an employee purchase arrangement with a vendor. Substantial discounts are often available under such programs.

Service and Support

If you purchase your personal computer from a specialized computer store, you are usually ensured of service and support. The store's staff can help you through the rough spots. Remember, however, that the excellent computer store personnel who were available during your purchase decision may not be there the next time you need service. In addition, equipment and software change rapidly, and sometimes personnel are not as knowledgeable as you might hope. Many stores also offer other services, such as training classes, warranty service, or a loaner while your computer is being repaired.

Maintenance Contract

When purchasing a computer, you may wish to consider a maintenance contract, which should cover labor and parts. Such contracts vary in comprehensiveness. Some cover on-site repairs (usually these contracts are available only to significant business customers); others require you to pack up the computer and mail it in.

Now That You Have It, Will You Be Able to Use It?

Once the proud moment has come and your computer system is at home or in the office with you, what do you do with it?

Documentation

Nothing is as important as documentation, the written manuals and instructions that accompany hardware and software. Unfortunately, some documentation is inadequate. Ask to see the documentation before you buy. On a machine in the store, try performing one of the procedures the user manual describes. The instructions should be simple to understand; too much jargon could cause you problems once you get your new hardware or software home.

BUYER'S
GUIDE
8

Training

Can you teach yourself? In addition to the documentation supplied with your computer, numerous books and magazines offer help and answer readers' questions. Consult these sources. Other sources are classes offered by computer stores, local colleges, and hardware manufacturers and tutorials offered on diskettes by software vendors. These tutorials, offering hands-on participation right on your own computer, may be the most effective teaching method of all.

SURVEY FOR THE PROSPECTIVE BUYER

Identify the activities you would like to do on your personal computer. Then, read computer magazines, check with friends, and visit retail stores for hardware and software options. Select software with your computer hardware in mind, and make certain that your software can be inexpensively and easily upgraded. Obtain comparative price information from many sources, including magazines, mail-order catalogs, and newspaper advertisements. Be prepared to comparison-shop.

▲ **Training.** Hardware and software purchases, especially in business, sometimes include classes provided by the dealer.

SURVEY FOR THE PROSPECTIVE BUYER

1. **Price Range.** I can spend:

___ under $1000
___ up to $2000
___ up to $3500
___ up to $5000
___ more

2. **Hardware Features.** I want the following features on my computer:

___ MS-DOS compatibility
___ OS/2 compatibility
___ Apple compatibility

___ 16-bit processor
___ 32-bit processor

___ 256 kilobytes of memory
___ 640 kilobytes of memory
___ 1 megabyte of memory
___ 2 megabytes of memory

___ Monochrome screen
___ Color screen
___ 80-column screen
___ Extra-large screen
___ Excellent screen readability

___ Color graphics capability
___ EGA graphics standard
___ VGA graphics standard
___ Tilt-and-swivel screen
___ Glare shield

___ Numeric keypad
___ Function keys
___ Detachable keyboard

___ Hard disk drive
___ 3 1/2-inch disk drive
___ 5 1/4-inch disk drive

___ Dot-matrix printer
___ Letter-quality printer
___ Ink-jet printer
___ Laser printer

___ Portability
___ Modem
___ Joy stick
___ Mouse
___ Scanner
___ Surge protector
___ Other

3. **Software Features.** I want the following software:

___ Word processing
___ Spreadsheet
___ Database management
___ Graphics
___ Desktop publishing
___ Communications
___ Information services
___ BASIC
___ Other programming languages
___ Games and recreation

4. **Other Features.** The following are important to me:

___ Manufacturer's reputation
___ Dealer's reputation
___ Service and support
___ Maintenance contract
___ Documentation quality
___ Training

PERSONAL COMPUTERS IN SYSTEMS

The original idea of personal computers emphasized the *personal* concept—one person, one computer. An island alone. Although this idea remains largely unchanged in the home environment, it has changed in a number of ways in business. Today, in companies large and small, personal computers may be linked in a network to each other and/or to a larger computer. As soon as a personal computer becomes part of a larger world in this way, it is part of a system. Furthermore, the personal computer user will deal with a person who plans systems, the systems analyst.

The System and the Systems Analyst

A **system** is an organized set of related components established to accomplish a certain task. There are natural systems, such as the cardiovascular system, but many systems have been planned and deliberately put into place by people. For example, the lines you stand in, stations you go to, and forms you fill out at the Department of Motor Vehicles compose a system to get qualified drivers their driver's licenses. A **computer system** is a system that has one or more computers as components.

A **systems analyst** analyzes existing systems and plans new, improved systems. **Systems analysis** is the process of studying an existing system to determine how it works and how effectively it meets user needs; **systems design** is the process of planning a new system.

Systems Analysis

Systems analysis lays the groundwork for improvements to a system. The analysis involves an investigation, which usually involves establishing relationships with the client for whom the analysis is being done and with the users of the system. The **client** is the person or organization contracting to have the work done. The **users** are people who will have contact with the system, usually employees and customers. For instance, in a college registration system, the client is the administration and the users are the school employees and the students.

The system to be analyzed may be a manual system or be automated already. In either case, computers will be components of the new system. Consider this example. Systems analyst Kit Mele responded to a request from Pacific Sound Technology, a chain of stores carrying a broad selection of television sets, VCRs, and sound system components. The company manager, Bob Butler, was disturbed about inventory problems, which caused frequent stock shortages and increasing customer dissatisfaction. Although the company had a minicomputer at the headquarters office, Mr. Butler envisioned more sophisticated technology to track inventory.

Ms. Mele's first task was to study, or analyze, the existing inventory system. Analysis techniques vary, but in this case she studied written records and used interviews and questionnaires to analyze the system. Her analysis uncovered several problems: a lack of information about inventory supplies; a tendency for stock to be reordered only when the shelf was empty; and, finally, no way to correlate order quantities with past sales records, future projections, or inventory situations. The system needed improvement; that called for systems design.

Systems Design

The process of developing a plan for an improved system, based on the results of systems analysis, is called systems design. In the Pacific Sound example, Ms. Mele, working with the users, planned a new system that featured personal computers in the individual stores. The personal computers were hooked together in a network and could communicate with each other and the headquarters computer. Information about inventory could now be collected in each store. Information about oversupply could be shared with the other stores but, more important, the reordering process could begin before the shelves were empty.

The Pacific Sound example is greatly oversimplified, but it does demonstrate two important points: (1) the old system must be analyzed before a new system can be designed, and (2) users of the system must be involved in both analysis and design.

The User Role

The systems analyst fills the role of **change agent.** That is, even though the initial idea may come from the boss, the analyst is the catalyst who overcomes the natural inertia and reluctance to change within an organization. The key to the analyst's success is involving the people of the client organization in the development of the new system. The common industry phrase is **user involvement,** and nothing could be more important to the success of a system. The finest system in the world will not suffice if users do not perceive it as useful. From your point of view, as a user, it is to your advantage to work with the systems analyst to make the system what you want it to be. Keep in mind that you know the subject matter intimately because you work with it on a daily basis. The systems analyst knows the technical end, but not how your business or department works. That is, the system analyst depends heavily on the user to supply information and to help design a new system that meets user needs.

▲   ▲   ▲

Someone once remarked, somewhat facetiously, that all top management—presidents, chief executive officers, and so forth—should be drawn from the ranks of computer specialists. After all, the argument went, computers pervade the entire company, and people who work with computer systems can bring broad experience to any job. Today, most presidents and CEOs still come from legal, financial, or marketing backgrounds. But as the computer industry and its professionals mature, that pattern could change.

CHAPTER REVIEW

SUMMARY AND KEY TERMS

- Some businesses in which personal computers are used include retailing, finance, insurance, real estate, health care, education, government, legal services, sports, politics, publishing, transportation, manufacturing, agriculture, and construction.

- The evolution of personal computers seems to fall into three phases: transformations of individuals, departments, and businesses.

- Personal computers will radically alter the business world for two reasons: (1) Computers are now cost-effective at a level affordable to most businesses, and (2) few businesses without computers can provide the levels of service their computerized competitors provide.

- Many workers must know how to use a personal computer to perform some part of a job. Today, if a job requires a personal computer, it is likely that the worker will receive some on-the-job training.

- By providing timely access to data, computers let us spend less time getting information and more time using it.

- An **information system (IS)** is a set of business systems, usually with at least one computer among its components, designed to provide information for decision making.

- The **information systems manager,** a person familiar with both computer technology and the organization's business, runs the Information Systems Department.

- Personal computer acquisition policies may include establishing standards for hardware and software, limiting the number of vendors, and limiting the hardware and software that the Information Systems Department will support.

- An **information center** typically offers employees classes on a variety of computer topics, advice on selecting software, help in getting data from corporate computer systems, and technical assistance on such matters as hardware purchases and requests to the Information Systems Department.

- The main concerns of a **personal computer manager,** also known as the **micro-computer manager,** are (1) avoiding technology overload, (2) monitoring all the expenses connected with personal computers, (3) being aware of potential data security problems when users download data from the corporate mainframe to their own personal computers, and (4) setting guidelines for personal computer use to combat user-abusers.

- As soon as a personal computer becomes part of a network, it is part of a **system,** an organized set of related components established to accomplish certain tasks. A **computer system** is a system that has one or more computers as components.

- A **systems analyst** studies existing systems and plans new, improved systems. **Systems analysis** is the process of studying an existing system to determine how it works and how it meets user needs; **systems design** is the process of planning the new system.

- The **client** is the person or organization contracting to have a system modified or created. The **users** are people who will have contact with the system, usually employees and customers of the client organization. For instance, in a college registration system, the client is the administration and the users are the school employees and the students.
- The systems analyst fills the role of **change agent,** the catalyst who overcomes reluctance to change within an organization. The key to system success is **user involvement.**

SELF-TEST

True/False

T F   1. A systems analyst is trained to design and then analyze systems.

T F   2. The information systems manager and the personal computer manager are usually the same person.

T F   3. In an organization, a client and a user could be the same person but usually are not.

T F   4. There are no security risks when data is downloaded.

T F   5. An information center function is to do users' work for them when they get overloaded.

T F   6. A computer system is a system that has one or more computers as components.

T F   7. In the future, most workers will not have to use computers on the job.

T F   8. In business, personal computers are usually found only in formal office environments.

T F   9. A systems analyst, sometimes called a change agent, overcomes an organization's reluctance to change.

T F 10. To be cooperative, a user should let the systems analyst decide how a new system should work.

Matching

_____ 1. download

_____ 2. PC manager

_____ 3. information center

_____ 4. user involvement

_____ 5. systems design

_____ 6. systems analysis

_____ 7. IS manager

_____ 8. systems analyst

_____ 9. system users

_____ 10. laptop

a. planning a new system

b. manages IS department

c. employees, customers

d. provides help for computer users

e. users help plan new system

f. send data from mainframe to personal computer

g. manages company personal computers

h. for on the road

i. studying an existing system

j. change agent

Fill-In

1. An organized set of components to accomplish a task:

   _____

2. Person or organization contracting to have a system created or modified:

   _____

3. To retrieve data from a mainframe and send it to a personal computer:

   _____

4. A set of business systems, usually with computers as components:

   _____

5. Computer abusers on the job are sometimes called:

   _____

6. A person who analyzes and designs systems: _____

7. A portable computer for the portable worker: _____

8. Studying an existing system with an eye to improving it:

   _____

9. The individual who monitors expenses of company personal computers:

   _____

10. Planning a new computer system: _____

Answers

True/False: 1. F, 3. T, 5. F, 7. F, 9. T

Matching: 1. f, 3. d, 5. a, 7. b, 9. c

Fill-In: 1. system, 3. download, 5. computer junkies, 7. laptop, 9. personal computer manager

CHAPTER 10

OVERVIEW

VIRUS

SECURITY, PRIVACY, AND ETHICS

PROTECTING HARDWARE, SOFTWARE, AND DATA

eslie Danner was electronic mail manager for Catalina Communications, a large telephone services company. Each Catalina staff member had a personal computer, which was linked to the corporate mainframe. Employees used electronic mail for nearly all their inter-office memos and for sharing documents. Leslie kept the mail running smoothly, helping users transfer files between their personal computers and the mainframe.

One afternoon Leslie's supervisor asked her to accompany him to the corporate board-room, where the three highest-ranking company executives were waiting. They swore Leslie to secrecy and gravely told her that the company's business plan for the next year had been leaked to the competition. It was an inside job, they assumed—and they wanted Leslie to search for evidence through the electronic mailboxes of all the employees. Struck by the executives' concern, she immediately agreed.

As she began to look at the archive of mail messages stored on the mainframe, however, she began to have second thoughts. She imagined how she would feel if another employee were sifting through her own e-mail. She realized that employees throughout the company presumed their e-mail was private. But the more "private" mail she read, the more Leslie began to feel that what she was doing was wrong. Leslie phoned a lawyer-friend and asked her opinion. Because the computer was

company-owned, the lawyer reasoned, all information on it belonged to the company. Legally then, given the permission of her bosses, Leslie was justified in searching through the files. Ethically, however, Leslie's friend agreed that there was reason for concern.

Leslie was in a dilemma. She was expected to snoop, but her instincts opposed snooping. She decided to ask her supervisor for advice. After hearing her out, he agreed that someone inside the company was not the appropriate person for the job. Knowing "secrets" about people she worked with could make Leslie regard her coworkers differently and give her an unfair advantage in business situations. They decided to hire a bonded private investigator to scan the e-mail archives.

As it turned out, no evidence was ever found in the archives and, under the terms of his contract, the detective revealed nothing else of what he had learned. Soon after the detective had finished, Leslie was assigned to draft policies concerning the e-mail system. She was sure to tell all the system's users exactly how much privacy they could expect and when the company felt it had the right to intrude. ❏

COMPUTER CRIME

• • • • • • • • • • • • • • • • • •

It was 5 o'clock in the morning and 14-year-old Randy Miller was startled to see a man climbing in his bedroom window. "FBI," the man announced, "and that computer is mine." So ended the computer caper in San Diego, where 23 teenagers, ages 13 to 17, had used their home computers to invade systems as far away as Massachusetts. The teenagers are **hackers,** people who gain access to computer systems illegally, usually from a personal computer, via a data communications network.

In this case, the hackers did not use the system to steal money or property. But they did change system passwords, preventing legitimate access to the computer accounts. They also created fictitious accounts and destroyed or changed some data files. The FBI's entry through the window was calculated—they figured that, given even a moment's warning, the teenagers were clever enough to warn each other via computer.

This story—except for the name—is true. Hacker stories make fascinating reading, but hackers are only a small fraction of the security problem. The most serious losses are caused by electronic pickpockets who are usually a good deal older and not half so harmless. Consider the following examples:

- A Denver brokerage clerk sat at his terminal and, with a few taps of the keys, transformed 1700 shares of his own stock worth $1.50 each to the same number of shares in another company worth ten times that much.

- A Seattle bank employee used her electronic funds transfer code to move certain bank funds to an account held by her boyfriend as a "joke"; both the money and the boyfriend disappeared.

- In an Oakland department store, a keyboard operator changed some delivery addresses to divert several thousand dollars worth of store goods into the hands of accomplices.

- A ticket clerk at the Arizona Veteran's Memorial Coliseum issued full-price basketball tickets, then used her computer to record the sales as half-price tickets and pocketed the difference.

These stories point out that computer crime is not always the flashy, front-page news about geniuses getting away with millions of dollars.

The problems of computer crime have been aggravated in recent years by increased access to computers (Figure 10-1). More employees now have access to computers in their jobs. In fact, computer crime is just white-collar crime with a new medium: Every time an employee is trained on the computer at work, he or she also gains knowledge that could be used to harm the company.

What motivates the computer criminal? The causes are as varied as the offenders; however, a few frequent motives have been identified. A computer criminal is often a disgruntled employee, possibly a long-time, loyal worker out for revenge after being passed over for a raise or promotion. In another scenario, an otherwise model employee may commit a crime while suffering from personal or family problems. Not

Disgruntled or militant employee could
- Sabotage equipment or programs
- Hold data or programs hostage

Competitor could
- Sabotage operations
- Engage in espionage
- Steal data or programs
- Photograph records, documentation, or CRT screen displays

Data control worker could
- Insert data
- Delete data
- Bypass controls
- Sell information

Clerk/supervisor could
- Forge or falsify data
- Embezzle funds
- Engage in collusion with people inside or outside the company

System user could
- Sell data to competitors
- Obtain unauthorized information

Operator could
- Copy files
- Destroy files

User requesting reports could
- Sell information to competitors
- **Receive unauthorized information**

Engineer could
- Install "bugs"
- Sabotage system
- Access security information

Data conversion worker could
- Change codes
- Insert data
- Delete data

Programmer could
- Steal programs or data
- Embezzle via programming
- Bypass controls

Report distribution worker could
- Examine confidential reports
- Keep duplicates of reports

Trash collector could
- Sell reports or duplicates to competitors

▲
Figure 10-1   The perils of increased access.
By letting your imagination run wild, you can visualize numerous ways in which people can compromise computer security. Computer-related crime would be far more rampant if all the people in these positions took advantage of their access to computers.

A GLOSSARY OF COMPUTER CRIME

Although the emphasis in this chapter is on preventing rather than committing crime, it is worthwhile being familiar with computer criminal terms and methods. Many of these words or phrases have made their way into the general vocabulary.

Data diddling: Changing data before or as it enters the system.

Data leakage: Obtaining copies of data from the system—without leaving a trace.

Logic bomb technique: Sabotaging a program by setting up a trigger that is activated by certain conditions—usually at a later date, perhaps after the perpetrator has left the company.

Piggybacking: Using another person's identification code or using that person's files before he or she has logged off.

Salami technique: Using a large financial system to embezzle small "slices" of money that may never be missed.

Scavenging: Searching trash cans for printouts and carbons containing not-for-distribution information.

Trapdoor technique: Leaving illicit instructions within a completed program; the instructions allow unauthorized—and undetected—entry.

Trojan horse: Tricking a user into running a destructive program by giving it the name of a trusted program.

Zapping: Bypassing all security systems with an illicitly acquired software package.

---

all motives are emotionally based, however. Some people are simply attracted to the challenge of the crime. In contrast, it is the ease of the crime that tempts others. In many cases the criminal activity is unobtrusive; it fits right in with regular job duties. The risk of detection is often quite low. Computer criminals think they can get away with it. And they do—some of the time.

Types and Methods of Computer Crime

Computer crime falls into three basic categories:

- Theft of computer time, either for personal use or with the intention of making a profit. Miscreants may, for example, perform computer tasks for outside clients, work on personal projects such as a hobby club budget or newsletter, or even write software for personal profit.
- Theft, destruction, or manipulation of programs or data.
- Alteration of data stored in a computer file.

Though it is not our purpose to be a how-to book on computer crime, the margin note called "A Glossary of Computer Crime" mentions some criminal methods as examples.

Discovery and Prosecution

Prosecuting the computer criminal is difficult because discovery is often difficult. Most computer crimes simply go undetected, and those that are detected are usually discovered by accident. Furthermore, an estimated 85% of the time, crimes that are detected are never reported to the authorities. By law, banks have to make a report when their computer systems have been compromised, but other businesses do not. Often they choose not to report because they are worried about their reputations and credibility in the community.

Even if a computer crime is detected, a prosecution is by no means assured. There are a number of reasons for this. First, some law enforcement agencies do not fully understand the complexities of computer-related fraud. Second, few attorneys are qualified to handle computer crime cases. Third, judges and juries are not educated in the ways of computers and may not understand the value of data to a company.

This situation is changing, however. In 1986 Congress passed the latest version of the **Computer Fraud and Abuse Act** to fight the problem on the national level. Furthermore, most states have passed some form of computer crime law. The number of safe places for computer desperados is dwindling fast.

SECURITY: KEEPING EVERYTHING SAFE

As you can see from the previous section, the computer industry has been extremely vulnerable in the matter of security. Computer security once meant the physical security of the computer itself—guarded and locked doors. But locking up the computer by no means prevents access, as we have seen.

What is security? We may define it as follows: **Security** is a system of safeguards designed to protect a computer system and data from deliberate or accidental damage or access by unauthorized persons. That means safeguarding the system against such threats as burglary, vandalism, fire, natural disasters, theft of data for ransom, industrial espionage, and various forms of white-collar crime.

Who Goes There? Identification and Access

How does a computer system detect whether you are a person who should be allowed access to it? Various means have been devised to give access to authorized people, without compromising the system. The means fall into four broad categories: what you have, what you know, what you do, and who you are.

- **What you have.** You may have a key or a badge or a plastic card to give you physical access to the computer room or a locked-up terminal. A card with a magnetized strip, for example, can give you access to your bank account via an automated teller machine.

- **What you know.** Standard what-you-know items are a system password or an identification number for your bank cash machine. Cipher or combination locks on doors require that you know the correct combination of numbers.

- **What you do.** Your signature is difficult but not impossible to copy. Signature-access systems are better suited to human interaction than machine interaction, however.

- **What you are.** Now it gets interesting. Some security systems use **biometrics,** the science of measuring individual body characteristics. Fingerprinting is old news, but voice recognition is relatively new. Even newer is the concept of identification by the retina of the eye, which has a pattern that is harder to duplicate than a voiceprint (Figure 10-2).

Some systems use a combination of the preceding four categories. For example, access to an automated teller machine requires both something you have—a plastic card—and something you know—a personal identification number (PIN).

When Disaster Strikes: What Do You Have to Lose?

In California, a poem, a pansy, a bag of Mrs. Field's cookies, and a message, "Please have a cookie and a nice day" were left at the Vandenberg Air Force Base computer installation—along with five demolished mainframe computers. Computer installations of any kind can be struck by natural or man-made disasters that can lead to security violations. What kinds of problems might this cause an organization?

Your first thoughts might be of the hardware, the computer and its related equipment. But loss of hardware is not a major problem in itself; the loss will be covered by insurance, and hardware can be replaced. The true problem with hardware loss is the diminished pro-

▲

Figure 10-2   Identification by retina.
The eye can be a means of personal identification. The security system shown here uses a person's unique retinal pattern to identify authorized system users.

cessing ability that exists while managers find a substitute facility and return the installation to its former state. The ability to continue processing data is critical. Some information industries, such as banking, could literally go out of business in a matter of days if their data processing operations were suspended.

Loss of software should not be a problem if the organization has heeded industry warnings—and used common sense—to make backup copies. A more important problem is the loss of data. Imagine trying to reassemble lost or destroyed master files of customer records, accounts receivable, or design data for a new airplane. The costs would be staggering. We will consider software and data security in more detail later in this chapter. First, however, let us present an overview of disaster recovery, the steps to restoring processing ability.

Disaster Recovery Plan

A **disaster recovery plan** is a method of restoring data processing operations if those operations are halted by major damage or destruction. There are various approaches. Some organizations revert temporarily to manual services, but life without the computer can be difficult indeed. Others arrange to buy time at a service bureau, but this may be inconvenient for companies in remote or rural areas. If a single act, such as a fire, destroys your computing facility, it is possible that a mutual aid pact will help you get back on your feet. In such a plan, two or more companies agree to lend each other computing power if one of them has a problem. This would be of little help, however, if there were a regional disaster and many companies needed assistance.

Banks and other organizations with survival dependence on computers sometimes form a **consortium,** a joint venture to support a complete computer facility. Such a facility is completely available and routinely tested but used only in the event of a disaster.

Computer installations regularly practice emergency drills. At some unexpected moment a notice is given that "disaster has struck," and the computer professionals must run the critical systems at some other site.

Software Security

Software security has been an industry concern for years. Initially, there were many questions. Who owns a program? Is the owner the person who writes a program or the company for which the author wrote the program? What is to prevent a programmer from taking copies of programs from one job to another? Or, even simpler, what is to prevent any user from copying personal computer software onto another diskette?

Many of these perplexing questions have since been answered. If a programmer is in the employ of an organization, the program belongs to the organization, not the programmer. If the programmer is a consultant, however, the ownership of the software produced should be spelled out specifically in the contract—otherwise, the parties enter extremely murky legal waters.

According to a U.S. Supreme Court decision, software can be patented. However, very little can be done to prevent the stealing of personal computer software. Although it is specifically prohibited by law, software continues to be copied as blatantly as music or video tapes. We will examine this issue more closely when we consider ethics later in the chapter.

Data Security

We have discussed the security of hardware and software. Now let us consider the security of data, one of an organization's most important assets. As we have noted before, the most important step in caring for files is to make backup copies of them. Large, medium, and even small organizations have procedures in place to make sure that copies of files are made on a regular basis. Users of personal computers tend not to be as reliable as mainframe users in regard to this issue, but they too are urged to back up their files.

In addition to the possible loss of data, there are problems related to its safety. What steps can be taken to prevent theft or alteration of data? Several data protection techniques are in common use; these will not individually (or even collectively) guarantee security, but at least they make a good start.

Secured Waste
Discarded printouts, printer ribbons, and the like can be sources of information to unauthorized persons. This kind of waste can be made secure by the use of shredders or locked trash barrels.

Passwords
Passwords are the secret words or numbers that must be typed on the keyboard to gain access to the system. In some installations, however, the passwords are changed so seldom that they become known to many people. Good data protection systems change passwords often and also compartmentalize information by passwords, so that only authorized persons can have access to certain data.

Internal Controls
Internal controls are controls that are planned as part of the computer system. One example is a transaction log. This is a file of all accesses or attempted accesses to certain data.

Auditor Checks
Most companies have auditors go over the financial books. In the course of an audit, auditors with special training may also review computer programs and data. From a data security standpoint, for example, auditors might check to see who has accessed data during periods when that data is not usually used. They may also be on the lookout for unusual numbers of data correction entries, usually a trouble sign. What is more, the availability of off-the-shelf audit software— programs that assess the validity and accuracy of a system's operations and output—promotes tighter security because it allows auditors to work independently of the programming staff.

Cryptography
Data being sent over communications lines may be protected by scrambling the messages—that is, putting them in code that can be broken only by the person receiving the message. The process of scrambling messages is called **encryption.** The American National

PERSONAL COMPUTERS IN ACTION

Your Own Security Checklist

With the subject of security fresh in your mind, now is a good time to consider a checklist for your own home computer and its software:

- Do not eat, drink, or smoke near the computer.
- Do not place the computer near open windows or doors.
- Do not subject the computer to extreme temperatures.
- Clean equipment regularly.
- Place a cable lock on the computer.
- Use a surge protector.
- Store disks properly in a locked container.
- Maintain backup copies of all files.
- Store copies of critical files off site.

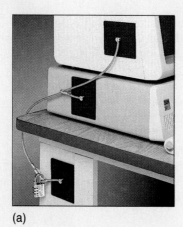

(a)

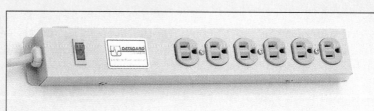

(b)

Security devices.
(a) Locking up your computer can help minimize theft. (b) A surge protector can protect your computer system and files from unpredictable electrical problems.

Standards Institute has endorsed a process called **Data Encryption Standard (DES),** a standardized public key that senders and receivers can use to scramble and unscramble their messages. Although the DES code has been broken, companies still use it because the method makes it quite expensive to intercept coded messages, forcing interlopers to use methods of gathering data that carry a greater risk of detection. Encryption software is available for personal computers. A typical package, for example, offers a variety of security features: file encryption, keyboard lock, and password protection.

Applicant Screening

The weakest link in any computer security system is the people in it. At the very least, employers should verify the facts that job applicants list on their resumes, to help weed out potentially dishonest applicants before they are hired.

Security Considerations for Personal Computers

One summer evening two men in coveralls with company logos backed a truck up to the building that housed a university computer lab. They showed the lab assistant, a part-time student, authorization to move 23 personal computers to another lab on campus. The assistant was surprised but not shocked, since lab use was light in the summer quarter. The computers were moved, all right, but not to another lab. There is an active market for stolen personal computers and their internal components. As this unfortunate tale indicates, personal computer security breaches can be pretty basic. One simple, though not foolproof, remedy is to lock personal computer hardware to the desk or table it sits on.

In addition to theft, personal computer users need to be concerned about the computer's environment. Personal computers in business are not coddled the way bigger computers are. They are designed, in fact, to withstand the wear and tear of the office environment, including temperatures set for the comfort of people. Most manufacturers discourage eating and smoking near computers and recommend some specific cleaning techniques, such as vacuuming the keyboard and cleaning the disk drive heads with a mild solution. The enforcement of these rules is directly related to the awareness level of the users.

Personal computer data is often stored on diskettes, which are vulnerable to theft and to damage from sunlight, heaters, cigarettes, abrasion, magnets, and dirty fingers. The data, consequently, is vulnerable as well. Hard disk drives used with personal computers are subject to special security problems too. If a computer with a hard disk is used by more than one person, your files on the hard disk may be available for anyone to access.

There are several precautions that can be taken to protect disk data. One is to use a **surge protector,** a device that prevents electrical problems from affecting data files. The computer is plugged into the surge protector, which is plugged into the outlet. Making backups is another security measure. As we noted earlier, all files should be backed up regularly to protect data. Hard disk files should be backed up onto diskettes or tape. Diskettes should be kept under lock and key.

Awareness of personal computer security needs is gradually rising. However, security measures and the money to implement them are directly related to the amount of the expected loss. Since the dollar value of personal computer losses is often relatively low in comparison to mainframe losses, personal computer security may be less than vigorous.

Worms and Viruses

These unpleasant little terms have entered the jargon of the computer industry to describe some of the bad things that can happen to computer systems and programs. A **worm** is a program that transfers itself from computer to computer over a network and plants itself as a separate file on the target computer's disks. One newsworthy worm, originated by a student at Cornell University, traveled the length and breadth of the land through an electronic mail network, shutting down thousands of computers. The worm was injected into the network and multiplied uncontrollably, clogging the memories of infected computers until they could no longer function.

A **virus,** as its name suggests, is contagious. That is, a virus, a set of illicit instructions, passes itself on to other programs with which it comes in contact. Figure 10-3 shows how one virus is transmitted and the result of the infection.

SOME GENTLE ADVICE ON SECURITY

Being a security expert is an unusual job because, once the planning is done, there is not a lot to do except wait for something bad to happen. Security experts are often consultants who move from company to company. Their advice often includes long and detailed checklists: Do this, do that, and you will be OK. We cannot include such a long set of lists, but here is a brief subset that includes some of the most effective approaches.

Beware of disgruntled employees. Ed Street was angry. Seething. How could they pass over him for a promotion again? Well, if they were not going to give him what he deserved, he would take it himself. . . . Ah, the tale is too common. Be forewarned.

Sensitize employees to security issues. Most people are eager to help others. They must be taught that some kinds of help, such as assisting unauthorized users with passwords, are inappropriate.

Call back all remote-access terminals. Don't call us, we'll call you. If, before your system accepts a call, it must check a list of phone numbers to ensure that the caller has valid access, you eliminate most intruders. In such an arrangement your computer has to call the caller back for the user to gain remote access, and your computer will do so only if the user's number is valid. The fact that the caller has your computer's phone number is irrelevant. What matters is does the computer have the caller's number?

Keep personnel privileges up to date. And, we might add, make sure they are enforced properly. Some of the biggest heists have been pulled by people who *formerly* had legitimate access to secured areas. In many cases, they can still get in because the guard has known them by sight for years.

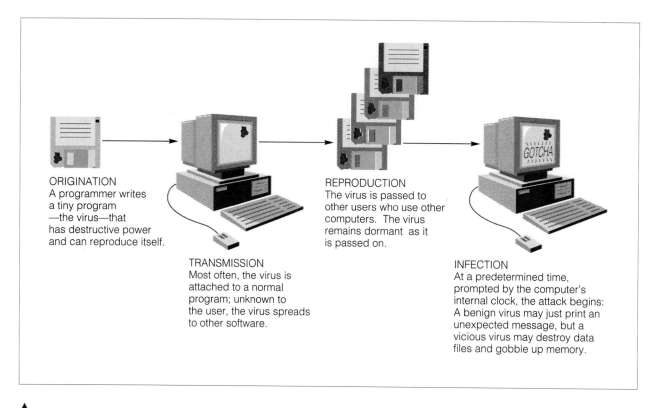

ORIGINATION
A programmer writes
a tiny program
—the virus—that
has destructive power
and can reproduce itself.

TRANSMISSION
Most often, the virus is
attached to a normal
program; unknown to
the user, the virus spreads
to other software.

REPRODUCTION
The virus is passed to
other users who use other
computers. The virus
remains dormant as it
is passed on.

INFECTION
At a predetermined time,
prompted by the computer's
internal clock, the attack begins:
A benign virus may just print an
unexpected message, but a
vicious virus may destroy data
files and gobble up memory.

▲
Figure 10-3   An example of a virus invasion.

Transmitting a Virus

Consider this typical example. A programmer secretly inserts a few unauthorized instructions in a personal computer operating system program. The illicit instructions lie dormant until these events occur together: (1) the disk with the infected operating system is in use; (2) a disk in another drive contains another copy of the operating system and some data files; and (3) a command, such as COPY or DIR, from the infected operating system references a data file. Under these circumstances, the virus instructions are now inserted into the other operating system. Thus the virus has spread to another disk, and the process can be repeated again and again. In fact, each newly infected disk becomes a virus carrier.

Damage from Viruses

We have explained how the virus is transmitted; now we come to the interesting part—the consequences. In this example, the virus instructions add 1 to a counter each time the virus is copied to another disk. When the counter reaches 4, the virus erases all data files. But this is not the end of the destruction, of course; three other disks have also been infected. Although viruses can be destructive, some are quite benign; one simply displayed a peace message on the screen on a given date.

Prevention

A word about prevention is in order. Although there are programs, called vaccines, that can prevent virus activity, protecting your computer from viruses depends more on common sense than on building a "fortress" around the computer. Although there have been isolated instances of viruses in commercial software, viruses tend to show up on free software acquired from friends or through electronic bulletin board systems. Test all such gifts by putting write protection on other disks, often accomplished by simply sliding the diskette's write-protect button into place. If an attempt is made to write on the protected disk, a warning message appears on the screen. In fact, it is wise to put write protection on all files that do not need to have data written on them.

PRIVACY: KEEPING PERSONAL INFORMATION PERSONAL

Think about the forms you have willingly filled out: paperwork for loans or charge accounts, orders for merchandise through the mail, magazine subscription orders, applications for schools and jobs and clubs, and on and on. There may be some forms you filled out with less delight—for taxes, military draft registration, court petitions, insurance claims, or a stay in the hospital. And consider all the people who can get your name and address from your checks—fund-raisers, advertisers, and petitioners. We have only skimmed the possible sources of data, but we can say with certainty where all this data went: straight to a computer file.

Where is that data now? Is it passed around? Who sees it? Will it ever be expunged? Or, to put it more bluntly, is anything private anymore? In some cases we can only guess at the answers to these questions. It is difficult to say where the data is now, and bureaucracies are not usually eager to enlighten us. It may have been moved, without your knowledge, to other files. In fact, much of the data is most definitely passed around, as anyone with a mailbox can attest. As for who sees your personal data, the answers are not comforting (Figure 10-4). Government agencies, for example, regularly share data that was originally filed for some other purpose. Many people are worried about the consequences of this kind of sharing. For one thing, few of us can be certain that data about us, good or bad, is deleted when it has served its legitimate purpose.

And, finally, for very little cost, it seems that anybody can learn anything about anybody—by accessing massive databases. There are matters you want to keep private. You have the right to do so. Although there is little you can do to stop data about you from circulating through computers, there are some laws that give you access to some of it.

Significant legislation relating to privacy began with the **Fair Credit Reporting Act** in 1970. This law allows you to have access to and gives you the right to challenge the information in your credit records. In fact, this access must be given to you free of charge if you have been denied credit.

Businesses usually contribute financial information about their customers to a community credit bureau, which gives them the right to review a person's prior credit record with other companies. Before the Fair Credit Reporting Act, many people were turned down for credit,

THE TALE TAXES TELL

Perhaps you have heard about personal computer software to keep track of income taxes. It's a bit of a nuisance, keying in data from all those receipts, but the payoff at tax time is gratifying: no rummaging through shoeboxes full of tiny papers, no stacking and sorting on the dining room table. Your computer gives you orderly printouts, according to the kinds of expenses represented.

But wait. What else could be done with those files? There has been some talk about—eventually—having people use their home computers to prepare income tax data that the IRS would access directly. This becomes a privacy issue. Suppose, for example, that the expense data was arranged not by type, but by date. As an outsider scrolled through the data, he or she could easily ascertain the times you went out, where you stayed, where you ate, whom you called, the books you purchased, and so forth. A virtual diary—devastatingly revealing—would come into focus. What other use might be made of that data? This is the kind of scenario privacy advocates have been warning about for years. We are not in danger of such intrusion yet, but the possibilities are food for thought.

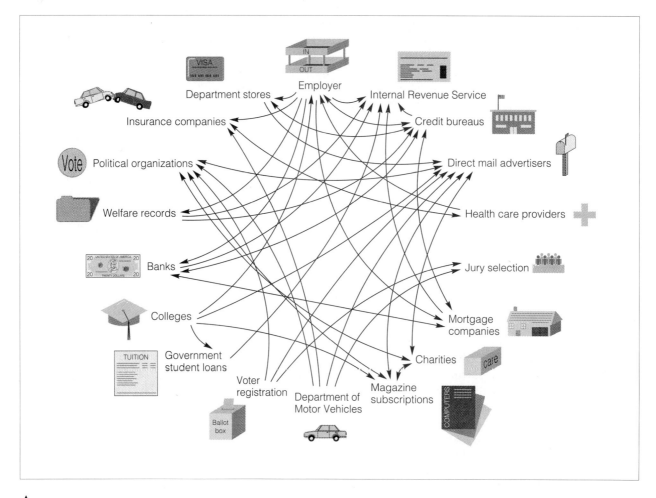

▲

Figure 10-4   Potential paths of data.
When an organization acquires information about you, it is often shared with—or sold to—other organizations.

without explanation, because of inaccurate financial records about them. Now people may check their records to make sure they are accurate. The **Freedom of Information Act** was also passed in 1970. This landmark legislation allows ordinary citizens to have access to data about them that was gathered by federal agencies (although sometimes a lawsuit has been necessary to pry data loose).

The most significant legislation protecting the privacy of individuals is the **Federal Privacy Act** of 1974. This act stipulates that there can be no secret personal files; individuals must be allowed to know what is stored in files about them, to know how the information is used, and to be able to correct it. The law applies not only to government agencies, but also to private contractors dealing with government agencies. These organizations cannot obtain data willy-nilly, for no specific purpose; they must justify obtaining it.

A more recent law is the **Video Privacy Protection Act** of 1988, which prevents retailers from disclosing a person's video rental records without a court order; privacy supporters want the same rule for medical and insurance files. Another step in that direction is the **Computer Matching and Privacy Protection Act** of 1988, which prevents the government from comparing certain records in an attempt to find a matchup. However, most comparisons are still unregulated. For example, the government routinely compares IRS records with draft registration records to catch those who have failed to register.

A MATTER OF ETHICS

The fact that professional computer personnel have access to files has always presented the potential for problems. In theory, those with access could do something as simple as snooping into a friend's salary on a payroll file or as complex as selling military secrets to foreign countries. But the problem has become more tangled as everyday people—not just computer professionals—have daily computer contact. They too have access to files. Many of those files are on diskettes and may be handled in a careless manner. As we noted earlier, data is the resource most difficult to replace, so increased access is the subject of much concern among security officers.

Where do you come in? As a student you could easily face ethical problems involving access and much more. Try some of these. A non-student friend wants to borrow your password to get access to the school computer. Or you know of a student who has bypassed computer security and changed grades for himself and some friends. Perhaps a "computer jock" pal collects software and wants you to copy a software disk used in one of your classes. And so on.

The problems are not so different in the business world. You will recognize that, whether you are a computer professional or a user, you have a clear responsibility to your own organization and its customers to protect the security and privacy of their information. Any compromise of data, in particular, is considered a serious breach of ethics. Many corporations have formal statements saying as much and present them to employees individually for their signatures.

COPYING SOFTWARE

Let us move from general ethical principles to a very individual problem: copying software. Have you ever copied a friend's music CD or tape onto your own blank tape? Many people do so without much thought. It is also possible to photocopy a book. Both acts are clearly illegal, but there is much more fuss over individual illegal software copying than over copying music or books. Why is this? Well, to begin with, few of us are likely to undertake the laborious task of reproducing *War and Peace* on a copy machine. The other part of the issue is money. A pirated copy of a top-20 tape will set the recording company and the artist back about $10. But pirated software may be valued at hundreds of dollars. The problem of stolen software has grown right along with the personal computer industry. Before we discuss industry solutions, we must distinguish among various kinds of software, based on its availability to the public.

OK If I Copy That Software?

Some software will not cost you a penny because it is free to all. Some such software is free because its generous maker, probably an individ-

COMPUTING HIGHLIGHTS

It's All Right to Be Just a Little Paranoid

Once you understand the relationship between computers and your name, it seems reasonable to be concerned. There is no place to hide in a computer society. Consider:

- Computers perform the equivalent of 100,000 calculations each second for every man, woman, and child in the United States.
- Your name pops up in some computer approximately 40 times a day.

- The National Security Administration eavesdrops 24 hours a day, seven days a week, on all overseas phone calls.
- Much of the data stored about you by banks and retailers is vulnerable to unauthorized access.
- Private companies and government agencies increasingly use powerful systems to link and compare different databases, including IRS files, credit ratings,

criminal records, bank records, telephone-call records, medical records, and records of drugs purchased at pharmacies.

- There are more than 2000 information retrieval services in the United States, each of which sells data gathered from various sources—often right off government computers.

ual at home or an educator, chooses to make it free. A variation on this theme is **shareware,** which is also given away free. However, the shareware maker hopes for voluntary monetary compensation—that is, the author requests that, if you like it, you send a contribution. Both completely free software and shareware may be copied freely and given to other people. However, the software that people use most often, such as a word processing or spreadsheet package, is **licensed software,** software that costs money and must not be copied without permission from the manufacturer.

Making illegal copies of licensed software is called **software piracy.** It is considered stealing because software makers do not get the revenues to which they are entitled. Furthermore, if software developers are not properly compensated, they may not find it worthwhile to develop new software for our use.

Why Those Extra Copies?

Copying software is not always illegal—there are lots of legitimate reasons for copying. To begin with, after paying several hundred dollars for a piece of software, you will definitely want to make a backup copy in case of disk failure or accident. You might want to copy the program onto a hard disk and use it—more conveniently—from there. Or, you might want to have one copy at the office and another to use at home. Software publishers have no trouble with any of these types of copying. But thousands of computer users copy software for another reason: to get the program without paying for it. And therein lies the problem.

Software publishers first tried to solve the problem by placing **copy protection** on their software—a software or hardware roadblock to make it difficult or impossible to make pirated copies. In effect, these devices punish the innocent with the guilty. There was vigorous opposition from software users, who argued that it was unfair to restrict paying customers just to outsmart a few thieves. Most software vendors have now dropped copy protection from their software, but they are still vigilant about illegal copies. Vendors have taken imaginative approaches to protecting their products and, at the same time, keeping customers happy.

Licensing Big Customers

An approach favored by some software makers is site licensing. Although there is no clear definition industrywide, in general a **site license** permits a customer to make multiple copies of a given piece of software. The customer needing all these copies is usually a corporation, which can probably obtain a significant price discount for volume buying. The exact nature of the arrangement between the user and the software maker can vary considerably. Typically, however, a customer obtains the right to make an unlimited number of copies of a product, agrees to keep track of who uses it, and takes responsibility for copying and distributing manuals to its own personnel.

Some software makers, however, oppose site licensing; they do not want to be bogged down in licensing negotiations. Industry leaders Microsoft Corporation and the Lotus Development Corporation favor **concurrent licensing,** a system that charges based on the number of users at a given time or perhaps at peak periods. Suppose, for example, that 20 users are on a network, but a maximum of 10 would be using Lotus at a given time. The company could pay for just ten copies of the software. However, once ten of the users are using the software at a given moment, an eleventh potential user is locked out.

▲ ▲ ▲

The issues raised in this chapter are often the ones we think of after the fact—that is, when it is too late. The security and privacy factors are somewhat like insurance that we wish we did not have to buy. But we do buy insurance for our homes and cars and lives because we know we cannot risk being without it. The computer industry also knows that it cannot risk being without safeguards for security and privacy. As a computer user, in whatever capacity, you can take comfort in the fact that the computer industry recognizes their importance.

Chapter Review

Summary and Key Terms

- A **hacker** is a person who gains access to computer systems illegally.
- Three basic categories of computer crime are (1) theft of computer time for development of software; (2) theft, destruction, or manipulation of programs or data; and (3) alteration of data stored in a computer file.
- In 1984 Congress passed the **Computer Fraud and Abuse Act,** which is supplemented by local laws in most of the states.
- **Security** is a system of safeguards designed to protect a computer system and data from deliberate or accidental damage or access by unauthorized persons.
- The means of giving access to authorized people are divided into four general categories: (1) what you have (a key, badge, or plastic card), (2) what you know (a system password or identification number), (3) what you do (by signing your name), and (4) what you are (by making use of **biometrics,** the science of measuring individual body characteristics such as fingerprints, voice, or retina).
- A **disaster recovery plan** is a method of restoring data processing operations if they are halted by major damage or destruction. Common approaches to disaster recovery include relying temporarily on manual services; buying time at a computer service bureau; making mutual assistance agreements with other companies; or forming a **consortium,** a joint venture with other organizations to support a complete computer facility.
- Common means of protecting data are securing waste, passwords, internal controls, auditor checks, cryptography, and applicant screening.
- Data sent over communications lines can be protected by **encryption,** the process of scrambling messages. The American National Standards Institute has endorsed a process called **Data Encryption Standard (DES).**
- Personal computer security includes such measures as locking hardware in place; providing an appropriate physical environment; and using a **surge protector.**
- A **worm** is a program that transfers itself from computer to computer over a network, planting itself as a separate file on the target computer's disks. A **virus** is a set of illicit instructions that passes itself on to other programs with which it comes in contact.
- The security issue also extends to the use of information about individuals that is stored in the computer files of credit bureaus and government agencies. The **Fair Credit Reporting Act** allows individuals to check the accuracy of credit information about them. The **Freedom of Information Act** allows people access to data that federal agencies have gathered about them. The **Federal Privacy Act** allows individuals access to information about them that is held not only by government agencies but also by private contractors working for the government. Individuals are also entitled to know how that information is being used. Other recent laws supporting privacy are the **Video Privacy Protection Act,** which prohibits retailers from disclosing a customer's video rental records, and the **Computer Matching and Privacy Protection Act,** which regulates comparison of records held by different branches of government.

- Some software is free because its maker, usually an individual at home or an educator, chooses to make it free. **Shareware** software is also free, but the maker hopes for voluntary monetary compensation. **Licensed software** costs money and must not be copied without permission from the manufacturer. Making illegal copies of copyrighted software is called **software piracy.** Many software publishers offer a **site license,** which permits a customer to make multiple copies of a given piece of software. **Concurrent licensing** allows a customer to use only a limited number of copies of a software product simultaneously.

SELF-TEST

True/False

T F 1. One category of computer crime is alteration of stored data.

T F 2. Computer security is achieved by physically restricting access.

T F 3. The loss of hardware is the most serious potential security problem.

T F 4. A disaster recovery plan is a scheme devised in anticipation of major software piracy.

T F 5. It is legitimate to make a copy of software for backup.

T F 6. Software can be patented.

Matching

_____ 1. access through knowing
_____ 2. consortium
_____ 3. virus
_____ 4. secured waste
_____ 5. free software
_____ 6. security

a. contagious
b. legally copyable
c. system of safeguards
d. provided by password
e. shredded
f. joint-venture computer facility

Fill-In

1. The most serious potential loss is loss of: _____

2. A system to protect a computer system and data from damage or unauthorized access: _____

3. Unauthorized copying of software is called: _____

4. Of violations of hardware, software, and data, the least damaging are:

   _____

5. Illicit instructions hidden within a completed program, allowing unauthorized entry: _____

6. A permit to make multiple copies of software, all of which can be used simultaneously: _____

Answers

True/False: 1. T, 3. F, 5. T   Matching: 1. d, 3. a, 5. b

Fill-In: 1. data, 3. software piracy, 5. trapdoor

CHAPTER 11

OVERVIEW

COMPUTERS ON THE CUTTING EDGE
ARTIFICIAL INTELLIGENCE, EXPERT SYSTEMS, AND ROBOTICS

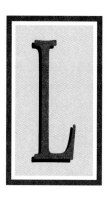

arry Northway had worked in metal fabrication for nearly 30 years. His specialty was precisely aligning crucial jet-engine components and spot-welding them together. Both he and his employers knew that the safety of thousands of airline passengers relied on the care he took each time he made a weld. Larry had heard about the coming of industrial robots. But he felt his job was secure. The welding he did required too much precision and human judgment to trust to a machine. Larry's managers, however, did not share his view. They were convinced that modern industrial robots could position metal parts more precisely than humans and that, due to the careful adjustment, their welds would be more consistently sound. The company contracted for a prototype robot-based welding system to test its theories.

To Larry's surprise and discomfort, management assigned him to work on the robot project. Because of Larry's skill, they asked him to provide the robot manufacturer's representatives with information about how the welding was done. The designers were eager to learn Larry's technique. At first, they just watched the way he worked. Then, with video cameras, they taped his movements—the way he manipulated the jigs that held the engine parts and the way he held and positioned the welder. Later, they interviewed Larry. How did he know when the parts were seated properly? What told him that the weld was complete and sound?

As predicted, it took some time to work the bugs out of the robot's computers, adjust its video-camera eyes to the right angles and exposures, and teach it to make perfect welds. But soon enough the machine was in operation and turning out products as fast as ten Larry Northways.

Happily, the robot's speed did not spell the end of Larry's employment. In fact, the robot needed his help. Whether produced by robot or human, the engine parts had to be tested. With the increased pace of production, more personnel were required to carry out the testing. Larry was the logical choice.

Although he is a little nostalgic for the old days, Larry is now the first to point out that the robot system produces consistently high-quality parts for his company's engines. Larry still takes great pride in his company's products. And he no longer flinches when his old coworkers refer to the robot by its nickname, Larry Junior. ◻

ARTIFICIAL INTELLIGENCE

• • • • • • • • • • • • • • • • •

Artificial intelligence (AI) is a field of study that explores how computers can be used for tasks that require the human characteristics of intelligence, imagination, and intuition. Computer scientists sometimes prefer a looser definition, calling AI the study of how to make computers do things that—at the present time—people can do better. The phrase "at the present time" is significant because artificial intelligence is an evolving science. As soon as a problem is solved, it is moved off the artificial intelligence agenda. A good example is the game of chess, once considered a mighty AI challenge. But now that most computer chess programs can beat most human competitors, chess is no longer an object of study by AI scientists.

Today the term *artificial intelligence* encompasses several subsets of interests (Figure 11-1):

- *Problem solving*, a field that covers a broad spectrum, from playing games to planning military strategy
- *Natural languages*, which involve a person-computer interface in unconstrained English language
- *Expert systems*, which present the computer as an expert on some particular topic
- *Robotics*, the study of endowing computer-controlled machines with machine equivalents of vision, speech, and touch

Although considerable progress has been made in these sophisticated fields of study, early successes did not come easily. Before we examine current advances in these areas, let us pause to consider some early moments in the development of artificial intelligence.

Early Mishaps

In the early days of artificial intelligence, scientists thought that the computer would experience something like an electronic childhood, in which it would gobble up the data in the world's libraries and then begin generating new wisdom. Few people talk like this today because the problem of simulating intelligence is far more complex than just stuffing facts into the computer. Facts are useless without the ability to interpret and learn from them.

One grand failure of artificial intelligence was the attempt to translate human languages via computer. Although scientists were able to pour vocabulary and rules of grammar into the machine, the literal word-for-word translations the machine produced were often ludicrous. In one infamous example, the computer was supposed to demonstrate its prowess by translating a phrase from English to Russian and then back to English. Despite the computer's best efforts, however, "The spirit is willing, but the flesh is weak" came back as "The vodka is good, but the meat is spoiled."

An unfortunate result of this widely published experiment was the ridicule of artificial intelligence scientists, who were considered dreamers who could not accept the limitations of a machine. Funding

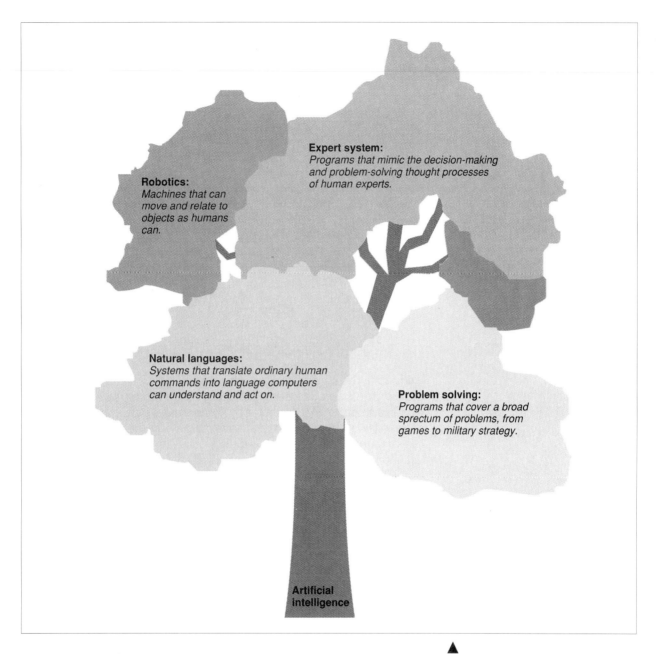

Expert system:
Programs that mimic the decision-making and problem-solving thought processes of human experts.

Robotics:
Machines that can move and relate to objects as humans can.

Natural languages:
Systems that translate ordinary human commands into language computers can understand and act on.

Problem solving:
Programs that cover a broad sprectum of problems, from games to military strategy.

Artificial intelligence

▲
Figure 11-1   The artificial intelligence family tree.

for AI research disappeared, plunging the artificial intelligence community into a slump from which it did not recover until expert systems emerged in the 1980s. Nevertheless, a hardy band of scientists continued to explore artificial intelligence, focusing on how computers learn.

How Computers Learn

The study of artificial intelligence is predicated on the computer's ability to learn—and to improve performance based on past errors. The two key elements of this process are the knowledge base and the inference engine. A **knowledge base** is a set of facts and rules about those facts. An **inference engine** accesses, selects, and interprets a set of rules. The inference engine applies the rules to the facts to make up

THE FIRST BOOK EVER WRITTEN BY A COMPUTER

The book billed as the first written by a computer comes with the unlikely title *The Policeman's Beard is Half Constructed*. As you might have guessed, the computer-author—via software named Racter—chose the name for its own book. *The Policeman's Beard* is a book of computer-generated poetry. Although most of the poems are quite daffy, the software does qualify as a sort of low-level artificial intelligence, because it does something that would normally be expected of human intelligence.

Some poems seem to show a certain flow that lends credibility. An example:

From water and from time
A visage bounds and tumbles
I seek sleep and need repose
But miss the quiet movement
Of my dreams.

The book describes the computer-generated output as "fascinating, humorous, and even aesthetically pleasing." You decide.

---

new facts—thus, the computer has learned something new. Consider this simple example:

Fact: Barbara is George's wife.
Rule: If X is Y's wife, then Y is X's husband.

The computer—the inference engine—can apply the rule to the fact and come up with a new fact: George is Barbara's husband. Although the result of this simplistic example may seem of little value, it is indeed true that the computer now knows two facts instead of just one. Rules, of course, can be much more complex and facts more plentiful, yielding more sophisticated results. In fact, artificial intelligence software is capable of searching through long chains of related facts to reach a conclusion—a new fact.

Further explanation of the precise way computers learn is beyond the scope of this book. However, we can use the learning discussion as a springboard to the question that most people ask about artificial intelligence: Can a computer really think?

The Artificial Intelligence Debate

To imitate the human mind, a machine with artificial intelligence must be able to examine a variety of facts, address multiple subjects, and devise a solution to a problem by comparing new facts to its existing storehouse of data from many fields. So far, artificial intelligence systems cannot match a person's ability to solve problems through original thought instead of familiar patterns.

There are many arguments for and against crediting computers with the ability to think. Some say, for example, that computers cannot be considered intelligent because they do not compose like Beethoven or write like Shakespeare; the rejoinder is that neither do most ordinary human musicians or writers—you do not have to be a genius to be considered intelligent.

Look at it another way. Suppose you rack your brain over a problem, and then—Aha!—the solution comes to you all at once. Now, how did you do that? You do not know, and nobody else knows either. A big part of human problem solving seems to be that jolt of recognition, that ability to see things suddenly as a whole. Experiments have shown that people rarely solve problems by using step-by-step logic, the very thing that computers do best. Most modern computers still plod through problems one step at a time. The human brain beats a computer at "Aha!" problem solving because the brain has millions of neurons working simultaneously. Now some scientists are taking that same approach with computers.

Brainpower: Neural Networks

A microprocessor chip is sometimes referred to as the "brain" of a computer. But, in truth, a computer has not yet come close to matching the human brain, which has trillions of connections between billions of neurons. What is more, the most sophisticated conventional computer does not "learn" the same way the human brain learns. But let us consider an unconventional computer, one whose chips are actually designed to mimic the human brain. These computers are called **neural networks**, or, simply, neural nets.

If a computer is to function more like the human brain and less like an overgrown calculator, it must be able to experiment and to learn from its mistakes. Researchers are developing computers with a few thousand brain-like connections that form a grid, much like a nerve cell in the brain. The grid enables the computer to recognize patterns rather than simply follow step-by-step instructions. For instance, a neural network with optical sensors could be "trained" to recognize the letter *A*.

At best, today's neural networks consist of only a few thousand connections—still a far cry from the billions found in the human brain.

The Famous Turing Test

So, can a computer think or not? Listen to Alan Turing. Several years ago, this English mathematician proposed a test of thinking machines. In the **Turing test**, a human subject is seated before two terminals that are connected to hidden devices. One terminal is connected to a different terminal run by another person, and the second terminal is connected to a computer. The subject is asked to guess, by carrying out conversations through the terminals, which is controlled by the person and which by the computer. If the human judge cannot tell the difference, the computer is said to have passed and is considered, for all practical purposes, a thinking machine.

But perhaps we are asking the wrong question: Will a computer ever *really* think? One possible answer: Who cares? If a machine can perform a task really well, does it matter if it *really* thinks? Still another answer is: Yes, machines will really think, but not as humans do. They lack the sensitivity, appreciation, and passion that are intrinsic to human thought.

Meanwhile, scientists are getting rather good at developing related areas of artificial intelligence. We will focus on some of the more visible results of recent research in natural languages, expert systems, and robotics.

THE NATURAL LANGUAGE FACTOR

· · · · · · · · · · · · · · · · · · ·

The language people use on a daily basis to write and speak is called a **natural language.** Natural languages are associated with artificial intelligence because humans can make the best use of artificial intelligence if they can communicate with the computer in their own language. Furthermore, understanding natural language is a skill thought to require intelligence.

Some natural language words are easy to understand because they represent a definable item: horse, chair, mountain. Other words, however—justice, virtue, beauty—are much too abstract to lend themselves to straightforward definitions. But abstractness is just the beginning. Consider the word *hand* in these statements:

ELIZA

In the 1960s, a computer scientist named Joseph Weizenbaum wrote a little program as an experiment in natural language. He named the program after Eliza Doolittle, the character in *My Fair Lady* who wanted to learn to speak proper English. The software allows the computer to act as a benign therapist who does not talk much but, instead, encourages the patient—the computer user—to talk.

The Eliza software has a storehouse of key phrases that the user's input triggers. For example, if a patient types "My mother never liked me," the software—cued by the word "mother"—can respond, "Tell me more about your family." If the patient's input does not contain a word the software can respond to directly, the computer responds neutrally with a phrase such as "I see" or "That's very interesting" or "Why do you think that?" If a patient gives yes or no answers, the computer may respond, "I prefer complete sentences." With party tricks like these, the program is able to move along quite nimbly from line to line.

Weizenbaum was astonished to discover that people were taking his little program seriously, pouring out their hearts to the computer. In fact, what he viewed as misuse of the computer radicalized Weizenbaum, who spent the next several years giving speeches and writing articles against artificial intelligence.

- Tim had a hand in the robbery.
- Tim had a hand in the cookie jar.
- Tim is an old hand at chess.
- Tim gave Dick a hand with his luggage.
- Tim asked Mary for her hand in marriage.
- All hands on deck!
- Look, Ma! No hands!

As you can see, natural language abounds with inconsistency; the word *hand* has a different meaning in each statement. In contrast, sometimes statements that appear to be different really mean the same thing:

- Alan sold Judy a book for five dollars.
- Judy bought a book for five dollars from Alan.
- Judy gave Alan five dollars in exchange for a book.
- The book that Judy bought from Alan cost five dollars.

It takes very sophisticated software (not to mention enormous computer memory) to unravel all these statements and see them as equivalent. A key function of the AI study of natural languages is to develop a computer system that can resolve such problems.

Feeding computers the vocabulary and grammatical rules they need to know is a step in the right direction. However, as we saw earlier in regard to the language translation fiasco, true understanding requires more: Words must be taken in context. Humans begin acquiring a context for words from the day they are born. Consider the statement "Jack cried when Alice said she loved Bill." From our own context, we could draw several possible conclusions: Jack is sad, Jack probably loves Alice, Jack probably thinks Alice does not love him, and so on. These conclusions may not be correct, but they are reasonable interpretations based on the context we supply. On the other hand, it would *not* be reasonable to conclude from the statement that Jack is a carpenter or that Alice has a new refrigerator.

One of the most frustrating tasks for AI scientists is providing the computer with context. Scientists have attempted to do this on specific subjects and found the task daunting. For example, a scientist who wrote software so the computer could have a dialogue about restaurants had to feed the computer hundreds of facts that any small child would know, such as the fact that restaurants serve food and that you are expected to pay for it.

A less formidable task is to give a computer enough information to answer questions on a given topic. For instance, a stockbroker's computer does not need to know what a stock is, only if associated numbers indicate it is time to buy. Such systems, which are categorized in a subset of artificial intelligence, are called expert systems.

EXPERT SYSTEMS

An **expert system** is software used with an extensive set of organized data that presents the computer as an expert on a particular topic. For example, a computer could be an expert on where to drill oil wells, or

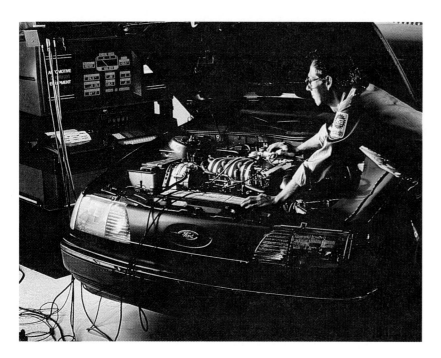

◀
Figure 11-2 An expert system on the job.
This expert system helps Ford mechanics track down and fix engine problems.

what stock purchase looks promising, or how to cook soufflés. The user is the knowledge seeker, usually asking questions in a natural—that is, English-like—language format. An expert system can respond to an inquiry about a problem—"What will happen if the bill of particulars is not received before the adjourned deadline?"—with both an answer and an explanation of the answer. (This is a legal question using a lawyer's "natural language," and the answer is probably "Prepare a motion to dismiss the case.") The expert system works by figuring out what the question means, then matching it against the facts and rules that it "knows" (Figure 11-2). These facts and rules, which reside on disk, originally come from a human expert.

Expert Systems in Business

For years, expert systems were no more than bold experiments found only within the medical and scientific communities. These special programs could offer medical diagnoses or search for mineral deposits or examine chemical compounds. But in the early 1980s, expert systems began to make their way into commercial applications. Today expert systems are slowly finding their place in big business. Consider these examples:

• The Campbell Soup Company has an expert system nicknamed Aldo, for Aldo Cimino, the human expert who knows how to fix cooking machines. Aldo was getting on in years and being run ragged, flying from plant to plant whenever a cooker went on the blink. How would the company manage when he retired? Now Aldo's knowledge has been distilled into an expert system that can be used by workers in any location.

• Nordstrom, a chain of stores selling high-quality clothing, uses an expert system to extend customer credit limits. Suppose, for example, that a customer wants to charge a coat whose cost pushes the

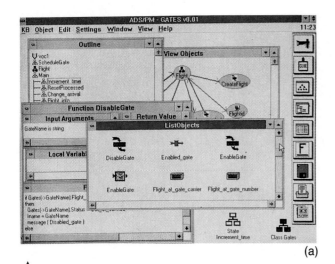
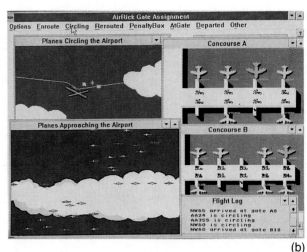

(a)   (b)

▲

Figure 11-3   Airline scheduling program produced with the aid of an expert system.
This system offers a graphical user interface to help solve a complex airport scheduling problem. (a) This screen illustrates the system's ability to display multiple views of objects in the knowledge-based system and the relationships between them. (b) Various screen windows show planes circling the airport, the number of planes circling the airport, gate information, and two concourses with planes at their gates.

total debt beyond the current credit limit. In the past, the salesperson phoned a human expert who reviewed credit records and made a decision; meanwhile, the customer waited. Now the decision process has been transferred to an expert system, which is faster and less expensive.

- Factory workers at The Boeing Company use an expert system to assemble electrical connectors for airplanes. In the old days, workers had to hunt through 20,000 pages of cross-referenced specifications to find the right parts, tools, and techniques for the job—approximately 42 minutes per search. The expert system lets them do the same thing in about 5 minutes.

- Employees at Coopers & Lybrand, a Big Eight accounting firm, use an expert system called ExperTax, which makes the knowledge of tax experts available to financial planners. The knowledge is, in fact, as close as their computers.

- About 400 flights per day land or take off from one of the 50 gates at the United Airlines terminal at O'Hare Airport in Chicago. Factors that complicate routing the traffic include the limitations of jumbo jets, which do not maneuver easily into some gates; weather; and heavy runway use, which can affect how quickly planes can get in and out. Airline employees used to track planes on a gigantic magnetic board. Now they keep track of gate assignments with an expert system that takes all factors into account (Figure 11-3).

The cost of an expert system can usually be justified in situations where there are few experts but great demand for knowledge. An expert system can be especially worthwhile where there is no margin for human failings, such as fatigue.

Building an Expert System

Some organizations choose to build their own expert systems to perform well-focused tasks that can easily be crystallized into rules. A simple example is a set of rules for a banker to use when making decisions about whether to extend credit. But very few organizations are capable of building an expert system from scratch. The sensible alternative is to buy an **expert shell**, a software package that consists of the basic structure used to find answers to questions. It is up to the buyer to fill in the actual knowledge on the chosen subject. You could think of the expert shell as an empty cup that becomes a new entity once it is filled—a cup of coffee, for instance, or a cup of apple juice.

In many cases, the most challenging task of building an expert system is deciding who the appropriate expert is and then trying to pin down his or her knowledge. Experts often believe that much of their expertise is instinctive and thus find it difficult to articulate just why they do what they do. However, the expert is usually following a set of rules, even if the rules are only in his or her head. The person ferreting out the information, sometimes called a **knowledge engineer**, must have a keen awareness and the skills of a diplomat. Sometimes cameras and tapes are used to observe the expert in action.

Once the rules are uncovered, they are formed into a set of IF-THEN rules: IF the customer has exceeded a credit limit by no more than 20% and has paid the monthly bill for six months, THEN extend further credit. After the system is translated into a computerized version, it is reviewed, changed, tested, and changed some more. This repetitive process could take months or even years. Finally, it is put into the same situations the human expert would face, where it should give equal or better service but much more quickly.

The Outlook for Expert Systems

Some industry analysts feel that expert systems are beginning to mimic the analytic processes of humans and that, as a result, these programs border on true artificial intelligence. Putting together the facets we have discussed so far, a computer having artificial intelligence should understand the facts it knows, come up with new facts, and be able to engage in a wide-ranging conversation about them in a natural language. By these standards, expert systems today are still rather dim-witted. Furthermore, each system has intelligence in only one specific area.

Expert systems will infiltrate companies department by department, much as personal computers did before them. Some expert systems are now available on personal computers. The main limitation of an expert system on a personal computer is that the expert system requires a substantial amount of memory. In addition, a large amount of data in terms of rules, facts, and program code must be stored, requiring the use of a hard disk. Even so, it seems likely that more expert systems for personal computers will appear in the near future.

ROBOTICS
. . . .

Many people smile at the thought of robots, perhaps remembering the endearing C-3PO of *Star Wars* fame and its "personal" relationship with humans. But vendors have not made even a small dent in the

A BATH FOR THE BIG GUY

Some of us spend part of an afternoon attacking a dirty car with a sponge and a pail of sudsy water. But how would you like the job of washing a jumbo jet? About once a month, airlines must remove the accumulated grime that can cause flight drag and cut into fuel efficiency. As a manual job, a jet bath takes 20 workers about four hours.

Enter the robots. Plane-cleaning robots, using 35 brushes and 17 TV cameras, can restore a plane's luster in approximately 80 minutes.

personal robot market—the much-heralded domestic robots have never materialized. So, where are robots today? Mainly in factories.

Robots in the Factory

Most robots are in factories, spray-painting, welding—and taking away jobs. The Census Bureau, after two centuries of counting people, has now branched out and today is counting robots. About 15,000 robots existed in 1985, and double that number in 1990. What do robots do that merits all this attention?

A loose definition of *robot* is a type of automation that replaces human presence. But a **robot** is more specifically defined as a computer-controlled device that can physically manipulate its surroundings. Some robots, as we will see later, can also manipulate themselves. Robots vary greatly in size and shape; each design is created with a particular use in mind. Often, a robot's job is a function that would be tedious or even dangerous for a human to perform. The most common industrial robots sold today are mechanical devices with five or six axes of motion so the machines can rotate into proper position to perform their tasks (Figure 11-4).

We mentioned spray-painting and welding as jobs for robots; a more intelligent robot can adapt to changing circumstances. For example, with the help of a TV-camera eye, a robot can "see" components it is meant to assemble. It is able to pick them up, rearrange them in the right order, or place them in the right position before assembling them.

Robot Vision

Recently, **vision robots** have been taught to see in living color—that is, to recognize multicolored objects solely from their colors. This is a departure from the traditional approach, whereby robots recognized

▼
Figure 11-4   Industrial robots.
(a) These standard robots are used in the auto industry to spray-paint new cars. (b) This robot is not making breakfast. Hitachi uses the delicate egg, however, to demonstrate that its visual-tactile robot can handle fragile objects. Its sensors detect size, shape, and required pressure, attaining sensitivity almost equal to that of a human hand.

(a)

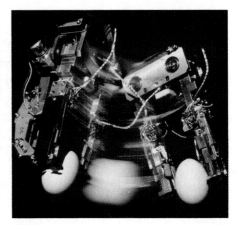
(b)

COMPUTING HIGHLIGHTS

Robot Tales

Like computers before them, robots will soon be everywhere. Here are some samples.

Robby the Robot steps out. NASA has developed a robot vehicle designed to explore Mars. In a recent outing Robby successfully picked its way along a dry, rocky riverbed, without human help. Eventually, Robby will be sent on his own to Mars to scout possible landing spots for a human mission.

My doctor the robot. If you have orthopedic surgery, you may find that a key player alongside the surgeon is a robot. For example, to make room for a hip implant, a robotic arm drills a long hole in a thigh bone. Robotic precision improves the implant, reduces pain after surgery, and speeds healing.

Robots on display. If you care to see robots in the workplace, here is your chance. At the General Motors manufacturing plant in Flint,

Michigan, 216 state-of-the-art robots labor side by side with their human coworkers on an assembly line. One of the most advanced robots places car seats on a conveyor belt, using its electronic eye to match each seat with the appropriate car model. Other robots weld in the body shop and install windshields. Tours are available for the public every Tuesday and Thursday.

Lending a hand. Robots may soon be of significant use to the disabled. Researchers have already developed a robot for quadriplegics. The machine can respond to a dozen voice commands by answering the door, getting the mail, serving soup, or performing other tasks.

Robots making computers. It seems most fitting that robots should be hard at work in factories that manufacture computers—and indeed they are. For example, in an IBM assembly plant, robots place memory boards inside computers,

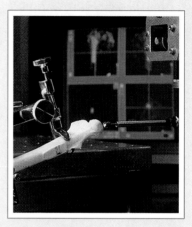

mount disk drives, screw in power supplies, and more.

Let the robots fight the next war. It has been suggested by some artificial intelligence researchers that countries send their most sophisticated robots into battle, declare a winner, and get on with living. Although this seems rather preposterous, it is food for thought.

objects by their shapes (Figure 11-5), and from vision machines that see a dominant color only. For example, a robot in an experiment at the University of Rochester was able to pick out a box of Kellogg's Sugar Frosted Flakes from 70 other boxes. Among the anticipated benefits of such visual recognition skills is faster supermarket checkout. You cannot easily bar-code a squash, but a robot might be trained to recognize it by its size, shape, and color.

Figure 11-5 The seeing robot.
Robots "see" by casting light beams on objects and identifying them by matching their shapes to those of "known" objects. In this machine-vision sequence, (a) objects are seen by the robot, (b) the objects are matched to known shapes, (c) inappropriate shapes are eliminated, and (d) the objects are recognized.

(a)

(b)

(c)

(d)

▲
Figure 11-6   Flying robot.
Can a robot really fly? Yes. Flying robots have both military and civilian uses. This Sentinel robot can soar up to 10,000 feet to spy on an enemy or to inspect high-voltage wires or spot forest fires.

Field Robots

Just think of some of the places you would rather not be: inside a nuclear power plant, next to a suspected bomb, at the bottom of the sea, or in the middle of a chemical spill. But robots readily go all those places. Furthermore, they go there to do some dangerous and dirty jobs. These days, robots "in the field"—called **field robots**—inspect and repair nuclear power plants, dispose of bombs, inspect oil rigs for undersea exploration, clean up chemical accidents, and much more. Space researchers look forward to the day when "astrobots" can be stationed in orbit, ready to repair faulty satellites.

Only a few years ago, there were just a handful of field robots commercially employed. Now there are hundreds, and soon there will be thousands. Field robots may be equipped with wheels, tracks, legs, fins, or even wings (Figure 11-6). Field robots have been largely overshadowed by factory robots, mainly because they lack the independent glamour of their manufacturing counterparts; field robots must be remotely controlled by human operators. Now, however, the poor-relative status of field robots is changing because enough computer power can be packed into a field robot to enable it to make most decisions independently. Field robots need all the power they can get. Unlike factory robots, which are bolted to the ground and blindly do the same tasks over and over again, field robots must often contend with a highly unstructured environment.

Although robots seem sophisticated, they cannot do many of the simple tasks that humans can do. Robots cannot yet tie shoelaces.

▲　▲　▲

The immediate prospect for expert systems and robots is growth and more growth. We can anticipate both increased sophistication and more diverse applications. The progress in the more esoteric applications of artificial intelligence will continue to be relatively slow. No one need worry just yet that any computer can capture the wide-ranging sophistication of the human mind.

However, even today computer professionals must sometimes convince people that computers cannot "take over." Will intensified publicity about intelligent computers and robots revive these concerns? If so, the answer remains the same: People are in charge of computers, not the other way around.

CHAPTER REVIEW

SUMMARY AND KEY TERMS

- **Artificial intelligence** (**AI**) is a field of study that explores how computers can be used for tasks that require the human characteristics of intelligence, imagination, and intuition. AI has also been described as the study of how to make computers do things that—at the present time—people can do better.

- *Artificial intelligence* is considered an umbrella term to encompass several subsets of interests, including problem solving, natural languages, expert systems, and robotics.

- In the early days of AI, scientists thought it would be useful just to stuff facts into a computer; however, facts are useless without the ability to interpret and learn from them.

- An early attempt to translate human languages via a computer using vocabulary and rules of grammar was a failure because the machine could not interpret context. This failure impeded the progress of artificial intelligence.

- Artificial intelligence applications are predicated on the computer's ability to learn—in particular, to improve performance based on past errors.

- A **knowledge base** is a set of facts and rules about those facts. An **inference engine** accesses, selects, and interprets a set of rules. The inference engine applies rules to the facts to make up new facts.

- People rarely solve problems by using the step-by-step logic used by most computers. The brain beats computers at solving problems, because it has millions of neurons working simultaneously.

- Computers whose chips are designed to mimic the human brain are called **neural networks**.

- In the **Turing test**, if a human judge cannot distinguish a human response from a computer response, the computer is said to be a thinking machine.

- **Natural language**—the language people use on a daily basis to write and speak—is associated with artificial intelligence because humans can make the best use of artificial intelligence if they can communicate with the computer in their own language. Furthermore, understanding natural language is a skill thought to require intelligence.

- A key function of the AI study of natural languages is to develop a computer system that can resolve linguistic ambiguities.

- An **expert system** is software used with an extensive set of organized data that presents the computer as an expert on a specific topic. The expert system works by figuring out what the question means, then matching it against the facts and rules that it "knows."

- For years, expert systems were the exclusive property of the medical and scientific communities, but in the early 1980s they began to make their way into commercial applications.
- Some organizations choose to build their own expert systems to perform well-focused tasks that can easily be crystallized into rules, but few organizations are capable of building an expert system from scratch. Some users buy an **expert shell**, a software package that consists of the basic structure used to find answers to questions. It is up to the buyer to fill in the actual knowledge on the chosen subject.
- A person working to extract information from a human expert is sometimes called a **knowledge engineer**.
- A **robot** is a computer-controlled device that can physically manipulate its surroundings. Most robots are in factories.
- **Vision robots** recognize objects by their shapes or by their color or colors.
- **Field robots** do jobs in environments that are too dangerous or unpleasant for humans. These robots inspect and repair nuclear power plants, dispose of bombs, inspect oil rigs for undersea exploration, clean up chemical accidents, and much more.

SELF-TEST

True/False

T F   1. An expert shell presents the computer as an expert on a specific topic.

T F   2. A human expert usually explains decision techniques to the robot replacement.

T F   3. Field robots are used mostly for farm assistance.

T F   4. Artificial intelligence is a broad field of study.

T F   5. An expert system is hardware that is an expert on some topic.

T F   6. Artificial intelligence software can rely on vocabulary and rules of grammar for language translation.

T F   7. The Turing test defines robot limitations.

T F   8. A robot is computer-controlled.

T F   9. Natural language ambiguities have largely been solved.

T F 10. An inference engine is part of an expert system.

Matching

_____ 1. expert shell   a. field robot
_____ 2. interprets rules   b. mostly in factories
_____ 3. Turing test   c. knowledge base
_____ 4. disposes of bomb   d. recognizes object shape
_____ 5. natural language   e. talks to expert
_____ 6. robots   f. inference engine
_____ 7. mimics the brain   g. neural network
_____ 8. facts, rules   h. Can the computer think?
_____ 9. vision robot   i. structure for expert system
_____ 10. knowledge engineer   j. context sensitive

Fill-In

1. The person who extracts what a human expert knows:

   _____

2. The test to determine if a computer is a thinking machine:

   _____

3. The field of study that explores how computers can do human tasks:

   _____

4. Software that presents the computer as an expert on a specific topic:

   _____

5. Accesses, selects, and interprets rules: _____

6. Software containing the basic structure used to find answers to questions:

   _____

7. A robot that can inspect a nuclear power plant:

   _____

8. A set of facts and rules for an expert system: _____

9. Computers that mimic the human brain: _____

10. Recognizes an object by shape or color: _____

Answers

True/False: 1. F, 3. F, 5. F, 7. F, 9. F

Matching: 1. i, 3. h, 5. j, 7. g, 9. d

Fill-In: 1. knowledge engineer, 3. artificial intelligence, 5. inference engine, 7. field robot, 9. neural networks

PART FOUR

INTERVIEW: Mark Ong—Side-by-Side Studios

ell us a little about your background as a designer. Did you have any specific training in the use of computers?

I graduated from college with a fine-arts degree, so I started out as a printmaker and a water-colorist. I went into graphic design as a way of supporting myself. I started with a company that designed brochures, posters, and books for the State Bar of California. I went free-lance in 1983 and started Side-by-Side Studios in 1987. My training was more toward traditional typography—all the old-style stuff, the letterpress, and all the really nice kinds of details.

In about 1986, I started using computers. It just seemed like there was no way that I could compete unless I knew how to use a computer. I still know designers who don't use computers at all. I don't see how they can get by, really—both in terms of their clients and in terms of the productivity of their work.

How did you learn to use a computer?

First of all, I had to learn how to type. Then I taught myself to use Word and PageMaker. Recently, I started taking courses, which have saved me a lot of time. The courses have mostly focused around Quark, because that's the main page-layout program that I favor. It's set up more for the way a book designer thinks. A book designer doesn't think in the same way that an advertising designer thinks. A book designer has to think in terms of regularity, a certain rhythm to the publication, very precise measures.

What types of computers do you use and why did you choose your current system?

I have a Macintosh SI, with a Radius two-page display. I was doing everything on a Mac Plus for a long time. Now that I have a two-page display, the screen on the Mac Plus just seems so incredibly small. I originally selected a Macintosh over a PC because the Mac was supposedly more user friendly, more intuitive. Since I was totally computer illiterate—in fact, keyboard illiterate—I wanted the safest thing possible.

How do you use computers in the day-to-day operation of your business?

I use the computer primarily for design layouts, word processing, and final output. There are times when I still may make some changes to a design by hand, because I can't do certain things with a computer or because certain things are just faster by hand. Because I'm coming from a traditional graphic-design standpoint, I'm using the computer to interface with what I know how to do already. I'm using it to express my traditional knowledge, not to shift everything over to a computer-based design approach.

What are the advantages of using a computer compared to traditional design methods?

I think the advantages are greater accuracy and greater control over type, layout, paging, and so on. I think designers are able to experiment more with typography in a way that they were not able to before. I'm able to use more fonts at the

▲
Mark Ong is a graphic designer and partner in Side-by-Side Studios. In addition to his primary work as a book designer, Mark is an accomplished artist and a published author. Here, he discusses how the use of personal computers is giving him a leg up in the competitive field of graphic design.

USING PERSONAL COMPUTER SOFTWARE

same time. There's more flexibility, accuracy, and speed.

Are there disadvantages to designing on computer?

I think if the operator doesn't have a sound knowledge of design, you'll get lousy design that's well produced and just looks terrible. My orientation has been very traditional, and I've done a lot of research into traditional ideas in typography and design, page layout, and so on. I think you have to have that kind of understanding before you can take this technology and manipulate it correctly. Having a computer, a lot of fonts, or a lot of illustration programs is not going to make you a good designer. It's the mind behind the computer that does it. The other problem is that a lot of clients then think that they know enough about design to start telling the designer what to do. I do think a designer has to be cooperative, but a designer is supposed to know his field.

So the disadvantage, first of all, is that there's a lot of bad design. Secondly, the computer is a neutral tool, and it won't give anyone design ability if they don't have it. Thirdly, I think there's a difference between looking at something on paper and looking at it on the screen. I can think of ideas on paper that I would never think of on the computer—and the other way around, too. The computer, perhaps, is less intuitive, shall we say? There's something about drawing with your hand that gives a different design. But the computer is also a lot more versatile and gives you options you might not be able to achieve otherwise.

Do you think your traditional background makes it harder for you to go to the computer first?

Yes. I think it will take a generation or two before we can really understand this, because now we're seeing people in art school and college who are trained on the computer and probably will use the computer more than they will use pencil and paper. So, in a sense I represent a transitional generation that is making the leap

> *In a sense, I represent a transitional generation that is making the leap from pencil and paper to the computer.*

from pencil and paper to the computer. On the one hand, I would hate to see all the old things thrown out. But on the other hand, those standards have entered the collective unconscious of this culture. You notice that computer print never became considered beautiful type. We've had to go back and ape all the traditional letter forms in order for computer-generated type to become acceptable in the culture and for people to feel comfortable with it. That to me says that,

culturally, we're still attuned to those older traditions. So I think designers, no matter how conversant they are on the computer, have to know those traditionally accepted forms and then manipulate from there. If they try to throw everything out, I don't think they'll get a lot of acceptance, because subconsciously people can't relate to it.

How do you think desktop publishing has changed your business?

I would say that it's been a very powerful tool, and it has allowed me to express design ideas I could not have expressed otherwise. From a business standpoint, it has allowed me to remain competitive in a very small field. Publishers in general are moving increasingly toward standardized design programs, eliminating the need for designers. So, having a computer has allowed me to have the speed and a technical look to my work that keep me competitive. ◻

CHAPTER 12

OVERVIEW

Word Processing and Desktop Publishing
Preparing Printed Communications

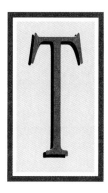

hough she is officially an employee of a university, scientist Della Vermeer does not teach. She is the principal investigator for a number of grant-funded projects, and she plays a dual role as business administrator and researcher. Della's job includes publishing research reports, writing grant proposals, and planning future research projects.

Few scientists are strangers to computers. For decades, scientists have used computing machines to collect and analyze data and to perform statistical tests. But for Della, the biggest breakthrough in computer technology was the word processing program. Before word processing, everything Della wrote had to be typed manually by a secretary. The work took forever, because each document had to be typed in its entirety, even though whole sections might be verbatim repetitions from earlier drafts or previously completed documents. It did not matter how often Della had used a phrase or an equation or a bibliographic citation. Each time it went down on paper, it had to be typed anew. What appeared in the grant proposal had to be typed again for next year's research plan. Later, much of that same information was retyped for a series of journal articles.

When the first personal computer word processing programs became available, the lab bought one. Della immediately found it to be a miracle of efficiency. Editing became easy—after a few quick on-screen changes, the com-

puter did all the work of printing a revised paper copy. Because revising documents had become a snap, Della did much of it herself, freeing her from dependence on her secretary's 9 to 5 schedule.

Once an idea was captured in words in the computer, Della found she could reuse the words in any context she liked. With the ability to move sections from one document into another, turning last year's grant proposal into this year's journal article was a vastly simpler task. Producing long lists of literature citations became easy; Della borrowed citations from one report and added them to another.

As her experience with computers grew and as the capabilities of computers and software advanced, Della found she could create tables, charts, and diagrams and electronically paste them into her work. Not only did the computer ease the ordeal of producing documents, but the appearance and overall quality of the documents improved noticeably.

Della is still a busy, successful administrator. But thanks to her computer and its word processing software, she has much more time for her first love: science. ◼

WORD PROCESSING AS A TOOL

Word processing is a software program that lets you create, edit, format, store, and print a text document. Let us examine each part of the definition. A *text document* is anything that can be keyed in, such as a letter. *Creation* is the original composing and keying in of the document. *Editing* is making changes to the document to fix errors or improve its content—for example, deleting a sentence, correcting a misspelled name, or moving a paragraph. *Formatting* refers to adjusting the appearance of the document to make it look appropriate and attractive. For example, you might want to center a heading, make wider margins, or use double spacing. *Storing* the document means saving it on a data disk, so that it can be accessed on demand. *Printing* is producing the document on paper, using a printer connected to the computer.

Some people think of word processing as just glorified typing. But consider the advantages of word processing over typing. Word processing lets you see on the screen what you type before you print it, remembers what you type and lets you change it, and prints the typed document at your request.

There are two notable differences between using a word processing program and using a typewriter. The first difference is the separation of typing from printing: When you use word processing, typing the document and printing the document do not occur at the same time; you print the document on paper whenever you like. Perhaps you want to print an intermediate draft, just to see how it looks, and then continue making changes. Or, you may choose to commit your work to paper only in the final version.

The second difference between word processing programs and typewriters is related to the first: When you use a word processing package, you can make changes as you go along, or even at some later time, and print out a revised—and perfect—copy. The key here is that only the changes themselves are retyped, not the entire document.

The ability to print at will and the ability to store work distinguish word processing from typing. But these are not the only two hallmarks. A word processing package is a sophisticated tool with many options; this chapter discusses many of them. We begin with an overview of how word processing works. This is followed by two simple case studies that explain how to use various processing features.

AN OVERVIEW: HOW WORD PROCESSING WORKS

Think of the computer's screen as a page of typing paper. On the screen the word processing program indicates the top of the page and left and right edges (margins) of the typed material. When you type, you can see the line of text you are typing on the screen—it looks just like a line of typing on paper. Remember that you are not really typing on the screen, however; the screen merely displays what you are entering into memory. As you type, the program displays a **cursor** to show

PERSONAL COMPUTERS IN ACTION

Writers Throw Off Their Chains

Although some resist, most people who write for a living have taken the plunge into word processing. So do people who have to write reports, memos, and so forth, as a component of their jobs. The statements of these people tell the story:

- **Mike Royko, columnist.** The machine terrifies me but I know enough to write my column on it. When the first typewriter came out, a lot of newspaper guys said they'd never write with "that monster." They'd rather write with a pen. When my newspaper brought in its [computer] system, I was the last guy writing with a typewriter; I didn't have time to learn to use the system. Then another reporter explained enough to me in simple English so I could do my columns.

- **Esther Dyson, editor and publisher.** The first PC I ever knew was a Wang word processor I single-handedly brought into the Wall Street firm where I was working. Everyone in the office was very suspicious of the machine, but by the time I left they were all standing in line to use it.

- **Alice Kahn, author.** For me, getting a computer meant the difference between being an amateur and a pro. I used to write on yellow pads and scribble the changes into the margin before I would even go near the typewriter. Now I turn out two pieces a week, and my writing income has increased 800 percent.

- **Andrew Tobias, author.** The PC has changed my life in several respects. I was already an established writer, but the computer has added a whole new dimension to my career. It would be dishonest of me not to acknowledge that it has bought me a va-

cation house and a lot of other nice things. . . . I didn't expect it to turn out that way, but it has.

- **Chris Pray, television writer.** I have a war with machines. I don't even drive. I have a Stone Age psychology and even have a Stone Age computer: no modem, no hard disk. The first month I had my computer, I found myself thinking like a computer after I turned it off: I'd think about deleting dumb remarks I'd made in a conversation, or inserting things, or moving things around.

- **Harvey Rosenfield, head of Ralph Nader's access to justice.** The special interests, with their infinitely greater resources, had access to computerized press lists and word processing. Then came the PC. Sensing vaguely what it could do for us, I took out a loan and bought a PC. It was a revolution among the revolutionaries. Suddenly, a position paper could quickly become legislative testimony; a press release, a newsletter. Most important, it helped even the odds for the consumer movement.

where the next character you type will appear on the screen (Figure 12-1). The cursor is usually a blinking dash or rectangle that you can easily see.

You can move the cursor around on the screen by using the **cursor movement keys** on the right side of the keyboard (Figure 12-2). The cursor movement keys are labeled with arrows that show the direction of cursor movement—up, down, left, and right. The Up Arrow and Down Arrow keys move the cursor up or down one line at a time. The **PgUp** and **PgDn** keys let you move the cursor up or down a whole page—as it would be printed—at a time. Furthermore, the Plus (+) key moves the cursor down a screen at a time, and the Minus key (−) moves the cursor up a screen at a time. Being able to move the cursor

▶

Figure 12-1 Entering text with word processing software.
As you type in your text, the position of the cursor (the dash just to the right of the last word in the paragraph) shows where the next character will be placed.

Cursor ────────────────

> A word processing program lets you use the computer's keyboard to enter text into the computer's internal memory. You can see what you are entering on the screen and make modifications to the text. Then the program lets you save the text._
>
> Doc 1 Pg 1 Ln 1.5" Pos 5.7"

to the top or bottom of a document is also handy—especially if the document is long. These cursor movements are caused by pressing specific cursor movement keys in sequence. To move the cursor to the top of the document, for example, press Home twice, then Up Arrow.

Scrolling

A word processing program lets you type page after page of material. Most programs show a line of dashes on the screen to mark where one printed page will end and another will begin; this line does not appear on the printed document. Most word processing programs also display the numbers of the line and page on which you are currently typing.

▼

Figure 12-2 A personal computer keyboard.
The cursor movement (arrow) keys, highlighted in blue, let you move the cursor around on the screen.

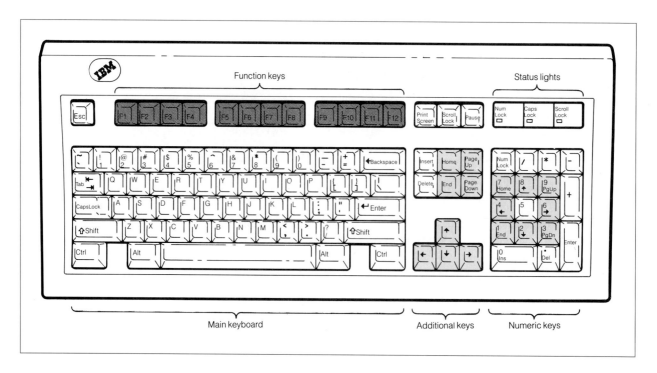

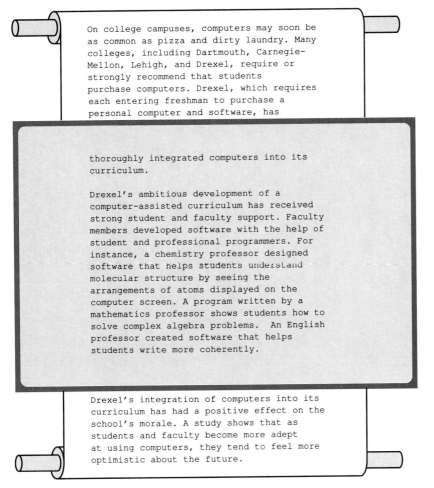

On college campuses, computers may soon be
as common as pizza and dirty laundry. Many
colleges, including Dartmouth, Carnegie-
Mellon, Lehigh, and Drexel, require or
strongly recommend that students
purchase computers. Drexel, which requires
each entering freshman to purchase a
personal computer and software, has

thoroughly integrated computers into its
curriculum.

Drexel's ambitious development of a
computer-assisted curriculum has received
strong student and faculty support. Faculty
members developed software with the help of
student and professional programmers. For
instance, a chemistry professor designed
software that helps students understand
molecular structure by seeing the
arrangements of atoms displayed on the
computer screen. A program written by a
mathematics professor shows students how to
solve complex algebra problems. An English
professor created software that helps
students write more coherently.

Drexel's integration of computers into its
curriculum has had a positive effect on the
school's morale. A study shows that as
students and faculty become more adept
at using computers, they tend to feel more
optimistic about the future.

◄ **Figure 12-3 Scrolling through a document.**
Although most documents contain many lines of text, the screen can display only about 24 lines at one time. You can use the cursor movement keys to scroll up and down through the document.

A screen can only display about 24 lines of text. Although the screen display size is limited, your document size is not. As you add new lines at the bottom of the screen, the lines you typed earlier move up the screen. Eventually, the first line you typed disappears off the top of the screen. But the line has not disappeared from the document or from the computer's memory.

To see a line that has disappeared from the top, use your cursor movement keys to move the cursor up to the top of the screen. Continue to press Up Arrow, and the line that had disappeared drops back down onto the screen. The program treats the text you are typing as if it were on a long roll of paper like a roll of paper towels or a scroll. You "roll the scroll" by moving the cursor, making different portions of the scroll visible on the screen. This process, called **scrolling,** lets you see any part of the document—but only 24 or so lines at a time (Figure 12-3).

No Need to Worry About the Right Side

After you start to type the first line of a document, you will eventually get to the right side of the screen. The word processing program watches to see how close you are to the edge of the "paper" (the right margin). If there is not enough room at the end of a line to complete the word you are typing, the program automatically starts that word at the left margin of the next line down. You never have to worry about running out of space on a line; the word processing program plans ahead for you. This feature is called **word wrap.** With word wrap you do not have to push a carriage return key (on the computer, Enter) at the end of each line as you would with a typewriter; in fact, you should *not* use a carriage return at the end of a line, or the word wrap feature will not work properly. However, you should use a carriage return—that is, you should press Enter—to provide a blank line or to signal the end of a paragraph.

Easy Corrections

What if you make a mistake while you are typing? No problem: Move the cursor to the position of the error and make the correction. Use the Backspace key to delete characters to the left or the Del key to delete the character under the cursor. Word processing programs let you delete characters or whole words or lines that you have already typed, and the resulting spaces are closed up automatically.

You can also insert new characters in the middle of a line or a word, without typing over (and erasing) the characters that are already there. The program moves the existing characters to the right of the insertion as you type the new characters. However, if you wish, the word processing program also lets you *overtype* (replace) characters you typed before. We will discuss these correction techniques in more detail later in this chapter.

Function Keys: At Your Command

The keyboard's function keys, shown in Figure 12-2, can save you a lot of time. The result of pressing each function key differs according to the word processing program you use. For example, if you are using WordPerfect and you want to indent a paragraph, you simply press F4. But if you are using another program, you might have to press a different function key or even a combination of keys to do the same task.

To help users remember which function key performs which task, software manufacturers often provide a sheet of plastic or paper that describes what each key does. This sheet, called a **template,** fits above the function keys (Figure 12-4).

Now you are ready to see how these concepts work in a word processing package.

GETTING STARTED:
USING A WORD PROCESSING PACKAGE

Carl Wade has just graduated with a business degree and is looking for an entry-level job in an advertising firm. Carl already has a resume, but he wants to use a word processing package to prepare a cover letter. Carl chooses WordPerfect, the word processing package that dominates both businesses and college campuses.

		Shell	Spell	Screen	Move	*Ctrl*	Text In/Out
WordPerfect® for IBM Personal Computers		Thesaurus	Replace	Reveal Codes	Block	*Alt*	Mark Text
Delete to End of Ln/Pg — End/Pg Dn / Delete Word — Backspace / Go To — Home / Hard Page — Enter / ◆Margin Release — Tab / Screen Up/Down — −/+ (num) / Soft Hyphen — − / Word Left/Right — ←/→		Setup	◆Search	Switch	◆Indent◆	*Shift*	Date/Outline
© WordPerfect Corp. 1988 TMXXENWPIID50—6/15/88 ISBN 1-55692-200-0		Cancel	◆Search	Help	◆Indent		List Files
		F1	F2	F3	F4		F5

Tab Align	Footnote	Font	*Ctrl*	Merge/Sort	Macro Define		
Flush Right	Math/Columns	Style	*Alt*	Graphics	Macro		
Center	Print	Format	*Shift*	Merge Codes	Retrieve		
Bold	Exit	Underline		Merge R	Save	Reveal Codes	Block
F6	F7	F8		F9	F10	F11	F12

When it is necessary to be specific in this example, we will use WordPerfect commands. In particular, we will use Version 5.1 of WordPerfect for the IBM personal computer and others like it.

Loading the Program

As always, Carl begins by booting the computer. (For information on booting, refer to Chapter 8, "Operating Systems.") After Carl boots the computer, he loads his word processing program from hard drive C and places his formatted data disk in drive B. (This scenario assumes that Carl is using a computer with a hard drive and two diskette drives, that the word processing software is already in drive C, and that he will keep his own files on a diskette in drive B.)

At this point, with the C> on the screen, Carl needs to type a command to get the word processing program started. The command varies with the program; examples are WP for WordPerfect, WS for WordStar, and WORD for Microsoft Word. After this command—and all others, in fact—he will press Enter. When the appropriate command is entered, the word processing program is loaded from disk drive C into the computer's memory. Depending on the word processing program used, a set of choices, called a **menu**, may appear on the screen. However, WordPerfect, the program Carl is using, immediately displays an almost blank screen to represent a blank sheet of typing paper (Figure 12-5).

Creating the Cover Letter

This section describes, in a general way, how Carl types, saves, and prints his letter. Although the specific keystroke instructions refer to WordPerfect Version 5.1, the general approach fits any word processing package. Once Carl has loaded the word processing program, he proceeds as follows.

▲
Figure 12-4   A function-key template. This template helps you remember which function keys perform which tasks. Without the template you would have to memorize numerous key combinations. The template is color-coded to match related keys: red for the Control (Ctrl) key, green for the Shift key, blue for the Alternate (Alt) key, and black for the function key alone. Examples: Press Shift-F7 (Shift and F7 simultaneously) to print, press Ctrl-F2 to check spelling, and press F6 by itself to mark text to print boldface. (To fit on this page the template has been split in half; normally, it fits above the function keys.)

▶
Figure 12-5   Getting started with WordPerfect.
When Carl first loads WordPerfect, the screen is almost as blank as a fresh sheet of paper. Note the cursor in the upper-left corner. The information at the bottom right of the screen is called the status line. The status line includes the document number, the page number, the position of the cursor in inches from the top of the page (Ln 1″), and the position of the cursor in inches from the left edge of the paper (Pos 1″).

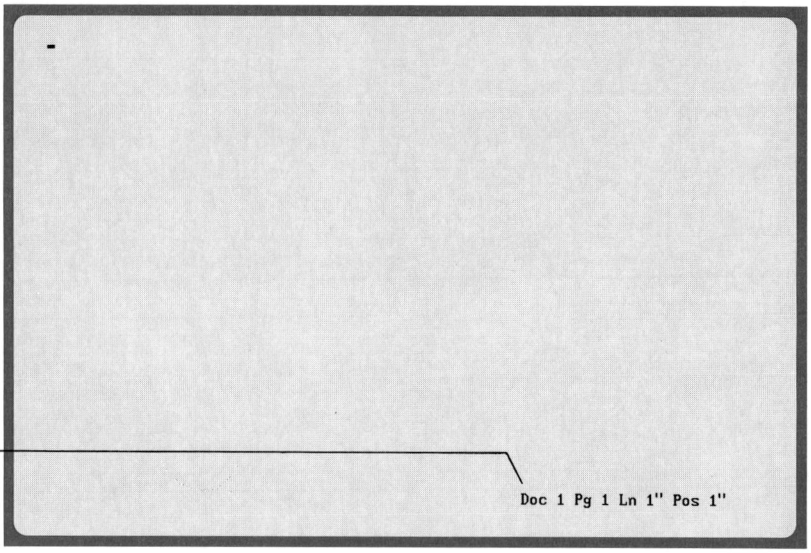

Status line ———————

Doc 1 Pg 1 Ln 1″ Pos 1″

Typing the Letter

Carl starts by typing the letter (Figure 12-6). He uses the computer keyboard much as he would a typewriter keyboard. He can see the results of his keystrokes on the screen. If he needs to make corrections, he can use the Backspace key or the Del key. Carl knows the letter is being stored in memory as he types; so, as he continues to use the word processing package, he can continue to make changes to any part of the letter.

Saving the Letter

After Carl finishes keying in the letter and corrects his mistakes, he stores—saves—the letter in a file on his data disk. He does this because memory keeps data only temporarily. To save the letter on disk, Carl presses the F10 function key. WordPerfect now asks him to name the file before it is saved. A file name lets DOS keep track of the file's location on the disk, so DOS can find the file when requested in the future. Carl types B:CLETTER—the B: tells the program which drive contains the disk to store the file on, and CLETTER (an abbreviation for *cover letter*) is the name of the file. Carl then presses Enter. By storing the letter on his data disk, Carl has a copy of the letter that he can access whenever he needs it.

Printing the Letter

Carl decides he wants to see a printed copy of what he has written so far. He turns on the printer and then holds down the Shift key while pressing the F7 function key. WordPerfect offers several printing options; Carl presses 1 (for choice 1) to print the whole document. This action sends the letter to the printer, and his letter is printed.

Exiting the Program

Once Carl finishes using the program, he gives the command to exit the program: He presses the F7 function key. Then, in response to WordPerfect's questions, he types N (no, do not save the file, since it is already saved), then Y (yes, do exit). This leads him back to the C>.

```
                                          18 Leroy Street
                                          Binghamton, NY   10037
                                          July 13, 1992


        Ms. Louise Graham
        Director of Personnel
        Charnley Advertising, Inc.
        1900 Corporate Lane
        Baltimore, Maryland   21200

        Dear Ms. Graham:

        I am writing to inquire about the possibility of a position in
        Charnley's accounts department.

        I recently graduated from Pennsylvania State University with a BA
        in business.  My area of interest was marketing.

        I became acquainted with your company through my intern work at the
        Dunhill Agency in New York.  I have always hoped to combine my
        background in business and my interest in marketing.  Charnley
        Advertising seems to offer the best opportunity for doing this.

        I will be in Baltimore on July 28 and 29.  Would it be possible for
        us to meet to discuss this further?  I can be reached at 600-623-
        4667.  I look forward to hearing from you.

        Sincerely,


        Carl Wade
```

Figure 12-6   The first draft of Carl's cover letter.
Carl uses WordPerfect to enter this draft and to make the changes described in this chapter.

If Carl wants to start a new file, without leaving the program he can clear the screen by typing N in response to the second question.

Editing the Letter

As we have noted, a significant payoff of word processing is the ease of making corrections to existing documents. Suppose Carl decides, for example, that his cover letter would be more effective if he made several changes. If he had typed the letter on a typewriter, he would have to retype the entire letter. In contrast, follow the word processing approach to making changes.

Because Carl exited the word processing program earlier, he types WP to load WordPerfect from disk drive C into the computer's memory, as he did before.

Retrieving the Letter

To retrieve the letter, Carl holds down the Shift key while pressing the F10 function key. When WordPerfect asks for the name of the document to retrieve, he types B:CLETTER, as illustrated in Figure 12-7. The current version of his letter, just as he last saved it on his data disk, is loaded into memory and then displayed on the screen.

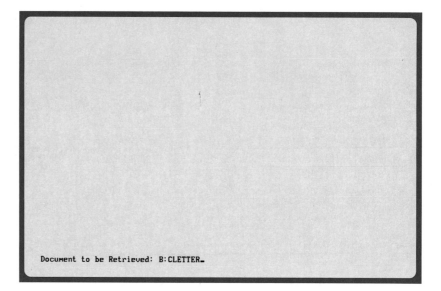

Document to be Retrieved: B:CLETTER_

▶
Figure 12-7   Retrieving the letter.
To retrieve a document, Carl must type in the name of the file he wants. He types B: to tell the computer the drive that holds the diskette with the file; CLETTER tells the computer the name of the file that holds the document.

Making the Changes

We have already described how existing text can be moved over to allow new text to be inserted. This is called the **insert mode** and is the standard way of inserting corrections in word processing. For example, suppose Carl wants to add the word "express" before the word "interest" in the second paragraph. All he has to do is move the cursor so it is below the "i" in "interest" and then type the word "express"; he finishes by pressing the Spacebar. This automatically adds the word to the sentence (Figure 12-8a).

Another correction option is to type right over the existing text. This feature, called **typeover mode,** replaces the existing text with the new text. Suppose Carl wants the word "special" instead of "express" in the second paragraph. He presses the insert (Ins) key, moves the cursor under the first "e" in "express," and types "special" (Figure 12-8b). Then he presses Ins again to turn off the typeover mode. It may seem odd that pressing Ins again turns off the typeover mode. This occurs because the Ins key is a **toggle switch,** which allows you to switch between two options—in this case, the two modes. The WordPerfect program starts with the insert mode as the **default mode**—a setting used by the word processing package unless deliberately changed by the user.

Carl also wants to add several sentences that explain his experience. He decides to insert the sentences between the third and fourth paragraphs. To insert the new sentences, Carl uses the cursor movement keys to position the cursor at the point where he wishes to add the new sentences. Then he types the sentences. He may, of course, make any other changes at this time. When he is finished, he presses Enter to provide the proper spacing at the end of the new paragraph. Compare the final version (Figure 12-9) with the original version (Figure 12-6).

Saving the Corrected Letter

As before, Carl presses the F10 key to save the letter on his disk. WordPerfect asks if Carl wants to replace the earlier version of the letter with the new version. Carl types Y for *yes*, and the letter is again

```
                                    18 Leroy Street
                                    Binghamton, NY  10037
                                    July 13, 1992


  Ms. Louise Graham
  Director of Personnel
  Charnley Advertising, Inc.
  1900 Corporate Lane
  Baltimore, Maryland 21200


  Dear Ms. Graham:

  I am writing to inquire about the possibility of a position in
  Charnley's accounts department.

  I recently graduated from Pennsylvania State University with a BA
  in business.  My area of express interest was marketing.

  I became acquainted with your company through my intern work at the
  Dunhill Agency in New York.  I have always hoped to combine my
  B:\CLETTER                                Doc 1 Pg 1 Ln 4.33" Pos 4.3"
```

(a)

◄

Figure 12-8 Editing the letter.
Carl uses the flexibility of word processing to edit his letter. (a) First he uses the insert mode to add the word "express" in the middle of a line. He positions the cursor and types in the word and a space. (b) Carl decides to use the typeover mode to change "express" to "special." As Carl keys in the new word, he types over the word he wants to replace. In the screen shown here, he has typed "spec" so far, so we still see the "ess" of "express."

```
                                    18 Leroy Street
                                    Binghamton, NY  10037
                                    July 13, 1992


  Ms. Louise Graham
  Director of Personnel
  Charnley Advertising, Inc.
  1900 Corporate Lane
  Baltimore, Maryland 21200


  Dear Ms. Graham:

  I am writing to inquire about the possibility of a position in
  Charnley's accounts department.

  I recently graduated from Pennsylvania State University with a BA
  in business.  My area of specess interest was marketing.

  I became acquainted with your company through my intern work at the
  Dunhill Agency in New York.  I have always hoped to combine my
  Typeover                                  Doc 1 Pg 1 Ln 4.33" Pos 3.9"
```

(b)

saved in a file named B:CLETTER. As an alternative, Carl could save the letter as part of the exit process: In this case, he would press the F7 key to exit, then Y to save the document, then Enter to indicate that the named document was the one to be saved, then Y to indicate that CLETTER was to be replaced, and finally Y to exit WordPerfect.

After you have practiced a bit, you will see that making changes with word processing is swift and efficient, even for a short document such as a letter. Given the volume of correspondence—or any kind of typing—in an office, the labor savings is significant.

FORMATTING: MAKING IT LOOK GOOD

Now that you know the basics of creating text with a word processing program, you can turn your attention to the appearance, or **format**, of the document. Formatting is not a trivial matter. In fact, one of the most appealing aspects of word processing is the capability it gives you

```
                                        18 Leroy Street
                                        Binghamton, NY  10037
                                        July 13, 1992


Ms. Louise Graham
Director of Personnel
Charnley Advertising, Inc.
1900 Corporate Lane
Baltimore, Maryland  21200


Dear Ms. Graham:

I am writing to inquire about the possibility of a position in
Charnley's accounts department.

I recently graduated from Pennsylvania State University with a BA
in business.  My area of special interest was marketing.

I became acquainted with your company through my intern work at the
Dunhill Agency in New York.  I have always hoped to combine my
background in business and my interest in marketing.  Charnley
Advertising seems to offer the best opportunity for doing this.

While I was in school, I prepared and monitored advertising
campaigns and tracked account budgets.  I am also familiar with
several types of computers and computer systems.

I will be in Baltimore on July 28 and 29. Would it be possible for
us to meet to discuss this further?  I can be reached at 600-623-
4667.  I look forward to hearing from you.

Sincerely,


Carl Wade
```

Figure 12-9   The corrected letter.
Carl prints out the corrected letter, knowing he can make further changes later if he wishes.

to adjust a document's appearance. With this capability you can present your company—or yourself—on paper in the best possible light.

Image is important. A multimillion-dollar company that relies on public opinion certainly wants to appear at its best on paper. So do little companies that do not have money to spend on fancy typesetting and printing. All these companies, big and small, can afford word processing.

The format of a document is the way the document appears on the page. *Format* refers to the size of the margins, indents, type size, margin alignment, the space between the lines, and all the other factors that affect appearance. Figure 12-10 shows some format considerations. Word processing software can control and vary these and many other format features.

To show you how formatting works, we return to Carl Wade, whose resume needs some work.

The Resume Example

Once Carl finishes his cover letter, he takes another look at a printed copy of his resume (Figure 12-11). He sees at a glance that it can use some improvement: The resume is bunched up at the top of the page,

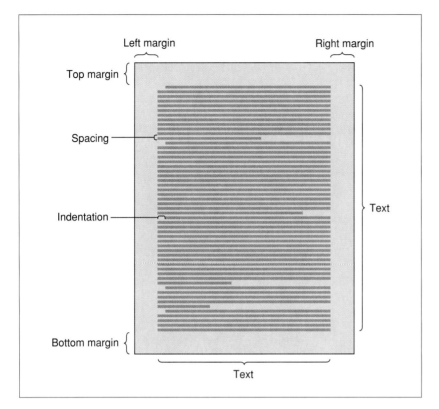

◄

Figure 12-10 Formatting considerations.
Word processing software lets you change the look of your document. For example, you can change the margins or center a page with just a few keystrokes. You can also alter the indentations, use double spacing, or make dozens of other style changes in a matter of seconds.

```
CARL WADE
18 LEROY STREET
BINGHAMTON, NY  10037
600-623-4667


CAREER OBJECTIVE
Challenging position with an advertising agency as an entry-level
account representative.  Seeking the experience that leads to a
career as an accounts manager.

EDUCATION
College: The Pennsylvania State University
Degree: Bachelor of Arts
Major: Business
Specialization: Marketing
GPA: 3.8

HONORS AND ACTIVITIES
Lloyd B. Trennon Honor Scholarship (2 years)
Kiwanis Achievement Scholarship (3 years)
Class Treasurer (Junior year)
President, Computer Club (Senior year)

EMPLOYMENT HISTORY
Junior Intern.  The Dunhill Agency, Binghamton, NY.  Earned one of
three student internships.  Assisted in preparing and monitoring
advertising campaigns.  Used Lotus 1-2-3 to track account budgets.
(Full time for two summers, part time senior year.)

Receptionist.  Martin Lumber Company, Binghamton, NY.
Responsibilities included greeting customers, coordinating
calendars and appointments, and taking community groups on company
tours.  (Summer job.)

REFERENCES
Available on request.
```

◄

Figure 12-11 The first draft of Carl's resume.
This is Carl's first draft of his resume. It is a good start, but he can make it much better. If Carl had to rely on a typewriter to make the corrections described in the text, he would have to retype the entire page.

giving it a short, squatty look. Carl wonders if the name and address lines would look better if they were centered. And he sees that the text runs together, making it hard to read. As Carl ponders various ways to fix the resume, he loads the original version from the disk and studies it on the screen.

Carl decides on several format changes to make the resume appear longer and more attractive. These changes are (1) adding a blank line after each major heading, (2) centering the name and address lines, (3) centering the text vertically on the page, (4) increasing the width of the margins, and (5) using boldface and underlining to highlight certain words.

Adding Blank Lines

The first change is easy enough: Carl positions the cursor at the end of the first major heading, "CAREER OBJECTIVE," and presses Enter. This action adds a blank line in the text. In the same way, Carl adds a blank line after each major heading.

Centering Lines

To center the name and address lines between the left and right margins of the page, Carl positions the cursor under the leftmost character of the first line and holds down the Shift key while pressing the F6 key. This automatically centers the line of text. He repeats this process for each of the next three lines. Figure 12-12 shows the results.

Vertical Centering

Carl's next improvement is to center the entire resume on the page, a process called vertical centering. **Vertical centering** adjusts the top and bottom margins so the text is centered vertically on the printed page. This eliminates the need to calculate the exact number of lines to leave at the top and bottom, a necessary process if using a typewriter.

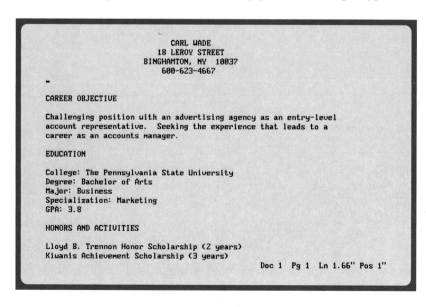

► **Figure 12-12   Easy centering.**
With word processing, Carl can center the top four lines without the risk of introducing typing errors.

To center the whole page vertically, the cursor must be at the top of the page. After Carl moves the cursor, he holds down the Shift key and then presses the F8 key. Next he types 2 to see the page format menu. He then types 1 to choose the option for vertical centering. Finally, he presses Enter twice to return to the document. The document does not look different on the screen, but when it is printed it will be centered vertically.

Changing Margins

When Carl first typed his resume, he left the margins—left and right, top and bottom—on their original settings. As we noted earlier, the original settings are called the default settings. Both the default left and right margins are usually 1 inch wide, leaving room for about 64 characters per line of text. Usually, the default top and bottom margins are also 1 inch each, allowing about 55 lines of text per page.

Documents are often typed using the default margin settings. However, if the document would look better with narrower or wider margins, the margin settings can be changed accordingly. Most packages even allow several different margin settings in various parts of the same document. Carl wants to widen the left and right margins for the entire resume by ½ inch on each side. To do this, he will move the cursor to the top of the document, then change each margin from its default of 1 inch to 1.5 inches. After the cursor is at the top of the document, he holds down the Shift key while pressing the F8 key. Next he presses 1 to get the line format menu, and then he presses 7 to choose the margin option. He types 1.5 and presses Enter to change the left margin; he again types 1.5 and presses Enter for the right margin. He presses Enter twice to get back to the document. The result is shown in Figure 12-13.

When the margin settings are changed, most word processing software automatically adjusts the text to fit the new margins. This process is called **automatic reformatting.** Notice in Figure 12-13 how WordPerfect automatically reformatted the resume so the text now fits

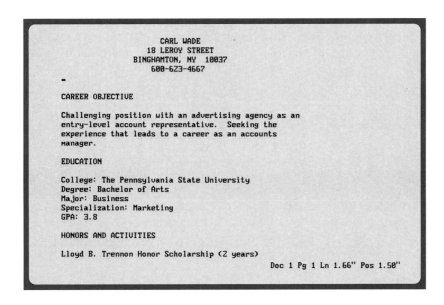

◄ **Figure 12-13   Changing the margins.**
When Carl widened the margins, WordPerfect automatically shifted the text to fit into the narrower space. Notice that the CAREER OBJECTIVE paragraph now takes up four lines rather than three.

in the new margin widths. With some word processing packages, you may have to press keys to initiate the reformatting.

Adding Boldface and Underlining

Finally, Carl decides to add a few special touches to his resume. He wants to use darker text, known as **boldface** text, for the address and name lines and the major headings. He wants to emphasize his job titles by underlining them.

To boldface words, Carl first positions the cursor at the beginning of the section he wants to be darker. He holds down the Alt key while pressing the F4 key. Then he moves the cursor to the end of the section to be boldface. This highlights the section (Figure 12-14a). Next Carl presses F6; the text to be boldface appears on screen as brighter, dimmer, or a different color than the surrounding words— the resulting on-screen effect depends on the word processing package and the type of monitor being used (Figure 12-14b). When the resume is printed, the marked words appear darker than the rest of the text. If Carl wants to enter the command to boldface text as he keys in a document, he can press F6 before he starts to type the words he wants to be boldface and then press F6 again after he has finished typing them.

Underlining is also easy. To underline already typed text, Carl first positions the cursor at the beginning of the section he wants to under-line. Next he holds down the Alt key and presses the F4 key. He then moves the cursor to the end of the text to be underlined, which high-lights the text. After he does this, he presses F8. The text assumes a different appearance on the screen—brighter or in another color or possibly even underlined, depending on the word processing program (Figure 12-14c). Once the document is printed, the text he wanted underlined is underlined. If Carl wants to underline while he is typing, he presses F8 to start the underlining command, then presses F8 again when he wants to stop the underlining.

The final printed version of Carl's resume is shown in Figure 12-15. As you can see, the resume is much more attractive and readable than the original version. As before, Carl saved his resume on the data disk, so he has the option of making more changes in the future. The changes can be format changes or changes to the substance of his resume; he can, for example, add job experience as he gains it.

TEXT BLOCKS: MOVING, DELETING, AND COPYING

A **text block** is a unit of text in a document. A text block can consist of one or more words, phrases, sentences, paragraphs, or even pages. Text blocks can be moved, deleted, copied, saved, and inserted. You can manipulate text blocks by using just a few keystrokes. To appreci-ate the power of text-block commands, imagine trying to move a para-graph to another place in a document if your only tool were a type-writer.

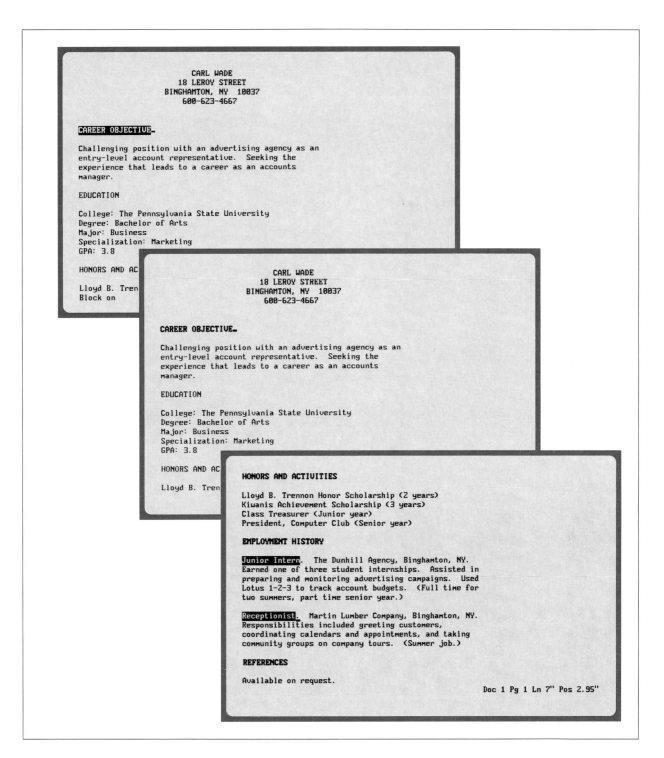

▲
Figure 12-14 Marking text.
(a) Carl marks—highlights—the text he wants in boldface. (b) When Carl presses F6 to make the text boldface, the marked text appears darker than the surrounding text. (c) Carl uses the F8 key to underline key words in his resume.

```
                          CARL WADE
                       18 LEROY STREET
                     BINGHAMTON, NY  10037
                       600-623-4667


     CAREER OBJECTIVE

     Challenging position with an advertising agency as an
     entry-level account representative. Seeking the
     experience that leads to a career as an accounts
     manager.

     EDUCATION

     College: The Pennsylvania State University
     Degree: Bachelor of Arts
     Major: Business
     Specialization: Marketing
     GPA: 3.8

     HONORS AND ACTIVITIES

     Lloyd B. Trennon Honor Scholarship (2 years)
     Kiwanis Achievement Scholarship (3 years)
     Class Treasurer (Junior year)
     President, Computer Club (Senior year)

     EMPLOYMENT HISTORY

     Junior Intern. The Dunhill Agency, Binghamton, NY.
     Earned one of three student internships. Assisted in
     preparing and monitoring advertising campaigns. Used
     Lotus 1-2-3 to track account budgets. (Full time for
     two summers, part time senior year.)

     Receptionist. Martin Lumber Company, Binghamton, NY.
     Responsibilities included greeting customers,
     coordinating calendars and appointments, and taking
     community groups on company tours. (Summer job.)

     REFERENCES

     Available on request.
```

▶
Figure 12-15   The final draft.
Compare this printed version of Carl's resume to his first draft in Figure 12-11.

The Survey Example

Shaunda Greene is taking her first sociology course at California College. Halfway through the term, she is asked to write a survey that evaluates people's eating and exercising habits. After class Shaunda goes to the school's computer lab, checks out WordPerfect, and sits down to write the survey.

After reading the first draft of her survey (Figure 12-16), Shaunda decides that it needs some changes. She wants to reverse the order of questions 4 and 5 so that all the eating-habit questions are together. She also wants to eliminate question 9, since it deals with hobbies rather than eating or exercising. And finally, she needs to type the Never-Always scale shown in question 1 for questions 2 through 8. Before Shaunda can do any of these tasks, however, she must first define—or **mark**—the text blocks she wants to manipulate.

```
Newspapers, magazines, and TV shows are filled with stories on
health and fitness.  But just how healthy are people today?  An
introductory sociology course at California College is conducting
a survey to evaluate community attitudes and activities.  We would
appreciate your helping us by answering the following questions.
Please circle the number that corresponds to the answer that best
describes your behavior.

  1.    Do you eat a variety of foods from each of the four food
        groups each day?
        Never          1     2     3     4     5          Always

  2.    Do you limit the amount of fat and cholesterol you eat?

  3.    Do you limit the amount of salt you eat?

  4.    Do you maintain your desired weight--being neither overweight
        nor underweight?

  5.    Do you limit the amount of sugar you eat?

  6.    Do you exercise vigorously for 15-30 minutes at least 3 times
        a week?

  7.    Do you walk to nearby locations rather than driving your car?

  8.    Do you take part in leisure activities that increase your
        level of fitness?

  9.    Do you participate in group activities or hobbies that you
        enjoy?

 10.    What is your age?
        a. under 18    b. 18-21    c. 22-35    d. 36-50    e. over 50

 11.    What is your sex?
        a.  male    b.  female

 12.    What is your marital status?
        a.  single       b.  married      c.  divorced
```

◄

Figure 12-16 The first draft of Shaunda's survey.
Shaunda enters this draft of her survey.

Marking a Block

Marking a block of text is done in different ways with different word processing software. In general, marking involves moving the cursor to the beginning of the chunk of text that constitutes the block and then either pressing a function key (or other keys) to place block markers there. Once the block is marked, it can be subject to a variety of block commands.

Since Shaunda is using WordPerfect, she positions the cursor at the beginning of question 4 (just under "4"), and holds down Alt while pressing F4. This turns on the Block command. WordPerfect reminds Shaunda that the command is on by flashing the words "Block on" in the lower-left corner of the screen. Next Shaunda moves the cursor until the entire question is highlighted. Now the block is marked (Figure 12-17).

Notice that the marked block stands out on the screen. Many word processing programs present marked blocks in **reverse video**—the print in the marked text is the color of the normal background and the background is the color of the normal text.

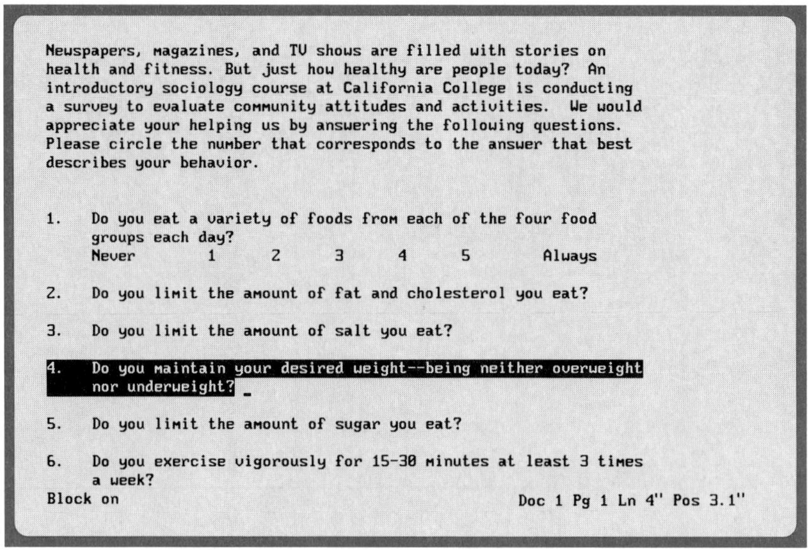

```
Newspapers, magazines, and TV shows are filled with stories on
health and fitness. But just how healthy are people today?  An
introductory sociology course at California College is conducting
a survey to evaluate community attitudes and activities.  We would
appreciate your helping us by answering the following questions.
Please circle the number that corresponds to the answer that best
describes your behavior.


1.    Do you eat a variety of foods from each of the four food
      groups each day?
      Never       1      2      3      4      5      Always

2.    Do you limit the amount of fat and cholesterol you eat?

3.    Do you limit the amount of salt you eat?

4.    Do you maintain your desired weight--being neither overweight
      nor underweight?

5.    Do you limit the amount of sugar you eat?

6.    Do you exercise vigorously for 15-30 minutes at least 3 times
      a week?
Block on                                    Doc 1 Pg 1 Ln 4" Pos 3.1"
```

▶

Figure 12-17   Marking a block of text.
Shaunda uses the Alt and F4 keys to mark
question 4.

Moving a Text Block

Once the text block is marked, Shaunda can use the Block Move command. The **Block Move** command removes a block of text from its
original location and places it in another location—the block still appears only once in the document. Moving a block from one location to
another is also called *cutting and pasting*, a reference to what literally
would have to be done if you were using a typewriter. WordPerfect
uses separate commands to achieve this end: one command that means
"cut," or delete the block from the current location, and another that
means "paste," or insert the block in the new location.

To move question 4 under question 5, Shaunda has already
marked question 4—the block she wants to move. Now she holds
down the Ctrl key and presses F4 to reveal the Block command options, which appear at the bottom of the screen (Figure 12-18a). She
presses 1 to indicate she is working with a block, then 1 to move the
block—that is, question 4. Question 4 disappears from the screen (Figure 12-18b). Shaunda now moves the cursor to the position where she
wants to insert question 4—under question 5. She presses the Enter
key to move the text to the current cursor location. Figure 12-18c
shows the survey after the question has been moved. Shaunda then
changes the numbering so the order is correct. Then she fixes the
spacing.

Deleting a Block

Shaunda is not done yet; she must get rid of question 9. In WordPerfect, the quickest way to delete a block is to mark the block and then
press the Del key. As she did before, Shaunda marks the block—in this
case, question 9—by positioning the cursor at the beginning of the text
to be marked, pressing Alt-F4, and moving the cursor to the end of the
text. She presses the Del key and the block disappears from the screen.
As before, Shaunda corrects the question numbers and fixes the
spacing.

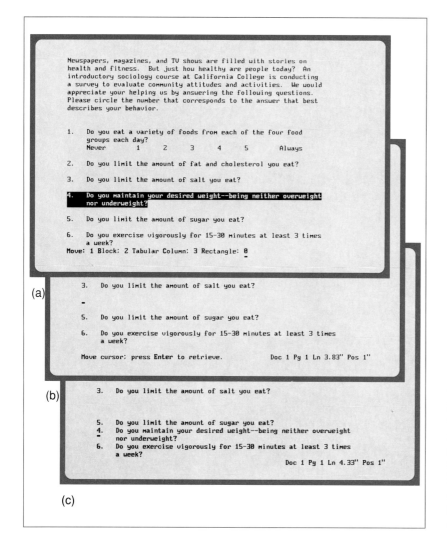

◀

Figure 12-18   Easy moves.
(a) After Shaunda marks the text she wants to move, she accesses the Block command options by pressing Ctrl-F4. (b) Shaunda presses 1 twice, and question 4 disappears from the screen. Shaunda then moves the cursor to the spot where she wants to insert the question. (c) When she presses Enter, question 4 appears in its new location.

Copying a Block

Now Shaunda wants to add the Never-Always scales. Because they are all the same, she can do this easily by using the Block Copy command. Similar to the Block Move command, the **Block Copy** command copies the block of text into a new location. However, the block stays in its original location—that is, the same text appears twice (or more) in the document. The Block Copy command comes in handy when similar material is needed repeatedly in the same document, since the text must be keyed in once only.

Shaunda has typed the scale once, as shown in Figure 12-16. As described, she presses Alt-F4 to mark the block of text and then presses Ctrl-F4 to display the Block command options. She presses 1 to indicate she is working with a block, then presses 2 to select the copy function. Next she moves the cursor to the position where she wants to insert the text—under question 2—and presses Enter to copy the text. She repeats these steps to copy the answer line under questions 3 through 8. (A shorter alternative for inserting the scale—a method that precludes remarking the block—is to place the cursor where the block is to be moved; press Shift-F10, for Retrieve; and then press Enter.) The final survey is shown in Figure 12-19.

Newspapers, magazines, and TV shows are filled with stories on
health and fitness. But just how healthy are people today? An
introductory sociology course at California College is conducting
a survey to evaluate community attitudes and activities. We would
appreciate your helping us by answering the following questions.
Please circle the number that corresponds to the answer that best
describes your behavior.

1.   Do you eat a variety of foods from each of the four food
     groups each day?
     Never   1   2   3   4   5   Always

2.   Do you limit the amount of fat and cholesterol you eat?
     Never   1   2   3   4   5   Always

3.   Do you limit the amount of salt you eat?
     Never   1   2   3   4   5   Always

4.   Do you limit the amount of sugar you eat?
     Never   1   2   3   4   5   Always

5.   Do you maintain your desired weight--being neither overweight
     nor underweight?
     Never   1   2   3   4   5   Always

6.   Do you exercise vigorously for 15-30 minutes at least 3 times
     a week?
     Never   1   2   3   4   5   Always

7.   Do you walk to nearby locations rather than driving your car?
     Never   1   2   3   4   5   Always

8.   Do you take part in leisure activities that increase your
     level of fitness?
     Never   1   2   3   4   5   Always

9.   What is your age?
     a. under 18   b. 18-21   c. 22-35   d. 36-50   e. over 50

10. What is your sex?
     a. male   b. female

11. What is your marital status?
     a. single   b. married   c. divorced

▶
Figure 12-19   The final draft.
Shaunda has made all the changes she wants at this time, so she prints the final draft of her survey.

SOME OTHER IMPORTANT FEATURES

Popular word processing packages offer more features than most people use. We cannot discuss every feature here, but we want to mention two that you will find handy—spacing and searching.

Spacing

Most of the time you will want your documents—letters, memos, reports—to be single spaced. But there are occasions when it is convenient or necessary to double space or even triple space a document. Word processing lets you do this with ease. In fact, a word processing program lets you switch back and forth from one type of spacing to another, just by pressing a few keys. A writer, for example, can print one single-spaced copy of a new chapter for his or her own use. Then a double-spaced copy of the same document can be printed for the editor, who will appreciate the space to make changes.

COMPUTING HIGHLIGHTS

Choosing a Software Package

We have said a lot about who is using what kind of software, and even why they are using it. But what are they using and how was the selection made? Some software brand names are well established. But much software—and certainly its price—is changing too frequently to be listed anywhere but in a weekly or monthly periodical. We can, however, address the selection process in a general way.

For any given application category, there are literally dozens or even hundreds of products for sale. Which way should you turn? Suppose you want to purchase a word processing package.

Hardware. If you already have a computer in mind, hardware is your first limitation. That is, you can only buy software that works on your machine. If your computer is an uncommon brand, your software choices are significantly narrowed.

If you have a brand for which there is a wide software selection, proceed with the search.

Standards. If you will be working with others, say, sending word-processed documents on disk for their perusal, then your choice of a word processing package is constrained by their choice. You must choose to agree. Sometimes selecting software is even more straightforward: If you work for an organization with established software standards, you use the package the organization has selected.

Recommendations. Everyone has an opinion. In particular, trade journals make it their business to have opinions, offering elaborate rating systems and survey results. Salespeople in retail software stores also have opinions and are usually happy to share them. And do not forget your friends and colleagues.

Join the crowd. Sometimes it is worth going with the most "popular" package just because all those people must be right, and at least you will share common ground. Many entrenched software packages stay that way, even when superior technology comes along. An established base, if it works adequately, is expensive to replace.

Search and Replace

Suppose you type a long report in which you repeatedly spell the name of a client as "Mr. Sullavan." After you submit the report to your boss, she sends it back to you with this note: "Our client's name is Sullivan, not Sullavan. Please fix this error and send me a corrected copy of the report."

You could scroll through the whole report looking for "Sullavan" and replacing the incorrect "a" with the correct letter. There is, however, a more efficient way—the **search and replace** function. You make a single request to replace one word or phrase with another. Then, search and replace quickly searches through the entire document, finding each instance of the word or phrase and replacing it with the word or phrase you designated. Most word processing programs offer **conditional replace,** which asks you to verify each replacement. In addition, the search function can be used by itself to find a particular item in a document.

EXTRA ADDED ATTRACTIONS
· · · · · · · · · · · · · · · · · · · ·

The popularity of word processing has encouraged the development of some very helpful programs that are used in conjunction with word processing software. These programs analyze text that has already been entered. The most widely used programs of this type check spelling or offer a thesaurus.

Spelling Checker Programs

A **spelling checker** program finds spelling errors you may have made when typing a document. The program compares each word in your document to the words it has in its "dictionary." A spelling checker's dictionary is a list of from 20,000 to 100,000 correctly spelled words. If the spelling checker program finds a word that is not on its list, it assumes that you have misspelled or mistyped that word. The WordPerfect spelling checker highlights the word by reversing the screen colors—the word in question appears blue on white instead of white on blue or in reverse video on monochrome screens. Then it displays words from its dictionary that are close in spelling or sound to the word you typed (Figure 12-20). If you recognize the correct spelling of the highlighted word in the list you are given, you can replace the incorrect word with the correct word from the list. If the word the program reads as misspelled is correct, you just leave it unchanged and signal the spelling checker to continue searching through your document.

Spelling checkers often do not recognize proper names, such as Ms. Waldo, or acronyms, such as NASA. So you must decide if the word is actually misspelled. If it is, you can correct it easily with the word processing software. If the word is correct, the software lets you signal that the word is acceptable.

▶

Figure 12-20   Spelling checker.
The highlighted word, "conjusion," is misspelled, so the spelling checker offers some alternatives in the area below the dashed lines. In this case, pressing A replaces the misspelled word with the correct spelling.

```
TYPES OF WORD PROCESSING PROGRAMS

* Business.  These programs duplicate the functions of the
dedicated word processors used in business offices.  Because so
many office personnel already know how to use the dedicated
machines, these packages sometimes cut down on conjusion and
reduce training costs.

* Professional.  These programs are designed to be used by people
whose jobs require a lot of text preparation, especially text
that will be published.  The functions included go far

--------------------------------------------------------------------
--------------------------------------------------------------------
   A. confusion           B. contusion           C. congestion


Not Found!  Select Word or Menu Option (0=Continue): 0
1 Skip Once; 2 Skip; 3 Add Word; 4 Edit; 5 Look Up; 6 Phonetic
```

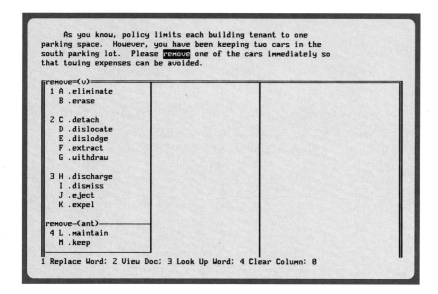

▲

Figure 12-21 A thesaurus program.
The words labeled A through K are synonyms for the highlighted word, "remove."

Thesaurus Programs

Have you ever chewed on the end of your pencil trying to think of just the right word—a better word than the bland one that immediately came to mind? Perhaps you were energetic enough to get a thesaurus to help you. A **thesaurus** is a book that gives synonyms (words with the same meaning) and antonyms (words with the opposite meaning) for common words. But never mind the big books. Now you can have a great vocabulary at your fingertips—electronically, of course. WordPerfect includes a thesaurus program.

Suppose you find a word in your document that you have used too frequently or that does not seem suitable. Place the cursor on the word. Then press the key to activate the thesaurus program. The program immediately provides a list of synonyms for the word you want to replace (Figure 12-21). You can then replace the word in your document with the synonym you prefer. It is easy, and it is even painlessly educational.

DESKTOP PUBLISHING: AN OVERVIEW

• • • • • • • • • • • • • • • • •

Would you like to be able to produce well-designed pages that combine elaborate charts and graphics with text and headlines in a variety of typefaces? Would you like to be able to do all this at your desk, without a ruler, pen, or paste? Now you can, with a technology called **desktop publishing.** You can use desktop publishing software to design sophisticated pages and, with a high-quality printer, print a professional-looking final document (Figure 12-22).

UPDATING SOFTWARE

From time to time, software makers offer new and improved versions of their software. If you are using an old version when a new version is made available, you have a decision to make: You can stick with the old or update to the new. Your decision will depend on a number of factors, not the least of which is whether you have the time to make the switch.

Suppose the new version has some features you could use. Are you willing to pay for the new version?

But money is not the primary consideration. Suppose you share files with a colleague who upgrades. Although your files—made with the older version—will probably still work with the upgraded version, files created by your colleague with the upgraded version may not work with your older version. This lack of compatibility is a powerful incentive to upgrade software.

Finally, are you willing to expend the time it takes to learn the new version? If you are well acquainted with the old version, the learning curve for the new version is usually not too steep. The decision is yours. Most users, both businesses and individuals, elect to update.

PRINCIPLES OF GOOD DESIGN

Desktop publishing programs put many different fonts and images at your disposal, but you can overwhelm a document if you crowd too much onto a page. The guidelines that follow will help get favorable reviews for you and your document:

- Do not use more than two or three typefaces in a document.

- Be conservative: Limit the use of decorative or unusual typefaces.

- Use different sizes and styles of one typeface to distinguish between different heading levels, rather than several different typefaces.

- Avoid cluttering a document with fancy borders and symbols.

- Do not use type that is too small to read easily just to fit everything on one page.

Figure 12-22   Desktop publishing.
With desktop publishing software and a high-quality laser printer, you can create professional-looking newsletters and documents.

Until recently, people who wanted to publish had just two alternatives—the traditional publishing process or word processing. Both processes have significant limitations. In the mid-1980s, however, the development of desktop publishing offered a new solution to the publishing problems of both large companies and individuals.

Consider the case of Andy Stokowski. Andy is an independent investment counselor who wants to send a newsletter to his clients. He wants to use the newsletter to outline conditions in investment markets, make investment recommendations, and describe some client success stories. In the past Andy tried to publish a newsletter by hiring conventional publishing services. But timing was a problem: By the time the newsletter was printed, the investment advice was out of date. Furthermore, using outside help to produce the newsletter was expensive. Andy tried to produce the newsletter himself, using word processing software, but the result was an unprofessional-looking flier.

With desktop publishing Andy can produce a newsletter that looks professional, without the cost and delay of going to outside services. Unlike word processing, desktop publishing gives the personal computer user the ability to do **page composition.** That is, Andy can decide where he wants text and pictures on a page, what typefaces he wants to use, and what other design elements he wants to include. He can also insert graphics into the text. Desktop publishing fills the gap between word processing and professional typesetting (Figure 12-23).

In the next two sections we present some publishing terminology and then discuss desktop publishing software.

▲
Figure 12-23   High-end desktop publishing.
This professional-looking magazine cover was produced entirely with computer software. The totem-pole art was created with graphics software. The type and layout were produced with desktop publishing software, which was also used to combine the text and art. In a separate step, the magazine cover was printed by a color printer.

THE PUBLISHING PROCESS

Sometimes we take the quality appearance of publications for granted. A great deal of activity goes on behind the scenes to prepare a document for publication. Writers, editors, designers, typesetters, and printers all contribute their knowledge and experience to complete a finished document. When you begin to plan your own publications, you will play several roles.

Desktop publishing gives the user full control over the editing and design of the document. Desktop publishing also eliminates the time-consuming measuring and cutting and pasting involved in traditional production techniques.

The Art of Design

Word processing programs can generate lines of text that look like a typed page, but if you are producing a brochure or newsletter, a more sophisticated appearance is expected. One part of the design is **page layout**—how the text and pictures are arranged on the page. For example, magazine publishers have found that text organized in columns and separated by a solid vertical line is an effective page layout. If pictures are used, they must be inserted into the text. Picture size needs to be adjusted for proper fit on the page. In addition to page layout, designers must take into account such factors as headings, type sizes, and typefaces. Are general headings used? Do separate sections or articles need their own subheadings? Does the size of the type need to be increased or decreased to fit a story into a predetermined space? What is the best typeface to use? Should there be more than one kind of typeface used on a page?

To help you understand how some of the decisions are made, we need to discuss some of the publishing terminology involved.

WINDOWS

Linking Arts and Letters

Microsoft Windows has opened up a whole new way of looking at things for those producing desktop-published documents using DOS-based computers. With word processing and graphics software packages designed specifically for Windows, producing attractive, professional-looking publications is faster and easier than ever.

Imagine that you are using a DOS-based computer and a laser printer to produce the monthly newsletter of the Daisy Hill Horticultural Society. One of the hallmarks of the newsletter is the exquisite botanical artwork that illustrates each issue. Without Windows, creating the text and graphics for the newsletter involves the following steps. First, you start up the word processing program and enter the newsletter text. Then you save the text file and quit the word processing program. At the DOS prompt you start up the graphics program, then design the illustration. When it is finished, you save the file and quit the graphics program. Back at the DOS prompt again, you start up the word processor a second time and find the point in the text where you want to insert the graphic. After pressing a few function keys, you type in the name of the graphics file. A note appears in the text, telling you that the illustration will be printed in that location after you send the text file to the printer. Finally, you print the

text file to see the illustration in its proper place on the page. If you decide the image is too large, for example, you have to go through the whole process again.

With word processing and graphics programs designed for Windows, you can link text and graphics much more efficiently. As before, you start up the word processor and key in the newsletter text. But when you are finished, you do not need to quit that program. Instead, you point with the mouse to a symbol (icon) on the screen that represents your graphics software. With two clicks of the mouse, the graphics software starts up in a separate window. You draw the illustration, then select the Copy option from the program's File menu.

Without quitting the graphics program, you put the mouse pointer back into the word processor window and click the mouse. Finding the place where you want the illustration to appear, you again point and click. Then you select Paste from the word processor's File menu. The illustration—not just a note about it—appears on the page just as it will appear on paper. If the artwork does not look right, you still have both applications open and can easily make changes.

Windows has not changed the tasks you can do with your computer, but it has simplified the process of doing the same chores. You can save time, save paper, and put out a better newsletter—all thanks to Windows.

Helvetica (12 pt)

Helvetica (18 pt)

Helvetica (24 pt)

Helvetica (36 pt)

Helvetica (48 pt)

▲

Figure 12-24 Different point sizes.
This figure shows a variety of different point sizes in the typeface called Helvetica.

Typefaces: Sizes and Styles

The type that a printer uses is described by its size, typeface, weight, and style. **Type size** is measured by a standard system that uses points. A **point** equals about $\frac{1}{72}$ inch. Point size is measured from the top of the letter that rises the highest above the baseline (a letter such as *b* or *l*) to the bottom of the letter that descends the lowest (a letter such as *g* or *y*). The text you are now reading was typeset in 10.5-point type; margin notes, however, were set in 9-point type. Figure 12-24 shows type in different sizes.

The shapes of the letters and numbers in a published document are determined by the typeface selected. A **typeface** is a set of characters—letters, punctuation, and numbers—of the same design. The typeface of the text you are now reading is called Janson. A typeface can be printed in a specific **weight**—such as boldface, which is darker than usual—or in a specific **style**—such as italic. Changes in typeface provide emphasis and variety. A **font** is a complete set of characters in a particular size, typeface, weight, and style.

As shown in Figure 12-25a, varying the size and style of the type used in a publication can improve the appearance of a page and draw attention to the most important sections. However, using too many different fonts or using clashing fonts can create a page that is unattractive and hard to read (Figure 12-25b). Combine fonts with discretion.

Most printers used in desktop publishing store a selection of fonts in a ROM chip in the printer. These are called the printer's **internal fonts.** Also, most desktop publishing programs provide a **font library** on a disk. A font library contains a wide selection of type fonts called **soft fonts.** A soft font can be sent—downloaded—from the library disk in the computer's disk drive to the printer. Then the printer can print type in the new font.

Leading and Kerning

Two terms you will encounter when you begin desktop publishing are *leading* and *kerning*. **Leading** (pronounced "ledding") refers to the spacing between the lines of type on a page. Leading is measured vertically from the base of one line of type to the base of the line above it.

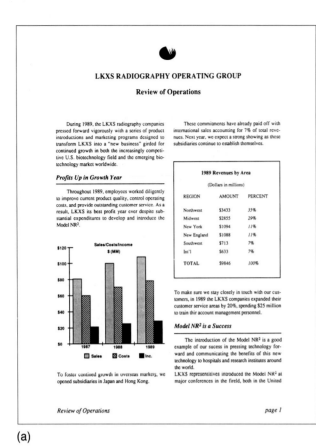

(a)

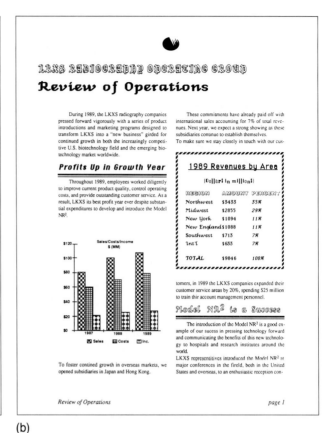

(b)

Figure 12-25 Sample designs.
(a) This example uses complementary typefaces to produce a professional-looking document. (b) The same page created with clashing typefaces.

The greater the leading, the more white space between lines. Leading—just like type size—is measured in points. **Kerning** refers to adjusting the space between the characters in a line. In desktop publishing software each font has a default kerning. Occasionally, you might want to change the kerning to improve the appearance of the final typeset work. An example of kerning is shown in Figure 12-26.

Halftones

Halftones, which resemble photographs, appear in newspapers, magazines, books, and documents produced by desktop publishing. Halftones are representations made up of black dots printed on white paper. Varying the number and size of dots in a given space produces shades of gray. As you can see in Figure 12-27, the smaller the dot pattern used, the clearer the halftone. At present, only the most expensive printers used in desktop publishing produce halftones that meet professional standards.

Now let us put this publishing background to work by examining desktop publishing in more detail.

(a) Unkerned:

WAVE

(b) Kerned:

WAVE

Figure 12-26 Kerning.
(a) In this example, the space between the characters is not altered. (b) Kerning, or adjusting the space between the characters, can improve the overall appearance of the word.

▲
Figure 12-27   Halftones.
Halftones consist of a series of dots. Reducing the size of the dots makes the
resulting halftone clearer.

DESKTOP PUBLISHING SOFTWARE

• • • • • • • • • • • • • • • • • •

Desktop publishing systems consist of the following software:

- A word processing program to create the text of the publication
- A graphics program to create and manipulate the graphics of the publication
- A page composition program

The page composition program is the key ingredient of a desktop publishing system.

Page composition programs, also called **page makeup programs** or **desktop publishing programs,** let you design each page, on the computer screen. You can determine the number and the width of the columns of text to be printed on the page. You can also indicate where pictures, charts, graphs, and headlines should be placed.

Once you have created the page design, you use the page composition program to combine the text files created by your word processing program with the graphics you produced with your graphics program; then the page composition program inserts them into the page design you laid out. Page composition programs also let you move blocks of text and pictures around on your page. If you are not satisfied with the way the page looks, you can change the size of the type or the pictures.

Page composition programs can also integrate **clip art**—images already produced by professional artists for public use—into your publication to enliven your text. You can purchase disks that contain various kinds of clip art. Figure 12-28 shows examples of illustrations in a clip art library.

IT USED TO BE SO EASY TO TELL THEM APART

Perhaps you have seen proposals or newsletters or contracts done with desktop publishing. They look so good. You want your work to look good too—crisp, professional, as if it just came from the typesetter. You want desktop publishing. Or do you?

Many people who think they want desktop publishing are actually attracted to quality printing—the output from a laser printer. Those same people may want only a few of the tricks of the trade—putting the word *memo* in inch-high letters across the top of the page or perhaps putting a heavy line across the bottom of the page, followed by the page number. These users may not want to switch to desktop publishing—it may not be worth their time or money. Word processing vendors, recognizing a need, are upgrading their products to include some desktop publishing features.

First there was word processing and then there was desktop publishing. What will the hybrid be called? High-end word processing? Superprocessing? Word publishing?

MACINTOSH

Another Way with Words

Because of its special screen technology, the Macintosh is best known for allowing people to create graphics—illustrations, charts, and diagrams. This capability also makes it a special kind of word processing program. Type can be virtually any size, for example. And, instead of waiting for your document to roll off the printer, you can get a good idea of just how a page will look from viewing portions of it on the Mac screen.

With the Macintosh you can format your text directly by using the mouse. Words that you want boldface or underlined show up that way on the screen, as shown in screen (a). True to the Mac's visual presentation, most word processing pro-

grams on the Mac have a ruler running across the top of the screen; you can use the ruler to set tabs, center or align text, and adjust margins.

The steps for moving text are the same in all Mac programs. Using the mouse to highlight the text you want to move, you first "cut" and then "paste" the text where you want it. The real advantage of this method is that you can copy selections from other documents and programs—spreadsheets, databases, even graphics. The Mac's "clipboard" stores the data while you change files or programs.

The Macintosh comes with several typefaces, but hundreds more are available; you can have a virtu-

ally unlimited choice in determining the look of your document. Type on the screen closely resembles what comes out on your printer. Using a laser printer, often available at copy centers and instant print shops, you can produce high-quality, professional-looking documents formatted to your liking. Most word processing programs for the Mac have special typographic effects like shadow and outline type, and more sophisticated programs allow you to create tables and multiple columns. With this kind of flexibility, you can create newsletters as well as eye-catching memos, reports, and term papers. On the Mac, word processing becomes more like typesetting and less like typewriting.

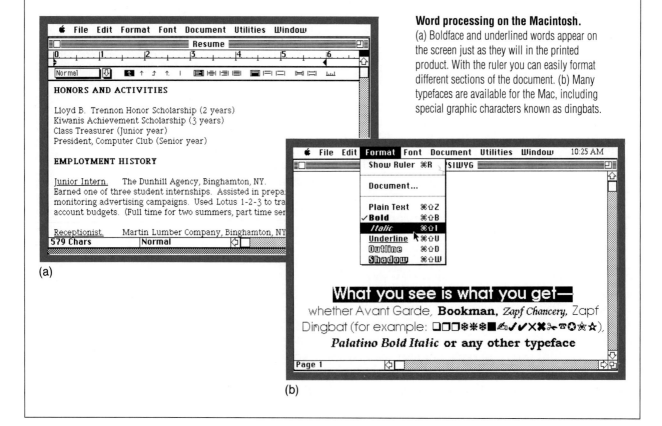

(a)

(b)

Word processing on the Macintosh.
(a) Boldface and underlined words appear on the screen just as they will in the printed product. With the ruler you can easily format different sections of the document. (b) Many typefaces are available for the Mac, including special graphic characters known as dingbats.

▲
Figure 12-28   Clip art.
A variety of clip art software can be purchased and used to improve the appearance of a document. Most clip art is mundane—standard sketches of everyday items such as cars, flags, food, and household implements. The items pictured here offer a little more visual enhancement than the usual clip art.

DESKTOP PUBLISHING: THE PAYOFF
• • • • • • • • • • • • • • • • • • •

The design, typesetting, and printing costs incurred by company publications are a major business expense. Many companies spend hundreds of thousands of dollars annually on publishing. Publications are a major expense for nonprofit organizations as well.

Desktop publishing users value the time and money savings the programs provide, but what they value even more is the control—the ability to see for themselves exactly how a change in the type size or layout looks by observing the results immediately on a computer screen. No more company newsletters filled with typos and amateurish drawings; most offices are moving to the greener pastures of desktop publishing.

▲   ▲   ▲

We hope you are convinced that word processing is a great time-saver, that it is easy to learn, and that it is one of the best software tools for personal computers. Most of all, we hope you are convinced that word processing is essential for your career, no matter what it is, and that desktop publishing is a valuable tool for individuals as well as businesses.

Some people, however, are much more interested in software that works with numbers rather than words. We are talking, of course, about spreadsheet software. This important topic is the subject of our next chapter.

CHAPTER REVIEW

SUMMARY AND KEY TERMS

- **Word processing** is the creation, editing, formatting, storing, and printing of a text document.

- As you type, the screen displays a **cursor** to show where the next character you type will appear; you can move the cursor by using **cursor movement keys.** The **PgUp** and **PgDn** keys move the cursor up or down a page at a time.

- **Scrolling,** done by moving the cursor, lets you see any part of the document on the screen.

- **Word wrap** automatically starts a word on the next line if it does not fit on one line.

- The purpose of each function key differs according to each application. A **template,** which fits above the function keys, briefly describes the use of each key.

- Some word processing packages offer a set of choices, called a **menu,** on the screen.

- After entering text and making corrections, save the document on a data disk.

- To edit a document, you must first retrieve it from the disk. The **insert mode** is the **default mode**—the setting used by the word processing package unless deliberately changed by the user. **Typeover mode** allows you to replace existing text with new text. The Ins key acts as a **toggle switch,** allowing you to switch between the insert mode and the typeover mode.

- The **format** of a document is the way it appears on the page: the choice of text, margin width, line spacing, boldface, underlining, and so on.

- **Vertical centering** refers to centering text between the top and bottom margins.

- **Automatic reformatting** means that the word processing software automatically adjusts the text to fit new margins.

- In a printed document, **boldface** words appear darker than the rest of the text.

- A **text block** can be moved, deleted, copied, saved, and inserted. To manipulate a block of text, you must first **mark** the block, which then usually appears in **reverse video** (in which the background color becomes the text color and vice versa).

- The **Block Move** command moves the text to a different location. The **Block Copy** command copies the block of text into a new location, leaving the text in its original location as well.

- The **search and replace** function searches through a document to find each instance of a certain word or phrase and replaces it with another word or phrase. A **conditional replace** asks you to verify each replacement.

- A number of special programs work in conjunction with a word processing package, analyzing text that has been entered already. These programs include a **spelling checker** program, which includes a built-in dictionary, and a **thesaurus** program, which supplies synonyms and antonyms.

- A **desktop publishing** program lets you produce professional-looking documents containing both text and graphics.
- One part of the overall design of a document is **page layout**—how text and pictures are arranged on the page. Adding type to a layout is called **page composition.**
- Printers offer a variety of type. Type is described by **type size, typeface, weight,** and **style.** Type size is measured by a standard system based on the **point.** A **font** is a complete set of characters in a particular size, typeface, weight, and style.
- Most printers used in desktop publishing contain **internal fonts** stored in a ROM chip. Most desktop publishing programs provide a **font library** on disk, containing a selection of type fonts called **soft fonts.**
- **Leading** refers to the spacing between the lines of type on a page. **Kerning** refers to adjusting the space between the characters in a line.
- A **halftone**—a representation made up of dots—can be produced by desktop publishing printers.
- The software requirements for desktop publishing include a word processing program, a graphics program, and a page composition program. **Page composition** programs, also called **page makeup** programs or **desktop publishing** programs, enable the user to design the page layout. Page composition programs also allow the incorporation of electronically stored clip art, professionally produced images for public use.

SELF-TEST

True/False

T   F   1. *Formatting* refers to adjusting the appearance of a document to make it look attractive.

T   F   2. A spelling checker program can detect spelling errors, typos, and improper use of language.

T   F   3. In WordPerfect, the default margins are $\frac{1}{2}$ inch.

T   F   4. In WordPerfect the Block Copy command moves text to another place and deletes it from its original place.

T   F   5. Text is centered vertically by adjusting the right margin.

T   F   6. A conditional replace goes through the program and automatically replaces each instance of a repeated error.

T   F   7. Text can be marked to be underlined when printed.

T   F   8. Most desktop publishing systems include an inexpensive dot-matrix printer.

T   F   9. Once a page layout has been planned using desktop publishing, the layout is very difficult to change.

T   F   10. *Kerning* refers to the space between lines.

Matching

_____ 1. cut and paste	a. default
_____ 2. word wrap	b. finds and corrects
_____ 3. file	c. clip art
_____ 4. thesaurus program	d. reorder text
_____ 5. boldface	e. synonyms
_____ 6. space between lines	f. computer-created document
_____ 7. composed of dots	g. leading
_____ 8. art stored on disk	h. darker print
_____ 9. original setting	i. "watches" right margin
_____ 10. search and replace function	j. halftone

Fill-In

1. A complete set of characters in a particular size, typeface, weight, and style is called: _____

2. A set of drawings stored on disk: _____

3. The fonts stored in the printer are called: _____

4. A feature that permits document viewing, about 24 lines at a time: _____

5. You can make a document shorter and wider by resetting the: _____

6. The feature that finds and changes text: _____

7. Words in darker type are: _____

8. Before a block of text can be copied or moved, it must be: _____

9. The computer's adjustment to fit text in new margin settings is called: _____

10. Italic is an example of this typeface characteristic: _____

Answers

True/False: 1. T, 3. F, 5. F, 7. T, 9. F

Matching: 1. d, 3. f, 5. h, 7. j, 9. a

Fill-In: 1. font, 3. internal fonts 5. margins 7. boldface, 9. automatic reformatting

CHAPTER 13

OVERVIEW

SPREADSHEETS AND BUSINESS GRAPHICS
FACTS AND FIGURES

arry Wailes earned his degree in accounting just before the revolution—the Computer Revolution, that is. He learned to balance corporate budgets by using a desktop calculator, a paper ledger, and a sharp pencil. He learned the value of double- and triple-checking his figures before inking them in on the final copy.

Barry did not actually lay eyes on an electronic spreadsheet until he had been on the job for several years. The first spreadsheet he saw was at a business convention, where all the activity was focused on the Apple exhibit. The flickering, black-and-white screen of an Apple II computer displayed VisiCalc, the first widely available electronic spreadsheet software.

Barry was not impressed at first. The little Apple screen showed only a few rows and columns of numbers. The only way to see the whole ledger at once was to print it. Yes, the machine-printed ledger was attractive. But a secretary could type a table of numbers on a typewriter and make it look even better. But there was something hypnotic about the shimmering computer display. Barry began to listen to the sales representative.

The first advantage of electronic spreadsheets that Barry noticed was that no erasers were required. When the sales rep made a mistake, he just backspaced over it and entered the correct number. But the greater advantage was one that had not been at all apparent at

first. The sales representative pointed out that not all the numbers in the spreadsheet had been keyed in manually; several of the columns of numbers had been calculated automatically by the computer. As the sales rep made changes to some of the manually entered numbers, Barry watched the automatically calculated figures change accordingly. A change in one number—an interest percentage, for instance—could result in the automatic updating of half the numbers in the spreadsheet.

Back at the office, Barry lobbied hard for a desktop computer and electronic spreadsheet software. Now, more than a decade later, Barry works on a personal computer 50 times more powerful than his first Apple II. He moves rows and columns of data with the click of the mouse. And he has a color screen that shows him high-quality graphs automatically constructed from the spreadsheet data.

Barry went from skeptic to computer enthusiast in one afternoon. Not everyone is that quick at seeing how to apply a computer-based tool to a particular line of work. However, once experienced, it is hard to live without the computer advantage. ◻

ELECTRONIC SPREADSHEETS

. . . .

A worksheet to present business data in rows and columns is called a **spreadsheet** (Figure 13-1a). The manually constructed spreadsheet has been used as a business tool for centuries. Spreadsheets can be used to organize and present business data, thus aiding managerial decisions. But spreadsheets are not limited to businesses. Personal and family budgets, for example, are often organized on spreadsheets. Furthermore, nonfinancial or even non-numerical data can benefit from a spreadsheet format.

Unfortunately, creating a large spreadsheet manually is time-consuming and tedious, even when you use a calculator or copy results from a computer printout. Another problem with manual spreadsheets is that making a mistake is too easy. If you do not discover the mistake, the consequences may be serious. If you do discover the mistake after

	JAN.	FEB.	MAR.	APR.	TOTAL	MIN	MAX
SALES	1750	1501	1519	1430	6200	1430	1750
COST OF GOODS SOLD	964	980	932	943	3819	932	980
GROSS MARGIN	786	521	587	487	2381	487	786
NET EXPENSE	98	93	82	110	383	82	110
ADM EXPENSE	77	79	69	88	313	69	88
MISC EXPENSE	28	45	31	31	135	28	45
TOTAL EXPENSES	203	217	182	229	831	182	229
AVERAGE EXPENSE	68	72	61	76	227	61	76
NET BEFORE TAXES	583	304	405	258	1550	258	583
FEDERAL TAXES	303	158	211	134	806	134	303
NET AFTER TAX	280	146	194	124	744	124	280

(a)

```
                      A        B       C      D      E      F      G      H      I
                 1            JAN     FEB    MAR    APR   TOTAL   MIN    MAX
                 2            ==========================================================
                 3   SALES            1750    1501   1519   1430   6200   1430   1750
                 4   COST OF GOODS SOLD 964     980    932    943   3819    932    980
                 5            ----------------------------------------------------------
                 6       GROSS MARGIN   786     521    587    487   2381    487    786
                 7
                 8   NET EXPENSE         98      93     82    110    383     82    110
                 9   ADM EXPENSE         77      79     69     88    313     69     88
                10   MISC EXPENSE        28      45     31     31    135     28     45
                11            ----------------------------------------------------------
                12       TOTAL EXPENSES 203     217    182    229    831    182    229
                13       AVERAGE EXPENSE 68      72     61     76    227     61     76
                14
                15   NET BEFORE TAX     583     304    405    258   1550    258    583
                16   FEDERAL TAXES      303     158    211    134    806    134    303
                17            ----------------------------------------------------------
                18       NET AFTER TAX  280     146    194    124    744    124    280
                19
                20
```

(b)

▶ **Figure 13-1 Manual versus electronic spreadsheets.**
(a) This manual spreadsheet is a typical spreadsheet consisting of rows and columns. (b) The same spreadsheet created with a spreadsheet program.

the spreadsheet is finished, you must manually redo all the calculations that used the wrong number.

An **electronic spreadsheet** is a computerized version of a manual spreadsheet (Figure 13-1b). Working with a spreadsheet on a computer eliminates much of the toil of setting up a manual spreadsheet. In general, an electronic spreadsheet works like this: You enter the data you want on your spreadsheet and then key in the types of calculations you need. The electronic spreadsheet program automatically does all the calculations for you, completely error-free, and produces the results. You can print a copy of the spreadsheet and store it on your disk so that the spreadsheet can be used again. But the greatest labor-saving aspect of the electronic spreadsheet is that, when you change one value or calculation on your spreadsheet, all the rest of the values on the spreadsheet are recalculated automatically to reflect the change.

SPREADSHEET FUNDAMENTALS

• •

Before you can learn how to use a spreadsheet, you must understand some basic spreadsheet features. The characteristics and definitions that follow are common to all spreadsheet programs. However, the examples presented are specific to a popular spreadsheet program called Lotus 1-2-3.

Cells and Cell Addresses

Figure 13-2 shows one type of spreadsheet—a teacher's grade sheet. Notice that the spreadsheet is divided into rows and columns, each

▼

Figure 13-2   Anatomy of a spreadsheet screen.
This screen shows a typical spreadsheet—a teacher's grade sheet. It provides space for 20 rows numbered down the side and eight columns labeled A through H. The intersection of a row and column forms a cell. When the cursor is on a cell, that cell is known as the active cell.

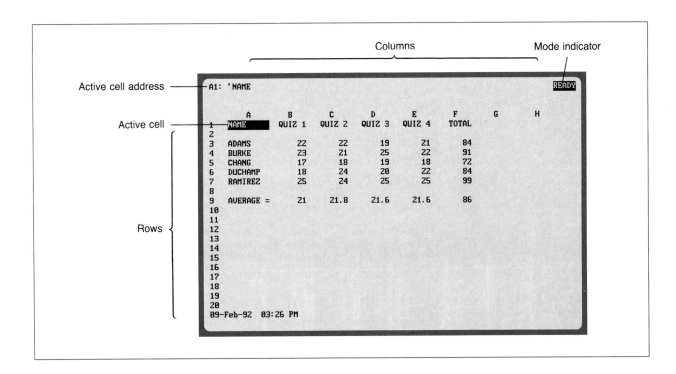

labeled with a number or a letter. The rows have *numeric labels* and the columns have *alphabetic labels.* There are actually more rows and columns than you can see on the screen; some spreadsheets have thousands of rows and hundreds of columns—more than you probably will ever need to use.

The intersection of a row and column forms a cell. **Cells** are the storage areas on a spreadsheet. When referring to a cell, you use the letter and number of the intersecting column and row. For example, in Figure 13-2, Cell B7 is the intersection of column B and row 7. This reference name is known as the **cell address.**

On a spreadsheet there is always one cell known as the **active cell,** or **current cell.** When a cell is active, you can enter data or edit the cell's contents. Typically, the active cell is marked by a highlighted bar called the spreadsheet **pointer.** The upper-left corner of the screen displays the active cell address. The active cell in Figure 13-2 is Cell A1.

Contents of Cells: Labels, Values, Formulas, and Functions

Each cell can contain one of four types of information: a label, a value, a formula, or a function. A **label** provides descriptive information about entries in the spreadsheet, such as a person's name. A cell that contains a label cannot be used to perform mathematical calculations. For example, in Figure 13-2, Cells A1, A9, and F1, among others, contain labels.

A **value** is an actual number entered into a cell to be used in calculations. A value can also be the result of a calculation. In Figure 13-2, for example, Cell B3 contains a value.

A **formula** is an instruction to the program to calculate a number.

FORMULA	MEANING
(A1+A2) or +A1+A2	The contents of cell A1 plus the contents of cell A2
(A2-A1) or +A2-A1	The contents of cell A2 minus the contents of cell A1
(A1*A2) or +A1*A2	The contents of cell A1 times the contents of cell A2
(A2/A1) or +A2/A1	The contents of cell A2 divided by the contents of cell A1
+A1+A2*2	The contents of cell A2 times the number 2 plus the contents of cell A1
(A1+A2)*2	The sum of the contents of cells A1 and A2 times 2
+A1+A2/4	The contents of cell A2 divided by the number 4 plus the contents of cell A1
(A1+A2)/4	The sum of the contents of cells A1 and A2 divided by 4
(A2-A1)*B1	The difference of the contents of cells A1 and A2 times the contents of cell B1
(A2-A1)/B1	The difference of the contents of cells A1 and A2 divided by the contents of cell B1

◀

Figure 13-3 Some spreadsheet formulas.
Spreadsheet formulas use arithmetic operators to perform calculations.

A formula generally contains cell addresses and one or more arithmetic operators: a plus sign (+) to add, a minus sign (−) to subtract, an asterisk (*) to multiply, and a slash (/) to divide. When you use a formula rather than entering the calculated result, the software can automatically recalculate the result if you need to change any of the values the formula is based on. All formulas must be enclosed in parentheses or begin with an operation symbol (such as +, −, *, or /); otherwise, the program will read the formula as a label. Formulas must be entered without spaces between the characters. Figure 13-3 shows examples of formulas.

A **function** is a preprogrammed formula. Functions let you perform complicated calculations with a few keystrokes. Two common functions are the @SUM function, which calculates sums, and the @AVG function, which calculates averages. Most spreadsheet programs contain a number of different functions. Figure 13-4 shows some common functions.

Ranges

Sometimes it is necessary to specify a range of cells to build a formula or perform a function. A **range** is a group of one or more cells arranged in a block shape; the program treats the range as a unit during an operation. Figure 13-5 shows some ranges. To define a range, you must indicate the upper-left and lower-right cells of the block. The cell addresses need to be separated by one or two periods. For example, in Figure 13-2, the QUIZ 1 range is B3.B7, and the ADAMS range is B3.E3. In the function @SUM(A4.G8), A4 through G8 is the range.

FUNCTION	MEANING
@SUM(range)	Calculates the sum of a group of numbers specified in an entire range. For example, the formula @SUM(A1.A10) calculates the sum of all numbers in cells A1 through A10.
@AVG(range)	Calculates the average of a group of numbers. For example, the formula @AVG(A1.A10) calculates the average of all the numbers in cells A1 through A10.
@SQRT(y)	Calculates the square root of a number. For example, @SQRT(A2) calculates the square root of the value contained in A2.
@COUNT(range)	Counts the number of *filled* cells in a range and displays the total number of cells containing a value. For example, the formula @COUNT(B1.B5) counts the number of cells in that range that contain values. If there are five of these cells in the range, the function will display the number 5.
@MIN(range)	Calculates and displays the smallest value contained in a range of values.
@MAX(range)	Calculates and displays the largest value contained in a range of values.
@PMT(principal,interest,term)	Calculates the individual payments on a loan with known principal, interest rate, and term. For example, the formula @PMT(A1,B1,C1) calculates the monthly payment by using the contents of A1 as the principal, the contents of B1 as the interest rate, and the contents of C1 as the term of the loan.
@IF(cond,x,y)	Determines whether a condition is true or false by using logical operators to compare numbers. Logical operators include equals (=), less than (<), greater than (>), less than or equal to (<=), and greater than or equal to (>=). The program then processes the data in a certain way, depending on whether the condition is true or false.
@COS(y)	Calculates the cosine of the value y.
@SIN(y)	Calculates the sine of the value y.
@TAN(y)	Calculates the tangent of the value y.

Figure 13-4   Some Lotus 1-2-3 functions.
This figure shows some of the built-in functions available in Lotus 1-2-3. These functions let you perform difficult or repetitive calculations with just a few keystrokes.

Moving the Pointer

To place data in a cell, you must first move the pointer to that cell. You can use the cursor movement (arrow) keys to move the pointer one row or column at a time. You can also use the cursor movement keys to scroll through the spreadsheet both vertically and horizontally.

However, moving around a large spreadsheet via the cursor keys can be tedious at times. Most programs let you zip around by pressing predefined keys and function keys. For example, if you press the Home key, the pointer moves "home" to Cell A1. Or you can go directly to a cell by pressing a designated **GoTo** function key, also known as the

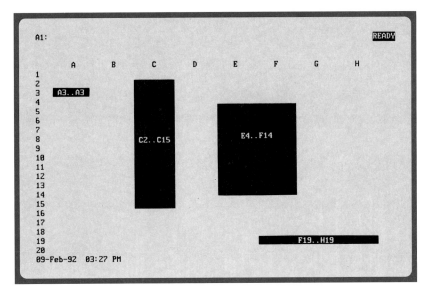

◀

Figure 13-5   Ranges.
A range is a group of one or more cells arranged in a rectangle. You can name a range or refer to it by using the addresses of the upper-left and lower-right cells in the group.

Jump-To function key. When you press this key, the software asks you for the desired cell address. You type in the address—for example, D7—and press Enter. The pointer immediately moves to Cell D7. Depending on the location of the pointer, using the GoTo function key may be the fastest way to get to a cell.

Operating Modes

A **mode** is the condition, or state, in which the program is currently functioning. It may be waiting for a command, for example, or presenting a selection of menu items. Most spreadsheets have three main operating modes: the READY mode, the ENTRY mode, and the MENU mode. The Lotus 1-2-3 spreadsheet screen displays a **mode indicator**—a message that tells you in what mode the spreadsheet is currently operating. The mode indicator is in the upper-right corner of the screen (Figure 13-2).

The READY Mode
Most spreadsheets are in the READY mode as soon as they are loaded into the system and the spreadsheet appears on the screen. The **READY mode** indicates that the program is ready for whatever action you want to take, such as moving the pointer, entering data, or issuing a command. As you begin entering data into a cell, you automatically leave the READY mode and enter the ENTRY mode.

The ENTRY Mode
When you are in the **ENTRY mode,** you can enter data into the cells. When you key in a label, the word "LABEL" appears as the mode indicator; the spreadsheet program recognizes your entry as a label because it begins with an alphabetic character (Figure 13-6a). The word "VALUE" appears as the mode indicator when you type in a number or formula (Figure 13-6b). After you key in the data and press Enter, the information is stored in the cell and the program returns to the READY mode.

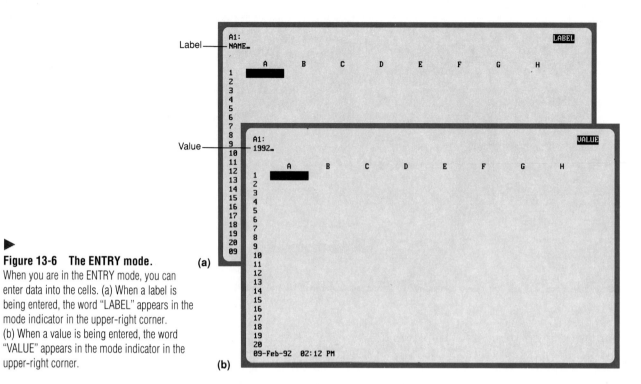

▶
Figure 13-6   The ENTRY mode.
When you are in the ENTRY mode, you can enter data into the cells. (a) When a label is being entered, the word "LABEL" appears in the mode indicator in the upper-right corner.
(b) When a value is being entered, the word "VALUE" appears in the mode indicator in the upper-right corner.

When you are in the ENTRY mode, the program does not let you jump or scroll around the spreadsheet—you can only enter data into empty cells or make changes to filled cells. The ENTRY mode lets you work on only one cell at a time. But sooner or later you will need to do things other than entering or editing cell contents. To do this, you need to enter the MENU, or COMMAND, mode.

The MENU Mode

The **MENU mode** lets you use commands to provide a wide range of spreadsheet functions. Programs display commands in a **command menu,** which is shown near the top of the screen (Figure 13-7). The

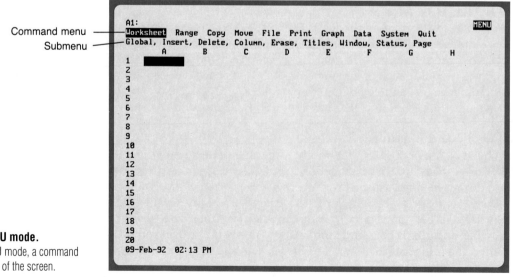

▶
Figure 13-7   The MENU mode.
When you are in the MENU mode, a command menu appears near the top of the screen.

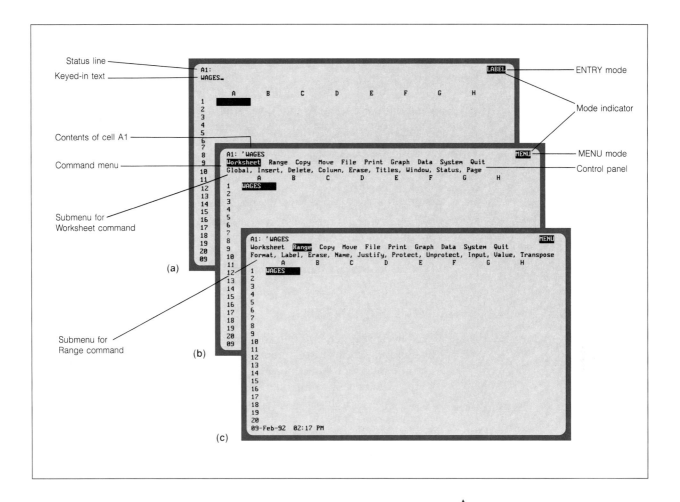

command menu contains a list, or menu, of different options, such as File and Move. The commands are very important, and we will discuss them in more detail later in the chapter. For now, all you need to know is that to enter the MENU mode, you press the Slash (/) key.

The Control Panel

Spreadsheets can get complicated. To help you keep track of what you are doing, most spreadsheet programs show a **control panel** at the top of the screen. The spreadsheet's control panel usually consists of three lines, as shown in Figure 13-8.

The First Line
The first line of the control panel is the status line. This line tells you the pointer location (the cell address) if you are in ENTRY mode (Figure 13-8a). In MENU mode, the first line also tells you the contents of that cell (Figure 13-8b). At times the status line shows the format—appearance—of the value or label in the cell and the width of the cell. (It is possible to change the appearance of the cell contents and also the cell's width, but that is beyond the scope of this text.)

To the far right of the status line is the mode indicator. As we mentioned earlier, this indicator tells you the spreadsheet's current mode of operation.

▲
Figure 13-8   The Lotus 1-2-3 control panel.
The first line of the control panel shows you the pointer location and the contents of that cell. (a) When you are in ENTRY mode, the second line of the panel displays the data you are typing in, before it is entered into the cell. (b) When you are in the MENU mode, the second line of the panel shows the current menu options, and the third line shows the submenu for the command that the pointer is on. (c) When you move the pointer to another command, the submenu changes.

The Second Line

The contents of the second line of the control panel vary, depending on the operating mode. If you are in the ENTRY mode, the line displays the data you are typing in, before it is actually entered into the cell. In Figure 13-8a, that data is WAGES. Being able to see the data lets you make changes and corrections before placing the data in the cell. If you are in the MENU mode, the line shows the current menu options (Figure 13-8b). This line is also occasionally used for prompts—that is, questions that ask you for information the program needs.

The Third Line

The control panel's third line appears only when the program is in the MENU mode. This line shows a **submenu,** a list of options for the command you have indicated with the pointer. Figure 13-8b shows the submenu for the Worksheet command.

Let us look at menus and submenus in more detail.

Menus and Submenus

We have already mentioned that you can select spreadsheet commands by choosing from the command menu. Sometimes, however, selecting a command from the menu does not cause a command to be executed; instead, you see a submenu. This is an additional set of options that refer to the command you selected from the command menu. For example, in Figure 13-8b, the second menu row shows the subcommands—Global, Insert, Delete, Column, and so forth—for the major command Worksheet. Moving the pointer to another major command, such as Range, causes a different set of submenu commands to appear (Figure 13-8c).

Submenus let you pick only the options that pertain to a particular command. Some of the choices on submenus have options of their own that are displayed on yet another submenu. This layering of menus and submenus lets you first give the computer the big picture with a general command, such as Print, and then select a particular option for the general command, such as Range, which allows you to print a particular set of cells.

Now that we have covered the basics of spreadsheets, let us pull this information together and see how you can use spreadsheet software for a practical application.

CREATING A SIMPLE SPREADSHEET

Learning to use an electronic spreadsheet program requires time. A good way to start is to read the manual that comes with the program and refer to it as you experiment with the program. Electronic spreadsheet programs have much greater capabilities than the average user will ever need. However, you can understand how such programs work by studying some examples. The examples we present in this section use Lotus 1-2-3. Lotus has established a standard approach to electronic spreadsheets; most popular spreadsheet programs work in a similar manner.

Lotus refers to the data keyed into the program as a **worksheet.** Lotus emphasizes the term by saving spreadsheet files with the file name extension WK1, WKE, or WKS, depending on which version you are using.

The Expense Sheet Example

Lyle Mayes teaches biology at Wilson High School. He recently bought Lotus 1-2-3 and uses it to keep track of his students' grades. Now he wants to use the program to keep track of his personal expenses. His expense sheet for the months of January through April is shown in Figure 13-9. Notice that each type of expense appears in a separate row of the expense sheet and each column is labeled with the name of a month. The amount of money spent on each item is entered in the cell at the intersection of the appropriate row and column.

The rightmost column of the spreadsheet contains the total amount spent on each item and the total income for the four-month period. At the bottom of each month's column, Lyle enters the total amount spent and the balance of his budget—the total amount of income minus the total amount of the expenses. As you can see, creating an expense sheet can be a time-consuming chore, and if a mistake is made, a number of recalculations must be done.

Now let us follow the steps that Lyle takes to create this spreadsheet with Lotus 1-2-3.

Loading the Program

To start his work, Lyle first boots the system. As in the word processing chapter, the software program, in this case Lotus 1-2-3, is on hard disk—drive C—and Lyle's formatted data disk is in drive B. At C⟩, he types the command to execute the program—either LOTUS or 123,

PLANNING YOUR
SPREADSHEET

1. Determine the results you want to display on your spreadsheet by mapping it out on paper.

2. Determine the data you have to input to your spreadsheet to calculate the results you want.

3. Write down the names of the input and output values that you will use in your spreadsheet and the equations you will use. Record the exact form in which you will enter them in your spreadsheet.

4. Write down the formulas for converting the spreadsheet's inputs to its outputs.

	JAN.	FEB.	MAR.	APR.	TOTAL
INCOME	2300	2300	2300	2300	9200
EXPENSES					
Rent	575	575	575	575	2300
Food	225	200	200	200	825
Phone	50	64	37	23	174
Heat	80	50	24	20	174
Insurance	100	100	100	100	400
Car	200	200	200	200	800
Leisure	105	120	95	125	445
TOTAL					
EXPENSES	1335	1309	1231	1243	5118
BALANCE	965	991	1069	1057	4082

◀

Figure 13-9   Lyle's expense worksheet.
This is Lyle's handwritten expense sheet. Notice that, if he makes any changes to one of the values—for example, the March food expense—he has to do numerous recalculations.

▶
Figure 13-10   A blank spreadsheet.
The blank display indicates that Lotus 1-2-3 is loaded and ready to accept data.

depending on his version of the program. Then he responds to the program prompts until he sees an empty spreadsheet with the pointer positioned in Cell A1 (Figure 13-10). Because a personal computer's screen can display only about 24 lines on a screen with 80 characters per line, the screen display shows only some of all the rows and columns that are available in the computer's memory. For the expense sheet, Lyle needs only columns A through F and rows 1 to 17.

Entering the Labels and Values

Since Lyle already knows what he wants to type into the spreadsheet, he starts by entering the labels—the names of the months and the types of expenses. Starting with Cell A3, Lyle types the word IN-COME. As he types, the mode indicator display changes from READY to LABEL. When Lyle finishes typing, the second line of the control

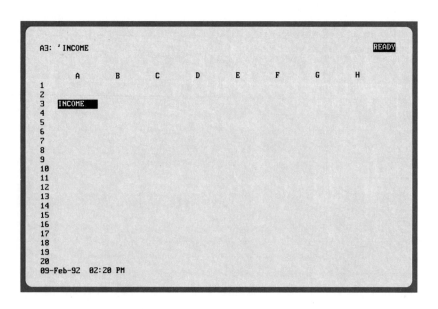

▶
Figure 13-11   Entering labels.
Lyle begins to set up his spreadsheet by entering the labels. When he presses Enter, the label is stored in the cell.

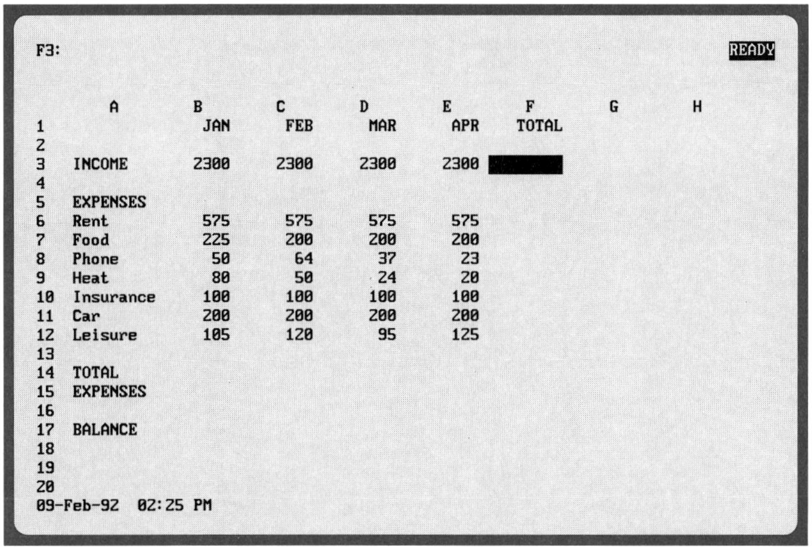

```
F3:                                                                    READY


            A         B         C         D         E         F       G       H
   1                 JAN       FEB       MAR       APR     TOTAL
   2
   3    INCOME      2300      2300      2300      2300  ██████████
   4
   5    EXPENSES
   6    Rent         575       575       575       575
   7    Food         225       200       200       200
   8    Phone         50        64        37        23
   9    Heat          80        50        24        20
  10    Insurance    100       100       100       100
  11    Car          200       200       200       200
  12    Leisure      105       120        95       125
  13
  14    TOTAL
  15    EXPENSES
  16
  17    BALANCE
  18
  19
  20
  09-Feb-92   02:25 PM
```

◄

Figure 13-12   Entering values.
This screen shows Lyle's spreadsheet with all
the labels and numbers entered.

panel displays " 'INCOME"; Lotus added an apostrophe before Lyle's
entry, to indicate that INCOME is a label. Lyle then presses Enter to
store his entry in the cell (Figure 13-11). When he does this, the mode
indicator immediately returns to READY.

To enter the rest of the labels and numbers, Lyle follows the same
procedure, moving the pointer from cell to cell by using the cursor
movement keys. If he makes a mistake as he is typing, he can use the
Backspace or Del key to make the correction before moving from the
cell. Remember that the pointer must be on a cell to store data in that
cell. Figure 13-12 shows Lyle's spreadsheet with all the labels and all
the numbers—except the totals—entered in their cells.

Entering the Formulas and Functions

Lyle must enter the total income for the four months in Cell F3. He
could create a formula including each value contained in row 3
(2300+2300+2300+2300), type it into Cell F3, and then press Enter.
The spreadsheet would calculate the total for him and enter the result
in F3. But if any of the values in the equation changed, Lyle would
have to retype them in the formula. Instead, Lyle uses a formula that
will add the contents of each of the four cells, regardless of their value.
The formula he uses is (B3+C3+D3+E3). This formula tells the program to add the values that appear in the cells B3, C3, D3, and E3.
Remember that all formulas must be enclosed in parentheses or begin
with an operation symbol; otherwise, the program will read the formula as a label. With the pointer at Cell F3, Lyle types the formula
(B3+C3+D3+E3) and presses Enter to store it in Cell F3.

If you look at Figure 13-13, you will see that Cell F3 does not
show the formula; instead, it shows the *result* of the formula. If the
pointer is on the cell, then the formula for that cell appears in the
upper-left corner of the screen. The result of the formula is the **displayed value** of the cell. The formula itself is the actual cell **contents.**
This is an important distinction to remember. Displayed values change
if other values in the spreadsheet change. A formula changes only if the
formula entered into the cell is edited or replaced.

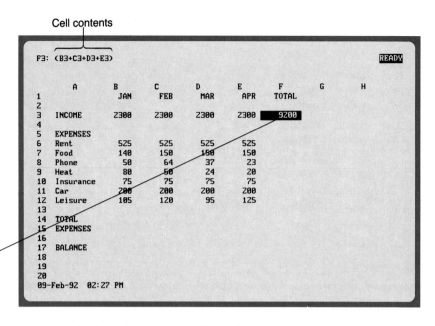

Figure 13-13   Entering formulas.
Lyle has entered the formula
(B3+C3+D3+E3) into Cell F3. Notice that
the displayed value of the cell is the result of
the calculation: 9200. When the pointer is on
Cell F3, you can see the actual contents of the
cell in the upper-left corner of the screen.

To calculate the totals in the other rows, Lyle could enter the formula (B6+C6+D6+E6) for row 6, and so on, for each of the Cells F6 to F12. However, Lotus 1-2-3 provides a simpler way of summing columns or rows: the @SUM function. For example, Lyle can key in @SUM(B6.E6) in Cell F6. This tells Lotus to add up the contents of Cells B6 through E6. (Lyle could have used this function for Cell F3 as well.) The @ symbol tells Lotus that Lyle is entering a function. The (B6.E6) part of the function is a range; recall that a range is a group of one or more cells arranged in a block. Lyle uses the @SUM function with the appropriate ranges to enter totals in Cells F6 through F12 and Cells B15 through F15. Figure 13-14 shows the result.

Finally, Lyle needs to use a formula to compute the monthly balance. Remember, the monthly balance is the monthly income minus the monthly total expenses. So, for January, Lyle places the formula (B3 − B15) in Cell B17. This tells Lotus to take the value of Cell B15

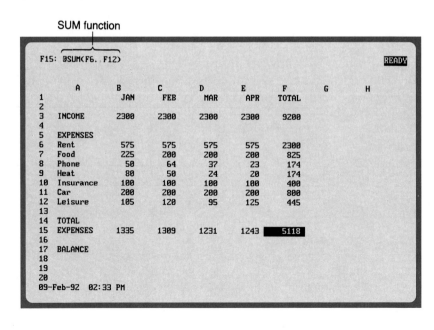

Figure 13-14   Entering functions.
Lyle has entered the Lotus 1-2-3 function
@SUM(F6.F12) in Cell F15. In this function
(F6.F12) is the range. As with formulas, the cell
shows the result of the calculation, and the
function is shown in the first line of the control
panel.

Balance formula

```
F17: (F3-F15)                                          READY

          A       B       C       D       E       F       G       H
1                JAN     FEB     MAR     APR    TOTAL
2
3        INCOME  2300    2300    2300    2300   9200
4
5        EXPENSES
6        Rent     575     575     575     575   2300
7        Food     225     200     200     200    825
8        Phone     50      64      37      23    174
9        Heat      80      50      24      20    174
10       Insurance 100    100     100     100    400
11       Car      200     200     200     200    800
12       Leisure  105     120      95     125    445
13
14       TOTAL
15       EXPENSES 1335    1309    1231    1243   5118
16
17       BALANCE   965     991    1069    1057   4082
18
19
20
09-Feb-92  02:38 PM
```

◄

Figure 13-15   A complete spreadsheet.
This screen shows Lyle's spreadsheet with all the labels, values, formulas, and functions in place.

and subtract it from the value of Cell B3. Lyle then fills in the rest of the balance row. Figure 13-15 shows the final spreadsheet.

Making Corrections

Suppose Lyle realizes that he made a mistake in his January food expense (the correct amount is 150). Also, he made a mistake in his April leisure expense (the correct amount is 123). The incorrect cells are already filled, so Lyle needs to position the pointer on the filled cell and type in the new data; the keyed-in changes will appear in the second line of the control panel. Then Lyle will press Enter to replace the incorrect data with the new data. Lyle moves the pointer over Cell B7, types in 150, and presses Enter. Then he moves the pointer to Cell E12, types in 123, and presses Enter.

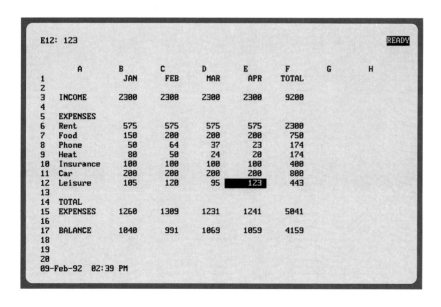

```
E12: 123                                               READY

          A       B       C       D       E       F       G       H
1                JAN     FEB     MAR     APR    TOTAL
2
3        INCOME  2300    2300    2300    2300   9200
4
5        EXPENSES
6        Rent     575     575     575     575   2300
7        Food     150     200     200     200    750
8        Phone     50      64      37      23    174
9        Heat      80      50      24      20    174
10       Insurance 100    100     100     100    400
11       Car      200     200     200     200    800
12       Leisure  105     120      95     123    443
13
14       TOTAL
15       EXPENSES 1260    1309    1231    1241   5041
16
17       BALANCE  1040     991    1069    1059   4159
18
19
20
09-Feb-92  02:39 PM
```

◄

Figure 13-16   Automatic recalculation.
Lyle enters in the changes for January's food expense and April's leisure expense. Lotus 1-2-3 automatically recalculates the affected totals and balances.

If the expense sheet were done manually, Lyle would also have to recalculate the totals for row 7 and row 12, and the total expenses and balances for columns B, E, and F. But since the expense sheet is an electronic spreadsheet, the spreadsheet program instantly recalculates the values. Figure 13-16 shows the result of typing only the two changed values. Nothing else has to be changed in the spreadsheet—it automatically adjusts all contents to reflect the changed values.

Automatic recalculation of a spreadsheet this size usually takes less than a second. This ability to recalculate a spreadsheet at the touch of a button is what has revolutionized the processes of budgeting and financial modeling. Now people who work with numbers can spend their time analyzing their spreadsheets rather than doing arithmetic.

Now that Lyle has created his spreadsheet, he can use the command menu to save, retrieve, and print it.

USING SPREADSHEET COMMANDS

• • • • • • • • • • • • • • • • • • •

Using the command menu and submenus can be a little tricky at first. To help make choosing easier, you can refer to a command tree. A **command tree,** so called because it has a "trunk" at the top and many "branches," shows choices from the main command menu and choices from the submenus (Figure 13-17). Some of the branches are short and simple, like the one for the Insert command. Others, like Global, have many branches. Each successive branch is reached by selecting from the submenu that precedes it.

▼
Figure 13-17   A command tree.
This command tree shows all the submenus associated with the Worksheet command. If you follow the Worksheet-Global path, there are many different choices you can make.

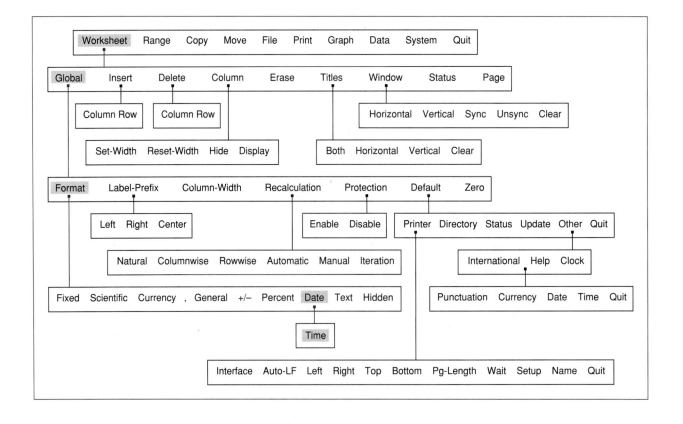

To take some action—to execute an instruction—on your spreadsheet, you must press the / key to obtain the command menu and then work your way out to the branch with the command you want. The commands along the way, as you go through the layers of menus, are merely vehicles for getting you to the instruction that takes the desired action. You must choose the right options from the submenus to get there. If you make a false step (get into the wrong submenu), you can get back to the next higher menu by pressing the Esc key. In fact, you can get out of the MENU mode completely by continuing to press the Esc key until you see READY in the mode indicator. You work your way down through the levels of submenus by moving the menu pointer to a selection and pressing Enter. You can undo a selection and work your way back up to a previous menu by pressing the Esc key.

Now let us show you the steps Lyle takes to use several of the important commands on the main menu.

The File Command

The File command lets you manipulate the Lotus 1-2-3 files on your data disk. You can use the File command to perform such tasks as saving files, retrieving files, erasing files, and listing files. Figure 13-18 shows the command tree for the File command. We will look at how to use the File command to save, retrieve, and list files.

Saving a File

Since Lyle is finished with his spreadsheet, he can save it on his data disk by using the File command. (In fact, Lyle can save the spreadsheet any time, whether or not it is finished.) To use this command, Lyle presses the / key to enter the MENU mode and obtain the command menu. Next he moves the menu pointer to the word "File" (Figure 13-19a). Notice that Save is one of the choices on the File submenu. With the pointer on File, Lyle presses Enter to access the File submenu. Now the submenu is the active menu. Lyle moves the pointer to "Save." When he does, the bottom line of the control panel shows a description of the Save option (Figure 13-19b). Lyle presses Enter to

Figure 13-18   The File command.
This figure shows the command tree for the File command.

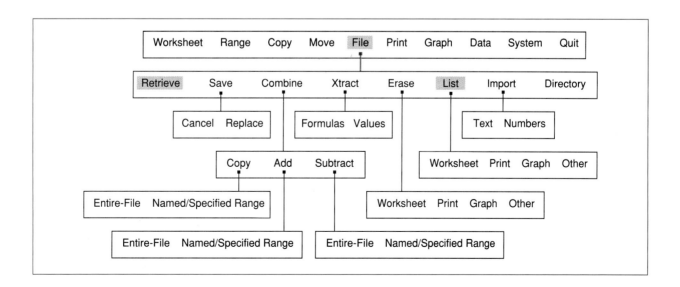

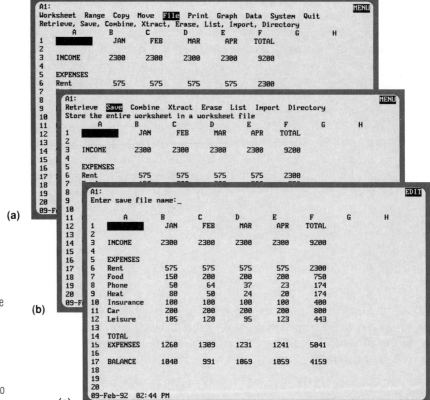

Figure 13-19   Saving a file.

(a) To select the File command, Lyle moves the pointer to the word "File." Note that the submenu now shows options for the File command. Then Lyle presses Enter. (b) Now the submenu becomes the active menu. Lyle moves the pointer to the word "Save" and presses Enter. (c) Lotus 1-2-3 then asks him to enter a file name.

select Save, and Lotus 1-2-3 prompts him for the file name he wishes to use (Figure 13-19c). File names can be up to eight characters long. Spreadsheet file names can contain letters, numbers, hyphens, and the underscore character. Lyle chooses the name B:EXPENSES, types it in, and presses Enter. (Lotus automatically adds an extension.) Since this is a new file, it is saved immediately.

There is another, faster way to make these types of menu choices: Just type the first letter of the option you want to use, rather than moving the pointer. For example, Lyle can save his file more quickly by typing / (to access the MENU mode), then F (for File), S (for Save), followed by the file name. So Lyle could type:

```
/FSB:EXPENSES
```

and press Enter to save his file. The shortcut method can be used for any of the menu commands.

Retrieving a File

Like the Save command, the Retrieve command is a File subcommand. If Lyle wants to retrieve the EXPENSES file, he needs to press the / key to enter the command menu. Then he selects the File command and the Retrieve subcommand. Lotus 1-2-3 then prompts Lyle for the name of the file he wants to retrieve. The program jogs Lyle's memory by listing the names of his stored files on the bottom line of the control panel (Figure 13-20). Lyle can either type in the name of one of the listed files and press Enter or he can move the pointer to that file name

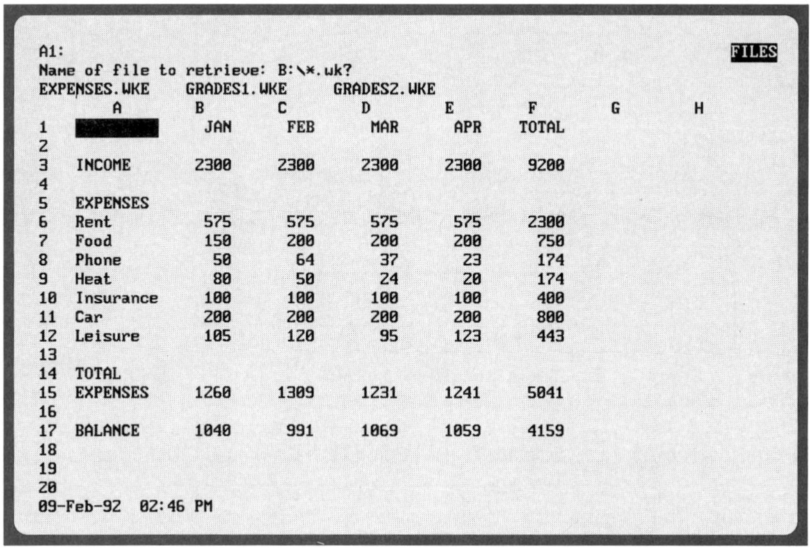

```
A1:                                                          FILES
Name of file to retrieve: B:\*.wk?
EXPENSES.WKE   GRADES1.WKE     GRADES2.WKE
            A       B       C       D       E       F       G       H
1                  JAN     FEB     MAR     APR    TOTAL
2
3        INCOME    2300    2300    2300    2300    9200
4
5        EXPENSES
6        Rent       575     575     575     575    2300
7        Food       150     200     200     200     750
8        Phone       50      64      37      23     174
9        Heat        80      50      24      20     174
10       Insurance  100     100     100     100     400
11       Car        200     200     200     200     800
12       Leisure    105     120      95     123     443
13
14       TOTAL
15       EXPENSES   1260    1309    1231    1241    5041
16
17       BALANCE    1040     991    1069    1059    4159
18
19
20
09-Feb-92  02:46 PM
```

◄

Figure 13-20   Retrieving a file.
When Lyle wants to retrieve a file, Lotus 1-2-3 displays a list of the worksheet files stored on Lyle's disk.

and press Enter. Either way, Lotus loads and displays the requested worksheet. Note that this process erases the current worksheet, if there happens to be one in memory that has not been saved. Usually, a user would save such a worksheet before retrieving a different one.

After Lyle enters the name of the file, the mode indicator flashes the word "WAIT"—this indicates that Lotus is loading the worksheet. When the worksheet appears on the screen, the mode indicator displays the word "READY."

Listing Files

If Lyle wants to check to see what worksheet files he has on his data disk, he can use the List subcommand. To do this, he types / and selects the File option. Then he selects List from the first submenu and Worksheet from the second submenu. Lotus then displays on the screen a list of the worksheet files on his data disk. When Lyle wants to return to the worksheet, he presses Enter.

The Print Command

Spreadsheet programs generally let you print a copy of the spreadsheet at any time during the session. The Print command provides options for printing all or part of a spreadsheet on paper. Figure 13-21 shows the command tree for the Print command.

Lyle wants to print a copy of his spreadsheet. To do this, he must tell Lotus 1-2-3 what part of the spreadsheet he wants to print and whether he wants the spreadsheet printed on paper or stored on a disk.

Lyle begins by selecting the Print option from the menu. Then he selects Printer from the first submenu because he wants to have a printed copy of the spreadsheet. When Lyle selects Printer, another submenu appears (Figure 13-22).

Now Lyle must tell Lotus how much of the spreadsheet he wants to print. Notice that there is a Range command in the second submenu. To tell Lotus which part of the spreadsheet he wants to print, Lyle must define the desired range. Notice that Lyle's work does not

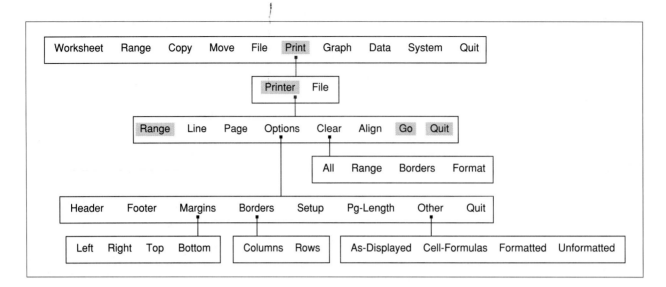

▲

Figure 13-21   The Print command.
This figure shows the command tree for the
Print command.

occupy the whole spreadsheet; rather, it is clustered in a small block.
The upper-left corner of the block is Cell A1. The lower-right corner
is Cell F17. The two cell addresses define the range of the worksheet
that needs to be printed.

To tell Lotus the range, Lyle selects the Range command. Then
he types A1 (the cell in the upper left of his worksheet) followed by one
or two periods and F17 (the cell in the lower right of his worksheet).
Lyle then presses Enter. This returns him to the menu he just left.
Next Lyle makes sure his printer is on and ready to print. Then he
selects Go from the second submenu to begin the printing.

As an alternative to highlighting and selecting the commands involved in the printing task, Lyle could have typed / (to access the
MENU mode), then P (for Print), P (for Printer), R (for Range), followed by the range to be printed. So Lyle could type:

```
/PPRA1.F17
```

Then he would press Enter and then type G for Go.

▶

Figure 13-22   Printing a worksheet.
After Lyle chooses the Print option from the
menu and the Printer option from the first
submenu, another submenu appears. This
submenu lets Lyle describe the range he
wishes to print, start the printing process, and
leave the Print menu.

```
A1:                                                                    MENU
Range Line Page Options Clear Align Go Quit
Specify a range to print
          A      B      C      D      E      F      G      H
1        ████   JAN    FEB    MAR    APR    TOTAL
2
3        INCOME 2300   2300   2300   2300   9200
4
5        EXPENSES
6        Rent   575    575    575    575    2300
7        Food   150    200    200    200    750
8        Phone  50     64     37     23     174
9        Heat   80     50     24     20     174
10       Insurance 100 100    100    100    400
11       Car    200    200    200    200    800
12       Leisure 105   120    95     123    443
13
14       TOTAL
15       EXPENSES 1260 1309   1231   1241   5041
16
17       BALANCE 1040  991    1069   1059   4159
18
19
20
09-Feb-92  02:47 PM
```

When the printing is completed, the second submenu is still the active menu. To return to the READY mode, Lyle must select the Quit command from the submenu. Figure 13-23 shows the final printed spreadsheet.

The Worksheet Erase Command

If Lyle wants to start another worksheet without leaving and reentering the Lotus 1-2-3 program, he can use the Worksheet Erase command. This command clears the worksheet in the computer's memory of any information that has been entered; an empty worksheet appears on the screen. The Worksheet Erase command does not erase any worksheets saved on a disk.

To use the Worksheet Erase command, Lyle presses the / key. Then he selects Worksheet from the menu and Erase from the submenu. Lotus asks if he really wants to erase the worksheet. This gives Lyle a chance to stop and think whether he saved his latest version on disk. Since he has saved the worksheet, Lyle types Y for *yes*, and a new blank worksheet appears on the screen.

The Quit Command

Lyle wants to leave the spreadsheet program and return to DOS. (Many spreadsheet programs do not automatically save the file currently in use when you use the command to quit, so always remember to save before you quit.) Since Lyle has already saved his file, he selects the Quit command from the command menu. Lotus 1-2-3 asks him to confirm the command with a Y (yes, leave the program) or an N (no, do not leave the program). Lyle presses Y, and the DOS prompt appears.

TRY LYING ON YOUR SIDE

When you are displaying your spreadsheet on your computer's screen, you can move the pointer along a row to see all the columns of data in that row. Even if your screen can display only 80 characters on a line, you can still scroll sideways along a line by moving the pointer. However, when a wide spreadsheet is printed, the columns that will not fit across the page appear on a separate page. This means that you will have to cut and paste—literally—to assemble the printed copy of your spreadsheet.

Most printers usually print 80 characters per line. When printing in compressed mode, they can print 132 characters per line. If this is still insufficient to print all the columns in your spreadsheet, you can purchase software that turns your spreadsheet sideways, printing the spreadsheet along the length of the printer paper. With the output from your spreadsheet in this form, you will have all the rows running continuously on the same piece of fanfold paper. This makes the printed spreadsheet much easier to read.

	JAN	FEB	MAR	APR	TOTAL
INCOME	2300	2300	2300	2300	9200
EXPENSES					
Rent	575	575	575	575	2300
Food	150	200	200	200	750
Phone	50	64	37	23	174
Heat	80	50	24	20	174
Insurance	100	100	100	100	400
Car	200	200	200	200	800
Leisure	105	120	95	123	443
TOTAL EXPENSES	1260	1309	1231	1041	5041
BALANCE	1040	991	1069	1259	4159

Figure 13-23 The printed worksheet.
For Lyle, getting a printed spreadsheet that shows his revisions takes only a few keystrokes. If he had been working with a handwritten ledger, making revisions would have been tedious and the result probably less attractive than this printed spreadsheet.

USING THE HELP KEY

The wide assortment of spreadsheet commands can be bewildering to the novice user. In fact, command choices can be confusing to an experienced user, too. But help is as close as your keyboard. When you are lost or confused, press the **Help key** (F1). Pressing the Help key places you in the HELP mode. You can press the Help key anytime, even in the middle of a command.

The HELP mode is useful in two ways. First, it is **context sensitive**—that is, it offers helpful information related to the command you were using when you pressed the Help key. Second, you can select the **help index,** which—for all practical purposes—gives you access to a reference manual right on your screen. Use the help index to select a topic, and the spreadsheet program supplies aid on that topic. It is easy to get out of the HELP mode: Press the Esc key once.

INTEGRATED PACKAGES

An **integrated package** of programs is an all-in-one set that includes word processing, spreadsheet, database, and graphics programs. Integrated packages are especially useful when numeric data must be included in textual reports or when a graphic representation of numbers can more easily show what the numbers mean.

Furthermore, with an integrated package you do not need to learn completely different programs that use different commands. Programs in an integrated package share a common methodology and command structure so that you do not have to begin anew each time you change programs; each has a familiar flavor.

Another advantage is the fast, easy transfer of data among the programs in the package. For example, with an integrated package it is easy to move a table of spreadsheet numbers into a word processing report. Graphs can be prepared using the graphics program, then easily inserted into text prepared using the word processing program. However, if you are using separate word processing, spreadsheet, and graphics programs, you will find that moving data from one to another is not simple. Even though your various files may be standard file types, the second program may not be able to store what you want to pass to it.

The First Integrated Package: Lotus 1-2-3

Although Lotus 1-2-3 does not have word processing capability, it does integrate with a powerful business graphics program and a limited database program. All three programs in the Lotus 1-2-3 package are based on storing data in a spreadsheet. After you enter the data in the spreadsheet, you can view the data graphically using the graphics program. You can also use commands available through the database program to sort the data in your spreadsheet or to find rows in the spreadsheet that match certain conditions.

Each program has a menu that lets you choose what task you want to perform. You can also move instantly from one program to another by making a selection from a menu. Furthermore, once your graphs and database are set up, you can stay in the spreadsheet program and see graphs of your data or select records from your database by simply pressing one key. Lotus also stores the graphs and database with the spreadsheet file on which they are based.

To Integrate or Not?

The popularity of Lotus 1-2-3 has led to the development of a number of different **integrated packages**—packages that, like Lotus 1-2-3, offer different program functions. Two different approaches have been taken by software developers:

- Including word processing, spreadsheet, graphics, and database capabilities in one program package. Some of the more popular programs of this type are Symphony, LotusWorks, and PFS: First Choice for the IBM PC and Microsoft Works for the Apple Macintosh.

- Allowing a user to purchase the individual word processing, spreadsheet, graphics, and database programs that are most appealing for that user. These **stand-alone programs** are then integrated by a **universal manager program** that coordinates the separate programs. The manager program also presents a common interface to the user and handles data transfer among the programs.

Despite their many advantages, sales of integrated packages have not skyrocketed. There are several reasons for this. First, the individual functions—such as word processing or graphics—within an all-in-one integrated package are not usually as strong as those in stand-alone packages. If you need state-of-the-art word processing and state-of-the-art database management, you would probably be better served by buying two stand-alone programs. Second, integrated packages are rather expensive, and you pay for all the functions in the package even if you really need only two or three. Third, integrated packages require more computer memory than one stand-alone program does. You may have to purchase additional memory for your computer to run an integrated package.

BUSINESS GRAPHICS
• • • • • • • • • • • • • • • • • • •

The change from numbers to pictures is a refreshing variation. But graphics software used in business is not a toy. Graphics can show words and numbers and data in ways that are meaningful and quickly understood. This is the key reason they are valuable. Personal comput-

Material	Units Sold Each Month			
	Jan.	Feb.	Mar.	Apr.
Copper	6	10	13	22
Bronze	18	28	36	60
Iron	9	15	19	32
Gold	32	52	64	110
Silver	20	32	40	68
Totals:	85	137	172	292

(a)

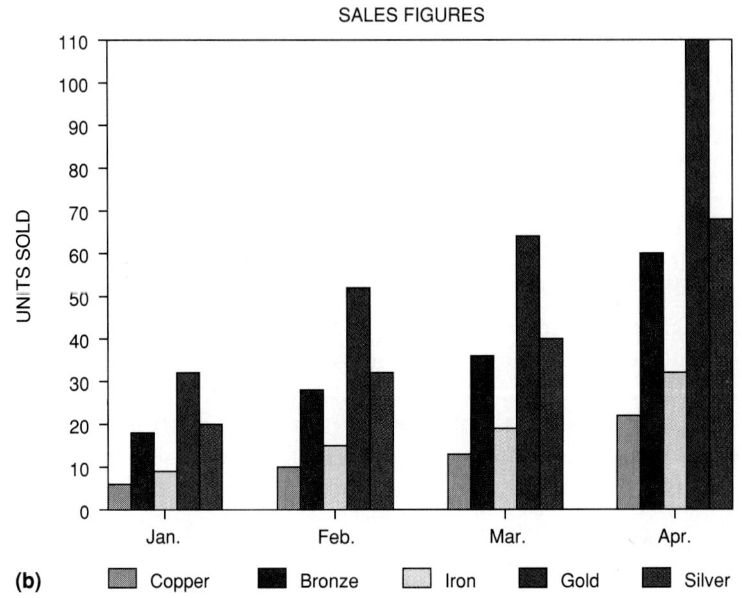

(b)

Figure 13-24   Business graphics.
(a) A large amount of data can be translated into (b) one simple, clear graph.

ers give people the capability to store and use data about their businesses. These same users, however, sometimes find it difficult to convey this information to others—managers or clients—in a meaningful way. **Business graphics**—graphics that represent data in a visual, easily understood format—provide an answer to this problem.

Why Use Graphics?

Graphics generate and sustain the interest of an audience by brightening up any lesson, report, or business document. In addition, graphics can help get a point across by presenting an overwhelming amount of data (Figure 13-24a) in one simple, clear graph (Figure 13-24b). What is more, that simple graph can reveal a trend that could be lost if buried in long columns of numbers. In addition, a presenter who uses graphics often appears more prepared and organized than one who does not. To sum up, most people use business graphics software for two reasons: (1) to view and analyze data and (2) to make a positive impression during a presentation. To satisfy these different needs, two types of business graphics programs have been developed: analytical graphics and presentation graphics.

PERSONAL COMPUTERS IN ACTION

Presentation Graphics Everywhere

W hy are people taking the trouble to get information all gussied up with fancy graphics when the unembellished numbers would be quite acceptable? The answer is that graphics are worth the trouble because they can clarify a concept and help the viewer get to the crux of the matter more quickly. Furthermore, studies show that graphics—especially color graphics—increase persuasiveness by as much as 50%.

As you can see from these representative samples, colorful graphics can be given a three-dimensional look and enhanced with drawings of related objects, such as planes and bottles.

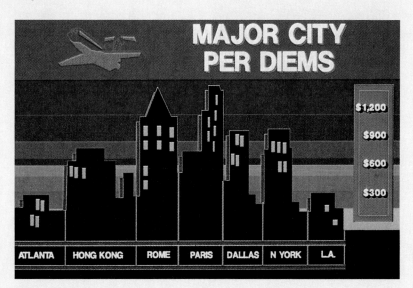

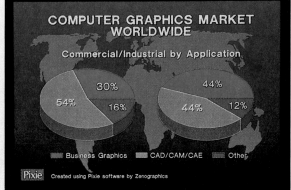

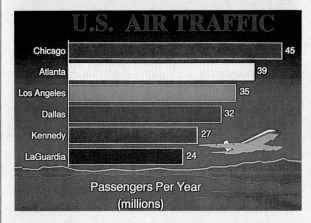

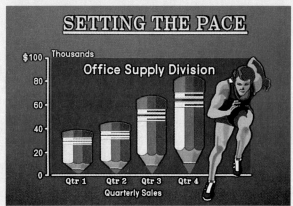

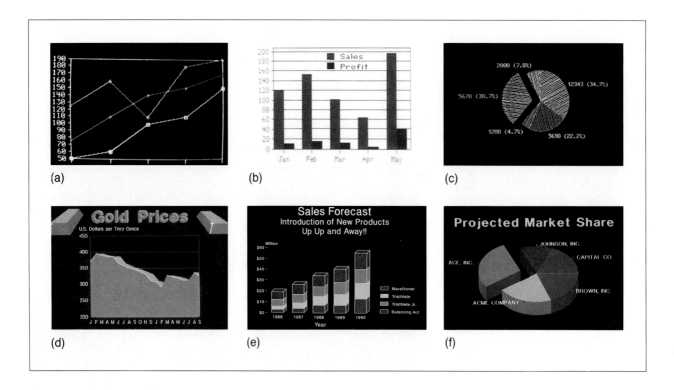

▲
Figure 13-25   Analytical graphics compared to presentation graphics.
Analytical graphics (a, b, and c) are certainly serviceable, but they lack the clarity and appeal of presentation graphics (d, e, and f). Compare the line graphs (a and d), bar graphs (b and e), and pie charts (c and f).

Analytical Graphics

Analytical graphics programs are designed to help users analyze and understand specific data. Sometimes called analysis-oriented graphics programs, these programs use already entered spreadsheet or database data to construct and view line, bar, and pie-chart graphs (Figure 13-25a–c).

Although analytical graphics programs do a good job of producing simple graphs, these programs are too limited and inflexible for a user who needs to prepare elaborate presentations. Lotus 1-2-3, for example, lets you choose from only a small number of graph types, and the programs's formatting features—which control graph size, color, and lettering—are limited. These limitations may be of little concern to some users. But those who require sophisticated graphics will want to consider presentation graphics.

Presentation Graphics

Presentation graphics programs are also called **business-quality graphics** or presentation-oriented desktop graphics programs. These programs let you produce charts, graphs, and other visual aids that look as if they were prepared by a professional graphics artist (Figure 13-25d–f). However, you can control the appearance of the product when you create it yourself, and you can produce graphics faster and make last-minute changes if necessary.

Most presentation graphics programs help you do three kinds of tasks:

• Edit and enhance charts created by other programs, such as the analytical graphs produced by Lotus 1-2-3.

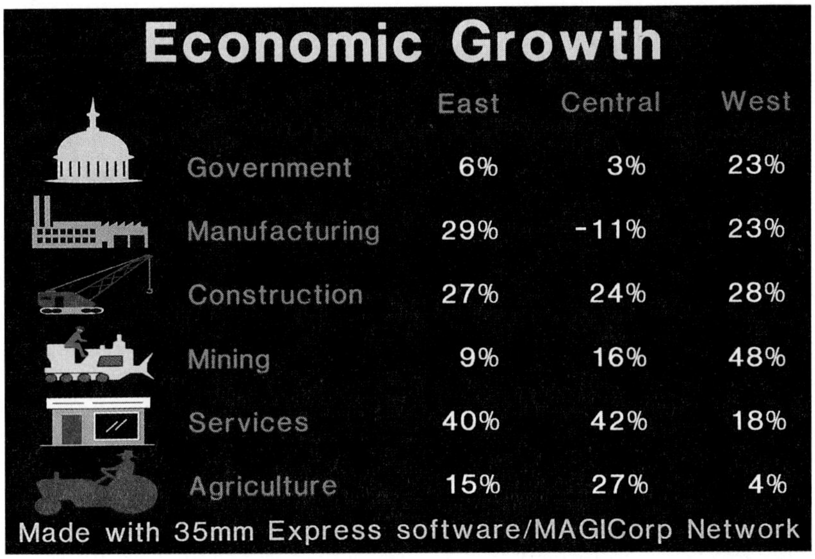

◄

Figure 13-26 Enhancing graphics with symbols.
Presentation graphics programs provide a library of symbols, which users can choose from. As shown here on the left, such symbols can add interest to columns of numbers.

- Create charts, diagrams, drawings, and text slides from scratch.
- Use a library of symbols, drawings, and pictures—called **clip art**—(Figure 13-26) that comes with the graphics program. Because the computer produces the "drawings" and manipulates them, even a nonartist can create professional-looking illustrations.

Presentation graphics can increase the impact of your message. They can make the information you are presenting visually appealing, meaningful, and comprehensible. Studies show that high-quality graphics increase both the amount that a listener learns in a presentation and the length of time that the listener retains the information. Also, an audience perceives you as more professional and knowledgeable when your presentation includes overhead graphics or slides. Although graphics hardware requirements vary, be aware that the requirements of presentation graphics include a high-resolution color monitor, possibly a color printer, and some method of transferring your computer-produced results to film.

SOME GRAPHICS TERMINOLOGY

· · · · · · · · · · · · · · · · · · ·

To use a graphics program successfully, you should know some basic concepts and design principles. Let us begin by exploring the types of graphs you can create.

Line Graphs

One of the most useful ways of showing trends or cycles over the same period of time is to use a **line graph.** For example, the graph in Figure 13-27 shows company costs for utilities, supplies, and travel during a five-month period. Line graphs are appropriate when there are many values or complex data. In the business section of the newspaper, line

MACINTOSH

Presentation Graphics: Mixing Business with Pleasure

The Macintosh is justly famous for its graphics capabilities. Little wonder, then, that the Mac has become the machine of choice for producing high-quality presentation graphics. If you need to make a presentation, graphics can make the crucial difference between communicating and not communicating. Products now available for the Mac go far beyond the mere dressing up of spreadsheet charts. Mac graphics products are highly integrated systems for organizing a presentation; designing illustrations; editing text and visual images; and producing colorful slides, overhead transparencies, and paper materials.

Here is a rundown of the basic features of good presentation graphics software for the Macintosh:

- Outlining tools supplied with many packages get you off to a good start, helping you organize—and easily reorganize—your thoughts before you commit them to paper.

- A set of standard templates provide basic layouts that you can copy, modify, and reuse. The templates guide you in using logos, titles, text, and illustrations effectively.

- Easy-to-learn tools allow you to create, edit, and embellish graph-

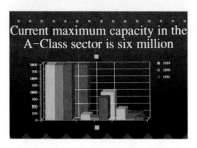

ics that are based on the data in a spreadsheet.

- An "overview" feature displays 20 or more reduced illustrations on the screen. You can access this feature while working on a specific graphic, and you are free to arrange and rearrange the reduced images in any sequence you like. Most packages also let you create speaker's notes and handouts based on these reduced images.

- Compatibility with a wide variety of devices allows output from simple black-and-white printers to color ink-jet, thermal, and

laser printers that produce near-photographic-quality images. Service bureaus in most major cities can take the files produced by presentation graphics software and, using machines called film recorders, create dazzlingly clear and colorful 35mm slides.

As computers become commonplace resources for creating visual aids, audiences come to expect more and more of presenters. You can take some comfort, then, in knowing that easy-to-use software is available to help you create a polished, first-class presentation.

graphs are used to show complex trends in gross national product, stock prices, or employment changes over a period of time. Also, corporate profits and losses are often illustrated by line graphs.

Notice the two solid lines in Figure 13-27—one that runs vertically on the left and one that runs horizontally across the bottom. Each line is called an **axis.** (The plural of *axis* is *axes.*) The horizontal line, called the **x-axis,** often represents units of time, such as days, months, or years; it can also represent characteristics, such as model number,

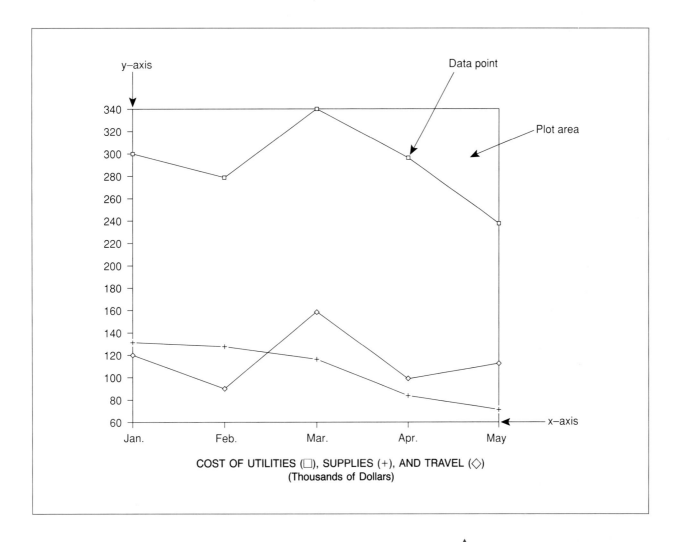

▲
Figure 13-27   A line graph.
Line graphs are useful for showing trends over a period of time. In many analytical programs, different symbols are used to show the different types of data being plotted.

brand name, or country. The vertical line, called the **y-axis,** usually shows measured values or amounts, such as dollars, staffing levels, units sold, and so on. The area inside the axes is called the **plot area**—the space in which the graph is plotted, or drawn.

Graphics programs automatically scale (arrange the units or numbers on) the x-axis and y-axis so the graph of your data is nicely proportioned and easy to read. When you become proficient with a graphics program, you can select your own scaling for the x- and y-axes.

Each dot or symbol on a line graph represents a single numerical quantity called a **data point.** You must specify the data to be plotted on the graph; many graphs are produced from the data stored in the rows and columns of spreadsheet files. This data is usually referred to as the *values.* The items that the data points describe are called **variables.** For example, in Figure 13-27, the variable Utilities includes the values 300, 280, 340, 300, and 240; the top line in the plot area shows how these values are graphed.

To make the graph easier to read and understand, **labels** are used to identify the categories along the x-axis and the units along the y-axis. **Titles** summarize the information in the graph and are used to increase comprehension.

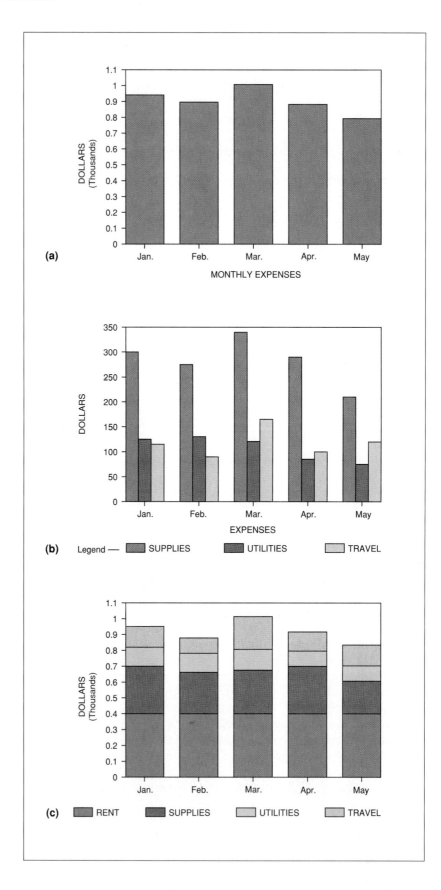

▶
Figure 13-28   Types of bar graphs.
(a) A single-range bar graph shows only one variable—in this case, monthly expenses. Multiple-range bar graphs show several variables. The other two graphs in this figure show the two basic types of multiple-range bar graph: (b) A clustered-bar graph shows several variables. (c) A stacked-bar graph shows the different variables stacked on top of one another.

Bar Graphs

Bar graphs are used for graphing the same kinds of data that line graphs represent. They are often used to illustrate multiple comparisons, such as sales, expenses, and production activities. Notice in Figure 13-28 that **bar graphs** shade an area up to the height of the point being plotted, creating a bar. These graphs can be striking and informative when they are simple. Bar graphs are useful for presentations, since the comparisons are easy to absorb. However, if there is a lot of data for each of several variables, the bars on the graph become narrow and crowded, making a confusing and busy graph; in such a case a line graph may be preferable.

In Figure 13-28, there are three different types of bar graphs. The first is a **single-range bar graph,** in which only one variable is involved; in this example the single variable is monthly expenses. The second type of bar graph is a multiple-range bar graph called a **clustered-bar graph.** In this graph, data values for three different variables—supplies, utilities, and travel—are plotted next to each other along the x-axis. Because clustered-bar graphs contain so much information, it is important to label each cluster clearly. You can also create a **legend,** or list, that explains different colors, shadings, or symbols in the graph. A legend is used at the bottom of Figure 13-28b. The third

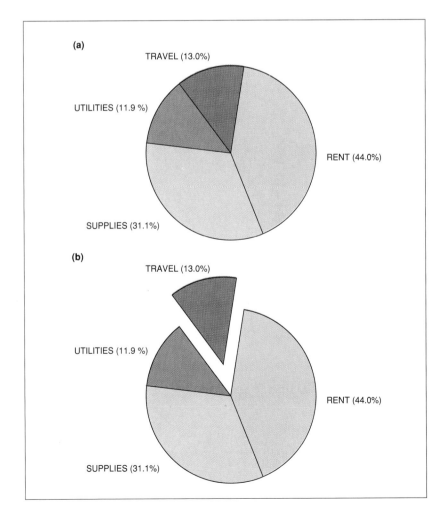

◄

Figure 13-29 Types of pie charts.
Pie charts are used to show how various values make up a whole. (a) A regular pie chart. (b) An exploded pie chart.

type of bar graph, the **stacked-bar graph,** is also a multiple-range bar graph. In this graph, however, the different variables are stacked on top of one another. All the data common to a given row or column appear in one bar.

Pie Charts

Representing just a single value for each variable, a **pie chart** shows how various values make up a whole. These charts really look like pies; the whole amount is represented by a circle, and each wedge of the pie—a portion of the whole—represents a value. Figure 13-29a shows a pie chart.

Pie charts can show only the data for one time period—January, in Figure 13-29. However, of all the graphics, the pie chart does the best job of showing the proportion of all expenses (the whole pie) that goes for rent, supplies, and so forth during that one month. Notice that pie charts often have the written percentage shown by each separate wedge of the pie. It is best to keep pie charts simple; if the pie contains more than eight wedges, you might consider using a bar graph or line graph instead.

Figure 13-29b shows one of the wedges pulled slightly away from the pie, for emphasis. This type of pie chart is called an **exploded pie chart.** This technique loses its effectiveness if more than one or two slices are separated. Not all graphics programs have the ability to produce an exploded pie chart.

▲   ▲   ▲

Thus far in the applications chapters, we have moved from words to numbers to pictures. Another powerful application is storing data so it is easily accessible in a database—the subject of our next chapter.

CHAPTER REVIEW

SUMMARY AND KEY TERMS

- Forms that are used to organize business data into rows and columns are called **spreadsheets.** An **electronic spreadsheet,** or **worksheet,** is a computerized version of a manual spreadsheet.

- The intersection of a row and column forms a **cell.** The letter and number of the intersecting column and row is the **cell address.**

- The **active cell,** or **current cell,** is marked by the spreadsheet's **pointer.**

- Each cell can contain one of four types of information. A **label** provides descriptive information about entries in the spreadsheet. A **value** is an actual number entered into a cell. A **formula** is an instruction to the program to perform a calculation. A **function** is a preprogrammed formula. Sometimes you must specify a **range** of cells to build a formula or perform a function.

- Use the cursor movement keys to scroll the spreadsheet horizontally or vertically. You may also use the **GoTo** function key, also known as the **Jump-To** function key.

- A **mode** is the condition, or state, in which the program is currently functioning. Most spreadsheets have three main operating modes: the **READY mode,** the **ENTRY mode,** and the **MENU mode.** The spreadsheet screen displays a **mode indicator,** which tells you the current mode.

- Spreadsheet programs display commands in a **command menu** shown near the top of the screen. The command menu contains a list, or menu, of different options.

- Most spreadsheet programs display a **control panel** to help you keep track of what you input. The first line is the status line; the second line is used in a variety of ways; and the third line shows a **submenu,** which lists options for the command you are choosing.

- A **command tree** shows all the choices from the main command menu and choices from associated submenus.

- To create a spreadsheet you enter labels, values, formulas, and functions into the cells. Formulas and functions do not appear in the cells; instead, the cell shows the result of the formula or function. The result is called the **displayed value** of the cell. The formula or function is the **contents** of the cell.

- The File command lets you manipulate the Lotus 1-2-3 files on your data disk. You can use the File command to save, retrieve, list, and erase files.

- The Print command provides options for printing all or part of a spreadsheet on paper or on disk.

- The Worksheet Erase command clears the current worksheet from memory, providing you with a blank worksheet. This command will not affect already saved worksheets.

- To leave the spreadsheet program and return to DOS, you must use the main Quit command from the command menu. Always save your file before you quit, since many spreadsheet programs do not automatically save files.

- The **Help key** places you in the HELP mode, which is **context sensitive** (it provides help about the command you are using). While in HELP mode, you can select the **help index,** which gives you access to an on-screen reference manual.

- Programs in an **integrated package** share a common methodology and command structure, which make learning and data transfer easier. **Stand-alone programs** can be integrated by a **universal manager program,** which presents a common interface to the user and handles data transfer among the programs.

- **Business graphics** represent business data in a visual, easily understood format.

- **Analytical graphics** programs help users analyze and understand specific data by presenting data in visual form. **Presentation graphics** programs, or **business-quality graphics** programs, produce sophisticated graphics. Presentation graphics programs also contain a library of symbols and drawings called **clip art.**

- A **line graph,** which uses a line to represent data, is useful for showing trends over time. A reference line on a line graph is an **axis.** The horizontal line is called the **x-axis,** and the vertical line is called the **y-axis.** The area inside the x-axis and y-axis is the **plot area.** Each dot or symbol on a line graph is a **data point.** Each data point represents a value. The items that the data points describe are called **variables.**

- **Bar graphs** show data comparisons by the lengths or heights of bars in columns or rows. In a **single-range bar graph,** only one variable is involved. A **clustered-bar graph** shows more than one variable. A **stacked-bar graph** also shows multiple variables, but the bars are stacked on top of one another. You can create a **legend** to explain the colors or symbols on a complex graph. **Labels** identify the categories along the x-axis and the units along the y-axis. **Titles** summarize the information in the graph.

- A **pie chart** represents a single value for each variable. A wedge of an **exploded pie chart** is pulled slightly away from the pie for emphasis.

SELF-TEST

True/False

T F   1. A manual spreadsheet can automatically recalculate totals when changes are made.

T F   2. Analytical graphics let you construct line graphs, bar graphs, and pie charts.

T F   3. Presentation graphics appear professionally produced.

T F   4. A Lotus 1-2-3 spreadsheet has a one-line control panel.

T F   5. Analytical graphics use a library of symbols to enhance output.

T F   6. The active spreadsheet cell is marked by the pointer.

T F   7. Labels identify categories along graph axes.

T F   8. On an exploded pie chart, one wedge is slightly removed from the pie for emphasis.

T F   9. In Lotus 1-2-3, the Help key is context sensitive.

T F 10. In a spreadsheet, a label cannot be used for calculations.

Matching

_____ 1. legend   a. saves, retrieves, lists, erases

_____ 2. File command   b. one value per variable

_____ 3. simple graphics   c. analytical

_____ 4. cell address   d. integrated package

_____ 5. cell   e. spreadsheet

_____ 6. common methodology   f. explanation

_____ 7. enhanced graphics   g. current cell

_____ 8. worksheet   h. presentation

_____ 9. pie chart   i. location on spreadsheet

_____ 10. active cell   j. row and column

Fill-In

1. The four types of information permitted in a spreadsheet cell are:

   _____, _____,

   _____, and _____

2. The screen entries Range, Copy, Move, and Print are part of what type of Lotus

   menu: _____

3. Enhanced graphics are called: _____

4. In a spreadsheet, a formula is called the cell contents; the calculated result is

   called: _____

5. The intersection of a row and column on a spreadsheet:

   _____

6. Plain line graphs are an example of what kind of graphics:

   _____

7. The user can see any part of a spreadsheet by using which keys:

   _____

8. Another name for the active cell: _____

9. A spreadsheet preprogrammed formula: _____

10. Stand-alone programs can be integrated by a: _____

Answers

True/False: 1. F, 3. T, 5. F, 7. T, 9. T

Matching: 1. f, 3. c, 5. i, 7. h, 9. b

Fill-In: 1. labels, numbers, formulas, functions, 3. presentation, 5. cell,
7. cursor movement keys, 9. function

CHAPTER 14

OVERVIEW

Database
Management Systems
Getting Data Together

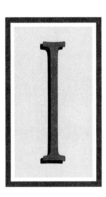

If you try to imagine the perfect job for a movie fanatic, you might come up with something very close to the job Jodie Pearson has. She is the chief executive and sole employee of Starcom Associates, a firm that provides capsule movie descriptions to newspapers, cable television franchises, and video rental shops.

On an average day, Jodie views four or five movies on TV or videotape, often watching two at a time on separate monitors. While she watches, she takes notes and consults a small library of books on domestic and foreign films. To stay current with new releases, she goes to a movie theater once a day. In addition, Jodie makes it a point to revise her descriptions once a year to fine-tune them and keep them fresh.

Jodie's job keeps her busy doing the thing she loves most. However, the job also makes less enjoyable demands on her time: She must organize and manage the thousands of movie descriptions that make up the Starcom Associates product set. As happens to most people who are responsible for the care and feeding of large sets of data, Jodie outgrew her paper filing system long ago. She eventually bought a personal computer with a high-capacity hard disk and set about creating a database.

Consider all the data items Jodie has to track: movie title, year of release, director, principal artists, supporting artists, quality rating, audience rating (G, PG-13, R, etc.), a one-sentence description, a two-sentence description, and a one-paragraph description.

Before she began using the computer database, Jodie had to type three paper descriptions for each movie, one description of each length. Anytime she revised or corrected a description, she had to retype the whole thing. When she received an order for a set of descriptions, she had to locate the correct ones in her file, sort and photocopy them.

Now that she has the data on her computer, things are much simpler. There is a single database entry for each movie. When she wants to change something, she just calls up the correct entry on the screen and edits it. And when a request arrives, she just types in the movie names; gives a command to the database software; and fresh, neatly formatted descriptions are printed.

Because computers are now so common in the publishing business, Jodie has begun to sell her customers copies of her entire database file on disk. With the disk they can extract movie descriptions from the computer file and enter them directly into their computer-generated publications. No intermediate paper version is produced in this process, and the publisher saves the cost of rekeying the information.

Database technology has really saved Jodie a lot of time. And if you think she spends it watching movies, you guessed right. ∎

GETTING IT TOGETHER: DATABASE PROGRAMS

A **database** is an organized collection of related data. In a loose sense you are using a database when you use a phone book or take papers from a file cabinet. Unfortunately, as the amount of data increases, creating, storing, changing, sorting, and retrieving data become overwhelming tasks.

For example, suppose you had a collection of names and addresses, each on a separate index card stored in a box (Figure 14-1). If you had only 25 cards, sorting the cards into alphabetical order or even finding all the people who have the same zip code would be fairly easy. But what if you had 100, or 1000, or 10,000 cards? What if you had several different boxes, one organized by names, one by cities, and one by zip codes? What if different file clerks added more cards each day, not knowing if they were duplicating cards already in the file? And what if another set of clerks were trying to update the data on the cards? As you can see, things might get out of hand. Enter computers and database management software.

A **database management system** (**DBMS**) is software that helps you organize data in a way that allows fast and easy access to the data. In essence, the program acts as an efficient and elaborate file system. With a database program you can enter, modify, store, and retrieve data in a variety of ways. In this chapter we will show you how to create and modify a database. But first we need to discuss some of the general terms used with databases.

USING DATABASE MANAGEMENT SOFTWARE

There are many DBMS programs on the market today. Covering all the operations, features, and functions of each package would be impossible. Therefore, throughout this chapter, we will discuss the characteristics and features of the database program called dBASE in its currently popular version, dBASE IV. This program has many features in common with other database software packages.

Database Models

The way a database organizes data depends on the type, or **model,** of the database. There are three main database models: hierarchical, network, and relational. Each type structures, organizes, and uses data differently. Hierarchical and network databases are usually used with mainframes and minicomputers, so we will not discuss them here. However, relational databases are used with personal computers as well as mainframes.

A **relational database** organizes data in a table format consisting of related rows and columns. Figure 14-2a shows an address list; in Figure 14-2b, this data is laid out as a table. A relational system can relate data in one file to data in another file, allowing a user to tie

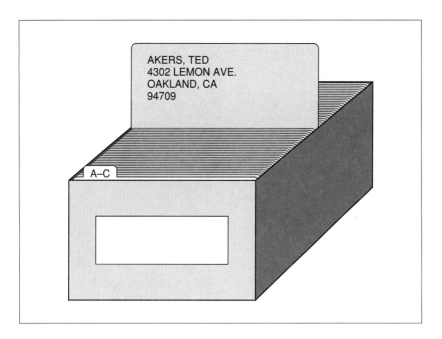

◀
Figure 14-1 An index-card database.
Each card in this index-card file contains one person's name and address. The cards are arranged alphabetically by last name.

together data from several files. However, relating files in this way is beyond the scope of this book. In this chapter we will focus on just one file, and see how it is entered and updated using dBASE IV software.

Fields, Records, and Files

Notice in Figure 14-2b that each box in the table contains a single piece of data, known as a **data item,** such as the name of one city. Each column of the table represents a **field,** which consists of data items.

▼
Figure 14-2 A relational database.
In this example the address list in (a) is organized as a relational database in (b). Note that the data is laid out in rows and columns; each field is equivalent to a vertical column and each record is equivalent to a horizontal row.

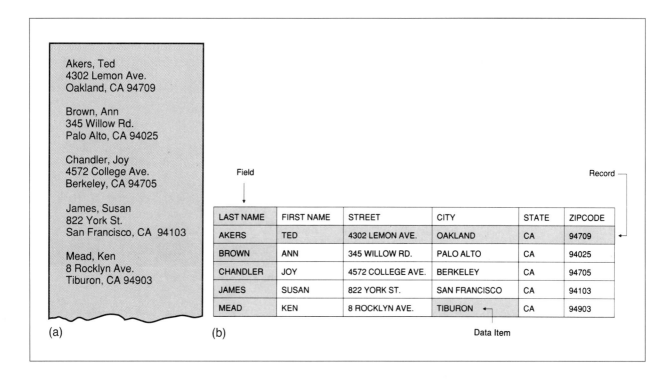

LAST NAME	FIRST NAME	STREET	CITY	STATE	ZIPCODE
AKERS	TED	4302 LEMON AVE.	OAKLAND	CA	94709
BROWN	ANN	345 WILLOW RD.	PALO ALTO	CA	94025
CHANDLER	JOY	4572 COLLEGE AVE.	BERKELEY	CA	94705
JAMES	SUSAN	822 YORK ST.	SAN FRANCISCO	CA	94103
MEAD	KEN	8 ROCKLYN AVE.	TIBURON	CA	94903

(a)

Akers, Ted
4302 Lemon Ave.
Oakland, CA 94709

Brown, Ann
345 Willow Rd.
Palo Alto, CA 94025

Chandler, Joy
4572 College Ave.
Berkeley, CA 94705

James, Susan
822 York St.
San Francisco, CA 94103

Mead, Ken
8 Rocklyn Ave.
Tiburon, CA 94903

(b)

Field

Record

Data Item

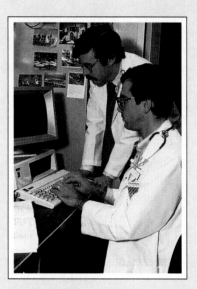

The specific data items in a field may vary, but each field contains the same type of data item—for example, first names or zip codes. The full set of data in any given row is called a **record.** Each record has a fixed number of fields. A collection of related records make up a **file.** In a relational database a file is also called a **relation.** There can be a variable number of records in a given relation; Figure 14-2b shows five records—one for each person.

File Structure

There are two steps to creating a database file: designing the structure of the file and entering the data into the file. To create the file structure, you must choose meaningful fields. The fields you choose should be based on the data you will want to retrieve from the database. For example, if you are creating a list of addresses, you might define fields for name, street address, city, state, and zip code. After you load the program and tell the software that you want to create a file structure, you see a structure input form on the screen. The program will ask for several types of information. Let us take a look at each one.

Field names
Names of the types of data you want to use are called **field names.** For example, a field called PHONE could be used to contain a phone number. Each field must have a unique name. A field name can be up

to ten characters long, must begin with a letter, and cannot contain a space or any punctuation. Letters, numbers, and underscores are permitted.

Field types

There are four commonly used types of fields: character fields, numeric fields, date fields, and logical fields. **Character fields** contain descriptive data such as names, addresses, and telephone numbers. **Numeric fields** contain numbers used for calculations, such as rate of pay. When you enter a numeric field, you must specify the number of decimal places you wish to use. **Date fields** are automatically limited to eight characters, including the slashes used to separate the month, day, and year. **Logical fields** accept only single characters. Logical fields are used to keep track of true or false conditions. For example, if you want to keep track of whether a bill has been paid, you can use a logical field and enter Y for *yes* or N for *no*.

Field widths

The **field width** determines the maximum number of characters or digits to be contained in the field, including decimal points.

Relational Operators

You will need to use a **relational operator** when entering instructions that involve making comparisons. Table 14-1 shows the relational operators that are commonly used. These operators are particularly useful when you want to locate specific data items. For example, to instruct a program to search through an address database and find the records of all the people who live in Wisconsin, you would enter the command

```
LIST FOR STATE = ''WI''
```

This command tells the program to look for the characters WI in the state field.

Now we can move on to using a DBMS to design and create a database. Consider Laurie Chang's problem—a problem that needs a database solution.

A Problem Fit for a Database

Laurie works as an intern for a public television station. One of her jobs is to keep track of people who have pledged to donate money to the station. In the current manual system, each person's name, city, and phone number is kept on a separate card, along with the amount pledged and the date the pledge was made. Laurie wants to place this data into a computer by using dBASE IV. She also wants to add another field—the PAID field—that tells whether each person has actually paid the pledged amount.

First Laurie sketches on paper the structure of the database—what kind of data she wants in each row and column (Figure 14-3).

Laurie has a copy of dBASE IV on the hard disk. Once she boots the system and sees the C > on the screen, she loads dBASE IV into the computer's memory. When the program has been loaded, dBASE displays a copyright notice; Laurie presses Enter to start the program.

Table 14-1 Relational Operators

Command	Explanation
<	Less than
>	Greater than
=	Equal to
< =	Less than or equal to
> =	Greater than or equal to
< >	Not equal to

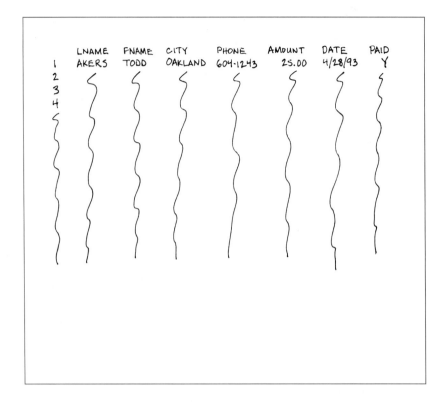

▶
Figure 14-3 Designing the file structure.
Laurie sketches the way she wants to set up her database. Note that she has seven fields: LNAME, FNAME, CITY, PHONE, AMOUNT, DATE, and PAID.

BUILDING A DATABASE

dBASE IV uses a system of menus called **work surfaces.** These menus let you edit, display, and manage your data. The most important menu is called the **Control Center.** This is the first menu Laurie sees after loading dBASE IV. The Control Center provides access to nearly all the features of dBASE IV. As shown in Figure 14-4, the Control Center menu consists of six **panels** that display various options. Users do

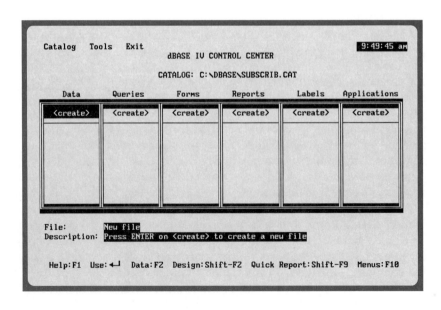

▶
Figure 14-4 dBASE IV Control Center screen.
The dBASE IV Control Center screen lets you access nearly all the features included in dBASE IV.

COMPUTING HIGHLIGHTS

A Computer Can Add Inches to Your Waistline

Just imagine coming home after a long day at work, tired and hungry. You do not feel like cooking. In some cities you can use your modem-equipped computer for a quick solution. A software package called Delivery Systems lets customers use their home computers to dial up local restaurants and fast-food outlets and make menu choices. The meals are delivered to their homes.

Typically, a customer's call goes to a central phone number that links the customer to a regional order-taking center, where operators route the order to the closest outlet. The only interaction with a human being is when the deliveryperson comes to the door.

Pizza firms have been leading the charge into computerized home delivery. Domino's, Godfather's, and Pizza Hut have developed large-scale computer systems. Pizza Hut has found that repeat customers order the same pizza 70% of the time, so the company keeps a database of customers' previous purchases; this information cuts the normal order-taking time in half. Information in the database is also used to market their product. The database can be interrogated to provide a listing of all customers that have not ordered in the past 60 days. The company then sends them a flyer with an incentive to order.

---

most of their work by using the Control Center. It is worth noting the words across the top of the screen: "Catalog, Tools, Exit." Each of these words represents a submenu. As Laurie works, she will often press F10, to activate whatever submenus are displayed across the top of the screen, and then type the first letter of the desired submenu, say, C for Catalog.

dBASE IV commands can be executed from the dot prompt, which is a period displayed on the screen. Some users, especially novices, prefer the menu system. The exercises in this section use the Control Center menu.

Laurie has sketched on paper the structure of the database—what data she wants in each row and column (Figure 14-3). To build the database in dBASE IV, the first step is to build a catalog.

Creating a Catalog

dBASE IV allows you to keep a **catalog,** a group of related files. For instance, once Laurie has created the database she is planning, she could create several reports associated with the database and perhaps design special forms for mailing labels. She would want to store all such files in the same catalog. Files can be added or deleted from a catalog. (However, a file that is deleted from a catalog listing is not deleted altogether; it is still on the disk.)

Before Laurie creates a database file structure in dBASE IV, she needs to create a catalog. Beginning from the Control Center, which is the first screen that appears when the system is accessed, she presses F10; the next screen shows the Catalog menu (Figure 14-5a). The menu selection "Use a different catalog"—the option that lets her make a new catalog—is already highlighted, so she presses Enter. A

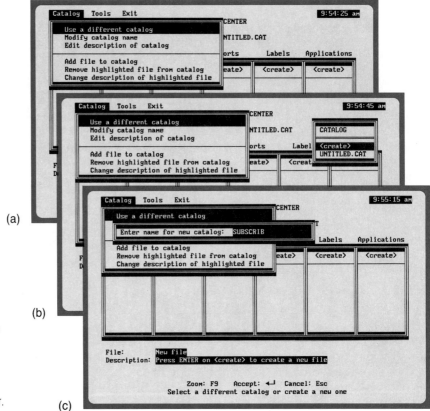

(a)

(b)

(c)

►

Figure 14-5   Creating a catalog.
(a) Laurie creates a new catalog by using F10 and typing C to access the Catalog menu. The highlight is on "Use a different catalog"; she presses Enter. (b) A new screen pops up. The highlight is on "〈create〉"; she presses Enter. dBASE prompts her for a catalog name.
(c) Laurie enters SUBSCRIB and presses Enter.

new window appears on the upper right of the screen (Figure 14-5b). The command "〈create〉" is already highlighted, so Laurie presses Enter. dBASE IV then prompts her for a catalog name. A catalog name can be from one to eight characters in length and contain letters, numbers, and underscores. Laurie enters SUBSCRIB (Figure 14-5c) and presses Enter, which returns her to the Control Center.

Creating the File Structure

To create the file structure, Laurie begins by using the Create command. On the Control Center screen, "〈create〉" in the Data panel on the left side of the screen is already highlighted, so Laurie presses Enter. dBASE IV then displays the database design work surface and presents a design screen (Figure 14-6). On paper, Laurie has already organized the database (see the sketch in Figure 14-3), so she begins to create the structure by entering the first field name.

Laurie types in LNAME for *last name* (dBASE does not accept spaces in field names) and presses Enter. The cursor moves to the Field Type column. There are two methods for entering the field type. Laurie can press the Spacebar until the appropriate field type is displayed in the column—"Character" appears first, as shown in Figure 14-6—and then press Enter, or she can enter the first character of the field type. Laurie types C for *character*; she does not press Enter. (Some other field type designators are N for numeric, D for date, and L for logical.) The cursor automatically moves to the Width column. Laurie

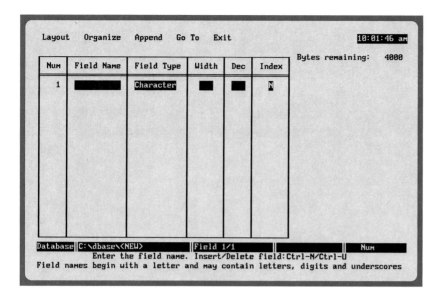

Figure 14-6   Creating the file structure.
To create a file structure, Laurie must fill in information about the field name, field type, and field width.

enters 10 and presses Enter. (The Dec (Decimal) column is automatically bypassed because Laurie is not defining a numeric field.) The cursor moves to the Index column, which we will ignore, since it is beyond the scope of this discussion; the N in the index column means that there is no index. Laurie presses Enter to begin a new line and a new field definition.

Laurie continues to enter the fields. The completed field structure is shown in Figure 14-7. Notice that she defined the PHONE field as a character field. Although a phone number contains numbers, it is not used in calculations and is therefore considered a character field. Laurie did not have to define a width for the DATE field or the PAID field, since the widths for date fields and logical fields are entered automatically when the field types are defined.

Before Laurie can save the file structure, she must use the cursor movement keys to move back to the last line of the file structure, so that she does not save a blank structure line by mistake. After she does

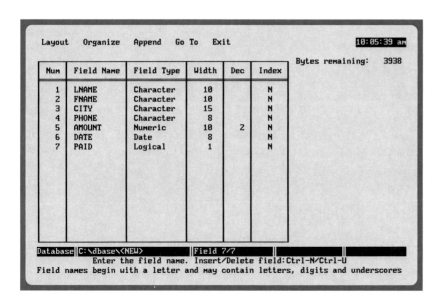

◄

Figure 14-7   The completed file structure.
Laurie has completed the file structure. Note the different field types. To save this structure, Laurie presses Ctrl-End. dBASE prompts her for a file name. Laurie types PLEDGE and presses Enter.

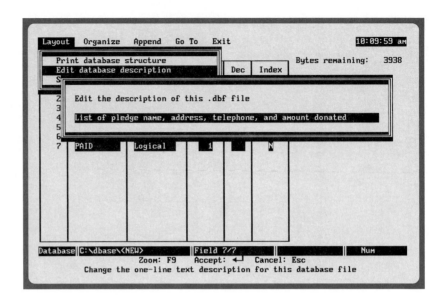

► **Figure 14-8 Entering the database description.**

After Laurie completes the structure, she must enter a description of the database. To do so, Laurie presses F10, which displays the Layout menu. She types E, and dBASE prompts her for the database description. Laurie types "List of pledge name, address, telephone, and amount donated"; then she presses Enter.

this, she saves the structure by pressing Ctrl-End. Laurie must name the database file; she types the name PLEDGE and presses Enter. The structure design screen reappears as soon as the save is completed.

Now Laurie needs to enter a database description, which will be displayed in the file description area whenever the file name is highlighted on the Control Center screen. To enter the description, Laurie presses F10. The Layout menu appears. She types E—for *Edit database description*—to display a prompt box. Laurie enters List of pledge name, address, telephone, and amount donated (Figure 14-8). Then she presses Enter, which redisplays the design structure.

Laurie then signals dBASE that she is done defining the structure by pressing F10. She uses the Right Arrow key to display the Exit menu, which highlights "Save changes and exit." dBASE displays the file name, PLEDGE, on the command line at the bottom of the screen. She presses Enter, which returns her to the Control Center. The new database file, PLEDGE is now included in the catalog called SUBSCRIB.

Viewing the Structure

From the Control Center, Laurie can view the completed file structure by pressing Shift-F2. The Organize menu appears. Laurie presses Esc, which clears the screen of the Organize menu and displays the structure screen shown in Figure 14-9. After reviewing the structure, Laurie presses Esc to return to the Control Center. dBASE responds with "Are You Sure You Want to Abandon this Operation?" Laurie enters Y, and the Control Center appears.

Entering the Data

To enter records into the database, Laurie must first specify the catalog to be used. Because she was using the SUBSCRIB catalog in her last session, the system has automatically retrieved it and the files associated with it. The PLEDGE file is displayed on the Data panel on the

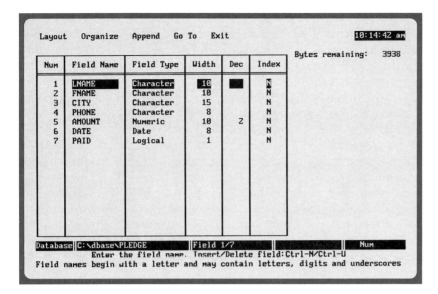

Num	Field Name	Field Type	Width	Dec	Index
1	LNAME	Character	10	▮	N
2	FNAME	Character	10		N
3	CITY	Character	15		N
4	PHONE	Character	8		N
5	AMOUNT	Numeric	10	2	N
6	DATE	Date	8		N
7	PAID	Logical	1		N

◀

Figure 14-9   Viewing the structure.
Laurie can view the completed file structure by pressing Shift-F2. The Organize menu appears. Laurie presses Esc to remove the menu and display the structure.

left side of the Control Center. Since the PLEDGE database file is already highlighted, Laurie presses F2, causing dBASE to display the Edit screen.

The Edit screen presents the fields vertically to provide an input form (Figure 14-10a). The designated width for each field is highlighted. Laurie fills in the blanks of the input form, beginning with the record about Ted Akers (Figure 14-10b). If the data item is shorter than the field length, Laurie presses Enter to move to the next field. However, if the width of the entry is exactly the size of the field, the program beeps and automatically advances to the next field. If Laurie

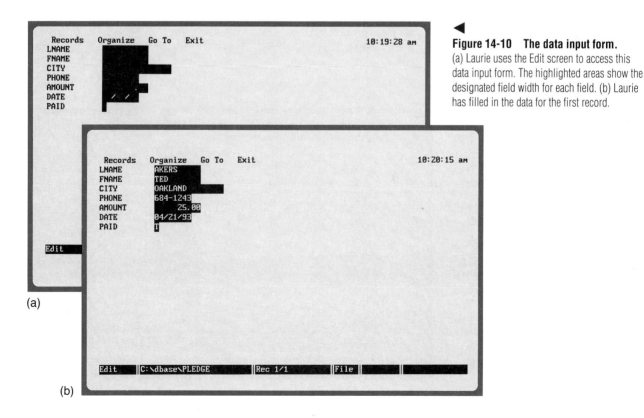

◀

Figure 14-10   The data input form.
(a) Laurie uses the Edit screen to access this data input form. The highlighted areas show the designated field width for each field. (b) Laurie has filled in the data for the first record.

makes a mistake while she is typing, she can use the Backspace key to make corrections. For the amount field, she types 25 followed by a decimal point; dBASE adjusts the field properly. If the numeric form of a month's name is a single digit, she must type 0 before typing the month number or shift the cursor to the right one place by using the Right Arrow key.

After Laurie has filled in all the data for the first record, dBASE automatically saves the record and displays another blank input form, so she can enter the data items for the fields in the second record. When Laurie completes the very last record, dBASE expects still another and again moves to a new empty form. Laurie should *not* save the file at this point, because the empty record would be added to the database. Knowing this, Laurie uses the Up Arrow key to move back to the last record in the database file. Then she presses Ctrl-End to save the file. dBASE stores all the records she created. The Control Center reappears on the screen.

Listing the Records

Laurie wants to check the records she just entered. The Browse screen will allow her to list the records horizontally on the screen and look for errors. Laurie presses F2. The Edit screen of the last record is automatically displayed because this was the last screen she used. Laurie presses F2 again to switch to the Browse screen. She then uses the Up Arrow key to move to the top of the file and thereby reveal all the records (Figure 14-11).

Laurie can print the file by using the **Quick Report** option. She presses Shift-F9 to display a printing submenu, then types B for the option Begin printing. Her printer produces a listing of the records she has just entered. The screen reverts to the Browse menu. Laurie leaves Browse by pressing F10 to get to the Browse submenu. She uses the cursor movement keys to move to Exit, then she presses Enter. The Control Center appears.

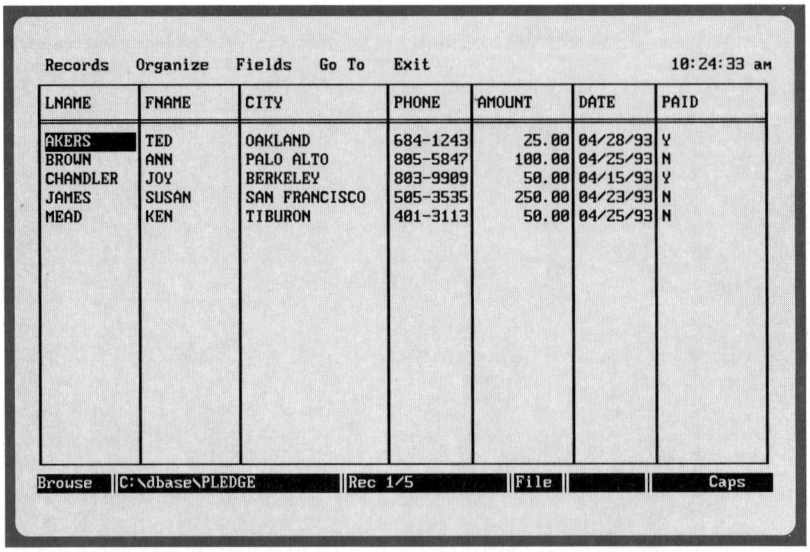

Records	Organize	Fields	Go To	Exit			10:24:33 am
LNAME	FNAME	CITY	PHONE	AMOUNT	DATE	PAID
AKERS	TED	OAKLAND	684-1243	25.00	04/28/93	Y
BROWN	ANN	PALO ALTO	805-5847	100.00	04/25/93	N
CHANDLER	JOY	BERKELEY	803-9909	50.00	04/15/93	Y
JAMES	SUSAN	SAN FRANCISCO	505-3535	250.00	04/23/93	N
MEAD	KEN	TIBURON	401-3113	50.00	04/25/93	N

Browse | C:\dbase\PLEDGE | Rec 1/5 | File | | Caps

▶
Figure 14-11 Viewing the records on the Browse screen.
Laurie uses the Browse screen, which lists records horizontally, to view the records in her database.

Listing Specific Fields

dBASE IV provides a method to create listings called **queries.** Laurie decides she wants to see a list that shows just the LNAME, PAID, and PHONE fields, in that order. Laurie begins from the Control Center. She highlights "(create)" in the Query panel and presses Enter. The PLEDGE database file is still active, so the fields in PLEDGE are displayed (Figure 14-12a). Notice that not all fields fit across the screen; those hidden to the right will appear when Laurie presses the Tab key. To move left, she can use Shift-Tab.

Laurie could automatically select all the fields in the database file for her query by pressing Enter within the first field, Pledge.dbf. However, Laurie wants to select specific fields only, so she must mark the fields she does *not* want. To do this, she uses the Tab key to move across the fields. As the cursor rests on a field, she presses F5 if she does not want to include that field in her query. Laurie simply "tabs

(a)

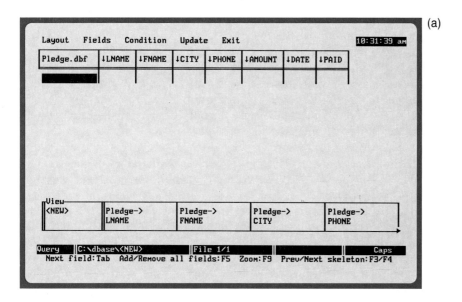

(b)

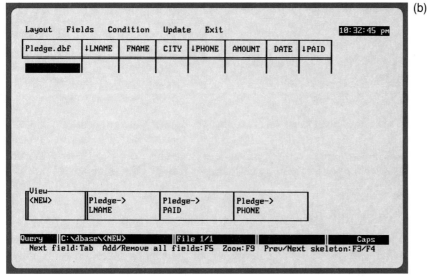

◄

Figure 14-12   Listing specific fields.
(a) Laurie begins the listing procedure from the Control Center, by highlighting "(create)" in the Query panel and pressing Enter. The fields in PLEDGE appear. By using F5, she marks the fields she does not want to include in her query. She skips over desired fields by pressing Tab. (b) The screen after Laurie marks the fields.

over" the fields she does want: LNAME, PAID, and PHONE. As the cursor passes each unmarked field, the field name appears on the lower half of the screen. After the fields have been marked, the screen looks like Figure 14-12b. To list the database records Laurie wants to see, she uses the Quick Report menu. She presses Shift-F9 and presses Enter.

After reviewing the list, she decides to save the list of selected fields, which is called a query. She presses F10 to return to the Layout menu, which is already highlighted. She moves the highlight to "Save this query." dBASE prompts her for the query name. She types PHONELST and presses Enter. To view this list again, Laurie presses F10 and uses the Right Arrow key to return to the Control Center. The Control Center screen now includes the file name PHONELST under the Query panel.

Closing the Files and Exiting the Program

In general, a file is *open* when it is available for commands and *closed* when it is not. dBASE automatically closed the PLEDGE database file at the completion of the query process. Laurie will open PLEDGE again, so that a simple closure can be demonstrated. To open the file, Laurie highlights the file name PLEDGE in the Data panel and presses Enter. A prompt box appears. It contains the option "Use file," an option that—if chosen—will allow her to reuse the last file she selected (Figure 14-13a). Because the option is already highlighted, she presses Enter to open the file.

Laurie can use a similar process to close the file: she highlights PLEDGE and presses Enter. A prompt box similar to the one in Figure 14-13a appears. Because the file is open, however, the prompt box expects a closure request (Figure 14-13b). "Close file" is already highlighted, so Laurie presses Enter to close the file; the dBASE session does not terminate. At this point Laurie can reopen PLEDGE, create another database file by highlighting ⟨create⟩ in the Data panel, or exit the program.

Now Laurie wants to exit the program and return to DOS. She does this by pressing F10 and then using the Right Arrow key to display the Exit menu. She highlights "Quit to DOS" (Figure 14-13c) and presses Enter.

CHANGING A DATABASE

. . . .

Over time, databases need to be changed. New records need to be added; others must be modified or deleted. dBASE IV allows you to add, delete, and change records by using the Edit and Browse menus. Laurie has some changes to make to the PLEDGE database.

Opening the Files

Laurie once again loads dBASE IV. She will begin by telling dBASE which file she wants to change. From the Control Center, Laurie uses the cursor movement keys to move the highlight to "PLEDGE"; she

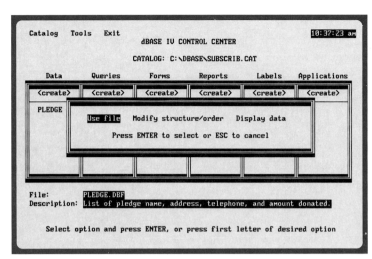

(a)

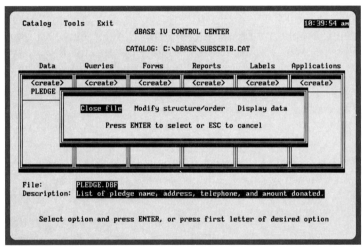

(b)

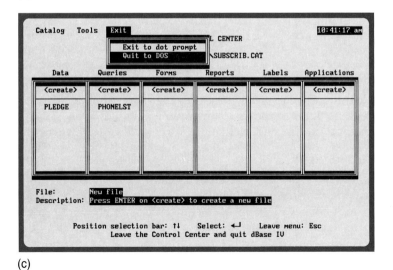

(c)

◄

**Figure 14-13   Closing a file and
exiting dBASE.**

(a) dBASE closed the file automatically when
Laurie saved her query. She knows this
because, when she highlights "PLEDGE," the
window in the Control Center displays "Use
file." (b) If the file had been open, the window
in the Control Center would have displayed
"Close file." (c) To exit dBASE IV, Laurie
presses F10 to get to the menus, selects "Exit,"
and highlights "Quit to DOS."

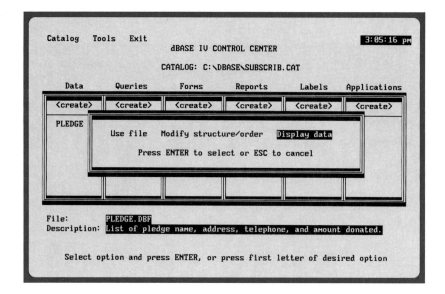

Figure 14-14   Opening a file and displaying the data.
Laurie wants to modify the records in the PLEDGE file. She highlights the file name in the Control Center and presses Enter. dBASE displays the screen shown here. Laurie highlights "Display data" and presses Enter.

presses Enter. dBASE opens PLEDGE, and a window containing three options appears (Figure 14-14). Laurie highlights "Display data" and presses Enter. The records are displayed within the Browse screen. Laurie can use either Browse or Edit to make changes to the file.

Modifying Existing Records

Laurie receives a list of pledge activity for the week. She sees that she needs to update record 1 because Ted Akers has a new phone number. Also, Ann Brown has paid, so Laurie needs to record the payment in record 2. Laurie decides to use the Edit screen to make the first change and the Browse screen for the other.

Using the Edit Screen

Laurie presses the F2 key to move to the Edit screen. The Edit screen allows editing of a data item in an individual record. Therefore, in most cases, Laurie must tell dBASE which record she wants to see. However, in this case, the first record she wants to modify already appears on the screen (Figure 14-15a). (There are several ways to access a record so it can be modified; the easiest is to simply move down the file using the cursor down arrow.) Laurie moves the cursor to the PHONE field, then types in the new phone number. (If necessary, she can also use the Ins and Del keys to make additional changes to the data.) Notice in Figure 14-15b that, in record 1, the new data has replaced the old data.

Once Laurie has used the Edit screen to access a particular record, she can edit previous or succeeding records in the file by pressing the PgUp or PgDn key. The PgUp key moves her to a previous record; the PgDn key moves her to the next record. If Laurie wanted to save these changes now, she would press Ctrl-End. Instead, Laurie decides to use the Browse menu to modify the next record.

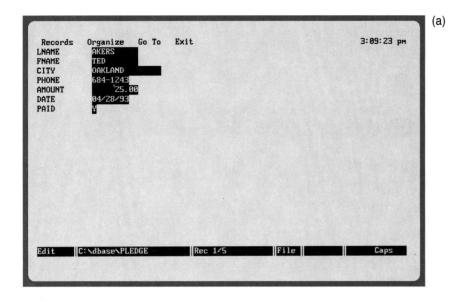

(a)

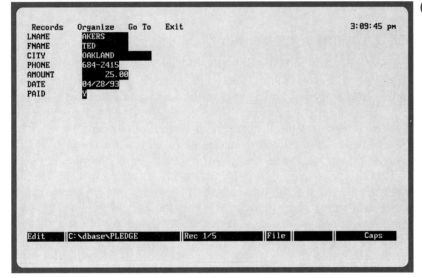

(b)

◀

Figure 14-15   Modifying records by using the Edit screen.
(a) Laurie uses the Edit screen to make changes to record 1. (b) As she types in the changes, new data replaces the old.

Using the Browse Screen

The Browse screen provides the same editing capabilities as the Edit screen. However, Browse displays all the records in the database. The program displays only as many records as will fit on the screen—usually about 12. Scrolling up or down by using the PgUp or PgDn key displays additional records. If there were a number of fields in a record, Laurie could **pan**—move horizontally across the screen—to the left or right by using the Tab or Enter key to move right, Shift-Tab to move left, and the Left or Right Arrow key.

The file is still open, so Laurie presses F2 to display the records in the Browse screen. Since there are currently only five records in her file, the screen displays all the records (Figure 14-16). To update record 2, Laurie moves the cursor down to record 2 and presses Enter to move over to the PAID field. Then she types Y. Now that she has made the change, she presses Ctrl-End to save the data and return to the Control Center.

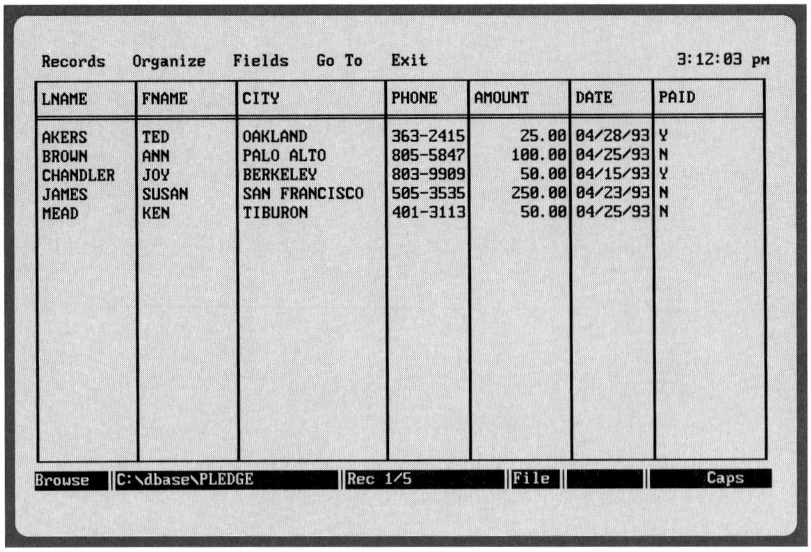

LNAME	FNAME	CITY	PHONE	AMOUNT	DATE	PAID
AKERS	TED	OAKLAND	363-2415	25.00	04/28/93	Y
BROWN	ANN	PALO ALTO	805-5847	100.00	04/25/93	N
CHANDLER	JOY	BERKELEY	803-9909	50.00	04/15/93	Y
JAMES	SUSAN	SAN FRANCISCO	505-3535	250.00	04/23/93	N
MEAD	KEN	TIBURON	401-3113	50.00	04/25/93	N

Figure 14-16 Modifying records by using the Browse screen.
In addition to the Edit screen, Laurie can use the Browse screen to make changes.

Adding Records

Laurie wants to add the records of two new subscribers: Mary Schwartz and Ted Greenlee. She can do this within the Browse screen or the Edit screen. Laurie can use the same steps in either screen.

To add the first new record—Mary Schwartz's—Laurie presses F2 twice to get back to the Edit screen. She then presses F10 to move to the Edit menu. In the Records submenu the choice "Add new records" is highlighted (Figure 14-17a), so she simply presses Enter. A blank data entry form for the PLEDGE file, just like the one used to add the original records, appears on the screen (Figure 14-17b). Laurie types in the data about Mary Schwartz. When another data entry form appears, she types in the data about Ted Greenlee. The completed screens are shown in Figures 14-17c and 14-17d. Laurie remembers to use the Up Arrow key to return to the last record. Then she saves the file and exits by pressing Ctrl-End. The Control Center appears.

Deleting Records

Sometimes a record must be removed—deleted—from a database file. Deleting records from a file is a two-step process. First, the specific records must be marked for deletion by using the Browse menu or the Edit menu. Second, the record must be permanently removed from the file by using the Pack command. The steps to delete records are the same within the Browse and Edit screens. Note that, once you remove a record by using the Pack command, the record cannot be recovered.

Laurie has been notified that Joy Chandler has moved and no longer wishes to donate to the station; the Chandler record needs to be deleted from the PLEDGE file. The PLEDGE file is already highlighted on the Control Center, so Laurie presses F2 twice. The Browse screen appears. Then she moves the cursor to Chandler's record and presses F10 to move to the Browse submenu. The Records menu is already highlighted; Laurie uses the cursor movement keys to move to "Mark record for deletion" (Figure 14-18a), then she presses Enter.

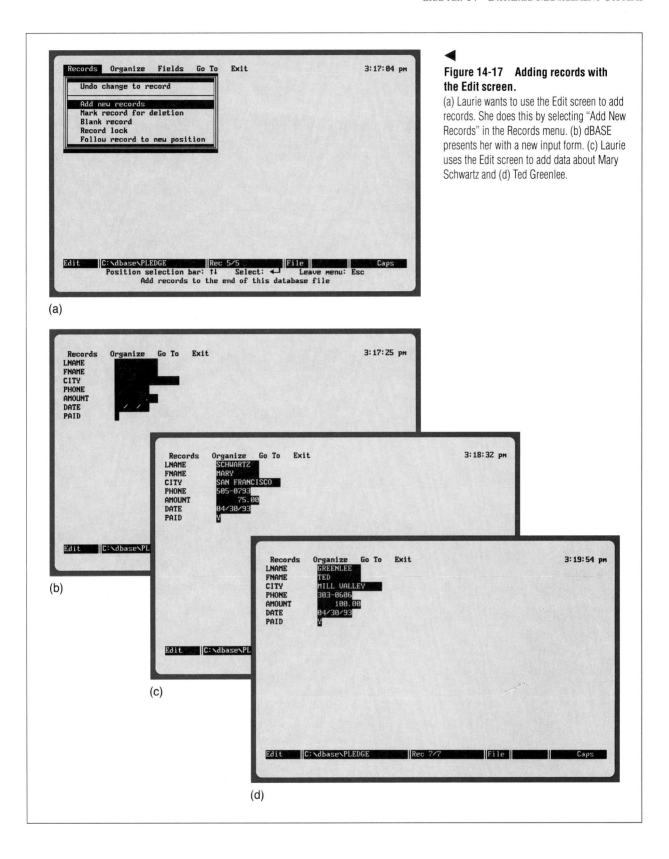

◀

Figure 14-17 Adding records with the Edit screen.

(a) Laurie wants to use the Edit screen to add records. She does this by selecting "Add New Records" in the Records menu. (b) dBASE presents her with a new input form. (c) Laurie uses the Edit screen to add data about Mary Schwartz and (d) Ted Greenlee.

▶

Figure 14-18   Deleting records with the Browse screen.
To delete a record, Laurie moves to the record she wants to remove and presses F10 to move to the Records menu. (a) She then highlights "Mark record for deletion" and presses Enter. (b) The word "Del" appears in the lower-right corner of the screen, and the Chandler record is highlighted.

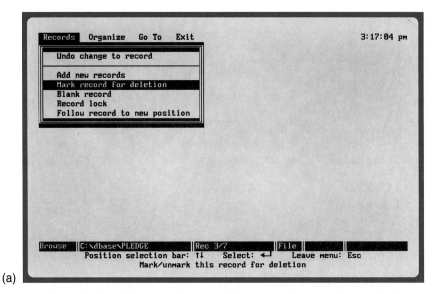

(a)

(b)

The word "Del" appears in the lower-right corner of the screen, and the cursor rests on the Chandler record (Figure 14-18b). The Chandler record is now marked for deletion.

To actually delete the record, Laurie must pack the file by using the Pack command. Laurie presses F10 to move to the Browse submenu. She moves to the Organize menu and, using the cursor movement keys, highlights "Erase marked records" (Figure 14-19a). dBASE displays the message "Are you sure you want to delete all marked records?" Laurie highlights "Yes" and presses Enter (Figure 14-19b). A new window appears, displaying the word "Pack." As records are deleted, they too are displayed in the window. When the operation is complete, the display panel at the bottom of the screen shows "1/6 records." This tells Laurie that there are now only six records in the PLEDGE file. The Chandler record is not one of them. Laurie can verify this by using Quick Report, as before, to list the records (Figure 14-19c). Laurie exits Quick Report and saves the changes with Ctrl-End. She then returns to the Control Center and Exits back to the DOS prompt.

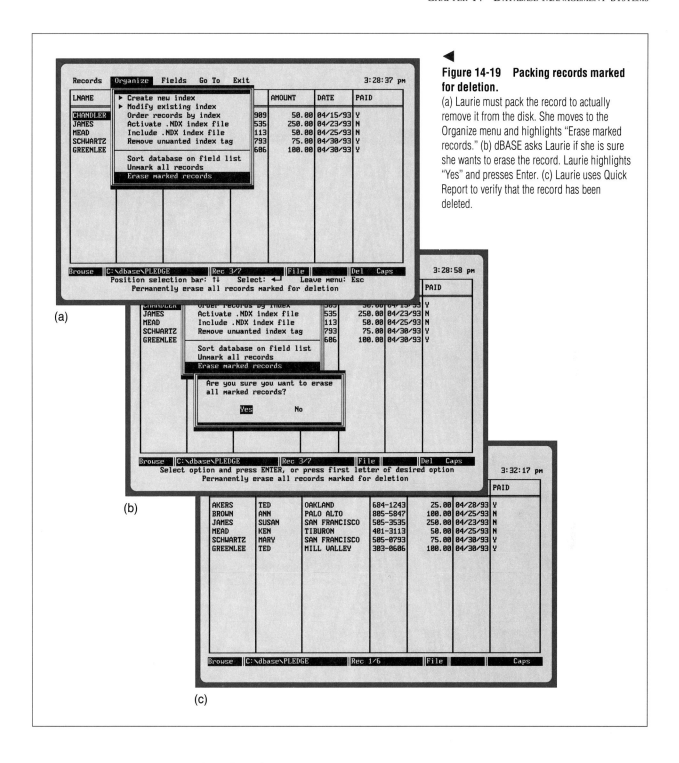

Figure 14-19 Packing records marked for deletion.

(a) Laurie must pack the record to actually remove it from the disk. She moves to the Organize menu and highlights "Erase marked records." (b) dBASE asks Laurie if she is sure she wants to erase the record. Laurie highlights "Yes" and presses Enter. (c) Laurie uses Quick Report to verify that the record has been deleted.

This chapter shows how simple yet powerful a database can be. However, there are many options beyond the basic features this chapter discussed. Those options are beyond the scope of this book, but we encourage you to learn all the bells and whistles of whatever database management package you may use in the future. The payoff in time-saving convenience will make your efforts worthwhile.

MACINTOSH

HyperCard: Linking Information Electronically

When Apple Computer introduced its HyperCard program for the Macintosh in 1987, a lot of people thought it was just a database manager with a big ego. But HyperCard, distributed free with every Mac sold, deliberately does not compete with the many database management programs available for the Mac.

HyperCard can be used as a personal information organizer. It comes with an electronic appointment calendar and an address file, as shown in (a).

The real power of HyperCard is its ability to link information. You place information on screen-size "cards," just as you would put information on index cards. Related cards are organized into "stacks." You can link cards or stacks by activating "buttons" on the screen. For example, the left side of screen (a) shows six buttons that take you from the address card stack to other stacks. HyperCard automatically transfers you to a new stack or a related card when you click a button (that is, when you move the screen arrow to the on-screen button and then press the button on the mouse).

HyperCard is an ideal educational tool. Using ready-made stacks, students can follow their own curiosity in pursuing a topic. For example, in the bird anatomy card shown in screen (b), clicking any part of the bird brings up a card with detailed text and graphical information about that part of the bird.

People have found some creative uses for HyperCard:

• The Voyager Company created a stack that runs a videodisc tour of 1500 images from the National Gallery of Art. You can take notes in HyperCard, and you can use the built-in index to search for a particular artist or period.

• Because HyperCard stacks can easily incorporate digitized speech, music, and other sounds as well as illustrations, many teachers have designed stacks to teach language—foreign-language pronunciation for Americans, English for nonnative speakers, and ABCs for preschoolers.

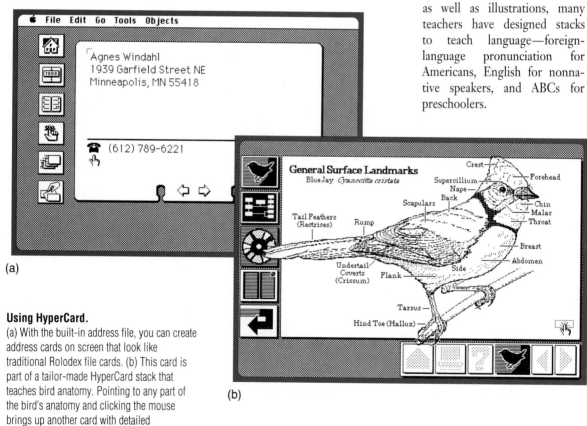

(a)

(b)

Using HyperCard.
(a) With the built-in address file, you can create address cards on screen that look like traditional Rolodex file cards. (b) This card is part of a tailor-made HyperCard stack that teaches bird anatomy. Pointing to any part of the bird's anatomy and clicking the mouse brings up another card with detailed information about that part of the bird.

CHAPTER REVIEW

SUMMARY AND KEY TERMS

- A **database** is an organized collection of related files. A **database management system** (**DBMS**) is software that creates, manages, protects, and provides access to a database.

- A database can store data relationships so that files can be integrated. The way the database organizes data depends on the type, or **model,** of database. There are three database models—hierarchical, network, and relational.

- A **relational database** organizes data in a table format consisting of related rows and columns. Each location in the table contains a single piece of data, known as a **data item.** Each column of the table represents a **field,** which consists of data items. The full set of data in any given row is called a **record.** Related records make up a **file.** In a relational database a file is also called a **relation.**

- There are two steps to creating a file: designing the structure of the file and entering the data. When a file structure is defined, many database programs require the user to identify the field types, **field names,** and **field widths.** There are four commonly used types of fields: **character fields, numeric fields, date fields,** and **logical fields.** The field width determines the maximum number of letters, digits, or symbols to be contained in the field.

- dBASE IV allows you to enter commands by using the Control Center or the dot prompt. The **Control Center** screen, consisting of six option **panels,** provides access to several menus, called **work surfaces,** used to design and work with databases. Each menu has several options.

- A **relational operator** is needed when making comparisons or when entering instructions. Relational operators include =, <, and >.

- Like most database programs, dBASE IV provides a number of commands that let you create a file structure, enter records, update records, delete records, edit records, and list records. These commands include Create, List Structure, Append, List, Edit, Browse, Delete, Use, and Pack.

- At times you may have to **pan**—move sideways across the screen—to view all the fields in a database record.

- In dBASE IV the **Quick Report** option allows you to print a file. A **query** is an on-screen list of particular fields.

- Deleting records from a file is a two-step process. The specific records must be marked for deletion by using one command. Then the record is removed from the file by using the Pack command.

- In dBASE IV the catalog allows you to store a database file and files associated with it (such as reports) under the same identifier, which is like a family name; within a catalog each file has a unique file name.

SELF-TEST

True/False

T   F   1. A database is an organized collection of related files.

T   F   2. In dBASE IV, a record can be added to a file by using the ⟨create⟩ command.

T   F   3. There are two commonly used types of fields: character and index.

T   F   4. In dBASE IV, the Control Center screen has six panels.

T   F   5. In dBASE IV, a record can be deleted by using the Append and Pack commands.

T   F   6. The pan operation moves sideways across the screen so all fields in a database can be viewed.

T   F   7. In dBASE IV, deleting records is a two-step process.

T   F   8. In dBASE IV, the field width is not adjustable.

T   F   9. The database model most commonly used on personal computers is the hierarchical model.

T   F   10. A relational operator—such as =, <, or >—is needed to locate specific data items.

Matching

_____ 1. Control Center   a. tests true/false conditions

_____ 2. record   b. produces reports

_____ 3. logical field   c. indicates the COMMAND mode

_____ 4. file structure   d. system of menus

_____ 5. dot prompt   e. opening menu

_____ 6. catalog   f. opens dBASE files

_____ 7. work surfaces   g. contains related dBASE files

_____ 8. Use command   h. deletes records from a database

_____ 9. Pack command   i. definition of fields in a record

_____ 10. Quick Report   j. all the data in any given row

Fill-In

1. The abbreviation for a database management system is:

   _____

2. The prompt that allows you to enter dBASE commands is called:

   _____

3. The command to open a database file: _____

4. Symbols such as =, >, and < are called: _____

5. The main menu displayed in dBASE IV is called:

   _____

6. The two editing menus in dBASE IV: _____,

   _____

7. Records to be deleted from the database must be marked and then:

   _____

8. The four most common field types: _____,

   _____, _____,

   _____

9. The rows and columns constitute the: _____

10. The database model usually used on personal computers:

    _____

Answers

True/False: 1. T, 3. F, 5. F, 7. T, 9. F

Matching: 1. e, 3. a, 5. c, 7. d, 9. h

Fill-In: 1. DBMS, 3. Use, 5. Control Center, 7. packed, 9. file structure

APPENDIX

OVERVIEW

DATABASE MANAGEMENT SYSTEMS

USING dBASE III PLUS

TO THE STUDENT

This appendix is the continuation of Chapter 14. First, read the beginning of Chapter 14, pages 310 through 313, for the explanation of the structure of a database. Then, turn to this appendix for an example that uses dBASE III PLUS in place of dBASE IV. In this appendix we will focus on just one file, and see how it is entered and updated using dBASE III PLUS software, a popular software package.

A Problem Fit for a Database

Laurie Chang works as an intern for a public television station. One of her jobs is to keep track of people who have pledged to donate money to the station. Currently, each person's name, city, and phone number is kept on a separate card, along with the amount pledged and the date the pledge was made. Laurie wants to place this data into a computer by using dBASE III PLUS. She also wants to add another column of data that tells whether each person has actually paid the amount he or she pledged.

First, Laurie sketches on paper the structure of the database—what data she wants in each row and column (Figure dB-1). Her next step is to enter this structure into the computer.

BUILDING A DATABASE

To use dBASE III PLUS, Laurie must first boot the system. Once she sees the A prompt (A>) on the screen, she places dBASE Disk #1 in drive A and her formatted data disk in drive B. Then she types DBASE and presses Enter. When the program has been loaded, dBASE displays a copyright notice and asks Laurie to press Enter to start the program. Then dBASE displays the instruction "Insert System Disk 2 and press Enter, or press Ctrl-C to abort."

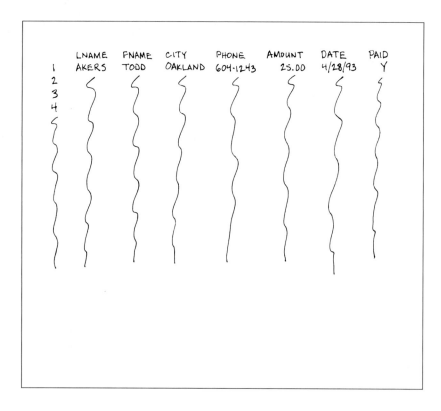

►
Figure dB-1 Designing the file structure.
Laurie quickly sketches how she wants to set up her database. Note that she has seven fields— LNAME, FNAME, CITY, PHONE, AMOUNT, DATE, and PAID.

Laurie removes Disk #1 and places Disk #2 in drive A. Then she presses Enter again, which causes the **Assistant menu** to appear on the screen.

Using the Assistant Menu

When Laurie first accesses dBASE, the Assistant menu appears on the screen, as shown in Figure dB-2. This menu offers a set of choices. Each selection on the top line of the menu has an associated **selection bar** that appears when the main selection is highlighted by the cursor. In Figure dB-2a, for example, the cursor rests on Set Up; the associated selection bar offers the choices "Database file," "Format for Screen," "Query," "Catalog," "View," and "Quit dBASE III PLUS." Laurie can use the Right and Left Arrow keys to move the cursor back and forth across the menu choices on the top line. When she wishes to select an option, she will highlight that option with the cursor and press Enter.

The dBASE program gives Laurie a second option for entering commands: She can type in commands directly by using the **COMMAND mode**. Throughout the rest of this chapter, Laurie will be using the COMMAND mode. (However, either method gets the job done.)

Using the COMMAND Mode

When Laurie is ready to issue commands directly to dBASE, she must first enter the COMMAND mode. To do this, she dismisses the Assistant menu, by pressing the Esc (Escape) key once. The menu screen

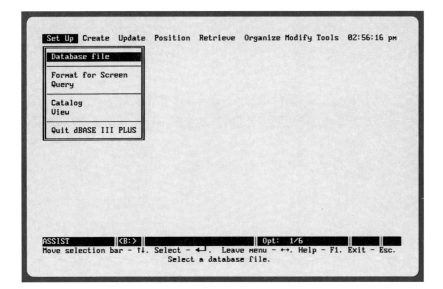

Figure dB-2   Telling dBASE III PLUS what to do.
The dBASE program gives Laurie two options for entering commands: (a) The Assistant menu offers her a series of choices. She can use the Right and Left Arrow keys and Enter to make her selections. (b) When she is in the COMMAND mode, she sees a dot—called the dot prompt—near the lower left of her screen. (With the limited-use version of dBASE III PLUS, the prompt is a dot followed by "(DEMO).") In this mode she simply types in the command she wants to use and then presses Enter.

(a)

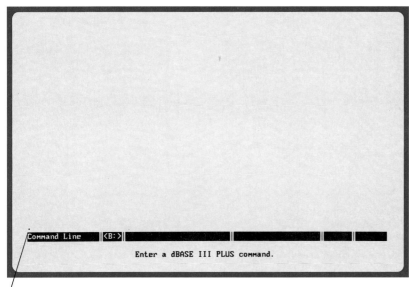

Dot prompt

(b)

disappears; a dot, called the **dot prompt**, appears near the lower left of her screen (Figure dB-2b). When the dot appears, the program is ready for her to type a dBASE command. The dot prompt is similar to A>, which signals that the operating system is ready for a DOS command. After typing each dBASE command, Laurie must press Enter.

Laurie can return to the Assistant menu any time by typing AS-SIST after the dot prompt and then pressing Enter. In fact, she can switch back and forth between the Assistant menu and the dot prompt whenever she wants to; as noted, Esc takes her from the menu to the dot prompt, and ASSIST takes her from the dot prompt to the Assistant menu.

Creating the File Structure

Laurie is ready to enter her data into dBASE III PLUS. First, she needs to create a file structure for her files. In the COMMAND mode, the dot prompt appears in the lower-left corner of the screen. This

▶

Figure dB-3   Creating the file structure.
(a) Once Laurie is in the COMMAND mode,
she types in CREATE after the dot prompt and
presses Enter. dBASE then asks her to name
the new file. (b) After Laurie enters the name
B:PLEDGES, a Create screen appears. The
lower highlighted line on the screen tells Laurie
several pieces of information (from left to
right): the mode she is in (CREATE), the disk
drive where her file will be stored (B), the name
of her file (PLEDGES), and the number of fields
currently in the file (1/1). The program uses the
last two lines to prompt Laurie regarding her
next step.

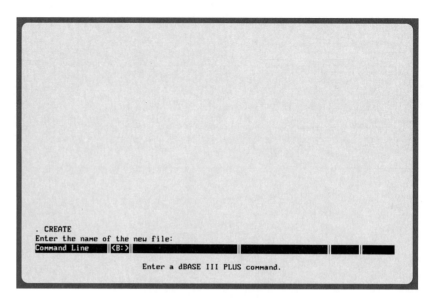

(a)

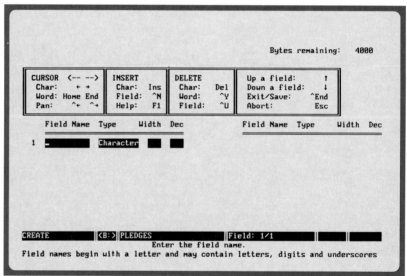

(b)

means that the program is ready for Laurie to enter a command. To create a file structure, she types CREATE and presses Enter. dBASE responds by asking for the name of the file she wishes to create (Figure dB-3a). Because Laurie wants to store the data file on her data disk in drive B, she types in B:PLEDGES and presses Enter. When she does this, a Create screen appears and the cursor flashes under the Field Name heading (Figure dB-3b). Notice that "CREATE" appears in the lower-left corner of the screen. dBASE uses this space to tell Laurie what command she is currently using. Under the lower highlighted bar, the program prompts Laurie regarding her next step. In this case, dBASE prompts her to enter a field name and also defines the guidelines for doing so.

Now Laurie fills in the blanks for each field in her database. She types in LNAME for *last name* (remember, dBASE does not accept spaces in field names) and presses Enter. The cursor moves to the Type column. In Figure dB-4a, notice the word "Character" under the Type column. If Laurie wanted to enter another type of field, she

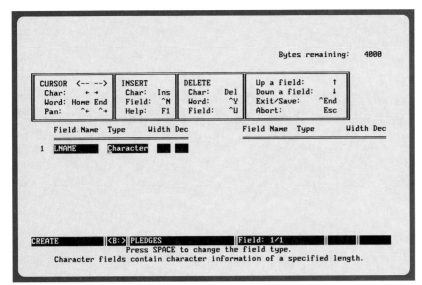

◀

Figure dB-4 Entering fields into the file structure.
(a) Laurie starts to fill in the definitions for the first field in her file. When she presses Enter, the cursor moves to the next column. (b) When Laurie has completed the information for one field, the cursor moves down to the next line.

(a)

(b)

could press the Spacebar until the appropriate field type appeared in the column. However, LNAME is a character field, so she simply presses Enter and the cursor moves on to the Width column. Laurie wants the width of the LNAME field to be ten characters wide, so she types 10. After she presses Enter, the cursor moves down to the next line (Figure dB-4b). Note that the decimal place column (Dec) was ignored, since LNAME is not a numeric field.

Laurie continues to enter the fields. The completed field structure is shown in Figure dB-5. Notice that she defined the PHONE field as a character field. Although a phone number contains numbers, it is not used in calculations and is, therefore, a character field. Laurie did not have to define a width for the DATE field or the PAID field; the widths for date fields and logical fields are entered automatically when the field types are defined.

Once Laurie has finished creating the file structure, she signals dBASE that she is done by pressing Enter without filling in any data. The program asks her to confirm her action by pressing Enter. When

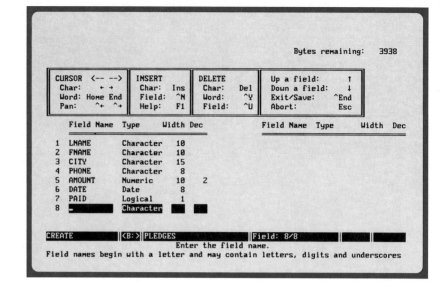

Figure dB-5   The completed file structure.
Laurie has filled in all the information on the file structure. To save this structure and return to the dot prompt, Laurie can press Enter or Ctrl-End.

she does, dBASE responds with the prompt "Input Data Records Now? (Y/N)." Laurie wants to double-check her file structure before she enters the data, so she types N. This returns her to the COMMAND mode.

Viewing the Structure

Laurie can view the completed file structure by using the List Structure command. At the dot prompt she types in LIST STRUCTURE and presses Enter. dBASE responds by displaying the screen shown in Figure dB-6. Notice that the number of data records shown is 0. When Laurie enters the data, this number will change to show the total number of records she has entered.

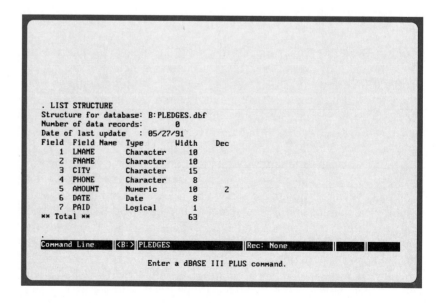

Figure dB-6   Viewing the structure.
Laurie uses the List Structure command to look at the structure of her data file. Notice that the total number of characters for this file is one more than the sum of the numbers in the Width column. The reason for this is that dBASE automatically adds a one-character field at the beginning of each record to make room for special symbols.

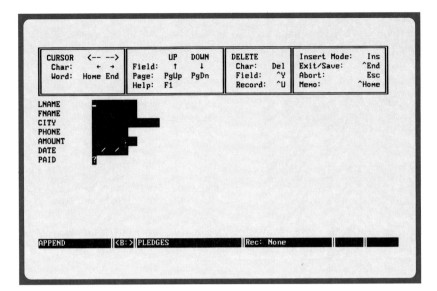

◄
Figure dB-7   The data input form.
Laurie uses the Append command to access a data input form for her file. The highlighted areas show the designated field width for each field.

Entering the Data

To enter records into the database, Laurie uses the Append command. When she sees the dot prompt, she types APPEND and presses Enter. dBASE uses the database structure—the field definitions she just typed in—to provide an input form, as shown in Figure dB-7. The designated width for each field is highlighted.

Using the input form is easy—all Laurie has to do is fill in the blanks. Each time Laurie finishes typing in an entry, she presses Enter to move to the next field. However, if the width of the entry is exactly the size of the field, the program automatically advances to the next field. If Laurie tries to enter too much data into the field, the system beeps or displays an error message. If Laurie makes a mistake while she is typing, she can use the Backspace key to make corrections. Once Laurie has filled in all the data for the first record (Figure dB-8),

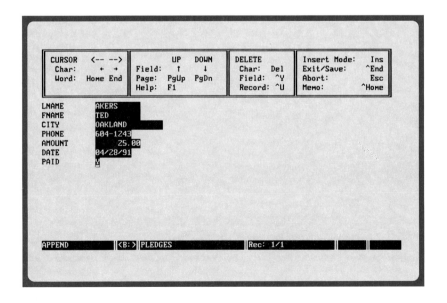

◄
Figure dB-8   Entering the data.
Laurie fills in the data for the first record.

dBASE displays another blank input form, so Laurie can enter the data items for the fields in the second record. She continues in this manner until all the data records are entered. Then she presses Enter or holds down the Ctrl key while pressing the End key. All the created records are stored automatically, and dBASE returns to the dot prompt.

Listing the Records

The entry screens are adequate for entering data, but it is hard to go through them to look for errors—especially if the database is very large. dBASE has a handy command for viewing the contents of a file—the List command. To see a list of all the records she just typed in, Laurie types LIST and presses Enter. A list of the records, as shown in Figure dB-9, appears on the screen. Notice that under the PAID column a "T" (true) or an "F" (false) appears, although Y or N was

(a)

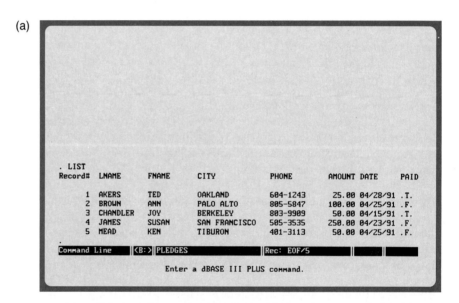

(b)

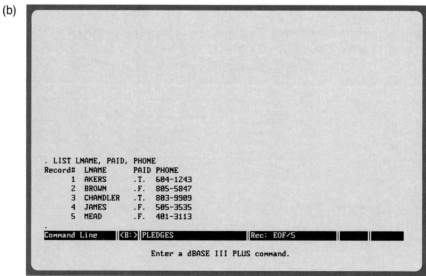

▶

Figure dB-9 Listing records.
(a) Laurie uses the List command to look at the records she has entered into the PLEDGES file.
(b) Laurie can use a variation of the List command to view data in specific fields. In this case she wants to see the data contained in the LNAME, PAID, and PHONE fields.

entered. Since the PAID column is a logical field, dBASE automatically translates the Y and N into T and F, respectively. After the listing appears, dBASE returns to the dot prompt.

Listing Specific Fields

Suppose Laurie wants to see only some of the fields in the database. She can use a variation of the List command to do this. At the dot prompt, she types LIST followed by the fields she wants to see in the order she wants to see them. For example, Laurie decides she wants to see a list that shows just the LNAME, PAID, and PHONE fields, in that order. To do this, she types:

```
LIST LNAME, PAID, PHONE
```

and presses Enter. dBASE then displays the list shown in Figure dB-9b.

Closing the Files and Exiting the Program

To close the file without leaving dBASE, Laurie types in USE at the dot prompt and presses Enter. The current file closes and the dot prompt reappears. Laurie can either reopen the file by typing USE again or create another database file by using the Create command.

Now Laurie wants to exit the program and return to DOS. She does this by typing QUIT. The Quit command closes all the files and returns Laurie to DOS.

Getting Help

If Laurie needs help when using dBASE III PLUS, she can use the F1 function key to access a help program. If she has the Assistant menu on her screen, she can get information on each choice by using the cursor movement keys to highlight a choice on the menu. Then she presses the F1 key. A help screen for that choice appears. She presses the Esc key to leave the help screen and resume her work.

When she is using dot prompt commands, she can get help by typing HELP followed by a space and then the command name. For example, if she wants help with the List command, she types:

```
HELP LIST
```

and presses Enter. The screen shown in Figure dB-10 appears.

CHANGING THE DATABASE

• • • • • • • • • • • • • • • • • •

Once a database file exists, it is unlikely to stay the same for very long. Over a period of time, new records are added, and others are changed or even deleted. Changes can be made to every record in the database, selected records, or one specific record. Most database programs pro-

BIRDS OF THE COMPUTER

Photo researchers specialize in finding just the right pictures for books and articles. Working from a list of photo requests, they contact their sources, which range from agencies that keep thousands of pictures on hand to an individual photographer who has taken a single exquisite picture. The job is time-consuming and the pressure is always on to make deadlines. But photo researchers now have a new tool: a visual archive, by way of computerized photo databases.

For example, a photo researcher can use a data communications system to retrieve the flamingo shown above from a distant photo database and view the photo on a computer screen.

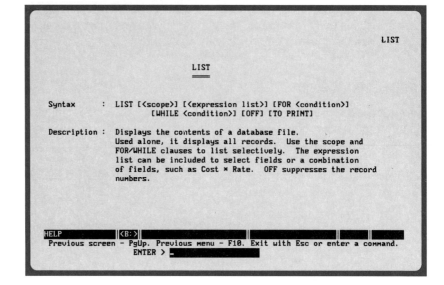

▶

Figure dB-10 A help screen.
The dBASE help feature provides an on-line user guide. In this example Laurie has asked for information about the List command by typing HELP LIST at the dot prompt, then pressing Enter.

vide a variety of commands for maintaining data. The main editing commands in dBASE are Edit, Browse, Append, and Delete. Let us return to Laurie Chang to see how these different commands work.

Opening Files

To add, edit, or delete data in a file, it is necessary to tell dBASE which file it needs to use. The Use command, followed by a file name, opens the desired file. Laurie presses the Esc key to access the dot prompt. Then she types USE B:PLEDGES, which tells dBASE to open the file called PLEDGES—that is, to make PLEDGES available for use. Then Laurie presses Enter. When a database file is open, the name of the file is displayed at the bottom of the screen.

Modifying Existing Records

When one of Laurie's coworkers hands her a list of pledge activity, she notices that one of her existing records, Record 1, needs to be updated—Ted Akers has a new phone number. She also notices that Ann Brown has paid, so Laurie needs to record the payment in Record 2. To modify these records, Laurie can use one of two commands: the Edit command or the Browse command. We will use the Edit command to change one record and then use Browse to change the other.

Using the Edit Command
The Edit command allows editing of data in an individual record. Therefore, to use it, Laurie must tell dBASE which record she wants to see. To edit Record 1, Laurie types EDIT 1 and then presses Enter. Record 1 appears on the screen (Figure dB-11a). Laurie moves the cursor to the PHONE field, then types in the new phone number. (If necessary, she can also use the Ins and Del keys to make additional changes to the data.) Notice in Figure dB-11b that the new data is

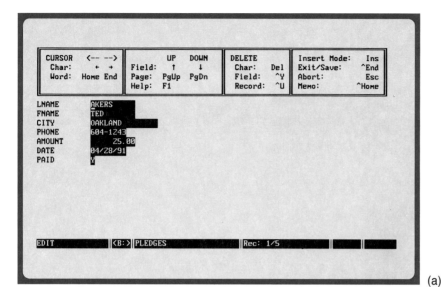

(a) Laurie uses the Edit command to make changes to Record 1. (b) As she types in the changes, the new data is written over the old.

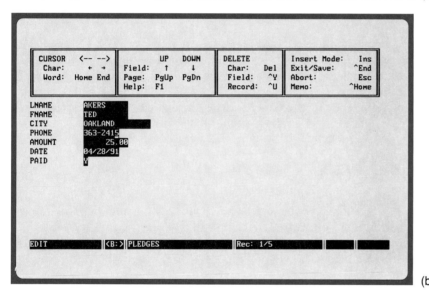

(b)

written over the old data. To store the changed record in the database and return to the dot prompt, Laurie presses Ctrl-End.

Once Laurie has used the Edit command to access a particular record, she can edit previous or succeeding records in the file by pressing the PgUp or PgDn key. The PgUp key moves her to a previous record; the PgDn key moves her to the next record.

Using the Browse Command

The Browse command provides the same editing capabilities as the Edit command. However, Browse displays all the records in the database. The program displays only as much data as will fit on the screen—usually about 12 records. To see records not shown on the screen, you can scroll up and down by using the PgUp and PgDn keys. If there are a number of fields in a record, you may have to **pan**—move horizontally across the screen—to the left or right by using the Ctrl key and the Left or Right Arrow key.

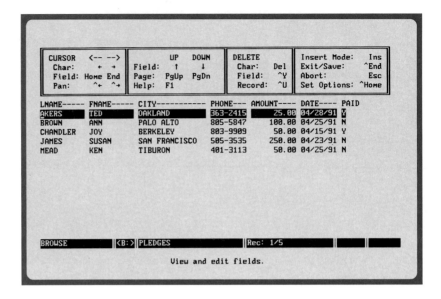

Figure dB-12   The Browse screen.
Laurie can use the Browse command to view and modify the records in her database.

To use the Browse command, Laurie types in BROWSE and then presses Enter. Since there are currently only five records in her file, the screen displays all the records (Figure dB-12). To update Record 2, Laurie moves the cursor down to Record 2 and over to the PAID field. Then she types Y. After she has made the change, she presses Ctrl-End to save the data and return to the dot prompt.

Adding Records

When Laurie wants to add new records to her database, she can use either the Append command or the Browse command. Suppose Laurie receives data on two new subscribers—Mary Schwartz and Ted Greenlee—to add to the database. Let us examine how she would use each command.

Adding Records with Append

To add the first new record—Mary Schwartz—Laurie types AP-PEND and presses Enter. A blank data entry form for the PLEDGES file, just like the one used to add the original records, appears on the screen. Laurie types in the data on Mary Schwartz, pressing Enter after typing data into each field. The completed screen is shown in Figure dB-13.

Before Laurie stores the data in the database, she wants to check to make sure everything is correct. Since the program automatically moved to the next record when Laurie filled in the PAID field, she has to use the PgUp key to return to Mary's record. After Laurie has checked over the data, she presses Enter, and a blank input screen appears. Laurie can continue adding records to the database in this manner. When she is finished, she presses Ctrl-End. The dot prompt reappears.

Adding Records with Browse

As we mentioned before, the Browse command displays a number of records at one time. To use this command to add records, Laurie types

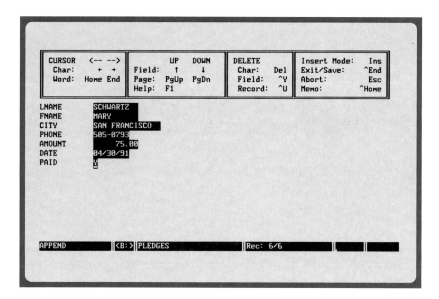

◀

Figure dB-13 Adding records with Append.
Laurie uses the Append command to add Mary Schwartz's record.

BROWSE and presses Enter. Then she moves the cursor to the last record in the file. Next Laurie presses the Down Arrow key to move beyond the last record (Figure dB-14a). dBASE asks her if she wants to add records. When she types Y for *yes*, a new blank record appears. Laurie types in the data on Ted Greenlee (Figure dB-14b). When she is done, she once again presses Ctrl-End to store the data.

Deleting Records

Sometimes a record must be removed—deleted—from a database file. Deleting records from a file is a two-step process. First, the specific records must be marked for deletion by using the Delete command or the Browse command. Second, the record must be permanently removed from the file by using the Pack command. Note that once a record is removed by using the Pack command, the record cannot be recovered.

Deleting with the Browse Command

Suppose Laurie receives a note indicating that Joy Chandler has moved and no longer wishes to donate to the station; the Chandler record needs to be deleted from the PLEDGES file. Laurie types BROWSE and presses Enter. Then she moves the cursor to Chandler's record and presses Ctrl-U. The word "Del" appears in the lower-right corner of her screen (Figure dB-15a). The Chandler record is now marked for deletion. If Laurie accidentally marks the wrong record, she can press Ctrl-U again, and the deletion mark will be removed.

Since Laurie wants to delete the Chandler record, she checks to see that the record is properly marked. First she exits the BROWSE mode by pressing Ctrl-End. Then she uses the List command. When the list of records is displayed, dBASE indicates a record marked for deletion by placing an asterisk in front of the record (Figure dB-15b).

To actually delete the record, Laurie will use the Pack command. At the dot prompt, she types in PACK and presses Enter. dBASE displays the message "6 records copied." This tells Laurie that there

▶

Figure dB-14   Adding records with Browse.
(a) To add a record by using the Browse command, Laurie must move beyond the last record in the file. (b) Then she can type in the new data.

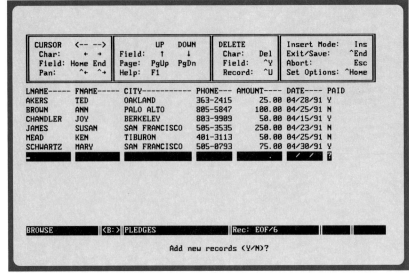

(a)

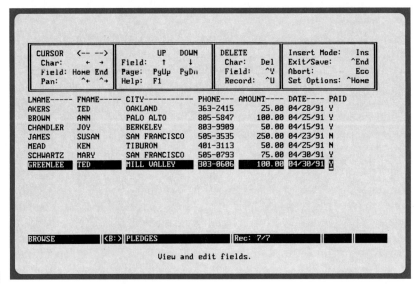

(b)

are now only six records in the PLEDGES file—the Chandler record is not one of them. Laurie can verify this by using the List command again (Figure dB-15c).

Deleting with the Delete Command

The Delete command is useful for deleting a specific record from a file when the record number is unknown. As with the Browse command, Laurie must first mark the record for deletion. To mark Ken Mead's record, for example, Laurie types:

```
DELETE FOR LNAME = ''MEAD''
```

Then she presses Enter. Notice the use of the relational operator in this command. This tells dBASE to search for the record in which the LNAME field contains the name MEAD. The quotation marks around MEAD indicate that MEAD is a character field. The program indicates the number of records marked for deletion—in this case, one record. As before, Laurie uses the List command to check that the proper record has been marked for deletion.

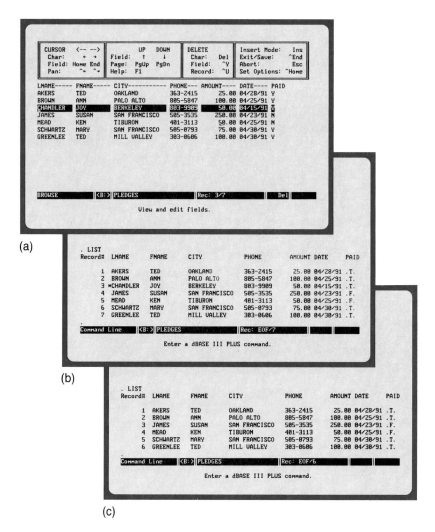

◀

Figure dB-15   Deleting records with Browse.

(a) To delete a record, Laurie moves the cursor to the record she wants to remove and presses Ctrl-U. Note that the word "Del" appears in the lower highlighted area of the screen. (b) When Laurie lists the records, the asterisk next to the Chandler record tells her that the record is marked for deletion. (c) After Laurie uses the Pack command to remove the record, the record is no longer listed.

If Laurie makes a mistake, she can use the Recall command to unmark the record she has marked. She would type:

```
RECALL FOR LNAME = ''MEAD''
```

and press Enter. When she uses the List command, the asterisk would no longer be next to the record. Recall is a useful command, but only if used *before* the Pack command is issued.

Now Laurie is ready to delete the record. As before, she types PACK and presses Enter. And as before, the program responds with the number of records copied.

When Laurie has finished with her editing, she types QUIT to close the file and exit the program.

▲ ▲ ▲

This chapter shows how simple yet powerful a database can be. However, there are many options beyond the basic steps of setting up and changing a database. Those options are beyond the scope of this book, but we encourage you to learn all the bells and whistles of whatever database management package you may use in the future; the payoff in time-saving convenience will make the learning curve worthwhile.

MACINTOSH

HyperCard: Linking Information Electronically

When Apple Computer introduced its HyperCard program for the Macintosh in 1987, a lot of people thought it was just a database manager with a big ego. But HyperCard, distributed free with every Mac sold, deliberately does not compete with the many database management programs available for the Mac.

HyperCard can be used as a personal information organizer. It comes with an electronic appointment calendar and an address file, as shown in (a).

The real power of HyperCard is its ability to link information. You place information on screen-size "cards," just as you would put information on index cards. Related cards are organized into "stacks." You can link cards or stacks by activating "buttons" on the screen. For example, the left side of screen (a) shows six buttons that take you from the address card stack to other stacks. HyperCard automatically transfers you to a new stack or a related card when you click a button (that is, when you move the screen arrow to the on-screen button and then press the button on the mouse).

HyperCard is an ideal educational tool. Using ready-made stacks, students can follow their own curiosity in pursuing a topic. For example, in the bird anatomy card shown in screen (b), clicking any part of the bird brings up a card with detailed text and graphical information about that part of the bird.

People have found some creative uses for HyperCard:

- The Voyager Company created a stack that runs a videodisc tour of 1500 images from the National Gallery of Art. You can take notes in HyperCard, and you can use the built-in index to search for a particular artist or period.

- Because HyperCard stacks can so easily incorporate digitized speech, music, and other sounds as well as illustrations, many teachers have designed stacks to teach language—foreign-language pronunciation for Americans, English for non-native speakers, and ABCs for preschoolers.

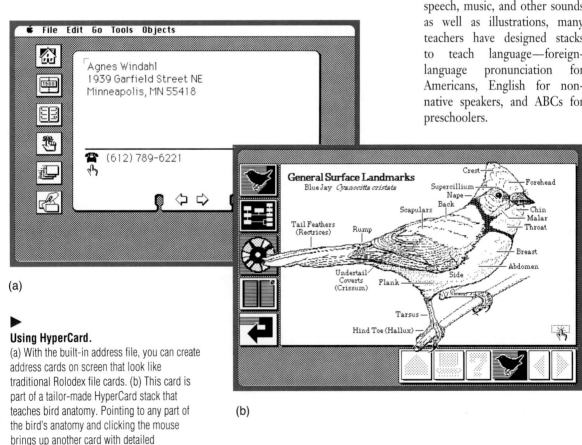

(a)

(b)

► **Using HyperCard.**
(a) With the built-in address file, you can create address cards on screen that look like traditional Rolodex file cards. (b) This card is part of a tailor-made HyperCard stack that teaches bird anatomy. Pointing to any part of the bird's anatomy and clicking the mouse brings up another card with detailed information about that part of the bird.

Appendix Review

Summary and key terms

- A **database** is an organized collection of related data. A **database management system (DBMS)** is software that creates, manages, protects, and provides access to a database.

- A database can store data relationships so that files can be integrated. The way the database organizes data depends on the type, or **model**, of database. There are three database models—hierarchical, network, and relational.

- In a **relational database**, data that is organized logically in a table is called a **relation**, or **file**. Each "box" in the table contains a piece of data known as a **data item**. Each column of the table represents an **attribute**, or **field**. All the data in any given row is called a **record**.

- There are two steps to creating a file: designing the structure of the file and entering the data. When a file structure is defined, many database programs require the user to identify the **field names**, the **field types**, and the **field widths**. There are four commonly used types of fields: **character fields, numeric fields, date fields**, and **logical fields**. The field width determines the maximum number of letters, digits, or symbols to be contained in the field.

- At times, a **relational operator** is needed when making comparisons or when entering instructions. Some commands generally used as operators include =, <, and >.

- dBASE III PLUS gives you two means of entering commands: the Assistant menu and the COMMAND mode. The **Assistant menu** has a number of options on the top line of the menu. Each option has an associated **selection bar**, which appears when the cursor highlights the main selection. When you are in the **COMMAND mode**, the menu screen disappears and a **dot prompt** appears.

- Like most database programs, dBASE III PLUS has a number of commands that let you create a file structure, enter records, update records, delete records, edit records, and list records. These commands include the Create command, the List Structure command, the Append command, the List command, the Edit command, the Browse command, the Delete command, the Use command, and the Pack command.

- If you need help when using the database program, you can press F1 to access a help screen.

- At times you may have to **pan**—move sideways across the screen—to view all the fields in a database.

- Deleting records from a file is a two-step process. The specific records must be marked for deletion by using one command. Then the record is removed from the file by using another command.

SELF-TEST

True/False

T F 1. A database is an organized collection of related files.

T F 2. In dBASE III PLUS, a record can be added to a file by using the Browse command.

T F 3. There are two commonly used types of fields: character and index.

T F 4. In dBASE III PLUS, commands can be entered using the Assistant menu or the COMMAND mode.

T F 5. In dBASE III PLUS, a record can be deleted by using the Append and Pack commands.

T F 6. The pan operation moves the cursor sideways across the screen so all fields in a database can be viewed.

T F 7. In dBASE III PLUS, deleting records is a two-step process.

T F 8. In dBASE III PLUS, the field width is not adjustable.

T F 9. The database model most commonly used on personal computers is the hierarchical model.

T F 10. A relational operator—such as =, <, or >—is needed to locate specific data items.

Matching

_____ 1. Append command

_____ 2. record

_____ 3. logical field

_____ 4. file structure

_____ 5. dot prompt

_____ 6. catalog

_____ 7. work surfaces

_____ 8. Use command

_____ 9. Pack command

_____ 10. List Structure command

a. tests true/false conditions

b. command to view completed file structure

c. indicates the COMMAND mode

d. system of menus

e. one of two commands needed to add records

f. opens dBASE files

g. contains related dBASE files

h. deletes records from a database

i. definition of fields in a record

j. all the data in any given row

Fill-In

1. The abbreviation for a database management system is:

   _____

2. The prompt that allows you to enter dBASE commands is called:

   _____

3. The command to open a database file is: _____

4. Symbols such as =, >, and < are called: _____

5. The main menu displayed in dBASE III PLUS is called:

    _____

6. The two editing menus in dBASE III PLUS are:

    _____ , _____

7. Records to be deleted from the database must be marked and then:

    _____

8. The four most common field types are: _____ ,

    _____ , _____ ,

    _____

9. The rows and columns constitute the: _____

10. The database model usually used on personal computers is:

    _____

Answers

True/False: 1. T, 3. F, 5. F, 7. T, 9. F

Matching: 1. e, 3. a, 5. c, 7. d, 9. h

Fill-In: 1. DBMS, 3. Use, 5. Assistant menu, 7. packed, 9. file structure

APPENDIX

OVERVIEW

HISTORY AND INDUSTRY:

THE CONTINUING STORY OF THE COMPUTER AGE

Although the story of computers has diverse roots, the most fascinating part—the history of personal computers—is quite recent. The beginning of this history turns on the personality of Ed Roberts the way a watch turns on a jewel. It began when his foundering company took a surprising turn.

Like other entrepreneurs before him, Ed Roberts had taken a big risk. He had already been burned once, and now he feared being burned again. The first time, in the early 1970s, he had borrowed heavily to produce microprocessor-based calculators, only to have the chip producers decide to build their own product—and sell it for half the price of Ed's calculator.

Ed's new product was based on a microprocessor too—the Intel 8080—but it was a *computer*. A little computer. The "big boys" at the established computer firms considered computers to be industrial products; who would want a small computer? Ed was not sure, but he found the idea so compelling that he decided to make the computer anyway. Besides, he was so far in debt from the calculator fiasco that it did not seem to matter which project propelled him into bankruptcy. Ed's small computer and his company, MITS, were given a sharp boost by Les Solomon, who promised to feature the new machine on the cover of *Popular Electronics*. In Albuquerque, New Mexico, Ed worked frantically to meet the publication deadline, and he even tried to make the machine pretty, so it would look attractive on the cover (Figure H-1).

Making a good-looking small computer was not easy. This machine, named the Altair (after a heavenly "Star Trek" destination), looked like a flat box. In fact, it met the definition of a computer in only a minimal way: It had a central processing unit (on the chip), 256 characters (a paragraph!) of memory, and switches and lights on a front panel for input/output. No screen, no keyboard, no storage.

But the Altair was done on time for the January 1975 issue of *Popular Electronics*, and Roberts made plans to fly to New York to demonstrate the machine for Solomon. He sent the computer on ahead by railroad express. Ed got to New York but the computer did not—the very first personal computer was lost! There was no time to build a new computer before the publishing deadline, so Roberts cooked up a phony version for the cover picture: an empty box with switches and

Figure H-1 The Altair.
The term *personal computer* had not even been invented yet, so Ed Roberts's small computer was called a "minicomputer" when it was featured on the cover of *Popular Electronics*.

355

▲
Figure H-2 Charles Babbage's difference engine.
This shows a prototype model. Babbage attempted to build a working model, which was to have been several times larger and steam-driven, but he was unsuccessful.

lights on the front panel. He also placed an inch-high ad in the back of the magazine: Get your own Altair kit for $397.

Ed was hoping for perhaps 200 orders. But the machine—that is, the box—fired imaginations across the country. Two thousand customers sent checks for $397 to an unknown Albuquerque, New Mexico, company. Overnight, the MITS Altair personal computer kit was a runaway success.

Ed Roberts was an important player in the history of personal computers. Unfortunately, he never made it in the big time; most observers agree that his business insight did not match his technical skills. But other entrepreneurs did make it. In this chapter, we will glance briefly at the early years of computers and then examine more recent history.

BABBAGE AND THE COUNTESS

Born in England in 1791, Charles Babbage was an inventor and mathematician. When solving certain equations, he found the hand-done mathematical tables he used filled with errors. He decided a machine could be built that would solve the equations better by calculating the differences between them. He set about making a demonstration model of what he called a **difference engine** (Figure H-2). The model was so well received that in about 1830 he enthusiastically began to build a full-scale working version, using a grant from the British government.

However, Babbage found that the smallest imperfections were enough to throw the machine out of whack. Babbage was viewed by his own colleagues as a man who was trying to manufacture a machine that was utterly ridiculous. Finally, after spending its money to no avail, the government withdrew financial support.

Despite this setback, Babbage was not discouraged. He conceived of another machine, christened the **analytical engine**, which he hoped would perform many kinds of calculations. This, too, was never built, at least by Babbage (a model was later put together by his son), but the analytical engine embodied five key features of modern computers:

- an input device
- a storage place to hold the number waiting to be processed
- a processor, or number calculator
- a control unit to direct the task to be performed and the sequence of calculations
- an output device

If Babbage was the father of the computer, then Ada, the Countess of Lovelace, was the first computer programmer (Figure H-3). The daughter of English poet Lord Byron and of a mother who was a gifted mathematician, Ada helped develop the instructions for doing computations on the analytical engine. Lady Lovelace's contributions cannot be overvalued. She was able to see that Babbage's theoretical approach was workable, and her interest gave him encouragement. In addition, she published a series of notes that eventually led others to accomplish what Babbage himself had been unable to do.

▲
Figure H-3 The Countess of Lovelace.
Augusta Ada Byron, as she was known before she became a countess, was Charles Babbage's colleague in his work on the analytical engine and has been called the world's first computer programmer.

◀

Figure H-4   Herman Hollerith's tabulating machine.
This electrical tabulator and sorter was used to tabulate 1890 census data.

HERMAN HOLLERITH: THE CENSUS HAS NEVER BEEN THE SAME

· · · · · · · · · · · · · · · · · · · ·

The hand-done tabulation of the 1880 United States census took seven and a half years. A competition was held to find some way to speed the counting process of the 1890 United States census. Herman Hollerith's tabulating machine won the contest. As a result of his system's adoption, an unofficial count of the 1890 population (62,622,250) was announced only six weeks after the census was taken.

The principal difference between Hollerith's and Babbage's machines was that Hollerith's machine used electrical rather than mechanical power (Figure H-4). Hollerith realized that his machine had considerable commercial potential. In 1896 he founded the successful Tabulating Machine Company, which, in 1924, merged with two other companies to form the International Business Machines Corporation—IBM.

WATSON OF IBM: ORNERY BUT RATHER SUCCESSFUL

· · · · · · · · · · · · · · · · · · · ·

For over 30 years, from 1924 to 1956, Thomas J. Watson, Sr., ruled IBM with an iron grip. Cantankerous and autocratic, supersalesman Watson made IBM a dominant force in the business machines market, first as a supplier of calculators, then as a developer of computers.

▲
Figure H-5   The ABC.
John Atanasoff and his assistant, Clifford Berry,
developed the first digital electronic computer,
nicknamed the "ABC" for *Atanasoff-Berry
computer.*

IBM's entry into computers was sparked by a young Harvard professor of mathematics, Howard Aiken. In 1936, after reading Lady
Lovelace's notes, Aiken began to think that a modern equivalent of the
analytical engine could be constructed. Because IBM was already such
a power in the business machines market, with ample money and resources, Aiken worked out a careful proposal and approached Thomas
Watson. In one of those make-or-break decisions for which he was
famous, Watson gave him $1 million. As a result, the Harvard Mark I
was born.

THE START OF THE MODERN ERA

Nothing like the **Mark I** had ever been built before. It was 8 feet high
and 55 feet long, made of streamlined steel and glass, and it emitted a
sound during processing that one person said was "like listening to a
roomful of old ladies knitting away with steel needles." Unveiled in
1944, the Mark I was never very efficient. But the enormous publicity
it generated strengthened IBM's commitment to computer development. Meanwhile, technology had been proceeding elsewhere on separate tracks.

American military officials approached Dr. John Mauchly at the
University of Pennsylvania and asked him to build a machine that
would rapidly calculate trajectories for artillery and missiles. Mauchly
and his student J. Presper Eckert relied on the work of Dr. John V.
Atanasoff, a professor of physics at Iowa State University. During the
late 1930s Atanasoff had spent time trying to build an electronic calculating device to help his students solve mathematical problems. He and
an assistant, Clifford Berry, succeeded in building the first digital computer that worked electronically; they called it the **ABC**, for
Atanasoff-Berry computer (Figure H-5).

After Mauchly met with Atanasoff and Berry in 1941, he used the
ABC as the basis for the next step in computer development. From this
association ultimately came a lawsuit, based on attempts to get patents
for a commercial version of the machine Mauchly built. The suit was
finally decided in 1974, when a federal court determined that Atanasoff
had been the true originator of the ideas required to make an electronic digital computer actually work. (Some computer historians dis-
pute this court decision.) Mauchly and Eckert were able to use the
principles of the ABC to create the **ENIAC**, for **Electronic Numerical Integrator and Calculator**. The main significance of the ENIAC
is that, as the first general-purpose computer, it was the forerunner of
the UNIVAC I, the first computer sold on a commercial basis.

THE COMPUTER AGE BEGINS

The remarkable thing about the computer age is that so much has
happened in so short a time. We have leapfrogged through four generations of technology in about 40 years—a span of time whose events

Figure H-6   Vacuum tubes.
Vacuum tubes were used in the first generation of computers. Vacuum tube systems could multiply two ten-digit numbers together in one-fortieth of a second.

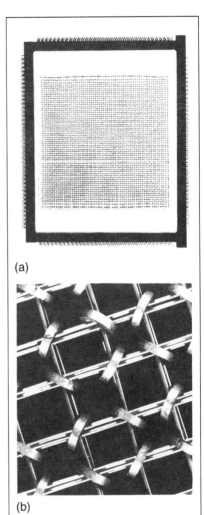

(a)

(b)

▲
Figure H-7   Magnetic cores.
(a) A 6- by 11-inch magnetic core memory. (b) Close-up of a magnetic core memory. A few hundredths of an inch in diameter, each magnetic core was mounted on a wire. When electricity passed through the wire on which a core was strung, the core could be magnetized as either "off" or "on." These states represented a 0 (off) or a 1 (on). Combinations of 0s and 1s could be used to represent data. Magnetic cores were originally developed by IBM, which adapted pill-making machinery to produce them by the millions.

are within the memories of many people today. The first three computer "generations" are pinned to three technological developments: the vacuum tube, the transistor, and the integrated circuit. Each has drastically changed the nature of computers. We define the timing of each generation according to the beginning of commercial delivery of the hardware technology. Defining subsequent generations has become more complicated because the entire industry has become more complicated.

The First Generation, 1951–1958: The Vacuum Tube

The beginning of the commercial computer age may be dated June 14, 1951. This was the date the first **UNIVAC**—*Universal Automatic Computer*—was delivered to a client, the U.S. Bureau of the Census, for use in tabulating the previous year's census. The date also marked the first time that a computer had been built for business applications rather than for military, scientific, or engineering use. The UNIVAC was really the ENIAC in disguise and was, in fact, built by Mauchly and Eckert, who in 1947 had formed their own corporation.

In the first generation, **vacuum tubes**—electronic tubes about the size of light bulbs—were used as the internal computer components (Figure H-6). However, because thousands of such tubes were required, they generated a great deal of heat, causing many problems in temperature regulation and climate control. In addition, although all the tubes had to be working simultaneously, they were subject to frequent burnout—and the people operating the computer often did not know whether the problem was in the programming or in the machine.

Another drawback was that the language used in programming was machine language, which uses numbers. (Present-day higher-level languages are more like English.) Using numbers alone made programming the computer difficult and time-consuming. The UNIVAC used **magnetic cores** to provide memory. These consisted of small, doughnut-shaped rings about the size of pinheads, which were strung like beads on intersecting thin wires (Figure H-7). To supplement primary storage, first-generation computers stored data on punched cards. In 1957 magnetic tape was introduced as a faster, more compact method of storing data.

The Second Generation, 1959–1964: The Transistor

Three Bell Lab scientists—J. Bardeen, H. W. Brattain, and W. Shockley—developed the **transistor,** a small device that transfers electric signals across a resistor. (The name *transistor* began as a trademark concocted from *tran*sfer plus re*sistor*.) The scientists later received the Nobel prize for their invention. The transistor revolutionized electronics in general and computers in particular. Transistors were much smaller than vacuum tubes, and they had numerous other advantages: They needed no warm-up time, consumed less energy, and were faster and more reliable.

During this generation, another important development was the move from machine language to **assembly languages**—also called **symbolic languages**. Assembly languages use abbreviations for instructions (for example, L for LOAD) rather than numbers. This made programming less cumbersome.

After the development of symbolic languages came **high-level languages**, such as **FORTRAN** (1954) and **COBOL** (1959). Both languages, still widely used today (in updated forms), are more English-like than assembly languages. High-level languages allowed programmers to give more attention to solving problems. Also, in 1962 the first removable disk pack was marketed. Disk storage supplemented magnetic tape systems and enabled users to have fast access to desired data.

All these new developments made the second generation of computers less costly to operate—and thus began a surge of growth in computer systems. Throughout this period computers were being used principally by business, university, and government organizations. They had not filtered down to the general public. The real part of the revolution was about to begin.

The Third Generation, 1965–1970: The Integrated Circuit

One of the most abundant elements in the earth's crust is silicon, a nonmetallic substance found in common beach sand as well as in practically all rocks and clay. The importance of this element to Santa Clara County, which is about 30 miles south of San Francisco, is responsible for the county's nickname: Silicon Valley. In 1965 Silicon Valley became the principal site for the manufacture of the so-called silicon chip: the integrated circuit.

An **integrated circuit** (abbreviated **IC**) is a complete electronic circuit on a small chip of silicon. The chip may be less than 1/8 inch square and contain thousands or millions of electronic components. Beginning in 1965 integrated circuits began to replace transistors in computers. The resulting machines were now called third-generation computers. An integrated circuit was able to replace an entire circuit board of transistors with one chip of silicon much smaller than one transistor.

Integrated circuits are made of silicon because it is a **semiconductor**. That is, it is a crystalline substance that will conduct electric current when it has been "doped" with chemical impurities implanted in its lattice-like structure. A cylinder of silicon is sliced into wafers, each about 6 inches in diameter, and the wafer is etched repeatedly with a pattern of electrical circuitry. Several layers may be etched on a single wafer. The wafer is then divided into several hundred small chips, each with a complete circuit so tiny it is half the size of a human fingernail—yet under a microscope it looks as complex as a railroad yard.

The chips were hailed as a generational breakthrough because they had desirable characteristics: reliability, compactness, and low cost. Mass-production techniques have made possible the manufacture of inexpensive integrated circuits.

The beginning of the third generation was trumpeted by the IBM 360 series (named for 360 degrees—a full circle of service), first announced April 7, 1964. The System/360 family of computers, designed for both business and scientific use, came in several models and sizes. The equipment housing was blue, leading to IBM's nickname, Big Blue.

The 360 series was launched with an all-out, massive marketing effort to make computers a business tool—to get them into medium-size and smaller business and government operations where they had not been used before. The result went beyond IBM's wildest dreams. The reported $5 billion the company invested in the development of the System/360 quickly repaid itself, and the system rendered many existing computer systems obsolete. Big Blue was on its way.

Software became more sophisticated during this third generation, permitting several programs to run in the same time frame, sharing computer resources. This approach improved the efficiency of computer systems. Software systems were developed to support interactive processing, which put the user in direct contact with the computer through a terminal. This kind of access caused the customer service industry to flourish, especially in areas such as reservations and credit checks.

Large third-generation computers began to be supplemented by minicomputers, which are functionally equivalent to a full-size system but are somewhat slower, smaller, and less expensive. These computers have become a huge success with medium-size and smaller businesses.

The Fourth Generation, 1971—Present: The Microprocessor

Through the 1970s computers gained dramatically in speed, reliability, and storage capacity, but entry into the fourth generation was evolutionary rather than revolutionary. The fourth generation was, in fact, an extension of third-generation technology. That is, in the early part of the third generation, specialized chips were developed for computer memory and logic. Thus, all the ingredients were in place for the next technological development, the general-purpose processor-on-a-chip, otherwise known as the **microprocessor**, which became commercially available in 1971.

Nowhere is the pervasiveness of computer power more apparent than in the explosive use of the microprocessor. In addition to the common applications of digital watches, pocket calculators, and personal computers, microprocessors can be anticipated in virtually every machine in the home or business—microwave ovens, cars, copy machines, television sets, and so on. Computers today are 100 times smaller than those of the first generation, and a single chip is far more powerful than ENIAC.

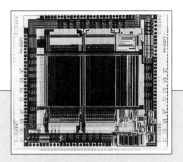

THE GREATEST INVENTION EVER

There was a time when an engineer who was also an inventor could look forward to fame as well as fortune. Thomas Edison, for example, was one of the best-known people in the world before he was 35. Today's famous people, however, tend to come from the entertainment industry. So it is that we have lost the names of Jack Kilby and Robert Noyce, who invented the device that operates your watch, oven, calculator, and computer: the integrated circuit. Some have called it the greatest invention ever. Let us make Kilby and Noyce just a little bit famous.

Kilby and Noyce come from America's heartland, Kansas and Iowa, respectively. Both were interested in electronics. But there the similarities end. Jack Kilby flunked the entrance exam at MIT and received only a single job offer when he graduated with an engineering degree from the University of Illinois. Robert Noyce, on the other hand, did get into MIT and stayed around to get a Ph.D.

Kilby and Noyce worked independently, each coming out with the integrated circuit on a chip in 1959—Kilby at Texas Instruments, Inc. and Noyce at Fairchild Semiconductor. Kilby went on to develop the first hand-held calculator and Noyce founded Intel Corporation to pursue the daring idea of putting the computer's memory on chips.

We can point with pride to Kilby and Noyce, the engineers who thought of the ingenious integrated circuit, the foundation of personal computers and many machines that make our lives easier.

PERSONAL COMPUTERS IN ACTION

The Software Entrepreneurs

Ever thought you'd like to run your own show? Make your own product? Be in business for yourself? Entrepreneurs are a special breed. They are achievement-oriented; like to take responsibility for decisions; and dislike repetitive, routine work. They also have high levels of energy and a great deal of imagination. But perhaps the key is that they are willing to take risks.

Entrepreneurs often have still another quality—a more elusive quality—that is something close to charisma. This charisma is based on enthusiasm, and it allows them to lead people, form an organization, and give it momentum. Study these real-life entrepreneurs, noting their paths to glory and—sometimes—their falls.

Steve Jobs

Of the two Steves who formed Apple Computer, Steve Jobs was the true entrepreneur. Although they both were interested in electronics, Steve Wozniak was the technical genius, and he would have been happy to have been left alone to tinker. But Steve Jobs would not let him alone for a minute—he was

always pushing and crusading. In fact, Wozniak had hooked up with an evangelist, and they made quite a pair.

When Apple was getting off the ground, Jobs wanted Wozniak to quit his job so he could work full-time on the new venture. Wozniak refused. His partner begged and cried. Wozniak gave in. While Wozniak built Apple computers, Jobs was out hustling, finding the best marketing man, the best venture capitalist, and the best company president. This entrepreneurial spirit paid off in a spectacular way as Apple rose to the top of the list of microcomputer companies.

Bill Gates

When Bill Gates was a teenager, he swore off computers for a year and, in his words, "tried to act normal." His parents, who wanted him to be a lawyer, must have been relieved when Bill gave up the computer foolishness and went off to Harvard in 1974. But Bill started spending weekends with his friend Paul Allen, dreaming about personal computers, which did not exist yet. When the MITS Altair, the first personal computer for sale, splashed on the market in January 1975, both Bill and Paul moved to Albuquerque to be near the action at MITS. But they showed a desire even then to chart their own course. Although

The Fifth Generation: Japan's Challenge

The term *fifth generation* was coined by Japan to describe its goal of creating powerful, intelligent computers by the mid-1990s. Since then, however, it has become an umbrella term encompassing many research fields in the computer industry. Key areas of ongoing research are artificial intelligence, expert systems, and natural language—topics discussed in detail in Chapter 11.

Japan's original announcement of the fifth generation captivated the computer industry. Some view the fifth generation as a race between Japan and the United States, with nothing less than world computer supremacy as the prize. However, the Japanese budget has been they wrote software for MITS, they kept the rights to their work and formed their own company. Their company was called Microsoft.

When MITS failed, Gates and Allen moved their software company to their native Bellevue, Washington. They employed 32 people in 1980 when IBM came to call. Gates recognized the big league when he saw it and put on a suit for the occasion. Gates was offered a plum: the chance to develop the operating system (a crucial set of software) for IBM's soon-to-be personal computer. Although he knew he was betting the whole company, Gates never hesitated to take the risk. He and his crew worked feverishly for many months to produce MS-DOS —Microsoft Disk Operating System. It was this product that sent Microsoft on its meteoric rise.

Mitch Kapor

Kapor did not start out on a direct path to computer fame and riches. In fact, he wandered extensively, from being a disk jockey to piano teacher to counselor. He had done some programming, too, but did not

like it much. But, around 1978, he found he did like fooling around with personal computers. In fact, he had found his niche.

In 1983 Kapor introduced a software package called Lotus 1-2-3, and there had never been anything like it before. Lotus added the term *integrated package* to the vocabulary; the phrase described the software's identity as a combination spreadsheet, graphics, and database program. Kapor's product catapulted his company to the top of the list of independent software makers in just two years.

Bill Millard

Bill Millard believed that nothing was impossible. It was his habit, for example, to give employees of his IMSAI company impossible assign-

ments and then exhort them to "make a miracle." IMSAI made one of the early personal computers. IMSAI employees were inspired and they did work hard, but nobody worked harder than Bill. Sales were phenomenal. The computer, unfortunately, was not. Quality control caught up with Bill and the company eventually failed.

But not Bill. He just struck out in a new direction. He realized that people would buy personal computers in stores, and he founded the Computerland chain in 1976. His net worth now is in the *billions*, and he describes himself as "the biggest winner of all in the microcomputer industry."

Champions of Change

Entrepreneurs thrive on change. Jobs, Wozniak, and Kapor all left their original companies to start new companies. Stay tuned for future breakthroughs from these and other personal computer entrepreneurs.

cut significantly in recent years, and enthusiasm over the project has waned somewhat.

THE SPECIAL STORY OF PERSONAL COMPUTERS

Personal computers are the machines you can "get closest to," whether you are an amateur or a professional. There is nothing quite like having your very own personal computer. Its history is very personal too, full of stories of success and failure and of individuals with whom we can readily identify.

▲
Figure H-8 Apple manual.
Shown here is a collector's item: the very first manual for operation of an Apple computer. Unfortunately, the early manuals were a hodgepodge of circuit diagrams, software listings, and handwritten notes. They were hard to read and understand and almost guaranteed to frighten away all but the most hardy souls.

▲
Figure H-9 The IBM PC.
Launched in 1981, the IBM PC took just 18 months to rise to the top of the best-seller list.

I Built It in My Garage

As we noted in the beginning of the chapter, the very first personal computer was the MITS Altair, produced in 1975. But it was a gee-whiz machine, loaded with switches and dials—and no keyboard or screen. It took two teenagers, Steve Jobs and Steve Wozniak, to capture the imagination of the public with the first Apple computer. They built it in that time-honored place of inventors, a garage, using the $1,300 proceeds from the sale of an old Volkswagen. Designed for home use, the Apple was the first to offer an easy-to-use keyboard and screen. Founded in 1977, Apple Computer was immediately and wildly successful. When its stock was offered to the public in December 1980, it started a stampede among investors eager to buy in. Apple has introduced an increasingly powerful line of computers, including the Macintosh, which continues to sell well. (Figure H-8 shows early documentation for the first commercial Apple computer.)

The other major player in those early years was Tandy Incorporated, whose worldwide chain of Radio Shack stores provided a handy sales outlet for the TRS-80 personal computer. Other manufacturers who enjoyed more than moderate success in the late 1970s were Atari and Commodore. Their number was to grow.

The IBM PC Phenomenon

IBM announced its first personal computer in the summer of 1981. IBM captured the top market share in just 18 months, and even more important, its machine became the industry standard (Figure H-9). This was indeed a phenomenal success.

IBM did a lot of things right, such as including the possibility of adding memory. IBM also provided internal expansion slots, so that peripheral equipment manufacturers could build accessories for the IBM PC. In addition, IBM provided hardware schematics and software listings to companies who wanted to build products in conjunction with the new PC. Many of the new products accelerated demand for the IBM machine.

Other personal computer manufacturers have hurried to emulate IBM, producing "PC clones," copycat computers that can run software designed for the IBM PC. Meanwhile, IBM has offered both upscale and downscale versions of its personal computer: PC XT, PC Portable, PC AT, and various models of the PS/2 (Personal System/2). A notable failure, however, was the ill-fated PCjr; this dud, however, caused hardly a ripple in IBM's financial picture, which continued rosy.

The story of personal computer history is ongoing, with daily fluctuations reflected in the trade press. The effects of personal computers are far-reaching, and they remain a key topic in the computer industry.

▲ ▲ ▲

History is still being made in the computer industry, of course, and it is being made incredibly rapidly. A book cannot possibly pretend to describe all the very latest developments. Nevertheless, as we indicated earlier, the four areas of input, processing, output, and storage describe the basic components of a computer system—whatever its date.

Appendix Review

Summary and key terms

- Charles Babbage, a nineteenth-century mathematician, is called "the father of the computer" because of his invention of two computation machines. His **difference engine,** which could solve equations, led to another calculating machine, the **analytical engine,** which embodied the key parts of a computer system—an input device, a processor, a control unit, a storage place, and an output device. Countess Ada Lovelace helped develop instructions for carrying out computations on Babbage's device.

- The first computer to use electrical power instead of mechanical power was Herman Hollerith's tabulating machine, which was used in the 1890 census in the United States. Hollerith founded a company that became the forerunner of International Business Machines Corporation (IBM).

- Thomas J. Watson, Sr., built IBM into a dominant force in the business machines market. He also gave Harvard professor Howard Aiken research funds with which to build an electromechanical computer, the **Mark I,** unveiled in 1944.

- John V. Atanasoff, with assistant Clifford Berry, devised the first digital computer to work by electronic means, the **Atanasoff–Berry Computer (ABC).**

- The **ENIAC (Electronic Numerical Integrator and Calculator),** developed by John Mauchly and J. Presper Eckert at the University of Pennsylvania in 1946, was the world's first general-purpose electronic computer.

- The first computer generation began June 14, 1951, with the delivery of the **UNIVAC (UNIVersal Automatic Computer)** to the U.S. Bureau of the Census. First-generation computers required thousands of **vacuum tubes,** electronic tubes about the size of light bulbs. First-generation computers had slow input/output, were programmed only in machine language, and were unreliable. The main form of memory was **magnetic core.** Magnetic tape was introduced in 1957 to store data compactly.

- Second-generation computers used **transistors,** developed at Bell Laboratories. Compared to vacuum tubes, transistors were small, needed no warm-up, consumed less energy, and were faster and more reliable. During the second generation, **assembly languages,** or **symbolic languages,** were developed. They used abbreviations for instructions, rather than numbers. Later, **higher-level languages,** such as **FORTRAN** and **COBOL,** were also developed. In 1962 the first removable disk pack was marketed.

- The third generation emerged with the introduction of the **integrated circuit (IC)**—a complete electronic circuit on a small chip of silicon. Silicon is a **semiconductor,** a substance that will conduct electric current when it has been "doped" with chemical impurities. The integrated circuits of 1965 progressed in 1970 to **large-scale integration (LSI),** with thousands of ICs on a single chip.

- With the third generation IBM announced the System/360 family of computers. During this period more sophisticated software was introduced that allowed several programs to run in the same time frame and supported interactive processing, in which the user has direct contact with the computer through a terminal.

- The fourth-generation **microprocessor**—a general-purpose processor-on-a-chip—grew out of the specialized memory and logic chips of the third generation. In 1975 **very large scale integration (VLSI)** was achieved. Microprocessors led to the development of microcomputers, expanding computer markets to smaller businesses and to personal use.

- In 1980 the Japanese announced a ten-year project to develop a fifth generation, radically new forms of computer systems involving artificial intelligence, expert systems, and natural language.

- The first microcomputer, the MITS Altair, was produced in 1975. However, the first successful computer to include an easy-to-use keyboard and screen was offered by Apple computer, founded by Steve Jobs and Steve Wozniak in 1977. IBM entered the microcomputer market in 1981 and captured the top market share in just 18 months.

- From 1950 to 1964 software was used mainly by large organizations to enable computers to perform clerical tasks. The period from 1965 to 1980 saw the development of interactive software, which enabled computers to respond to input data more efficiently than people could. Generic software, programs that could be used by different user organizations, led to the development of the software industry.

SELF-TEST

True/False

T F 1. The analytical engine embodied the five key concepts of a computer system.

T F 2. The ENIAC, made operational in 1946, was the world's first electronic digital computer.

T F 3. The first generation, characterized by the vacuum tube, encompassed all computer development prior to 1960.

T F 4. The transistor of the second generation was faster and more reliable than the vacuum tube but used more energy.

T F 5. Both assembly languages and higher-level languages were developed during the second generation.

T F 6. Integrated circuits, ICs, marked the advent of the third generation.

Matching

_____ 1. Howard Aiken   a. assembly language

_____ 2. Thomas Watson   b. Mark I

_____ 3. symbolic language   c. transistor

_____ 4. Bell Laboratories   d. vacuum tubes

_____ 5. Herman Hollerith   e. IBM

_____ 6. UNIVAC   f. tabulating machine

Fill-In

1. The technology of the second generation: _____

2. Who built IBM into a dominant force in the business machine market?

   _____

3. What machine was used in the U.S. Census of 1890?

   _____

4. The first commercial computer, delivered in 1951:

   _____

5. What was the principal form of technology used for primary storage for the first two decades of the computer age? _____

6. What was the first microcomputer called? _____

Answers

True/False: 1. T, 3. F, 5. T

Matching: 1. b, 3. a, 5. f

Fill-in: 1. transistor, 3. Hollerith's tabulating machine, 5. magnetic core

APPENDIX

NUMBER SYSTEMS

Data can be represented in the computer in one of two basic ways: as **numeric data** or as **alphanumeric data.** The internal representation of alphanumeric data—letters, digits, special characters—was discussed in Chapter 2. Recall that alphanumeric data may be represented using various codes; EDCDIC and ASCII are two common codes. Alphanumeric data, even if all digits, cannot be used for arithmetic operations. Data used for arithmetic calculations must be stored numerically.

Data stored numerically can be represented as the binary equivalent of the decimal value with which we are familiar. That is, values such as 1050, 43218, and 3 that we input to the computer will be converted to the binary number system. In this appendix we shall study the binary number system (base 2) and two related systems, octal (base 8) and hexadecimal (base 16).

NUMBER BASES
• • • • • • • • • • • • • • • • • •

A number base is a specific collection of symbols on which a number system can be built. The number base familiar to us is base 10, upon which the **decimal** number system is built. There are ten symbols—0 through 9—used in the decimal system.

Since society uses base 10, that is the number base most of us understand and can use easily. It would theoretically be possible, however, for all of us to learn to use a different number system. This number system could contain a different number of symbols and perhaps even symbols that are unfamiliar.

Base 2: The Binary Number System

Base 2 has exactly two symbols: 0 and 1. All numbers in the **binary** system must be formed using these two symbols. As you can see in column 2 of Table 1, this means that numbers in the binary system become long quickly; the number 1000 in base 2 is equivalent to 8 in base 10. (When different number bases are being discussed, it is common practice to use the number base as a subscript. In this case we could say $1000_2 = 8_{10}$.) If you were to continue counting in base 2, you would soon see that the binary numbers were very long and unwieldy. The number 5000_{10} is equal to 10011100010000_2.

The size and sameness—all those zeros and ones—of binary numbers make them subject to frequent error when they are being manipulated by humans. To improve both convenience and accuracy, it is common to express the values represented by binary numbers in the more concise octal and hexadecimal number bases.

Base 8: The Octal Number System

The **octal** number system uses exactly eight symbols: 0, 1, 2, 3, 4, 5, 6, and 7. Base 8 is a convenient shorthand for base 2 numbers because 8 is a power of 2: $2^3 = 8$. As you will see when we discuss conversions, one octal digit is the equivalent of exactly three binary digits. The use of octal (or hexadecimal) as a shorthand for binary is common in printed output of main storage and, in some cases, in programming.

Look at the column of octal numbers in Table 1. Notice that, since 7 is the last symbol in base 8, the following number is 10. In fact, we can count right through the next seven numbers in the usual manner, as long as we end with 17. Note, however, that 17_8 is pronounced *one-seven*, not *seventeen*. The octal number 17 is followed by 20 through 27, and so on. The last double-digit number is 77, which is followed by 100. Although it takes a little practice, you can see that it would be easy to learn to count in base 8. However, hexadecimal, or base 16, is not quite as easy.

Table 1   Number bases 10, 2, 8, 16: First values

Base 10 (decimal)	Base 2 (binary)	Base 8 (octal)	Base 16 (hexadecimal)
0	0000	0	0
1	0001	1	1
2	0010	2	2
3	0011	3	3
4	0100	4	4
5	0101	5	5
6	0110	6	6
7	0111	7	7
8	1000	10	8
9	1001	11	9
10	1010	12	A
11	1011	13	B
12	1100	14	C
13	1101	15	D
14	1110	16	E
15	1111	17	F
16	10000	20	10

Base 16: The Hexadecimal Number System

The **hexadecimal** number system uses exactly 16 symbols. As we have just seen, base 10 uses the familiar digits 0 through 9, and bases 2 and 8 use a subset of those symbols. Base 16, however, needs those ten symbols (0 through 9) and six more. The six additional symbols used in the hexadecimal number system are the letters A through F. So the base 16 symbols are: 0, 1, 2, 3, 4, 5, 6, 7, 8, 9, A, B, C, D, E, and F. It takes some adjusting to think of A or D as a digit instead of a letter. It also takes a little time to become accustomed to numbers such as 6A2F or even ACE. Both of these examples are legitimate numbers in hexadecimal.

As you become familiar with hexadecimal, consider the matter of counting. Counting sounds simple enough, but it can be confusing in an unfamiliar number base with new symbols. The process is the same as counting in base 10, but most of us learned to count when we were too young to think about the process itself. Quickly—what number follows 24CD? The answer is 24CE. We increased the right-most digit by one—D to E—just as you would have in the more obvious case of 6142 to 6143. What is the number just before 1000_{16}? The answer is FFF_{16}; the last symbol (F) is a triple-digit number. Compare this with 999_{10}, which precedes 1000_{10}; 9 is the last symbol in base 10. As a familiarization exercise, try counting from 1 to 100 in base 16. Remember to use A through F as the second symbol in the teens, twenties, and so forth (. . . 27, 28, 29, 2A, 2B, and so on).

CONVERSIONS BETWEEN NUMBER BASES

It is sometimes convenient to use a number in a base different from the base currently being used—that is, to change the number from one base to another. Many programmers can nimbly convert a number from one base to another, among bases 10, 2, 8, and 16. We shall consider these conversion techniques now. Table 2 summarizes the methods.

To Base 10 from Bases 2, 8, and 16

We present these conversions together because the technique is the same for all three.

Let us begin with the concept of positional notation. **Positional notation** means that the value of a digit in a number depends not only on its own intrinsic value but also on its location in the number. Given the number 2363, we know that the appearance of the digit 3 represents two different values, 300 and 3. Table 3 shows the names of the relative positions.

Using these positional values, the number 2363 is understood to mean:

```
2000
 300
  60
   3
----
2363
```

Table 2 Summary conversion chart

From Base	To Base			
	2	**8**	**16**	**10**
2	——	Group binary digits by 3, convert	Group binary digits by 4, convert	Expand number and convert base 2 digits to base 10
8	Convert each octal digit to 3 binary digits	——	Convert to base 2, then to base 16	Expand number and convert base 8 digits to base 10
16	Convert each hexadecimal digit to 4 binary digits	Convert to base 2, then to base 8	——	Expand number and convert base 16 digits to base 10
10	Divide number repeatedly by 2; use remainders as answer	Divide number repeatedly by 8; use remainders as answer	Divide number repeatedly by 16; use remainders as answer	——

Table 3 Digit positions

Digit	2	3	6	3
Position	**Thousand**	**Hundred**	**Ten**	**Unit**

This number can also be expressed as:

$$(2 \times 1000) + (3 \times 100) + (6 \times 10) + 3$$

We can express this expanded version of the number another way, using powers of 10 (note that $10^0 = 1$).

$$2363 = (2 \times 10^3) + (3 \times 10^2) + (6 \times 10^1) + (3 \times 10^0)$$

Once you understand the expanded notation, the rest is easy: You expand the number as we just did in base 10, but use the appropriate base of the number. For example, follow the steps to convert 61732_8 to base 10:

1. Expand the number, using 8 as the base:

$$61732 = (6 \times 8^4) + (1 \times 8^3) + (7 \times 8^2) + (3 \times 8^1) + (2 \times 8^0)$$

2. Complete the arithmetic:

$$61732 = (6 \times 4096) + (1 \times 512) + (7 \times 64) + (3 \times 8) + 2$$
$$= 24576 + 512 + 448 + 24 + 2$$

3. Answer: $61732_8 = 25562_{10}$

The same expand-and-convert technique can be used to convert from base 2 or base 16 to base 10. As you consider the following two examples, use Table 1 to make the conversions. (For example, A in base 16 converts to 10 in base 10.)

Convert $C14A_{16}$ to base 10:

$$C14A_{16} = (12 \times 16^3) + (1 \times 16^2) + (4 \times 16^1) + 10$$
$$= (12 \times 4096) + (1 \times 256) + (4 \times 16) + 10$$
$$= 49482$$

So $C14A_{16} = 49482_{10}$.

Convert 100111_2 to base 10:

$$100111_2 = (1 \times 2^5) + (1 \times 2^2) + (1 \times 2) + 1$$
$$= 39$$

So $100111_2 = 39_{10}$.

From Base 10 to Bases 2, 8, and 16

These conversions use a simpler process but more complicated arithmetic. The process, often called the *remainder method*, is basically a series of repeated divisions by the number of the base to which you are converting. You begin by using the number to be converted as the dividend; succeeding dividends are the quotients of the previous division. The converted number is the combined remainders accumulated from the divisions. There are two points to remember:

1. Keep dividing until you reach a zero quotient.
2. Use the remainders in reverse order.

Consider converting 6954_{10} to base 8:

```
8|6954
 8|869      2
  8|108     5
   8|13     4
    8|1     5
     0      1
```

Using the remainders backwards, $6954_{10} = 15452_8$.

Now use the same technique to convert 4823_{10} to base 16:

```
16|4823
 16|301     7
  16|18     13 (=D)
   16|1     2
     0      1
```

The remainder 13 is equivalent to D in base 16. So $4823_{10} = 12D7_{16}$.

Convert 49_{10} to base 2:

```
2|49
2|24      1
2|12      0
 2|6      0
 2|3      0
 2|1      1
  0       1
```

Again using the remainders in reverse order, $49_{10} = 110001_2$.

To Base 2 from Bases 8 and 16

To convert a number to base 2 from base 8 or base 16, convert each digit separately to three or four binary digits, respectively. Use Table 1 to make the conversion. Leading zeros may be needed in each grouping of digits to fill out each to three or four digits.

Convert 4732_8 to base 2:

4	7	3	2
100	111	011	010

So $4732_8 = 100111011010_2$.

Now convert $A046B_{16}$ to base 2:

A	0	4	6	B
1010	0000	0100	0110	1011

Thus $A046B_{16} = 10100000010001101011_2$.

From Base 2 to Bases 8 and 16

To convert a number from base 2 to base 8 or base 16, group the binary digits from the right in groups of three or four, respectively. Again use Table 1 to help you make the conversion to the new base.

Convert 111101001011_2 to base 8 and base 16:

In the base 8 conversion, group the digits three at a time, starting on the right:

111	101	001	011
7	5	1	3

So $111101001011_2 = 7513_8$.

For the conversion to base 16, group the digits four at a time, starting on the right:

1111	0100	1011
F	4	B

$111101001011_2 = F4B_{16}$.

Sometimes the number of digits in a binary number is not exactly divisible by 3 or 4. You may, for example, start grouping the digits three at a time and finish with one or two "extra" digits on the left side of the number. In this case, just add as many zeros as you need to the front of the binary number.

Consider converting 1010_2 to base 8. By adding two zeros to the front of the number to make it 001010_2, we now have six digits, which can be conveniently grouped three at a time:

001	010
1	2

So $1010_2 = 12_8$.

GLOSSARY

• • • • • • • • • • •

Access arm   A mechanical device that can access all the tracks of one cylinder in a disk storage unit.

Active cell   The cell currently available for use on a spreadsheet. Also called the current cell.

Address   A number used to designate a location in memory.

AI   Artificial intelligence.

ALU   Arithmetic/logic unit.

Analog transmission   The transmission of computer data as a continuous electric signal in the form of a wave.

Analytical engine   A mechanical device of cogs and wheels, designed by Charles Babbage, that embodied the key characteristics of modern computers.

Analytical graphics   Traditional line graphs, bar charts, and pie charts used to illustrate and analyze data.

ANSI   American National Standards Institute.

Applications software   Programs designed to perform specific tasks and functions.

Arithmetic/logic unit (ALU)   The electronic circuitry in a computer; it executes all arithmetic and logical operations.

Arithmetic operations   Mathematical calculations the ALU performs on data.

Artificial intelligence (AI)   The field of study that explores computer involvement in tasks requiring intelligence, imagination, and intuition.

ASCII (American Standard Code for Information Interchange)   A coding scheme using 7-bit characters to represent data characters.

Assembler program   A translator program used to convert assembly-language programs to machine language.

Assembly language   A second-generation language that uses abbreviations for instructions. Also called symbolic language.

Atanasoff-Berry computer (ABC)   The first electronic digital computer, designed by John V. Atanasoff and Clifford Berry, in the late 1930s.

ATM   Automated teller machine.

Audio-response unit   A device that converts data in main storage to sounds understandable as speech to humans. Also called a voice synthesizer or a voice-output device.

Automated teller machine (ATM)   An input/output device connected to a computer used by bank customers for financial transactions.

Automatic reformatting   In word processing, automatic adjustment of text to accommodate changes.

Auxiliary storage   Storage, often disk, for data and programs; separate from the CPU and memory. Also called secondary storage.

Axis   A reference line of a graph. The horizontal axis is the x-axis. The vertical axis is the y-axis.

Bar code reader   A stationary photoelectric scanner that reads bar codes by means of reflected light.

Bar codes   Standardized patterns (Universal Product Code) of vertical marks that identify products.

Bar graph   A graph made up of filled-in columns or rows that represent the change of data over time.

BASIC (Beginner's All-purpose Symbolic Instruction Code)   A high-level programming language that is easy to learn and use.

Batch processing   A data processing technique in which transactions are collected into groups, or batches, for processing.

BBS   Bulletin board system.

Binary system   A system in which data is represented by combinations of 0s and 1s, which correspond to the two states off and on.

Biometrics   The science of measuring individual body characteristics; used in some security systems.

Bit   A binary digit.

Block copy command   The command used to copy a block of text into a new location.

Block delete command   The command used to erase a block of text.

Block move command   The command used to remove a block of text from one location in a document and place it elsewhere.

Boldface   Printed characters in darker type than the surrounding characters.

Booting   Loading the operating system into memory.

Branch   In a flowchart, the connection leading from the decision box to one of two possible responses. Also called a path.

Bulletin board system (BBS)   Telephone-linked personal computers that provide public-access message systems.

Business graphics   Graphics that represent data in a visual, easy-to-understand format.

Business-quality graphics program   A program that allows a user to create professional-looking business graphics. Also called a presentation graphics program.

Bus network   A type of local area network that assigns a portion of network management to each computer but preserves the system if one node fails.

Byte   A string of bits (usually 8) used to represent one data character—a letter, digit, or special character.

C   A sophisticated programming language invented by Bell Labs in 1974.

CAD/CAM   Computer-aided design/computer-aided manufacturing.

Cathode ray tube (CRT)   The most common type of computer screen.

CD-ROM   Compact disk read-only memory.

Cell   The intersection of a row and a column in a spreadsheet. Entries in a spreadsheet are stored in individual cells.

Cell address   In a spreadsheet, the column and row coordinates of a cell.

Cell contents   The label, value, formula, or function contained in a spreadsheet cell.

Centering   The word processing feature that places a line of text midway between the left and right margins.

Centralized data processing   Keeping hardware, software, storage, and computer access in one location.

Central processing unit (CPU)   The electronic circuitry that executes stored program instructions. It consists of two parts: the control unit and the arithmetic/logic unit.

Change agent   A systems analyst who, acting as a catalyst, overcomes the reluctance to change within an organization.

Character   A letter, number, or special character (such as $).

Chief information officer (CIO)   The manager of an MIS department.

Client   An individual or organization contracting for systems analysis.

Clip art   Illustrations stored on disk that are used to enhance a graph or document.

Clustered-bar graph   A bar graph comparing several different but related sets of data.

Coaxial cable   Bundles of insulated wires within a shielded enclosure that can be laid underground or undersea.

COBOL (COmmon Business-Oriented Language)   An English-like programming language used primarily for business applications.

Command   A name that invokes the correct program or program segment.

Command menu   The list of commands in an applications software program such as Lotus 1-2-3.

Command tree   A hierarchical diagram that shows all the choices from a main command menu and the associated submenus.

Compact disk read-only memory (CD-ROM)   Optical data storage technology using disk formats identical to audio compact disks.

Compare operation   An operation in which the computer compares two data items and performs alternative operations based on the comparison.

Compiler   A translator that converts the symbolic statements of a high-level language into computer-executable machine language.

CompuServe   A major information utility that offers program packages, text editors, encyclopedia reference, games, and a software exchange as well as services such as banking, travel reservations, and legal advice.

Computer   A machine that accepts data (input) and processes it into useful information (output).

Computer-aided design/computer-aided manufacturing (CAD/CAM)   The use of computers to create two- and three-dimensional pictures of manufactured products.

Computer conferencing   A method of sending, receiving, and storing typed messages within a network of users.

Computer Fraud and Abuse Act   A law passed by Congress in 1984 to fight computer crime.

Computer literacy   Awareness, knowledge of, and interaction with computers.

Computer operator   A person who monitors the console screen, reviews procedures, and keeps peripheral equipment running.

Computer programmer   A person who designs, writes, tests, and implements programs.

Computer system   A system that has one or more computers as components.

Computing Services   A department that manages computer resources for an organization. Also called Information Services or Management Information Systems.

Conditional replace   A word processing function that asks the user whether to replace copy each time the program finds a particular item.

Connector A symbol used in flowcharting to connect paths.

Consortium A joint venture to support a complete computer facility to be used in an emergency.

Context sensitivity The software feature that allows a user to access information about the application or command the user is currently using.

Control Center In dBASE IV, the main menu, which gives access to several menu options.

Control panel The upper portion of a spreadsheet screen; it consists of status, entry, and prompt lines.

Control unit The circuitry that directs and coordinates the entire computer system in executing stored program instructions.

Copy protection A software or hardware block that makes it difficult or impossible to create unauthorized copies of software.

CPU Central processing unit.

CRT Cathode ray tube.

Current cell The cell currently available for use on a spreadsheet. Also called the active cell.

Current drive The disk drive currently being used by the computer system. Also called the default drive.

Cursor A flashing indicator on the screen; it indicates where the next character will be inserted. Also called a pointer.

Cursor movement keys The keys on the computer keyboard that allow the user to move the cursor on the screen.

DASD Direct-access storage device.

Data The raw material to be processed by a computer.

Database A collection of interrelated files stored together with minimum redundancy.

Database management system (DBMS) A set of programs that create, manage, protect, and provide access to a database.

Data collection device A device that allows direct data entry in such places as factories and warehouses.

Data communications The process of exchanging data over communications facilities.

Data communications systems Computer systems that transmit data over communications lines, such as public telephone lines or private network cables.

Data Encryption Standard (DES) The standardized public key by which senders and receivers can scramble and unscramble their messages.

Data entry operator A person who prepares data for computer processing.

Data item Data in a relational database table.

Data point A single value represented by a bar or symbol in a graph.

Date field A field used for dates and automatically limited to eight characters, including slashes used to separate the month, day, and year.

DBMS Database management system.

DDP Distributed data processing.

Debugging The process of detecting, locating, and correcting mistakes in a program.

Decision box The standard diamond-shaped box used in flowcharting to indicate a decision.

Default drive The disk drive to which commands refer in the absence of any specified drive. Unless instructed otherwise, an applications program stores files on the memory device in the default drive. Also called the current drive.

Default settings Settings automatically used by a program unless the user specifies otherwise.

Demodulation The process of converting a signal from analog to digital.

DES Data Encryption Standard.

Desk-checking A programming phase in which the logic of the program is mentally checked to ensure that it is error-free and workable.

Desktop publishing The use of a personal computer, special software, and a laser printer to produce very high-quality documents that combine text and graphics. Also called electronic publishing.

Desktop publishing program A software package for designing and producing professional-looking documents. Also called a page composition program or a page makeup program.

Diagnostic message A message that informs the user of programming-language syntax errors.

Difference engine A machine designed by Charles Babbage to solve polynomial equations by calculating the successive differences between them.

Digital transmission A data transmission method that sends data as distinct electrical (on or off) pulses.

Digitizer A graphics input device that converts images into digital data that the computer can accept.

Direct access The immediate access to a record in secondary storage, usually on a disk. Also called random access.

Direct-access storage device (DASD) A storage device in which a record can be accessed directly.

Direct-connect modem A modem connected directly to the telephone line.

Disaster recovery plan A method of restoring data processing operations if those operations are halted by major damage or destruction.

Disk drive A device that allows data to be read from a disk and written on a disk.

Diskette A single magnetic disk on which data is recorded as magnetic spots. Available in both 5¼-inch format and 3½-inch format.

Disk pack A stack of magnetic disks assembled together.

Displayed value 1. The calculated result of a formula or function in a spreadsheet cell. 2. A number in a cell; it is displayed according to a user-specified format.

Distributed data processing (DDP) A data processing system in which processing is decentralized, with the computers and storage devices in dispersed locations.

Documentation 1. A detailed written description of the programming cycle and specific facts about the program. 2. The instruction manual for packaged software.

Dot-matrix printer A printer that constructs a character by activating a matrix of pins to produce the shape of a character on paper.

Dot prompt In dBASE, the prompt that tells the user that the program is ready for a command.

Download The transfer of data from a mainframe or large computer to a smaller computer.

EFT Electronic fund transfer.

Electronic disk A chip that lets the computer regard part of its memory as a third disk drive. Also called a RAM disk or phantom disk.

Electronic fund transfer (EFT) Paying for goods and services by using electronically transferred funds.

Electronic mail (e-mail) The process of sending messages directly from one terminal or computer to another. The messages may be sent and stored for later retrieval.

Electronic publishing The use of a personal computer, special software, and a laser printer to produce very high-quality documents that combine text and graphics. Also called desktop publishing.

Electronic spreadsheet An electronic worksheet used to organize data into rows and columns for analysis.

E-mail Electronic mail.

Encryption The process of encoding communications data.

End-user A person who buys and uses computer software or who has contact with computers.

ENIAC (Electronic Numerical Integrator And Computer) The first general-purpose electronic computer, which was built by Dr. John Mauchly and J. Presper Eckert, Jr., and was first operational in 1946.

ENTRY mode The spreadsheet mode that lets the user enter data.

Equal to (=) condition A logical operation in which the computer compares two numbers to determine equality.

Erasable optical disk An optical disk on which data can be stored, moved, changed, and erased, just as on magnetic media.

Erase head The head in a magnetic tape unit; it erases any previously recorded data on the tape.

Ethernet A popular local area network; this system accesses the network by listening for a free carrier signal.

E-time The execution portion of the machine cycle.

Expansion slots The slots inside a computer that allow a user to insert additional circuit boards.

Expert shell Software having the basic structure to find answers to questions; the questions can be added by the user.

Expert system A software package that presents the computer as an expert on some topic.

Exploded pie chart A pie chart with a "slice" that is separated from the rest of the chart.

External direct-connect modem A modem that is separate from the computer, allowing it to be used with a variety of computers.

External DOS commands Commands that access DOS programs residing on the DOS disk as program files. The programs must be read from the disk before they can be executed. These program files are not automatically loaded into the computer when it is booted. See *internal DOS commands*.

Facsimile technology (fax) The use of computer technology to send digitized graphics, charts, and text from one facsimile machine to another.

Fair Credit Reporting Act Legislation passed in 1970; it allows individuals access to and the right to challenge credit records.

Fax board A circuit board that fits inside a personal computer and allows the user, without interrupting other applications programs, to transmit computer-generated text and graphics.

Federal Privacy Act Legislation passed in 1974; it stipulates that no secret personal files can be kept by government agencies and that individuals can have access to all information about them that is stored in government files.

Fiber optics Technology that uses light instead of electricity to send data.

Field A set of related characters. In a database, also called an attribute.

Field name   In a database, the unique name describing the data in a field.

Field robot   A robot that is used on location to inspect nuclear plants, dispose of bombs, clean up chemical spills, and so forth.

Field type   A category describing a field; it's determined by the kind of data the field will accept. Common field types are character, numeric, date, and logical.

Field width   In a database, the maximum number of characters that can be contained in a field.

Fifth generation   A term coined by the Japanese; it refers to new forms of computer systems involving artificial intelligence, natural language, and expert systems.

File   1. A repository of data. 2. A collection of related records. 3. In word processing, a document created on a computer.

File command   A command selection on the main menu of Lotus 1-2-3; it allows file manipulation: saving, retrieving, and erasing.

Firmware   Read-only memory used to store programs that will not be altered.

Floppy disk   A flexible magnetic diskette on which data is recorded as magnetic spots.

Flowchart   The pictorial representation of a step-by-step solution to a problem.

Font   A complete set of characters in a particular size, typeface, weight, and style.

Font library   A variety of type fonts stored on disk.

Format   The specifications that determine the way a document or worksheet is displayed on the screen or printer.

Formula   In a spreadsheet, an instruction to calculate a value.

FORTRAN (FORmula TRANslator)   The first high-level language, introduced in 1954 by IBM; it is scientifically oriented.

4GL   Fourth-generation language.

Fourth-generation language   A nonprocedural language. Also called a 4GL or a very high-level language.

Freedom of Information Act   Legislation passed in 1970; it allows citizens access to personal data gathered by federal agencies.

Function   A built-in spreadsheet formula.

Function keys   Special keys programmed to execute commonly used commands.

GB   Gigabyte.

Gigabyte (GB)   One billion bytes.

GIGO   Garbage in, garbage out: The quality of the output is directly dependent on the quality of the input.

GoTo function key   In a spreadsheet, the key used to get to another cell. Also called the Jump-To function key.

Graphical user interface (GUI)   A software feature that uses screen icons invoked by pointing and clicking a mouse.

Graphics   Pictures or graphs.

Greater than (>) condition   A comparison operation that determines if one value is greater than another.

GUI   Graphical user interface.

Hacker   A person who gains access to computer systems illegally, usually from a personal computer.

Halftone   A reproduction of a black-and-white photograph; it is made up of tiny dots.

Hard copy   Printed paper output.

Hard disk   An inflexible disk, usually in a pack, often in a sealed module.

Hard magnetic disk   A metal platter coated with magnetic oxide and used for magnetic disk storage.

Hardware   The computer and its associated equipment.

High-level languages   English-like programming languages that are easier to use than older symbolic languages.

Host computer   The central computer in a network.

Icon   A small picture on a computer screen; it represents a computer activity.

Impact printer   A printer that forms characters by physically striking the paper.

Inference engine   In artificial intelligence systems, software that accesses, selects, and interprets a set of rules.

Information   Processed data; data that is organized, meaningful, and useful.

Information center   A company unit that offers employees computer and software training, help in getting data from other computer systems, and technical assistance.

Information Services   A department that manages computer resources for an organization. Also called Computing Services or Management Information Systems.

Information system (IS)   A set of business systems, usually with computers among its components, designed to provide information for decision making.

Information systems manager   The person who runs the Information Systems department.

Information utilities   Commercial consumer-oriented communications systems, such as The Source, CompuServe, and Prodigy.

Initializing Setting the starting values of storage locations before running a program.

Ink-jet printer A printer that sprays ink from jet nozzles onto the paper.

Input Raw data that is put in to the computer system for processing.

Input device A device that puts data in machine-readable form and sends it to the processing unit.

Insert mode In word processing, a text input mode in which text is inserted at the current cursor position without overwriting any text already in the document.

Integrated circuit A complete electronic circuit on a small chip of silicon.

Integrated package A set of software that typically includes related word processing, spreadsheet, database, and graphics programs.

Interactive Data processing in which the user communicates directly with the computer, maintaining a dialogue.

Internal DOS commands Commands that access DOS programs that are loaded into the computer when the system is booted. See *external DOS commands*.

Internal font A font built into the read-only memory of a printer.

Internal modem A modem on a circuit board; it can be installed in a computer by the user.

Internal storage The electronic circuitry that temporarily holds data and program instructions needed by the CPU. Also called memory, main memory, primary memory, primary storage, and main storage.

IS Information system.

Iteration The repetition of program instructions under certain conditions. Also called a loop.

I-time The instruction portion of the machine cycle.

Joy stick A graphics input device that allows fingertip control of figures on a CRT screen.

Jump-To function key The key used to get to a distant part of a file. Also called the GoTo function key.

Justification Aligning text along left and/or right margins.

K Kilobyte.

Kerning Adjusting the space between characters to create wider or tighter spacing.

Keyboard A common input device similar to the keyboard of a typewriter.

Kilobyte (K) 1024 bytes.

Knowledge-based system A collection of information stored in a computer and accessed by natural language.

Knowledge engineer A computer professional who extracts information from a human expert to design an expert system based on that information.

Label In a spreadsheet, data consisting of a string of text characters.

LAN Local area network.

Laptop computer A small portable computer that can weigh less than 10 pounds.

Laser printer A printer that uses a light beam to transfer images to paper.

LCD Liquid crystal display.

Leading The vertical spacing between lines of type.

Legend The text beneath a graph; it explains the colors, shading, or symbols used to label the data points.

Less than (<) condition A logical operation in which the computer compares values to determine if one is less than another.

Librarian A person who catalogs processed disks and tapes and keeps them secure.

Licensed software Software that costs money and must not be copied without permission of the manufacturer.

Light pen A graphics input device that allows the user to interact directly with the computer screen.

Line graph A graph made by using a line to connect data points.

Link A physical data communications medium.

Link/load phase The phase during which prewritten programs may be added to the object module by means of a link/loader.

Liquid crystal display (LCD) The flat display screen found on some laptop computers.

Load module The output from the link/load step.

Local area network (LAN) A network designed to share data and resources among several computers.

Logical field A field used to keep track of true and false conditions.

Logical operations Comparing operations. The ALU is able to compare numbers, letters, or special characters and take alternative courses of action.

Logic chip A general-purpose processor on a chip; it was developed in 1969 by an Intel Corporation design team headed by Ted Hoff. Also called a microprocessor.

Logic error A flaw in the logic of a program.

Loop The repetition of program instructions under certain conditions. Also called iteration.

Machine cycle   The combination of I-time and E-time.

Machine language   The lowest level of language; it represents information as 1s and 0s.

Magnetic core   A flat doughnut-shaped piece of metal used as an early memory device.

Magnetic disk   An oxide-coated disk on which data is recorded as magnetic spots.

Magnetic-ink character recognition (MICR)   A method of machine-reading characters made of magnetized particles.

Magnetic tape   A medium with an iron-oxide coating that can be magnetized. Data is stored on the tape as extremely small magnetized spots.

Magnetic tape unit   A data storage unit used to record data on and retrieve data from magnetic tape.

Mainframe   A large computer that has access to billions of characters of data and is capable of processing data very quickly.

Main memory   The electronic circuitry that temporarily holds data and program instructions needed by the CPU. Also called memory, primary memory, primary storage, main storage, and internal storage.

Main storage   The electronic circuitry that temporarily holds data and program instructions needed by the CPU. Also called memory, main memory, primary memory, primary storage, and internal storage.

Management Information System (MIS)   1. A set of formal business systems designed to provide information for an organization. 2. A department that creates or maintains such systems. Also called Computing Services or Information Services.

Mark   The process of defining a block of text before performing block commands.

Mark I   An early computer; it was built in 1944 by Harvard professor Howard Aiken.

Master file   A semipermanent set of records.

MB   Megabyte.

Megabyte (MB)   One million bytes.

Memory   The electronic circuitry that temporarily holds data and program instructions needed by the CPU. Also called main memory, primary memory, primary storage, main storage, and internal storage.

Menu   An on-screen list of command choices.

MENU mode   The spreadsheet mode that allows the user access to command menus.

MICR   Magnetic-ink character recognition.

Microcomputer   The smallest and least expensive class of computer. Also called a personal computer.

Microcomputer manager   A person who manages microcomputers. Also called personal computer manager.

Microprocessor   A general-purpose processor on a chip; it was developed in 1969 by an Intel Corporation design team headed by Ted Hoff. Also called a logic chip.

Microsecond   One-millionth of a second.

Microwave transmission   The line-of-sight transmission of data signals through the atmosphere from relay station to relay station.

Millisecond   One-thousandth of a second.

Minicomputer   A computer with storage capacity and power less than a mainframe's but greater than a personal computer's.

MIS   Management Information System.

MIS manager   The manager of an MIS department.

MITS Altair   The first microcomputer kit; it was offered to computer hobbyists in 1975.

Mode   The state in which a program is currently functioning. In a spreadsheet program, there are usually three modes: READY mode, ENTRY mode, and MENU mode.

Mode indicator   A message displayed on the screen by a spreadsheet program; it tells the user the program's current mode of operation.

Model   A type of database, each type representing a particular way of organizing data. The three database models are hierarchical, network, and relational.

Modem   The term short for *modulate/demodulate*. A modem converts a digital signal to an analog signal or vice versa. Used to transfer data over analog communication lines between computers.

Modulation   The process of converting a signal from digital to analog.

Monochrome   A computer screen that displays information in only one color.

Mouse   A hand-held computer input device whose rolling movement on a flat surface causes corresponding movement of the cursor on the screen.

Multiple-range graph   A graph that plots the values of more than one variable.

Multipoint line   A line configuration in which several terminals are connected on the same line to one computer.

Multiuser, multitasking personal computer   A supermicro with a high-speed microprocessor and significantly increased memory and hard disk capacity

Nanosecond   One-billionth of a second.

Natural language   A programming language that resembles human language.

Near–letter quality   The printing produced by dot-matrix printers with 24-pin printheads.

Network A computer system that uses communications equipment to connect two or more computers and their resources.

Neural network Computer chips designed to mimic the human brain.

Node A device—such as a personal computer, hard disk, printer, or another peripheral—that is connected to a network.

Nonimpact imprinter A printer that prints without striking the paper.

Nonprocedural language A language that states what task is to be accomplished but does not state the steps needed to accomplish it.

Numeric field A field that contains numbers used for calculations.

Object module A machine-language version of a program; it is produced by a compiler or assembler.

OCR devices Optical-character recognition devices.

OCR-A A standard typeface for optical characters.

Office automation The use of technology to help achieve the goals of the office.

OMR devices Optical-mark recognition devices.

On-line Processing in which terminals are directly connected to the computer.

Operating environment An operating system environment in which the user does not have to memorize or look up commands.

Operating system A set of programs through which a computer manages its own resources.

Optical-character recognition (OCR) devices Input devices that use a light source to read special characters and convert them to electrical signals to be sent to the CPU.

Optical disk Storage technology that uses a laser beam to store large amounts of data at relatively low cost.

Optical-mark recognition (OMR) devices Input devices that use a light beam to recognize marks on paper.

Optical read-only memory (OROM) Optical storage media that cannot be written on but can be used to supply software or data.

Optical-recognition system A system that converts optical marks, optical characters, handwritten characters, or bar codes into electrical signals to be sent to the CPU.

OROM Optical read-only memory.

Output Raw data that has been processed into usable information.

Output device A device, such as a printer, that makes processed information available for use.

Packaged software Software that is packaged and sold in stores.

Page composition Adding type to a layout.

Page composition program A software package for designing and producing professional-looking documents. Also called a page makeup program or a desktop publishing program.

Page layout In publishing, the process of arranging text and graphics on a page.

Page makeup program A software package for designing and producing professional-looking documents. Also called a page composition program or a desktop publishing program.

Pan To move the cursor across a spreadsheet.

Panel In dBASE IV, a portion of the Control Center screen that offers menu options.

Pascal A structured, high-level programming language named for Blaise Pascal, the seventeenth-century French mathematician.

Path In a flowchart, the connection leading from the decision box to one of two possible responses. Also called a branch.

Peripheral equipment Hardware devices attached to a computer.

Personal computer The smallest and least-expensive class of computer. Also called a microcomputer.

Personal computer manager The manager in charge of personal computer use. Also called a microcomputer manager.

Phantom disk A chip that lets the computer regard part of its memory as another disk drive. Also called a RAM disk or an electronic disk.

Picosecond One-trillionth of a second.

Pie chart A pie-shaped graph used to compare values that represent parts of a whole.

Pixel A picture element on a computer display screen. Pixels are the individual points of light that make up screen images.

Point A typographic measurement equaling approximately $\frac{1}{72}$ inch.

Pointer A flashing indicator on a screen that shows where the next user-computer interaction will be. Also called a cursor.

Point-of-sale (POS) terminal A terminal used as a cash register in a retail setting. It may be programmable or connected to a central computer.

Point-to-point line A direct connection between each terminal and the computer or between computers.

Portable computer A self-contained computer that can be easily carried and moved.

POS terminal Point-of-sale terminal.

Presentation graphics program   A program that allows a user to create professional-looking business graphics. Also called a business-quality graphics program.

Primary memory   The electronic circuitry that temporarily holds data and program instructions needed by the CPU. Also called memory, primary storage, main storage, internal storage, and main memory.

Primary storage   The electronic circuitry that temporarily holds data and program instructions needed by the CPU. Also called memory, primary memory, main storage, internal storage, and main memory.

Print command   A command that provides options for printing a spreadsheet.

Printer   A device for generating output on paper.

Procedural language   A language used to present a step-by-step process for solving a problem.

Process box   In flowcharting, a rectangular box that indicates an action to be taken.

Processor   The central processing unit (CPU) of a computer.

Prodigy   A major information utility offering access to a broad range of services, including a variety of news, business, and shopping applications.

Program   A set of step-by-step instructions that directs a computer to perform specific tasks and produce certain results.

Programmer/analyst   A person who performs systems analysis functions in addition to programming.

Programming language   A set of rules that can be used to tell a computer what operations to do.

Prompt   A signal that the computer or operating system is waiting for data or a command from the user.

Pseudocode   An English-like way of representing structured programming control structures.

Public-domain software   Software that is free.

Ragged right margin   The nonalignment of text at the right edge of a document.

RAM   Random-access memory.

RAM disk   A chip that lets the computer regard part of its memory as a third disk drive. Also called an electronic disk or a phantom disk.

Random access   The immediate access to a record in secondary storage, usually on a disk. Also called direct access.

Random-access memory (RAM)   The memory that provides temporary storage for data and program instructions.

Range   A group of one or more cells, arranged in a rectangle, that a spreadsheet program treats as a unit.

Read   To bring data outside the computer into memory.

Read-only memory (ROM)   Memory that can be read only and remains after the power is turned off. Also called firmware.

Read/write head   An electromagnet that reads the magnetized areas on magnetic media and converts them into the electrical impulses that are sent to the processor.

READY mode   The spreadsheet mode indicating that the program is ready for whatever action the user indicates.

Real-time processing   Processing in which the results are available in time to affect the activity at hand.

Record   A collection of related fields.

Reformatting   The readjustment of visual aspects of a word processing document, including the accommodation of additions and deletions.

Relation   A table in a relational database model.

Relational database   A database in which the data is organized in a table format consisting of columns and rows.

Relational model   A database model that organizes data logically in tables.

Relational operator   An operator (such as $<$, $>$, or $=$) that allows a user to make comparisons and selections.

Resolution   The clarity of a video display screen or printer output.

Reverse video   The feature that highlights on-screen text by switching the usual text and background colors.

Ring network   A circle of point-to-point connections of computers at local sites, with no central host computer.

Robot   A computer-controlled device that can physically manipulate its surroundings.

ROM   Read-only memory.

Satellite transmission   Data transmission from earth station to earth station via communications satellites.

Scanner   A device that reads text and images directly into the computer.

Screen   A television-like output device that can display information.

Scrolling   A word processing feature that allows the user to move to and view any part of a screen document in 24-line chunks.

Sealed module   A sealed disk drive containing disks, access arms, and read/write heads. Also called a Winchester disk.

Search-and-replace function A word processing function that finds and changes each instance of a repeated item.

Secondary storage Additional storage, often disk, for data and programs; it is separate from the CPU and memory. Also called auxiliary storage.

Security A system of safeguards designed to protect a computer system and data from deliberate or accidental damage or access by unauthorized persons.

Semiconductor A crystalline substance that conducts electricity when it is "doped" with chemical impurities.

Semiconductor storage Data storage on a silicon chip.

Server The central computer in a network; it is responsible for managing the LAN.

Shareware Software that is given away free, although the maker hopes that satisfied users will voluntarily pay for it.

Shell An operating-environment layer that separates the operating system from the user.

Single-range bar graph A graph that plots the values of only one variable.

Single-range graph A graph that plots the values of only one variable.

Site license A license permitting a customer to make multiple copies of a piece of software.

Soft copy Computer output displayed on a screen.

Soft font A font that can be downloaded from disk files in a personal computer to a printer.

Software Instructions that tell a computer what to do.

Software piracy Unauthorized copying of computer software.

The Source A major information utility offering access to a broad range of services, including electronic games and a variety of news and business applications.

Source data automation The use of special equipment to collect data and send it directly to a computer.

Source document Data, on paper, to be prepared as input to a computer.

Source module A program as originally coded, before being translated into machine language.

Source program listing The printed version of a program as the programmer wrote it.

Speech recognition The process of presenting input data to the computer through the spoken word.

Speech recognition device A device that accepts the spoken word through a microphone and con-

verts it into digital code that can be understood by a computer.

Speech synthesis The process of enabling machines to talk to people.

Spelling checker program A word processing program that checks the spelling in a document.

Spreadsheet An electronic worksheet divided into rows and columns that can be used to analyze and present business data.

Stacked-bar graph A bar graph in which all data common to a given row or column appear stacked in one bar.

Stand-alone programs Individual programs, such as word processing and spreadsheet programs.

Star network A network consisting of one or more smaller computers connected to a central host computer.

Start/stop symbol An oval symbol used to indicate the beginning and end of a flowchart.

Style The way a typeface is printed, for example, in *italic*.

Submenu An additional set of options related to a prior menu selection.

Supercomputer The largest and most powerful category of computers.

Supermicro A multiuser, multitasking microcomputer that has a high-speed microprocessor, increased memory, and hard-disk storage.

Supermini A minicomputer at the top end of capacity and price.

Surge protector A device that prevents electrical problems from affecting data files.

Symbolic language A second-generation language that uses abbreviations for instructions. Also called assembly language.

Syntax The rules of a programming language.

Syntax errors Errors in the use of a programming language.

System An organized set of related components established to perform a certain task.

Systems analysis The process of studying an existing system to determine how it works and how it meets user needs.

Systems analyst A person who plans and designs individual programs and entire computer systems.

Systems design The process of developing a plan for a system, based on the results of a systems analysis.

Tape drive The drive on which reels of magnetic tape are mounted when their data is ready to be read by the computer system.

Telecommunications The merger of communications and computers.

Telecommuting The home use of telecommunications and computers as a substitute for working outside the home.

Teleconferencing A system of holding conferences by linking geographically disbursed people through computer terminals or personal computers.

Terminal A device that consists of an input device, an output device, and a communications link to the main terminal.

Text block A continuous section of text in a document.

Thesaurus program With a word processing program, this program provides a list of synonyms and antonyms for a word in a document.

Title The caption on a graph that summarizes the information in the graph.

Toggle switch A keystroke that turns a software function on or off.

Topology The physical layout of a local area network.

Touch screen A computer screen that accepts input data by letting the user point at the screen to select a choice.

Transaction file A file that contains all the changes to be made to a master file: additions, deletions, and revisions.

Transaction processing The technique of processing transactions one at a time in the order in which they occur.

Transistor A small device that transfers electrical signals across a resistor.

Translator A program that translates programming language into machine language.

Transponder A device in a communications satellite that receives a transmission from earth, amplifies the signal, changes the frequency, and retransmits the data to a receiving earth station.

Twisted pairs Wires twisted together in an insulated cable. Twisted pairs are frequently used to transmit information over short distances. Also called wire pairs.

Typeface A set of characters—letters, symbols, and numbers—of the same design.

Typeover mode A text-entry mode in which each character typed overwrites the character at the cursor position.

Type size The size, in points, of a typeface.

Underlining Underscoring text.

UNIVAC I (UNIVersal Automatic Computer) The first computer built for business purposes.

Universal manager program A program that uses a common interface to coordinate separate stand-alone programs.

Universal Product Code (UPC) A code number, unique to a product, represented on the product's label in the form of a bar code.

Update To keep files current by changing data as appropriate.

Upload To send a file from one computer to a larger computer.

User A person who uses computer software or has contact with computer systems.

User friendly Refers to software that is easy for a novice to use.

User involvement The participation of users in the systems development life cycle.

Vacuum tube An electronic tube used as a basic component in the first generation of computers.

Value In a spreadsheet, data consisting of a number representing an amount, a formula, or a function.

Variable 1. A storage location in memory. 2. On a graph, the items that the data points describe.

VDT Video display terminal.

Vertical centering A word processing feature that adjusts the top and bottom margins so that text is midway between the top and the bottom of the page.

Very high-level language A nonprocedural language. Also called a 4GL or a fourth-generation language.

Videoconferencing Computer conferencing combined with cameras and wall-size screens.

Video display terminal (VDT) A terminal with a screen.

Video graphics Computer-produced animated pictures.

Videotex Data communications merchandising.

Virus A set of illicit instructions that passes itself on to other programs in which it comes in contact.

Vision robot A robot that can recognize an object by its shape or color.

Voice input The process of presenting input data to the computer through the spoken word. Also called speech recognition.

Voice mail A system in which the user can dictate a message into the voice mail system, where it is digitized and stored in the recipient's voice mailbox. Later the recipient can dial the mailbox, and the system delivers the message in audio form.

Voice-output device See *Voice synthesizer*.

Voice synthesizer A device that converts data in main storage to sounds understandable as speech to humans. Also called an audio-response unit or a voice-output device.

Volatile Refers to the loss of data in semiconductor storage when the current is interrupted or turned off.

WAN Wide Area Network.

Wand reader An input device that scans the special letters and numbers on price tags in retail stores.

Weight The variation in the heaviness of a typeface; for example, type is much heavier when printed in **boldface.**

Wide Area Network (WAN) A network of geographically distant computers and terminals.

Winchester disk A sealed disk drive containing disks, access arms, and read/write heads. Also called a sealed module.

Wire pairs Wires twisted together in an insulated cable. Wire pairs are frequently used to transmit information over short distances. Also called twisted pairs.

Word processing Computer-based creation, editing, formatting, storing, and printing of text.

Word wrap A word processing feature that automatically starts a word at the left margin of the next line if there is not enough room for it on the current line.

Worksheet Erase command The command that clears the current spreadsheet from memory, leaving a blank worksheet.

Workstation 1. A supermicro. 2. A personal computer attached to a LAN.

Worm A program that transfers itself from computer to computer over a network, then plants itself as a file on the target computer's disk.

WORM Write-once, read-many media.

Write-once, read-many media (WORM) Media that can be written on only once; then it becomes read-only media.

x-axis The horizontal reference line of a graph; it usually represents units of time.

y-axis The vertical reference line of a graph; it usually represents values or amounts, such as dollars, staffing levels, or units sold.

INDEX

• • • • • • • • • • • •

NOTE: Page numbers in italics indicate illustrations or tables separated from accompanying text.